# POLITICS in an ISLAND STATE

## *Wills O. Isaacs* and Jamaica's Struggle for Development

Diane Austin-Broos

The University of the West Indies Press
Mona • St Augustine • Cave Hill • Global • Five Islands

First published in Jamaica, 2024 by
The University of the West Indies Press
7A Gibraltar Hall Road,
The UWI, Mona Campus,
Kingston 7, Jamaica
www.uwipress.com



ISBN: 978-976-640-958-6 (Hardback)
978-976-640-959-3 (Paperback)
978-976-640-960-9 (epub)

**A catalogue record of this book is available from the National Library of Jamaica.**



Cover and Book Design by Christina Moore Fuller
Printed and Bound in the United States of America

*Cover Image*: "They came from the countryside to downtown Kingston." Painting by David Pottinger (author's private collection).

# CONTENTS

# POLITICS
## *in an* ISLAND STATE

**Wills O. Isaacs circa 1938.**
Courtesy of the Isaacs family.

# Synopsis

This biography of Wills O. Isaacs addresses some of Jamaica's most important challenges in the mid-twentieth century; a time when its governments sought both to decolonize and to revamp an economy weakened by the decline of sugar, British underdevelopment, the Great Depression and two world wars. The study involves a focus on rural-to-urban migration, mass unemployment, and the effort to industrialize. These elements combined to shape both Kingston's and Jamaica's struggles and troubles throughout subsequent decades, reaching into the twenty-first century. Wills Isaacs' experience as Jamaica's first full-term Minister of Trade and Industry provides a lens through which to examine these and related issues, including the heated clashes and policy debates within and between the rival political parties. The work concludes with a summation of its two major themes: the life and times of Isaacs, a notable Jamaican, and some comment on the obstacles to development faced by a small island state with limited resources.

# Preface

A chance encounter in Sydney, Australia aroused my interest in Wills Isaacs. In 1979, I met the late Nadine Isaacs, a prominent architect and daughter of Isaacs. At the time, Nadine was engaged in postgraduate study at the University of Sydney, where I was about to take a position. I had returned to Australia following doctoral studies at the University of Chicago. My ongoing research concerned two East Kingston neighbourhoods, Rollington Town and Harbour View.

Nadine and I became good friends. On news of her father's failing health, she returned to Jamaica just months before he passed away. However, these events did not scotch our friendship. We continued to converse, and I continued my trips to Jamaica, pursuing further research outside Kingston. I also began to work with Indigenous groups in central Australia. On her own, Nadine returned to Australia and visited various such communities. We discussed the fact that housing was an issue that loomed large both in Jamaica and remote Australia. She introduced me to projects that involved the provision of sites and services for community-based construction. I felt that the schemes Nadine had fostered in Jamaica could also work in central Australia, where training and jobs for youth were paramount. During our discussions, she related her father's views on housing. As a Kingston and St Andrew councillor, he first raised the issue of public housing in the 1940s.

Regrettably, Nadine's untimely death cut short our plan for an Australian initiative, but not my engagement with the Isaacs family. As the years passed, I met other family members, including Isaacs' widow, Gloria, and four of Nadine's sisters. Her brother, William, also known as Vunnie, I had known in Rollington Town even before I met Nadine. At the time, he was the Member of the House of Representatives for Kingston East in Michael Manley's government. Isaacs, I never met. Still, Nadine and her younger sister, Christine, regaled me with stories of "Pa" and the people south of Torrington Bridge whom he represented. In time, I began to connect two seemingly different worlds: of those I knew downtown and of Wills Isaacs, a prominent mid-century politician. This biography grew out of intersections between my own pursuits and those of many Jamaican friends from various walks of life. The work is something more than a research project, though it was shaped by the Jamaica I first came to know in the 1970s.[1]

# Acknowledgements

I extend my thanks to Wills Isaacs' family, who shared numerous insights with me. Nadine Isaacs triggered my interest, William elaborated, and Christine Gore (née Isaacs) gave me access to her father's collected papers. Thanks also to those who contributed to the collected papers. Marguerite Curtin's unpublished essays on Isaacs' early life were of great assistance. I also acknowledge the small band who interviewed a number of family members, comrades and colleagues. The late Claudette Carby (née Isaacs) started the interviews in 1978. Abby Majendie-Wynter continued in 2001, and then Michael Burke in 2002 and 2003. Many of those who were interviewed had passed away by the time I began my research.

My gratitude to Julian Wilson and Anthony Lloyd, the librarian and the orderly, respectively, at Jamaica's Parliamentary Library. During the months I spent there, they were always helpful and encouraging. Thanks also to Dr Deborah Hickling Gordon and her small team who accessed Public Opinion at the National Library of Jamaica when I could not travel due to the pandemic. I am deeply indebted to my late friend and colleague Gaynor Macdonald, who worked on illustrations. Sheree Rhoden (the Gleaner Company) and Tasheka Parkes and Adolphus Depass (Jamaica National Library) also helped with photographs.

There are many more to thank in their various capacities: Arnold Bertram, Brandon Burke, Janice Casserly, the late Barry Chevannes, Leroy Cooke, Evie Czapla, Peter Espeut, Ainsley Henriques, Barry Higman, Leighton Holness, Antonio Lauria-Perricelli, the late Bruce McFarlane, Kathleen Monteith, Patrick Neveling, Jahlani Niaah, Don Nonini and Sandy Smith-Nonini, the Honourable P.J. Patterson, Peter Phillips, Don Robotham, Sonjah Stanley-Niaah, the late Connie Sutton, Deborah Thomas, Ronnie Thwaites, Gina Ulysse, Brackette Williams and Swithin Wilmot. Anyone I have overlooked, please forgive me.

Special thanks go to Christine Randle (University of West Indies Press); and to three Rollington Town friends – Winifred Davis, Sam King and Noel Patrick – who, from the start, always pushed me to ask more questions. My debt to Frank and Harry Broos is beyond measure. Notwithstanding all this support, final responsibility for this work lies with the author.

# Introduction

Wills O. Isaacs was a prominent member of the People's National Party from its early days. For a few decades in the mid-twentieth century, he was one of Jamaica's most controversial figures; loved by many, but also reviled by some. Isaacs joined the PNP soon after its official launch in 1938. He quickly became a leading nationalist, and a strategist within the party. His early work was in union organization and building local constituency groups, including one intended to attract the commercial class.[1] Another, Group 69, formed in downtown Matthews Lane, brought him notoriety. In later years, Group 69 was sometimes seen as a precursor to Kingston's neighbourhood garrisons and the wars between supporters of the rival political parties. Isaacs' first elected position was to the Kingston and St Andrew Corporation council (1943 to 1954). Elected to Parliament in 1949, he held a Central Kingston seat until 1967. In that year, he was elected to the rural seat of St Ann North East and re-elected in 1972.

Under Norman Manley's leadership, the PNP assumed government in 1955. Isaacs became Minister of Trade and Industry and held the position until 1962. He was the first minister to serve a full term in the portfolio, one that played a pivotal role in Jamaican development. To expand the economy and address unemployment, the society needed to industrialize and revamp agriculture. This seemed to be the only way to absorb the many rural residents trekking into Kingston in search of work and a better life. While others attended to mining and agriculture, Isaacs saw to the expansion of tourism and manufacturing. Both could reduce unemployment, while tourism would also be a 'US dollar earner' of foreign exchange for much-needed imported goods. The trade component of his portfolio involved regulation at home, and the search for markets and suppliers abroad. As a minister, he travelled widely and dispatched trade missions to Eastern Europe and Asia.

Isaacs' task, and that of his comrades in government, proved much harder than they imagined. In office, they struggled to reduce unemployment and address the issue of agricultural land. Far too much estate land was still being used to grow sugar cane, a commodity of decreasing value; and far too many Jamaicans remained unemployed, landless or both. The PNP was defeated in 1962 and, at that time, Isaacs' aspirations to lead the party were put aside. The defeat followed a period of highly contested politics around the West Indies Federation. There was disagreement within the PNP and, despite Manley's efforts, the Jamaica Labour Party prevailed. The JLP's position was that the federation, with its financial demands, would increase Jamaica's inequality, only mitigated to a degree by the PNP government.

From 1962, Isaacs sat on the Opposition benches and shadowed the Trade and Industry portfolio. In government, he (and Robert Lightbourne of the JLP) embraced the policy of "industrialization by invitation" to foreign investment, albeit with some unease on Isaacs' part. He was first and foremost a nationalist, and an economic nationalist as well. However, domestic reluctance to invest in Jamaica, and the restrictions of the sterling area, drew him and the party to seek foreign capital, mainly from the United States. It proved a problematic course. Despite the frustrations, Isaacs did expand both manufacturing and tourism, while creating more employment in construction as well. Along with mining, these developments saw the economy grow and diversify. Isaacs' terms in office also brought a more acute awareness of Jamaica's dependence on imports. The need to import food staples for the people and raw materials for industrial development made the society vulnerable to external conditions. In the 1970s, with International Monetary Fund pressure on Jamaica to devalue and lower wages, self-reliance became a central issue.

In 1972, Isaacs returned briefly to government in Michael Manley's first Cabinet, sharing a Commerce and Industry portfolio with P.J. Patterson, whose career he had fostered. Patterson attended mainly to trade while Isaacs addressed Commerce and Consumer Affairs. In that year, he was part of the response to the impact of worldwide inflation on Jamaica; a major factor that triggered the government's destabilization. In 1973, at the age of seventy-one, Isaacs retired from Parliament and became Jamaica's High Commissioner to Canada. Following a tumultuous time abroad, he returned home in 1975. Three years later, he was made a life member of the PNP. This recognition followed earlier awards for his service to the nation. Always the party man, he was deeply disappointed when the PNP lost the election in 1980. By that time, he was seriously ill. He died early in 1981.

Isaacs received his life membership at a mass meeting to celebrate the first forty years of the PNP. Fourteen surviving founding members of the party related their stories of struggle. His account was among the most vivid: "I remember the harassment of our leadership. I remember the internment of the Hill boys, Domingo, Samuel Marquis and others. I remember the shooting of Adina Spencer in cold blood." Isaacs evoked the world war years, the days of battles between unions, and the neighbourhood fights of the 1940s. The party had retaliated as the JLP sought to muscle PNP supporters off the streets. He also recalled his own personal travail during the 1949 Hearne Commission concerning events in Gordon Town. The Chief Justice reviled him for his remark, "A broken skull or two does not matter much in the growth of a nation." Responding, Michael Manley acknowledged Isaacs for his spirit and strength in the party's early days. He noted that, though times had changed, "the essential struggle" remained the same: "And I say to the memory of all those who died, I say to the founders who are still with us [...], our generation has been blessed with an inspiration that is given to very few political movements." At that moment, Isaacs was a hero of the party. He was the one who braved the attacks from both colonial officials and Bustamante.[2]

Yet, his role within the PNP was a contentious one. Throughout his career, Isaacs was a nationalist and a social democrat who identified as a socialist. As a champion of the unemployed and the racially vilified, he condemned capitalism's social failures. He also condemned the market failures involved in merchant cartels and private monopolies. Consequently, he supported some nationalization, especially of Jamaica's central services. Yet, he did not foreclose on capitalism and looked for a détente between the classes. His main target was totalitarianism, of both the right and the left, and of the various nineteenth- and twentieth-century imperialisms. Isaacs' nationalist ire was raised equally by British treatment of African peoples of the transatlantic slave trade, and by the fate of Europeans overwhelmed in turn by Nazi Germany and Stalin's Russia. He described the path of the PNP as one between "the red shirts" and "the black shirts".[3]

His views placed him at odds with the party's democratic socialists. They proposed that government should either own or largely control the means of production, while the role of a private sector should be minimal. Some voiced strong support for the Soviet Union and, in the 1960s, others argued for rapid land redistribution. These positions seemed to entail a command economy – albeit with an emphasis on labour unions and cooperatives, and on worker inclusion in management. The more constructive elements of democratic socialism, however, were lost in translation due to the ideological tenor of the times. Cold War tensions meant that, in Jamaica, support for the Soviet system as a paradigm of socialism became problematic once the search was on for foreign capital investment, especially from the United States.[4]

These matters pervaded debate within the PNP for most of Isaacs' career. Democratic socialism came to the fore when the PNP first declared itself socialist in 1940. Initially, Norman Manley endorsed the position, though he added that the party's socialism would be incremental and tailored to suit Jamaica. Retreat to a more moderate position preceded the party's election to government in 1955. Following the 1962 defeat, a policy review in 1964 reintroduced the more radical position fiercely debated for two years. That position was modified and then modified further through the PNP's years in Opposition. Assuming power on a platform of economic nationalism, Michael Manley reasserted democratic socialism in 1974. Though some have attributed the subsequent demise of his government to economic policy alone, the politics of that decade were transnational and more complex. By the 1970s, Isaacs stood at a distance from the cut and thrust of intra-party debate. Nonetheless, he still discussed policy with Manley, even as his life ebbed away.[5]

If Isaacs was a nationalist and a social democrat, he was also called a populist – with good reason. He was a man of the people, entirely fluent in patois when many of his middle-class comrades were not. He was known as the "stormy petrel" of Jamaican politics, passionate and mercurial, but also called "Bishop" for his biblical turn of phrase.[6] He was a committed Roman Catholic and, in this regard, a conservative. Nonetheless, his humour, faith and warmth buttressed his mass appeal. He was always at the forefront in election campaigns. Michael Manley captured him well: "Now Wills at his greatest was a poet, at his greatest was an absolute poet on the platform, and yet he also had this tremendous capacity for a warm rapport with an audience. To slide into the vernacular, to crack a joke and have them popping up with laughter. The magnetism with which he spoke created almost the atmosphere of a cathedral."[7] Short of stature, spectacled and balding, Isaacs had charisma.

Writing of a youthful Michael Manley, Anthony Payne cites three components of Jamaican populism: a commitment to multi-class coalitions, charismatic nationalism and an embrace of "redistributive, neo-socialist ideas".[8] This description conjoins a social democratic stance with a passionate appeal to Jamaicanness. Michael and Isaacs were from different generations and differed greatly as politicians. Still, these elements were common to their politics. Michael Manley – and his father, to some degree – sought to embrace the new black nationalism of the 1960s. Isaacs, on the other hand, stood for integration, and an accord between the classes.[9] Yet he remained a trenchant critic of racist state violence, both at home and abroad. He also retained a profound belief in the abilities of those who suffered most.

This biography addresses the words and actions that made Wills Isaacs notorious: his streetcorner politics in downtown Kingston and his outspoken nationalism turned to serve the cause of independence. It also addresses those disputes within the PNP in which he was prominent. However, the book's central focus is his public debates and policy positions as they pertained to Jamaica's majority – the masses and the sufferers, also known as the downpressed. Of the issues he addressed, his commitment to racial justice and Jamaican independence is well-known. Less well-known is the fact that, among his comrades in government, he was at the forefront in promoting development as the means to reduce unemployment – a cause he first made his own on the Kingston and St Andrew Corporation council. In addition, he turned his attention to the cost of staples that fed the masses. He sought to undermine the cartels that controlled imported necessities, thereby paving the way for needed regulation. And it was this concern with protecting his own people that shaped his ambivalence towards a federation. Later, in retirement from Parliament, he made his thoughts known on inflation and its management, and on Jamaica's circumstances as a commodity producer. He spoke up for a New International Economic Order and for the rights of Caribbean immigrants in Canada. His story is one of a distinctive life in Jamaican politics, and his concerns during those four decades shed new light on central aspects of the island's economy during the twentieth century.

Following World War II, Jamaica's unemployed comprised close to 30 per cent of the labour force. This was the legacy of the Great Depression, war and British underdevelopment over centuries.[10] When Jamaican slaves were freed, they were also left bereft of their previous means of production and destined to occupy the less productive land not used by the planter class. One response came with the Morant Bay Rebellion in 1865, when land-hungry Jamaicans staged a revolt. It was put down brutally by the British. A second response came soon after as workers sought regional employment in Panama, Costa Rica, Cuba and the United States. Beginning in the 1920s, however, these itinerants were pushed back to Jamaica, bringing, in turn, waves of internal migration. Kingston's population burgeoned as men and women deserted land unable to support them.[11] Sadly, many migrants found that they had simply moved from rural to urban poverty. By the mid-point of the twentieth century, depression and two world wars had made the situation acute; one that was barely relieved by a few short years of post-war emigration. Britain's decision to grant independence to its colonies, and radically curtail West Indian immigration, merged with these events. As Wills Isaacs entered politics, these were the challenges that he and his compatriots faced.[12]

A central task was to address unemployment. The outline of an effective response seemed to be at hand in the work of W. Arthur Lewis. Born in St Lucia, he studied at the London School of Economics and was awarded the Nobel Prize in 1979. A pioneer in development economics, his early publications addressed the Caribbean. He argued that Jamaica needed to industrialize – to absorb the unemployed off the land and, in the longer term, to raise productivity in the countryside. Plantation agriculture was caught in a roadblock of minimal innovation and low wages due to British preferences, and to reliance on a subsistence sector for its seasonal labour. His concern was rural productivity, and Jamaica's vast number of casual workers, rural and urban. He deemed its unemployment the worst in the Caribbean and among the worst of all the British colonies.[13]

Lewis also criticized Jamaica's low level of corporate saving. He termed the situation one of "entrepreneurial failure" over generations, and recommended incentives to foreign capital investment that could secure markets for Jamaica abroad.[14] The objective was to use the initial advantage of low wages to produce competitive exports. As manufacturing increased and drew more labour, agriculture would start to respond. The island's own resources would be put to better use and, importantly, bring greater self-sufficiency in food production. As overall activity increased, so would wages. In popular form, these views were canvassed in Jamaica through the late 1940s and the 1950s.

As Minister of Trade and Industry, Isaacs' role was to develop, first and foremost, manufacturing and tourism. With the help of a booming bauxite industry and emigration to Britain, the PNP government had some success in the 1950s. Fewer Jamaicans were unemployed. However, the cost of foreign capital proved disproportionate to the benefit and impeded crucial expenditure on infrastructure and services. Moreover, job-creating industries were hard to sustain, especially in rural parishes. Without the assistance of major emigration, two JLP governments saw unemployment rise again and a restive downtown population become more violent. Foreign investment in bauxite mining barely alleviated these realities and the government became increasingly oppressive. The PNP was returned to power in 1972.

During the 1960s, the policy of industrialization by invitation had been subject to mounting critique. The writings of Walter Rodney and George Beckford were especially influential. Rodney discussed underdevelopment in Africa and Beckford plantation dependency in the Caribbean.[15] Their influence turned the focus away from industrialization and towards growth in endogenous agriculture. This view rejected an emphasis on raw material extraction, processed rural exports, and the pursuit of foreign capital. The last, it was argued, simply entrenched dependency. Self-reliance should be paramount, led by a small farmer movement producing first and foremost for home consumption.

These issues took centre-stage in the 1970s as the members of the Organization of the Petroleum Exporting Countries (OPEC), in response to the Yom Kippur War, restricted the sale of oil on the international market. This action, and the worldwide inflation that followed, hit Jamaica hard. Struggling to shore up the government's reforms, and the economy, Michael Manley revived the PNP's democratic socialism. Manley's stance combined the old and the new. Domestically, it involved a mixed economy focused on self-reliance to obviate the need for capital from abroad. In foreign affairs and trade, Manley embraced a non-aligned stance. He also advocated for a New International Economic Order that might bring fairer trade between the consumers of the North and the commodity-producing South. The issue of foreign capital, and of capital per se, had a new iteration when, with declining foreign reserves, Jamaica turned to the IMF. The conditionalities required for the fund's assistance conflicted with major aspects of the government's programme. That programme, however, rested in part on bank finance from abroad – which required that the IMF provide Jamaica with its imprimatur.[16] The impasse undid the government.

Following the crisis of the 1970s, Jamaican governments struggled with low or no economic growth, over-reliance on imports, debt and IMF-imposed austerity. The re-privatization of previously acquired foreign banks hastened the growth of domestic finance. But, lacking both regulation and responsible corporate management, the financial sector was soon in crisis. Between 1996 and 1997, numerous firms collapsed, incurring widespread losses, not least among numerous workers who had invested in small building societies. Structural adjustment and mass suffering followed. By 2009, the government, which had sought to help, was faced with massive debt. Radical measures to reduce the interest paid on the debt left Jamaica at the mercy of the IMF again.[17] In the first two decades of the twenty-first century, unemployment dropped to single-digit figures as numerous Jamaicans, rural and urban, engaged in marginal farming and casual services to sustain a precarious existence. And subsequently, the long-term effects of a global financial crisis, serious flooding and a pandemic have underlined Jamaica's vulnerability as a small state.

With the passage of time, views on development have been blunted to a degree. It is rare today for socialists to advocate for a command economy, or for control of the "commanding heights" – though neoclassical economists still insist that minimal government is always best. In reality, most economies are mixed and likely to remain so for generations.[18] When it comes to international agencies, and to the IMF in particular, few would rule out assistance today, if the need arises. However, the operations of the IMF remain subject to intense debate. In particular, its quota system of funding and votes gives a major voice to the United States and other wealthy nations. The conditionalities for support are still demanding, and the implications for the sovereignty of client states remain unresolved. Where Jamaica and international finance are concerned, debates over sovereignty, the politics involved, and their impact on the masses, have ramified to this day.

In a far-reaching comparative study, Giovanni Arrighi notes that the prospects for development among peripheral states are poor in comparison to core states. For those on the semi-periphery, like

Jamaica, transfers abroad of capital and skills add to the adverse effects of unequal exchange. His conclusion is that industrialization of the type pursued in Jamaica in the 1950s and 1960s does not ensure development.[19] Kari Polanyi Levitt, too, has spoken of barriers to development. She describes a situation familiar to the PNP from the 1950s through to the 1970s: national priorities in health, education and employment being made secondary to investors' rights; unfair terms of trade; and an ever-growing set of conditionalities linked to international finance. Since that post-war period, "globalization has devalued sovereign equality and stripped states of economic and administrative policy instruments". Commodity prices continue to fall and those with relatively open economies have borne the full human cost of adaptation. With reference to Jamaica, Levitt, like Norman Girvan, notes that, for Arthur Lewis, rural reconstruction was always as important as industrialization. Yet, in Isaacs' time and beyond, neither party found a viable path to major rural restructuring.[20] In this regard, zealous reports of downtown Kingston's periodic violence hardly convey the ongoing struggle – social, political and economic – that has produced these manifestations.

In sum, and for all concerned, it is extremely difficult to create change in a small, open economy with limited natural resources. Many of the lessons learned, and some still to be addressed, were spelt out during Isaacs' time. They informed his debates with comrades, the merchant class, and his various political opponents. Isaacs talked and bantered with them all. His biography provides a lens through which to see some of Jamaica's central dilemmas played out in the concerns of a mid-century maverick.[21] Indeed, the perennial nature of these concerns transports the past into the present, and who dares look away? Known as Wills O. and Bishop (for the hymns and prayers), Isaacs himself preferred the nickname Stormy Petrel, one who, with a fierce resolve, served the people and his party.

# Abbreviations

| | |
|---|---|
| ADC | Agricultural Development Corporation |
| ALCAN | Aluminium Company of Canada |
| ALCOA | Aluminium Company of America |
| BOJ | Bank of Jamaica |
| B&ATU | Builders and Allied Trades Union |
| BITU | Bustamante Industrial Trade Union |
| CARICOM | Caribbean Community |
| CARIFTA | Caribbean Free Trade Association |
| CASEA | Canadian Atlantic Saltfish Exporters Association |
| CCC | Caribbean Cement Company |
| CD&WA | Colonial Development and Welfare Act |
| CHA | Central Housing Authority |
| CPU | Central Planning Unit (of the 1955 PNP Government) |
| DFC | Development Finance Corporation |
| DLP | Democratic Labour Party (of the West Indies) |
| EEC | European Economic Community (European Common Market) |
| EU | European Union |
| FTAA | Free Trade Area of the Americas (discontinued in 2005) |

| | |
|---|---|
| GATT | General Agreement on Tariffs and Trade |
| IBRD | International Bank of Reconstruction and Development |
| IDB | Inter-American Development Bank |
| IDC | Industrial Development Corporation (aka Jamaica Industrial Development Corporation) |
| ISER | Institute of Social Economic Studies (SALISES) |
| IMF | International Monetary Fund |
| JAS | Jamaica Agricultural Society |
| JCC | Jamaica Chamber of Commerce |
| JDP | Jamaica Democratic Party |
| JDX | Jamaica Debt Exchange |
| JHA | Jamaica Hotels Association |
| JIA | Jamaica Imperial Association |
| JLP | Jamaica Labour Party |
| JMA | Jamaica Manufacturers Association |
| JMMB | Jamaica Money Market Brokers |
| JPL | Jamaica Progressive League |
| JPSC | Jamaica Public Services Company |
| JTA | Jamaica Teachers' Association |
| JTB | Jamaica Tourist Board |
| JTC | Jamaica Telephone Company |
| KSAC | Kingston and St Andrew Corporation |
| MHR | Member of the House of Representatives |
| MLC | Member of the Legislative Council |
| NAFEL | Newfoundland Associated Fish Exporters Limited |
| NAFTA | North American Free Trade Agreement |
| NAT | National Housing Trust |
| NAFEL | Newfoundland Associated Fish Exporters Limited |
| NATO | North Atlantic Treaty Organization |
| NCB | National Commercial Bank |

| | |
|---|---|
| NEC | National Executive Council (of the PNP, aka National Council) |
| NHT | National Housing Trust |
| NIEO | New International Economic Order |
| NWU | National Workers' Union |
| OPEC | Organization of Petroleum Exporting Countries |
| PHR | Proceedings of the House of Representatives (*Hansard*) |
| PNP | People's National Party |
| PPP | People's Political Party (one formed by Marcus Garvey in the early 1930s; the other by Millard Johnson in the early 1960s) |
| PSOJ | Private Sector Organization of Jamaica |
| RCCWI | Regional Consultative Council of the West Indies |
| SALISES | Sir Arthur Lewis Institute of Social and Economic Studies |
| STC | State Trading Corporation |
| TUAC | Trade Union Advisory Council |
| TUC | Trade Union Council (from 1946, Trade Union Congress) |
| TT&GWU | Tramways, Transport and General Workers' Union |
| UCWI | University College of the West Indies (since 1962, UWI) |
| UNCTAD | United Nations Commission on Trade and Development |
| UNIA | Universal Negro Improvement Association |
| UWC | Unemployed Workers' Council |
| WFTU | World Federation of Trade Unions |
| WIF | West Indies Federation |
| WIFLP | West Indies Federal Labour Party |
| WISCO | West Indies Sugar Corporation |
| WTO | World Trade Organization |
| YSL | Young Socialist League |

# SECTION I
# THE EARLY YEARS

## Chapter 1

# A Political Awakening

*Dominating all internal migration in the years 1921–43 was the movement towards Kingston. Not only the city but also the suburban parts of St Andrew grew at a phenomenal rate.* – Gisela Eisner, 1961.

*[T]he worst economic and social conditions to be met with anywhere in Jamaica are to be found in some parts and among some classes of the people of Kingston.* – Lord Olivier, 1936.[1]

Wills Ogilvy Isaacs was born on 8 February 1902 at Chester Castle in southeast Hanover. His mother was Catherine Reckard Cridland, daughter of Simon Cridland, who would inherit from his father a nearby estate called Retirement. Her mother, Catherine Campbell, is identified by Isaacs' family as the direct descendant of slaves, possibly working over generations at Retirement or nearby. Born in 1871, Catherine was baptised in the Church of England in 1872, and thereafter grew up mainly in the care of her father's parents. When she reached a marriageable age, he gave her a piece of land in Westmoreland bringing in some £15 a month. She married John Alexander Isaacs in 1896 at Green Island on the Hanover coast.

John Alexander's father – also John – may have been a postmaster and registrar of births in the Chester Castle district. His son was born around 1873. Although the extent of his education is unknown, he is said to have worked as a private tutor to the children of the rural middle class. He also kept a shop in Chester Castle where, on occasion, he traded with young Wills by his side. The Cridlands kept shops as well, adjacent to their land. These small concerns probably garnered steady though modest returns. In the 1890s, the parish capital, Lucea, and Green Island, declined when railways were constructed between Montego Bay and the main banana parishes. Montego Bay became the hub of an export industry in tropical fruit. Still, proximity to Panama and Cuba meant that the Hanover ports maintained a trade in farm-grown produce. Returns to farmers from coconut oil and bananas brought a continuing demand for dry goods and groceries imported from Kingston. John Isaacs and his son were involved in this trade.[2]

Later in life, Wills Isaacs inherited his mother's piece of land, which he sold in order to secure his position as a commission agent in Kingston. His only foray into agriculture came once he had entered politics and terminated his business partnership. In the 1950s, with his wife, Gloria, he acquired land at Sligoville, on which they maintained a family home and a small venture raising pigs destined for market.

In sum, Isaacs was rooted in Jamaica's brown middle class and in the parish where he was born. Two other prominent Jamaican politicians, Alexander Bustamante and P.J. Patterson, were also Hanoverians. He had a rapport with both. Like them, however, he stood at a distance from Jamaica's educated urban elite. He shared that elite's opposition to Britain's dispossession of the enslaved, and their descendants. Yet, his life course was different. For the sake of his siblings and mother, Isaacs sought work from an early age. His experience gave him a common touch and nurtured an engagement with commerce. Both would inform his career in politics.

For the duration of Isaacs' childhood, his family enjoyed a comfortable life. One of eight – three boys and five girls – he was the favoured son. He rode a horse to school and, with his mother and siblings, travelled in a buggy to church. Sunday meals were substantial. Though baptized in the Anglican Church, Catherine Isaacs later became a devout Presbyterian and raised her children in that faith. In his reminiscences Isaacs recalled that, where religion was concerned, his mother made it clear that he was her son, drawing "a thick curtain between me and her Jewish husband". Nonetheless, he loved his father, whom he described as the "kindest" of men whose charity "knew no bounds". In 1917, however, a large family and diminishing means led John Isaacs to migrate to the United States. He returned some years later and remarried in 1932, following Catherine's death. In 1945, aged seventy-two, John Isaacs died at Hopewell in Hanover. He had become a local notable and member of the parish board.[3] In the interim Isaacs grew up, entered the workforce and migrated to Kingston.

He attended Pondside Elementary School in central Hanover. Pondside had a Presbyterian church, established as an outreach from Lucea. Aged fourteen and having passed his second pupil/teacher exam, Isaacs became a pupil teacher at the school on a salary of 6/8d a month. In 1917, he passed his third exam. His parents did not intend him to become a teacher in a country school. His father hoped he would study law, while his mother's wish was that he would enter the ministry. The local pastor supported her, impressed by Isaacs' bible knowledge and oratorical skills. For a time, he pursued private study, but his father's departure put an end to these aspirations.

In his late teenage years, Isaacs found employment as a bookkeeper on a Westmoreland estate. Apart from record-keeping, the position involved supervision of work in the fields and, at crop time, in the still house. The estate may well have been Roaring River where a Thomas Cridland had been an attorney and overseer during the century's first decade. His mother's land was in the vicinity, and Isaacs was tasked with collecting the rent to be sent back home.

In later years, he wrote of his journey on horseback away from Chester Castle. Leaving Hanover behind, in time he arrived at a vast estate. Cane stretched as far as the eye could see, while the factory's billowing smoke cast a pall across the land.[4]

Though Isaacs remained there barely two years, his time in Westmoreland was formative.

Later in life, he attested to the fact that he "could write a book about my experiences on that sugar estate, [...] of innocence destroyed [and] of exploitation in the raw". An exuberant youth, he copied the ways of his peers and became, as he termed it, a "libertine". Advised to employ a maid, she became his bed mate and confidante. Within six months, he was "seasoned" to the life.[5] Yet, Isaacs also saw the conditions under which men and women worked. Of the senior overseer he remarked,

> He was without doubt a very cruel man. He would have been a most trusted employee of Anne Palmer in her day. He used to ride around with a cow skin whip, and if the occasion arose, he did not hesitate to use it on any of the labourers.
>
> One day however he spoke to a woman who was gathering trash for the boiling house, and she evidently gave an answer he thought impertinent. She was heavy with child, but that did not deter him from kicking her [...].

As Isaacs recounted,

> The woman held her stomach with her hands for a while, and when she could speak, she looked at him and said, 'Busha, you kick me, see God there. I am the last woman you kick.' He was about to kick her again when she said, 'You better kick me quick for you is as good as dead.'
>
> He was a man over six feet tall and looking at him he was the embodiment of good health, but nine days later, he was dead. My Christian concepts of life did not allow me to mourn his passing although he was engaged to a half-sister of mine.[6]

Isaacs would contrast the sugar workers' lot with that of the farmers he knew as a child. The farmers were less alienated, and able to sustain a community based, co-operative spirit. His daughter, Nadine, remarked that the contrast between the two situations impressed her father: "He was moved by the way in which the workers were treated on the estate. He really sincerely wanted to make a better life for them. [As a self-educated] man of his colour, there were few options for respectable occupations. It was basically to become a pastor or a politician."

Isaacs was also introduced to *bone dice*, a game of chance, at which he lost heavily. On one fateful day he wagered and lost £45 rent, and his horse. Shamed by his recklessness, he conferred with his maid and decided to run away to Kingston. With him he took her generous donation of £3, arriving in Kingston with just 2/6d. The year was 1922.[7]

For Isaacs and other newcomers to the island's capital, jobs were scarce and would become more so as the years passed. Between 1881 and 1921, emigration to Panama, Cuba and the United States had reduced the rate of Jamaica's population growth. Coupled with a proliferation of small farms, this factor slowed Kingston's expansion. Soon, however, regional migration tapered off and the land available for small cultivations reached its limit. Concurrently, after a short resurgence, sugar prices and production resumed a long-term decline. The trek from rural parts to the city quickened as new arrivals spread across the parishes of Kingston and St Andrew. A former governor, Lord Olivier, remarked that by the mid-1930s, the city had become "the sink of the landless, casual labouring folk of most of the Island". This circumstance affected both men and women, many of whom remained unemployed or confined to casual work.[8]

Initially, Isaacs had no place of abode and suffered hardship. After a month or so, he had some luck. In Kingston he met a man he had known in Westmoreland. The still house worker had inflated his wages due, and then fled the estate, destined for Cuba. Isaacs had borrowed £5 from a family friend to help him on his way. Now returned prosperous, the man repaid Isaacs ten times over. With £50 in hand, he was able to find stable lodging and employment. Eight weeks after his arrival in Kingston, he began work as a proof reader at the Gleaner Company. He earned £2 a week and stayed with the company for almost a year. However, the hours were long and left little time for a social life.

He sought employment as a customs clerk and then moved on to clerk for a dry goods merchant. The position was demanding. "There wasn't a day when night did not catch [us] in the store and you had to come to work by seven o'clock in the morning." There were no lunch breaks. All day the clerks toiled while others called out the orders: "Ten pieces of KD4 Khaki Drill, ten by forty yards at ten pence." The owner's son took over the business and sought to cut wages. Isaacs tried and failed to persuade his fellow clerks to strike. Finally, he appealed to the father, who told his son to desist. Isaacs noted the quiescence of his workmates, afraid to risk their jobs.[9]

Soon thereafter, he began to tour parishes as a sales representative. His suppliers included Nathans, the Issas and the Hannas, all importers of manufactured, mostly dry goods. When Isaacs had arrived in Kingston, Nathan and Company was already established as a wholesale and retail firm. By contrast, E.A. Issa & Bros and R. Hanna and Sons were just beginning to make their mark. The founders of both these family firms had their roots in the Middle East; Elias Issa in Palestine and Edward Rasheed Hanna Sr. in Lebanon, then part of Syria. Both families were Christian and socially conservative. Elias Issa, father of entrepreneur and tourism promoter Abe Issa, came to the Americas and to Jamaica with his father in the pursuit of commercial success.[10] In 1893, they attended the Chicago World Trade Fair, where they learned of Kingston's recent international exhibition. Travelling by way of Central America to Kingston, they arrived and soon established a mainly wholesale store in 1894. Two years later, they moved to

Orange Street. Wiped out by the 1907 earthquake, Elias rebuilt and became sole proprietor of his firm in 1916, the year that his elder son, Abe, entered St George's College. Abe would go on to study in the United States and travel abroad as an agent for his father – to London, North America, Europe and the Far East. Though they were of similar age, Abe and Isaacs were worlds apart. Initially, at least, Isaacs felt Elias to be a more kindred spirit: "He never forgot that he was once poor."[11]

Isaacs had a more immediate rapport with Edward (Eddie) Rasheed Hanna. Eddie was born in 1894 to Rasheed Hanna Sr. and his wife, Jamilie. The family resided in Matthews Lane, just a short remove from Kingston's commercial centre.[12] Eddie's father found employment as an itinerant peddler and, from earnings saved, opened a shop close to Orange Street. The year was 1900. Income from his father's shop allowed Eddie to complete elementary school and attend Wolmer's Secondary School in Kingston. The Hannas' shop was also destroyed in 1907. While Rasheed sought to rebuild the business, Eddie, with his mother and brothers, went to New York. Eddie worked at odd jobs. In 1917, he entered the US Navy, but soon thereafter returned to Jamaica, where his father and a brother had established a haberdashery.

In 1934, R. Hanna and Sons Ltd. became a registered company. By that time the firm had twenty-one shops in Kingston – both wholesale and retail – and seven stores in strategic parish towns, including Port Maria, Balaclava, Oracabessa and Montego Bay. Eddie Hanna also moved into manufacturing. In 1942, he became a partner in and later, owner, of Jamaica Knitting Mills. After World War II he invested in garment, furniture and shoe manufacture.

The initial period of Hanna's expansion coincided with the years in which Isaacs sought to secure a livelihood. Although he sourced merchandise from all three suppliers – the Nathans, the Issas and Hanna – it was the last in particular who provided Isaacs with contacts and a range of products to sell in the countryside. As the 1920s unfolded, Isaacs applied himself and repaid his mother the money he had gambled away. Two decades later, as the PNP's Minister of Trade and Industry, he would work with Abe Issa to revamp tourism in Jamaica, and support Eddie Hanna's initiatives in manufacturing. His early interest in trade and commerce would continue for a lifetime.

Isaacs married for the first time on 1 June 1926. His wife was Ivy Lucille, daughter of a Mr and Mrs Louis Davis of Kingston. Their first child, a son, was born on 22 June 1927 and their second son, on 9 September 1928. The boys' respective middle names, Aloysius and Ignatius, Roman Catholic saints, reflected Isaacs' conversion to Catholicism following his Presbyterian childhood. A third son, William Isaacs, followed, but then, tragedy struck. The two elder brothers passed away and, late in 1931, Ivy died in childbirth, while delivering twin girls. The funeral notice for his wife gave the family's address as 39 Molynes Road, Half Way Tree. At 5pm on 17 December, mourners would proceed from there to Calvary Cemetery. The infant girls barely survived their mother. Six months later they died in Ramble, Hanover, just a few weeks apart. Only young William would remain, just one year old when his mother died. A malaria epidemic possibly explains the comprehensive loss of both the twins and the boys. It had raged in Jamaica, beginning in late 1930 and continuing throughout 1931. Unusually heavy rain in the early 1930s, and poor drainage, had brought mosquitoes in abundance. It was worst in some rural parts, in Red Hills and in some of Kingston's slums.[13]

To add to this personal crisis, on 14 September 1931, the *Daily Gleaner* carried a notice inserted by E.A. Issa & Bros that Mr W.O. Isaacs is "no longer connected with our Firm". Isaacs confirmed that rising misfortune had left him dazed and demoralized over an extended period. William relates a conversation with his father in later years. It concerned Isaacs' situation and the good news brought by a certain doctor:

> Him say, 'William, after your mother and four brothers and sisters died and you alone were left and not expected to live, I went to pieces. I lost control of my life. I lost my job. And Dr Stockhausen found me drunk one Sunday morning at 8 o'clock at a bar at the foot of King Street. Dr Stockhausen went next door and paid six pence for a condensed can of black coffee. He gave it to me and I vomited it up [and a second can as well]. Now William, at that stage a normal man would say, 'To hell with it!' He went and paid a third six pence for a third can of coffee. I drank it and kept it down. He took one pound out of his pocket. [....] He gave the pound to me and said, 'Go and clean up yourself. Meet me at the hospital at 3 o'clock. Your son is out of danger.'
>
> [....] Him say, 'William, I put you under my left arm and I bent down and took your coffin from under the bed.' (The coffin was made.) 'And with you under my left arm and the coffin under my right, we walked out of there.'[14]

Isaacs suffered further losses during this period. His sister, Ellen, had married a Presbyterian pastor, who ministered to the congregation at Ebenezer Church in Spur Tree, southwest of Mandeville. Catherine Isaacs came to this daughter, acutely ill with cancer. Several months later, on 13 October 1930, she died, leaving "a husband and 8 children – three sons and five daughters – and several grandchildren, to mourn their irreparable loss". Almost two years later, it was from the same Ebenezer Manse that Isaacs and his sister gave notice of the death of a younger sibling, Sarah Platt Isaacs, aged twenty-six. The notice ended with the passage, "And the Lord God chose the best of them."[15] Barely thirty, Isaacs had lost his mother, his wife, four infant children and a sister. He had worked and travelled throughout the parishes in order to insert himself into Kingston's commercial life. He did, however, rekindle relations with his father, who had returned to Hanover from the United States.

Events soon took a more promising turn. Isaacs inherited and quickly sold his mother's land. While William remained in the care of his sister at the Manse, Isaacs used part of the proceeds to make a trip to England. His return was detailed in the *Daily Gleaner*'s shipping lists, where it was reported that the steamship *Coronado* had docked from Avonmouth (a port of Bristol), on 31 August 1933. Among the passengers listed were some well-known Jamaican names: DaCosta, Henriques, Jacobs and de Lisser. If Wills had determined to take this trip following his sister's death in August 1932, he may have been away for around half a year. And notwithstanding his offhand comment – that "I went to England and had a good time" – it is likely that the trip secured the contacts that enabled him to start a business.[16]

He began to receive imported goods to distribute in Jamaica on commission. He formed a partnership with Ferdinand 'Ferdy' Samms. The agency was known as Samms, Isaacs & Sons, the latter in anticipation of the day when William would join the firm. Their office was located at 21 Port Royal Street in downtown Kingston. It remained Isaacs' business address for many years, and also a venue for various PNP activities. According to William, Britain and Japan were the firm's main suppliers of diverse merchandise. Samms advertised in the *Daily Gleaner* as an agent for bicycles produced by the Runwell Cycle Company of Birmingham. Runwell described its product as a "bicycle for all purposes" that "won't wear out", a plus in Jamaica's rough terrain. In 1940, the *Gleaner* noted that Isaacs had as one of his principals in Manchester, England, Messrs David Midgley, Donner & Co. For many generations, the Midgley family, based in Keighley, Bradford, was a prominent textile manufacturer. Isaacs also engaged in riskier ventures. One involved a shipment of cement tombstones destined for Jamaica that sank mid-Atlantic during World War II. Notwithstanding, with more than a decade's experience in his trade, he was modestly successful. A regular letter writer to the *Gleaner*, he was often referred to as a "Kingston businessman".[17]

He also changed his residential address from Molynes Road to Kingston Gardens, southeast of Race Course. Built in the last three decades of the nineteenth century, initially it housed a mostly white elite. However, as Kingston and southwest St Andrew became the destination of rural migrants, members of the colonial elite moved north to upper St Andrew. Colin Clarke remarks that "during the 1920s the exodus, which originally affected only the growing commercial centre, extended to the whole of Kingston parish". By the late 1930s, Kingston Gardens had become a residential site for the brown middle class, including minorities of Syrian, Jewish and some Chinese merchants.[18]

In time, William would complete his elementary schooling at Blake's Preparatory and enter the prestigious Jamaica College. In first form he and Michael Manley, both keen athletes, formed an enduring friendship. William, since those days called 'Vunnie', said of JC: "We were the first real PNP group. The head boy was David Coore." He also observed that as Samms, Isaacs & Sons faltered through the 1940s, "Samms migrated to America and my father came under the spell of Norman Manley and he entered politics."

The late 1920s was a rousing time for politics in Kingston. Marcus Garvey returned from the United States near the end of 1927 and launched his People's Political Party in 1928. The Sixth World Convention of Negro Peoples was held in 1929 at Edelweiss Park. Garvey spoke of an end to British rule, world war, and the need for Jamaicans to engage with the world. A few years later, in 1934, two men who would be heroes of labour, St William Grant and Alexander Bustamante, returned as well. Bustamante's family, the Clarkes, resided in Hanover and likely knew the Isaacs family. Indeed, of all those involved in twentieth-century Jamaican politics, Isaacs may have shared most with Bustamante: a rural middle-class background, a knockabout youth and early adulthood, a populist appeal, political nous and a flair for performance. There were differences, of course. Isaacs was a nationalist and, even then, something of a Christian socialist engaged in commerce. Bustamante was socially less conservative but, with regard to the British and capitalism, less critical than Isaacs.[19]

This mustering of forces in the early 1930s surely influenced Isaacs. However, his interest in politics in fact began earlier and was more parochial. Two men stood out in his memory. One was the often-comical Dr Alfred Mends and the other, the rather more sober H.A.L. Simpson. Mends was a nativist and activist, while Simpson was a nationalist and served as an elective member of the Legislative Council, and as mayor of Kingston.[20] In the mid-1920s, Isaacs was often in the audience periodically entertained by Dr Alfred Mends expounding his views from Coke Chapel steps. A number of these gatherings were meetings of the Jamaica Reform Club, formed in 1923 by Mends, along with S.P. Radway. With its motto, "Jamaica for Jamaicans", the club maintained a critical stance towards crown colony rule.[21] The *Daily Gleaner* attacked it accordingly. In this milieu, Isaacs found support for his nascent nationalist views and meshed his own exuberant style with the idiom of the street corner crowd. Watching Mends, he also grasped the importance of theatre as a means to hold an audience. His recollection of Dr Mends and the issues he raised combined substance with high farce.

In those days there was no loudspeaker and no electric lights at Coke Chapel steps so, if there was an issue to be ventilated in public, Dr Mends would come down with his lantern and prevail on someone to lend him a table.

> The very first issue that I can remember that he took up was when the streets of Kingston were to be paved. That night he began by demanding that the workers should be given a dollar a day. Of course in those days, 1/6d was the maximum that a working man got. [....][22]
>
> He was an outstanding orator, and when he made a point that demanded an applause from his audience, he had a habit of turning his back and only turned around when the applause was finished. One night he made one of these telling points and the audience roared their approval, and as he turned his back...a man called out – 'Doctor, your trouser batty tear', as quick as lightning, he turned to his audience and shouted, 'I say a dollar a day!' [....]

> It must be said of him however, that [...] the KSAC raised the salary of the working man who paved the streets of Kingston to 2/6d per day.

Isaacs also recalled the Darling Street riot of 1924. He remarked of the clash between police and workers, "In those days the police would shoot people at the slightest provocation, and one man was shot dead." Mends responded with a protest meeting, but others charged him with causing the riot – due to his catch cry "A dollar a day".[23] Certainly, in May 1924, he had addressed his followers on the issue of wages, and also on the need for a governor to replace the unpopular Leslie Probyn. As reported in the *Gleaner*, Mends said:

> If the labourers got higher wages the stores and all professional men and traders would be better off and there would not be so many bankruptcies because the commodities for sale would be bought up by the working people. The landlords would get their rents paid up to them more regularly. [....] In fact, the Corporation should set the pace agoing for a higher state of living and better citizenship. The squalor, poverty, hunger and dirt would be overcome. People would wear better clothes and perform all their duties of citizenship to the State, and this would bring about contentment and harmony between the Government and the people.

On the matter of a governor, Mends observed that the island required a replacement for Probyn drawn from the ranks of British Labour; one who would "harmonize best with the people" and not waste money on expatriate officials. He proposed Ben Tillett, a British Labour politician and recent visitor to the island. Tillett had deplored the fact that many women in Jamaica broke stones for a living, a task performed in England only by male convicts.[24]

Born in 1871, Mends had managed and edited a number of popular newssheets. He was also active in early trade unionism. He became a follower of Marcus Garvey and joined the Universal Negro Improvement Association. His prominence grew, however, when he split from that organization. He formed the Jamaica Reform Club, taking with him the Libertarian Chapter of the UNIA. The chapter's leader had remarked that Dr Mends "had come out boldly and squarely" for Jamaica. "Africa must be redeemed, but we must redeem Jamaica first."[25]

The Reform Club was at its height when the Darling Street riot occurred. The club would soon peter out and Dr Mends moved on. In 1935, he began to manage and edit the pro-Ethiopian newspaper, *Plain Talk*, which aroused popular feeling in the years that preceded the labour rebellion of 1938. Under Mends, the paper aired the demands of shopkeepers, merchants and small manufacturers who believed they were threatened by "alien competition".[26] In 1936 a new column, "Jamaica for Jamaicans", pursued this theme: "We have all sorts of nationalities infesting this Island to the detriment of the native Jamaicans not being able to obtain employment. The Capitalists do not care whether the peasants, workers, suffer hunger, starve and die as long as their several interests are protected." In 1939, Alfred Mends sent his own memorandum to the Moyne Royal Commission into labour unrest across the West Indies. Some years later, he died in obscurity. Isaacs helped to fund his funeral and was one of the few who attended.[27]

Despite his affection for Dr Mends, in the mid-1920s Isaacs was a strong supporter of H.A.L. Simpson, who had been mayor of Kingston during the Darling Street riot. When, for a time, Simpson withdrew from politics following his defeat in the Kingston mayoral election of 1925, supporters across the island organized a testimonial fund for him. It grew to £400. Isaacs donated five shillings.[28]

Born in 1872, Simpson attended the Kingston Collegiate School, which admitted boys of any colour shade, provided their families could pay the fees. In 1902 the school closed, but not before Hubert Ashton Laselve Simpson secured an education that would allow him to become a solicitor and enter politics. He became a Kingston councillor in 1908 and in 1911 was elected to the Legislative Council. In 1912 he was elected mayor of Kingston for the first time. He would serve two periods as mayor, 1912–1925 and 1935–1937. He was awarded an OBE for his services during World War I.

In fact, Simpson was more radical than his elections to office suggest. He was a member and sometime president of the National Club, which was founded in 1909 by S.A.G. (Sandy) Cox, also a lawyer, and Alexander Dixon. Jamaica's first nationalist group, the club became a vehicle for middle-class activism. Members were required to be 'native born' and pledged to self-government. Although it was short lived (1909–1911), the National Club had other illustrious members. Both Marcus Garvey and W.A. Domingo, who later founded the Jamaica Progressive League in New York, served as assistant secretaries. Simpson remained an associate of Garvey and, in 1930, contested the seat of Kingston for Garvey's People's Political Party. Unsuccessful in that year, in 1935 he was elected again to the Legislative Council and again became Kingston's mayor. Simpson was also a social reformer. In the Legislative Council, he introduced a Shop Assistants Bill which became law in May 1912. Pertaining to hours of work and employment of minors, it was an early instance of labour regulation in Jamaica. Equally progressive, he saw through Council legislation on women's suffrage, albeit subject to age and income provisions.[29]

Two further aspects of Simpson's career would have engaged Isaacs. One, his volatile relationship with the barrister and nationalist J.A.G. Smith. In 1921, when both were electives of the Legislative Council, they formed rival associations to promote their respective approaches to constitutional reform. Smith had proposed a return to the 1865 constitution that was terminated when crown colony rule was introduced. His view entailed a restricted suffrage at the outset and brought considerable opposition including, some twenty years later, from PNP members Wills Isaacs and Ivan Lloyd. They debated with Smith in the press.[30]

Isaacs also followed the mayoral elections that Simpson contested. Simpson's principal opponent in each case was supported by J.A.G. Smith. These opponents, Altamount DaCosta and Lewis Ashenheim, were respectively, a director and the chairman of the Gleaner Company. Both were white representatives of capital. The 1925 election was bitterly fought. Personal insults were traded, and meetings of the candidates were disrupted by partisan henchmen. The election involved Norman Manley's first appearance on a political platform – at the Ward Theatre and in support of Simpson. Simpson lost, due mainly to votes cast for DaCosta by the St Andrew middle class.[31]

Ten years later and running again, Simpson made his position on J.A.G. Smith and Ashenheim clear. In December 1934 he launched his campaign declaring, "Mr Ashenheim is being brought forward by the Hon. J.A.G. Smith; a gentleman whom Jamaica respects and esteems [...]. No one can say that Mr Smith has not done some good work at some time in Jamaica. But Mr Smith has done some bad work also. Mr Smith gave you Mr DaCosta ten years ago. [....] Mr Smith gave you Mr DaCosta five years ago. [....] Do you want anybody else that Mr Smith recommends?" Simpson continued: "What has Mr Ashenheim ever done for the people of Kingston? Has he ever identified himself with the public affairs of the parish? Has he ever associated himself with the sufferings and needs and wants of the people? He is too busy for that, controlling the capital of this country."

The large crowd at Old Wolmer's Yard gave Simpson rousing applause.[32] Eight years later, Isaacs campaigned at this site, among others, for his own election to the KSAC council. On election, he would thank Norman Manley who, from early days, had moulded his politics. Although with different foci and strategies, the two shared both with Simpson and Mends a passionate nationalist outlook, a critique of imperial power, and a commitment to the people of Jamaica.

A further sense of Isaacs' evolving politics comes from his letters to the *Daily Gleaner*. Initially, these addressed debates regarding

Roman Catholicism, to which he had converted. Throughout his adult life, Isaacs was avid in his defence of the faith although, from time to time, he criticized the organization. His idea of the church was quite specific. He advocated for it as a universal one beyond the distinctions of colour, class, race and nation, and the various denominations. For him, the church embodied a spiritual and moral touchstone outside politics.

In March 1925, a debate emerged in the letters section of the *Daily Gleaner* concerning the relative merits of Protestantism and Catholicism. One letter argued that the Reformation was a matter of politics, rather than religion. Another proposed that social conditions in Spanish-speaking countries would deter almost anyone from being a Catholic. At age twenty-three, Isaacs entered the fray, noting that he was both a Catholic and a "first-time" contributor to the *Gleaner*. He argued that the *New Testament* assumed one unified church. Moreover, depressed conditions were a failure of the nation, not the church. Charged with Catholic arrogance, Isaacs extolled a church with a universal reach, rather than a bounded one, such as the Church of England. Notwithstanding the anti-slavery stance of some nonconformists, the English Protestant church, as a state church, had a sordid history:

> "Let us examine for a moment the foundation of the Anglican Church [and whether it bears] the characteristics of heaven-sent reformers. King Henry, the murderer of his wives, continued by Somerset, the murderer of his brother, and completed by Elizabeth the murderer of her guest [...] a religion of such an evil origin cannot be the work of God."

Where human welfare was concerned, the "admirable achievements" of some Protestants were minor compared with those of the Catholic Church. Attending Holy Trinity Cathedral on North Street at the time, Isaacs extolled the work of priests amongst the poor.[33]

A decade later, debates around Catholicism were couched in terms of the Spanish Civil War. In 1936, a new face in Jamaica's politics, Bustamante, gave an address in Kingston on the background to the war. He underlined the suffering of the masses under King Alfonso and the Catholic Church. In 1938, and just prior to the labour rebellion, the *Gleaner* featured remarks on the Spanish war by Cardinal Patrick Hayes, archbishop of New York. He endorsed General Franco, noting that Republicans were controlled by the communists. He also questioned the accuracy of reports that Italian fascists, in alliance with Franco, had bombed Barcelona, killing hundreds. The *Gleaner* article was followed by an opinion piece and letters devoted to the nature of communism, fascism, and the British position on Spain. Among them were virulent charges that the "reds" had "set to work to remodel Spain". Isaacs responded with the question, "Why Communism?" – in Spain or elsewhere:

> Governments and readers of religious thought take a great amount of pleasure in telling of the horrors of Communism but none seem to be honest enough to ask and answer the question [Why?] and the only answer that can be given is that it is a natural re-action to the system of Capitalism which is far more vicious than Communism, for while Communism will murder those who oppose its principles, for centuries Capitalism has caused millions to live in hunger, poverty and want with diseased minds and bodies languishing for years to find relief only in the grave [...]. Under this latter system the people of Spain suffered for centuries and the Church not only upheld the ends of the Capitalists, but by their vast possessions and wealth could rightly be termed a Capitalistic Church.

He counselled against support for Franco. "Had the early Church in its infancy half a dozen adherents with the principles of General Franco they would have dragged its fair name in the dust."[34]

His letter was published on 4 May 1938, just five days after Jamaica's labour rebellion had erupted among sugar workers at Frome. Four were killed and fourteen, including five policemen, were wounded. Eighty-five people were arrested. The uprising would be reignited on 23 May, when Kingston dockers led a strike that was joined by hundreds of the city's service workers. Not long after these events, the *Daily Gleaner* published a detailed account of a lecture on communism by Father Joseph Krim SJ. He proposed to provide the history of Russian communism since World War I; a history of savagery, murder, starvation and martyrdom. Now clearly influenced by Jamaica's own rebellion, Isaacs responded: "It is a waste of time telling of the atrocities of Communism, when the people are aware of the fact that there is no atrocity imputed to Communism of which the Christian Church is not guilty. What we Christians should do is to take the beam out of our own eye before trying to pluck the mote out of our brother's eye."[35]

On 13 June, the *Daily Gleaner*'s editorial described the rebellion as a "reign of terror" by a "hooligan element" unwilling "to labour for one day or one week". Those who rebelled should not be considered workers at all. The paper proposed that a fund be collected island-wide to express appreciation to Jamaica's constabulary. Well aware of labour conditions in Kingston and at Frome, a Westmoreland estate, the *Gleaner*'s proposal riled Isaacs. Albeit in terms more restrained than usual, he raised a crucial point: "If my memory serves me right, public officers are not allowed to receive presents from private individuals or corporations and to my mind it is a very dangerous precedent [...]. We might as well subscribe a very tidy amount and make a presentation to the several magistrates in the Colony who performed very well their duties when they sentenced rioters to prison."

On 12 December 1938, his last such letter for the year concerned a recent appointment by the governor to Jamaica's Privy Council, a representative of landowners' interests. It was the council that offered advice to the governor on fiscal policy and, he explained, the landowners had been without a voice on the Council for some time. Isaacs responded: "I take it that the interests of the various sections of this community, judging from his Excellency's remarks, ought to be represented on the Privy Council. Would you be good enough to let me know whether the thousands who comprise the labouring classes in this country are represented in the Privy Council?"[36]

Almost twenty years after his arrival in Kingston, Isaacs had become politically aware. In the 1920s and 1930s, he was confronted by the suffering he saw in Westmoreland and Kingston. He also faced personal loss of a magnitude uncommon in his class. He became a committed Catholic. A largely self-educated man, he reflected on political systems – capitalism, fascism and communism. He engaged with Kingston's municipal politics and with a range of local reformers. Those to whom he was drawn were invariably nationalists. His experience is captured in two quite different designations. One was "Kingston businessman" – applied to him as a partner in Samms, Isaacs & Sons, a member of the Chamber of Commerce, and a contributor to the *Gleaner*. The second was "the Catholic Communist" – used by some due to his views on Franco, the church, and capitalism and communism.[37] The two designations attest to Isaacs' early career, which involved a breadth of experience unusual among fellow activists. Early on, he presented as a critic of exploitation and later, as a social democrat, especially when his concerns turned to unemployment. He maintained these views throughout his life.

## Chaper 2

# Becoming an Activist

*Wills O. was the spark plug that moved others and the party to action. He was accepted by the masses as a man who eschewed the advantages given to men of his class in Jamaica. He worked for them and without condescension, the stormy petrel so badly needed.*
– Dudley Thompson, 2002.

*He was the most interesting person of the time. Because, you know, the commercial community was not always supportive, at the best, of the PNP.* – Howard Cooke, 2002.[1]

In the course of the 1930s, Isaacs secured his position in Kingston's middle class as a resident of Kingston Gardens and a partner in Samms, Isaacs & Sons on Port Royal Street. He also played his part in lettered associations.[2] Along with Florizel Glasspole, he was prominent in the Kingston and St Andrew Literary and Debating Association, which was formed in 1931. He became a member of the Readers and Writers Club, of which H.G. de Lisser, editor of the *Gleaner* and secretary of the Jamaica Imperial Association, was patron. De Lisser soon withdrew, confronted by more progressive members, including a young Frank Hill. In 1938, Richard Hart founded a Kingston branch of the British-based Left Book Club. The branch had among its participants Isaacs, Glasspole and Arthur Henry, as well as Hart. Members of the National Reform

Association – instigated in 1937 by Frank's brother, Ken – were also participants in the Book Club.[3] This group was the nationalist core of Jamaica, a number of whom believed that socialism should prevail not only over fascism, but capitalism as well. Some were communists. The Spanish Civil War and the growth of fascist sympathies among England's upper class fuelled these allegiances. The racism increasingly explicit in Nazism was anathema to Jamaica's nationalists.

The labour rebellion of 1938 jolted this constellation of thinkers into action. Previously reluctant to engage in politics, Norman Manley now became the leader of a party.[4] This development marked a shift from the small, ephemeral groups of Laselve Simpson's time, and overtook Hill's National Reform Association. The Jamaica Progressive League of New York, with a branch in Kingston from 1937, became an affiliated group. The People's National Party was formally launched in Kingston one Sunday afternoon, 18 September 1938. About two thousand were seated in the Ward Theatre while loudspeakers enabled the five thousand more outside to hear the proceedings. Manley took centre stage and outlined the party's aims. It would be the vanguard of a push for self-government under a new constitution. As a mass democratic party, it would also foster a "widespread campaign of education" and a programme of "development planning". A planned economy was at the heart of the party's rationale, Manley explained:

> It is called the People's Party because it will unswervingly aim at all those measures which will serve the masses of the country [...]. It is perfectly true that the interests of all classes of people are bound together. But it is equally true that there is a common mass in this country whose interest must predominate above and beyond all other classes, because [...] the object of civilization is to raise the standard of living and security of the masses of the people.

Manley called on Jamaicans to embrace a post-colonial stance, accepting "the burden and responsibility of guarding our own destiny".[5]

A few months later, in January 1939, Alexander Bustamante registered the Bustamante Industrial Trade Union.[6] He called a general strike and Governor Richards threatened to arrest him, declaring a state of emergency. Bustamante said the strike was in response to antagonism towards his union. However, he and unionist A.G.S. Coombs had a personal rivalry. Manley convened a meeting of interested parties and proposed a Trade Union Advisory Council to mediate between unions.[7] His move diverted Richards from confrontation with Bustamante. In time, the TUAC would discard its advisory role and, as the Trade Union Council, form a group of sixteen small unions linked with the PNP. Coombs and Ken Hill, who was at the time a unionist with the BITU, aligned with the TUC and the PNP.[8]

The party's constitution provided for a tiered, community-based structure. It was comprised on the one hand of district groups and wards feeding into parochial committees and, on the other, of an executive consisting of a general council and an executive committee. Both rank and file and the executive answered to the party's annual conference. Membership in the party could be sought through a district group or through affiliated groups, including as well as the JPL, the Jamaica Union of Teachers, and the Citizens' Associations. It is likely that Isaacs joined the PNP via the Metropolitan Group, along with Hart, the Hill brothers, Arthur Henry and W.A. McBean, also of the left Book Club. Historically known as the group that harboured the PNP's left, by late 1938 Isaacs' stated views revealed like sympathies.[9] The following notice in the *Gleaner* on 9 August 1939 suggests that Isaacs wished to identify with the left: "The Kingston Group of the Left Book Club will be addressed by Mr. Wills Isaacs at 8 o'clock tonight […] at 4 Central Avenue Kingston Gardens and will be open to the public. The subject of the address will be 'Does Roman Catholic Philosophy justify my Leftist tendency?'"

Less than a month later, on 3 September 1939, Britain declared war on Germany. The next day the PNP announced a moratorium on its self-government campaign. The primary focus would be on fighting fascist doctrine which denied "the equality of all races".[10] A state of war quickly underlined the vulnerability of those whom Manley saw as the party's chief concern. Disruptions to shipping brought inflation. The price of staples – including cornmeal, flour, imported fish and meat – rose rapidly; while the cost of kerosene and firewood went up by almost 25 per cent. The poor suffered. The first issue of Frank Hill's *Evening News* came out on 19 September. The paper launched a lively critique of the way in which the war was being used to subordinate labour. BITU industrial inaction was noted. Two months later, the *Evening News* was banned under War Emergency Regulations introduced just ten days before the war was declared.

At the PNP's first annual conference, 21–22 December 1939, Richard Hart moved a motion, seconded by Isaacs, that the party's executive oppose "the extraordinary censorship" of the *Evening News.* The motion was lost, in part due to the fact that country members were unfamiliar with the paper. There was also a view that the leftist *News* reflected poorly on the party. The left's disappointment was eased, however, when Isaacs – on behalf of the Metropolitan Group – moved another motion: that the party press for elections to the Legislative Council (delayed by the war) to be held within one month. The success of this motion reflected an upbeat mood. The PNP would not "agitate" for constitutional reform, but it would mobilize on related issues.

Post notes that at this conference Hart was the only leftist member of the party elected to the General Council, along with just one other of like mind. He remarks of Isaacs at this time that he "was not of the left". Nonetheless, as a "partner in a small trading company, Isaacs had emerged as a radical nationalist, who was prepared to work with the self-confessed communists; in this he typified what might be called a radical centre position in the PNP." Isaacs was already active in the drive to build up groups across the island. His name appeared often in the Meetings column of the *Daily Gleaner*, speaking in Spanish Town and beyond.[11]

He was not among the small inaugural group that ushered in a party on 28 August 1938, or one of those who helped to draft the PNP constitution. However, he was at the Ward Theatre launch, along with Glasspole, whom he knew through the LBC and other associations. Soon thereafter, both joined the PNP. Like Glasspole, Isaacs would be called a "foundation" member.[12] Years later, Edna Manley would write in her diary of "the early political pioneers". "The first ones that spring to mind are always Fairclough, Nethersole, Arnett, Glasspole, Wills Isaacs – and looking back after all these years, they seem as vivid, as real, to use a funny word, as valid." She also listed "the men of the left wing", the Hills and Hart, and the notable women, Edith Dalton-James, Iris King and Amy Bailey. [13]

Following the labour rebellion, in February 1940, advice from the *Moyne Royal Commission Report* was tabled in the British parliament. Although not part of the commission's brief, the recommendations for Jamaica included some pertaining to constitutional reform: universal adult suffrage, fewer appointed members of the Legislative Council, a more representative executive, and a new advisory committee to the governor on policy.[14] The recommended economic measures would be enacted by the Colonial Development and Welfare Office, formed the same year. The measures for Jamaica were modest: to increase small-farmer productivity, improve education and housing, and support trade union development. The sugar industry drew little comment and urban industrialization was deemed unfeasible.[15] In short, there was no real alternative imagined for Jamaica's unemployed and under-employed. Welfare measures were emphasized instead.

By contrast, *Public Opinion*[16] advocated an immediate response with regard to the island's unemployed: "Now is the time for the cement works [...]. Now is the time to start our beef-canning and bacon-curing, our boot and shoe factory and all other new efforts and new crops."[17] These measures would be part of Isaacs' agenda. The *Moyne Commission Report* was notable for the fact that, implicitly, it endorsed some central planning for the island's economy. However, it left intact an export industry based on rent-seeking agriculture; the off-shore repatriation of profits; lax taxation on capital gains; and intermittent charity in the place of welfare support. Norman Manley remarked on the commission's "futile proposal to make charitable social services do duty for economic, political and social reform". The recommendations offered only "palliatives" in the place of "work, wages and homes" for the people. And from this critique came the PNP view that Jamaica required both responsible government and a socialist programme to address the masses' needs. At the party's annual conference from 28 to 29 August 1940, Manley remarked on their close connection: "Any real programme for development of the Country is dependent upon our being responsible for our own Government and able to introduce measures which could never obtain the approval of the Colonial Office dominated as the British Government is by the financial interests in England." Herewith socialism, as the path to a just society, became a central aim of the nationalist movement. And notwithstanding war, Manley now recommitted the party to work for responsible government.[18]

These matters were addressed in a draft statement circulated to all groups one week before the annual conference. The statement received critique from the left and especially from members of the Metropolitan Group, who had caucused with others in the urban area. There was reason for their unease. The decision for socialism by Manley had been taken without prior consultation. The draft interpreted socialism in a fashion consistent with continuing support for Britain's war. As such, the PNP's socialism would be closely aligned with that of the British Labour Party. Manley endorsed state planning and government ownership of the means of production, but his rendering of policy came in evolutionary terms requiring step-by-step education. He failed to address the extensive nationalization implied. Policies concerning private land, profits, trade and international finance were not spelt out.[19]

When support for the statement was moved at the conference, Frank Hill brought a substantial amendment. Manley overruled him, arguing that the amendment was in fact a separate proposal. A subsequent motion to refer the statement back to the executive committee also failed. Among those who voted against were Isaacs, W.A. McBean and the Jamaica Progressive League's representative. Some other left delegates were absent. In his address to the conference, Manley referred good-naturedly to the party's "intellectual communists". He assured those present, and the world, that the PNP's socialism was neither anti-Christian nor revolutionary. He endorsed the view that Christian social principles were in fact socialist ones. He remarked that party intellectuals should "work with and for the party and not for secret aims of their own, be they socialist or otherwise". The remarks were prescient. He wanted party members to forego "rigid dogma" and respond to "particular conditions". He wanted a Jamaican socialism for Jamaica.[20]

In the year that followed Britain's declaration of war, Isaacs worked with the Metropolitan Group and also courted the commercial class. He was a member of the Chamber of Commerce and a regular attendee at meetings. He also proposed some attention-grabbing schemes, as reported in the *Gleaner.* One involved an island-wide gathering of clergy in Kingston to discuss challenges posed by the war; an unusual idea, but not entirely without foundation. The International Missionary Council had produced an informed report on socio-economic conditions following the 1938 rebellion. From this initiative came the Jamaica Christian Council, with its extensive network across the island. The council's organizational reach was at least equal to each of the parties. In June 1940, six months after this suggestion, Isaacs made another: that merchants who did business with Britain should allow their principals to retain half of their commissions to be paid to a British war fund. The *Gleaner* extolled Isaacs' patriotism and confirmed his own offer to Messrs David Midgley, Donner & Co. in England. The company had cabled back, "Deeply appreciate your message in this our hour of trial." In its account, the *Gleaner* noted that Isaacs was "a member of the General Council of the People's National Party and Vice President of the Metropolitan Group of the Party".[21] However, he would soon redirect his activities.

On the evening of 3 February 1941, the inaugural meeting of the Kingston Commercial Group took place at Edmondson Hall. Isaacs was elected president of the group and Manley addressed the gathering. Soon after, at an emergency meeting on 10 March, the group moved a no-confidence motion against the government. The motion would be put in the Legislative Council by elective member, J.A.G. Smith. The group's resolution expressed "our entire disapproval of totalitarian methods adopted by the Government" and underlined the "lack of interest and fair-play towards the workers of the Colony by the administration". Senior civil servants, expected to maintain political neutrality, were censured for "indulging in political speeches".[22] Finally, the group provided support for the central labour issue of the time: the PNP's Kingston Commercial Group gave its "wholehearted support to the just demands of the Bustamante Industrial Unions for an increase in pay to all sugar workers throughout the island". In June, Isaacs chaired a large gathering in Coke Memorial Hall addressed by visiting Englishman E.H.J. King on "Education and the Social Order". The talk reflected Manley's emphasis on the role of education in preparing citizens for self-government. In his remarks, Isaacs noted that one hundred thousand Jamaican children still did not go to school.[23]

Later in the year, the Commercial Group announced the formation of a study circle charged with producing at least twenty "active workers", who would strive to establish groups in rural parishes. The Commercial Group itself had grown by two hundred members due to its outreach, "taking the party doctrine into the homes of [...] people who would not under ordinary circumstances have attended meetings". In short, the Kingston Commercial Group was adopting the activism more commonly associated with the left – of small study circles, lectures and debates – to recruit the middle class. These activities proceeded "under the direction" of Isaacs. The group held its first annual general meeting on 28 May 1942, where, as president, he remarked that the Commercial Group had the largest membership in the PNP and "also contributed more to party funds than any other group". The membership stood at around three hundred. Also in 1942, Noel Nethersole would provide three lectures to the group on "Political Theory and Economy".[24]

Less than two weeks after the PNP's 1940 annual conference, Alexander Bustamante was interned indefinitely by Governor Richards. The reason was an island-wide speech addressed to sugar workers and banana loaders, carriers and boatmen. Bustamante called a strike in response to the refusal of producers to increase wages. He predicted industrial paralysis and that blood might flow. Responding, Richards claimed that his decision to intern Bustamante was due to the speech's inflammatory nature. He acted in accord with the War Emergency Regulations, which gave the power to forbid meetings and detain individuals without trial. The strike began on 8 September. The next day, Bustamante was interned and Richard Hart, Frank Hill and another man were arrested for protesting the detention. Brought before a magistrate, Manley successfully defended them, but Bustamante remained interned. A week later, the PNP's General Council condemned his arrest. The party and the TUC met with the BITU executive, offered support and set up a contact committee that would co-operate while Bustamante remained interned.[25]

Following these events, opposition to the suppression of civil liberties grew. A further order went out from Richards in March

1941 for the arrest of PNP activist Samuel Marquis, and W.A. Williams of the BITU's maritime section. Marquis was also a member of the Negro Workers' Education League. Grounds for the arrests were described in vague terms concerning speech that was "prejudicial" to the war. In May, an English journalist at the *Daily Gleaner*, G. St C. Scotter, was arrested. Ten days later, Sam Hinds, a leader of the NWEL, was due for arrest. He absconded and was chased across three parishes. Malnourished and ill, he returned to Kingston and was placed under surveillance. Even the governor was embarrassed by the treatment of an innocent man. The arrest that drew most attention was that of JPL leader, W.A. Domingo. He was apprehended on board a ship in Kingston Harbour before he had even set foot in Jamaica. The detention order accused Domingo of fostering anti-British and defeatist sentiments, exciting opposition to US bases in Jamaica, and promoting "feelings of colour prejudice and racial animosity". Nor would Richards have liked his socialist views.[26]

Leslie Ashenheim protested the arrest of Scotter in the *Daily Gleaner*. The paper noted the arbitrary nature of Jamaica's war regulations compared to the British ones. A Council for the Protection of Civil Liberties was formed and held its first Kingston meeting in June. Along with Ashenheim, H.G. de Lisser was present. Others included J.A.G. Smith and E.E.A. Campbell, both electives of the Legislative Council; Florizel Glasspole of the TUC; and H.M. Shirley of the BITU.[27] Another large crowd gathered for a meeting in the parish of St Ann in July. Among those seated on the platform were Ivan Lloyd, Isaacs, Leslie Ashenheim and George Desnoes, a prominent businessman.

Isaacs' was among the speeches reported by the *Gleaner*, including one section directed at the Colonial Secretary, who had defended the recent internments. Isaacs remarked, "He said it was a few disloyal people in the country. [...] Who were the people who were disloyal? If they were disloyal, what were the crimes committed?"

He coyly suggested that surely the government was lax to have let such crimes occur at all. He concluded that despite the island's poverty, Jamaicans had made generous donations to the war. They knew that "Nazi rule would be worse than slavery". The Secretary's words were "stupid and idle".[28] The United States consul general seemed to agree. He reported to Washington just a week later that "so far as is known", none of those interned "is in any way pro-German; probably none of them is anti-British in the broad sense of the term; all of them are bitter critics of the present Government of Jamaica."[29]

In the midst of this civil liberties debate, a constitutional one resurfaced in the *Daily Gleaner*. The debate concerned J.A.G. Smith's stance on steps towards representative government. His view that the process should begin with a return to the 1865 constitution was contentious.[30] In October 1941, the *Daily Gleaner* published an extended statement from Smith. His position also left the governor's reserve powers in place and therefore begged the question of internment without trial. The PNP's Ivan Lloyd called him to account. Isaacs weighed in. Turning to banter, he noted that Smith's proposal would prolong the governor's power. He suggested that Smith rename his model "Reprehensible Government", for it was neither representative nor responsible.[31]

During 1941 and 1942, the PNP – through its TUC affiliate – became more active in union affairs. With Bustamante in detention, co-operation with the BITU brought closer and more effective relations between the industrial and political arms of Jamaica's labour movement. The BITU was able to secure favourable Labour Department awards for both sugar workers and dockers. The agreements were negotiated by Noel Nethersole, chairman of the TUC and PNP vice president. He was supported by Glasspole, the TUC's secretary.[32] Bustamante was released in February 1942. As Bertram recounts, his release, in all likelihood, reflected concerns of the governor beyond the war, including the apparent consolidation of a socialist front involving the PNP and the BITU; awareness that Jamaica, with its newly confirmed bauxite deposits, would become a strategic possession; and his distaste for the PNP's critique of imperialism. Bustamante's subsequent break with Manley, and with BITU officials who had engaged with the PNP, created a fissure in this political bloc.[33] The fissure widened when, on 8 July 1943, Bustamante launched his Jamaica Labour Party.

These events strengthened the PNP's resolve to build a bridge between the party and the working class. With the BITU well established among manual workers, the TUC turned its attention to skilled workers, with a focus on those in government employment. The following unions became TUC affiliates: Postal and Telegraph Workers, Printers and Allied Workers, Public Works Employees, Fruit Selectors and Tally Clerks, and the Jamaica Railways Union. These joined earlier affiliates – the Tramways, Transport and General Workers' Union, and Builders and Allied Trades.[34]

Whilst not first and foremost a unionist, Isaacs was active in union affairs. In August 1942, he mobilized the Kingston Commercial Group to petition the governor on the TT&GW's behalf. The issue involved a rival strike-breaking union within the privately owned Jamaica Public Services Company. The petition stated that the company union was "striking at the vitals" of trade unionism and named the leader of this rogue union, J. Coleman Beecher. A year or so later, Isaacs would face Beecher as a rival candidate for a KSAC council seat. Following submissions, the Labour Department ruled that the TT&GW, by virtue of its extensive membership, should have sole bargaining rights at JPSC for motormen and conductors. The representation of shed men, however, would be shared with the BITU.[35] Beecher's rogue union did not figure in the ruling. Where the two main unions were concerned, the outcome was amicable, but foreshadowed things to come. As competition between the TUC and BITU grew, the Bustamante union would use demarcation disputes to disrupt the activity of TUC unions.[36]

Isaacs was also active in the B&ATU. The union grew rapidly, not least because it represented workers at the newly established US bases at Sandy Gully, Salt Creek and Goat Island. He became union president in March 1943 and claimed substantial credit for the union's expansion from fifteen members to "500 odd", with four hundred artisans in work and "all of them financial". Isaacs was also vice president of the Postal and Telegraph Workers Union and active in the Fruit Selectors and Tally Clerks Union, becoming president of the latter in 1944. The four most effective union organisers were Richard Hart, Arthur Henry, and Frank and Ken Hill. Isaacs worked most closely with Ken, holding office in four different unions where Ken was president, secretary, or the leading organiser.[37]

The activities of the 4Hs, as they became known, were disrupted by Governor Richards in October 1942. Using his powers under the newly enacted Authorized Associations (Defence) Regulations, Richards declared three trade unions illegal. Jamaica Railways, Public Works Employees, and Postal and Telegraph Workers were each deemed to be engaged in acts that could prejudice transport and communications. Soon after, on 2 November, the 4Hs were interned. The union leaders were alleged to have "political aims and ideals […] so markedly anti-British and revolutionary in character that their dissemination in war time must inevitably prejudice public safety and defence."[38] In addition, six of the PNP's more active workers were also interned, making it clear that the governor's action was both against an industrial movement and a socialist party.

At the direction of the Secretary of State for the Colonies, the relevant Associations Act was soon rescinded and the unions reinstated. However, those interned had longer to wait and, in that period, Isaacs redirected his activities. For the duration of Ken's internment, he acted as president of the TT&GW and, some months later, resigned from the Kingston Commercial

Group, effective March 1943. Isaacs stated his intent to pay more attention to the trade union movement. In retrospect, Ken observed that "[Isaacs] was influenced by the detentions that took place of Domingo, Marquis and the 4Hs, and then he decided to join in and throw his weight into the movement".[39] Soon thereafter, on 18 March, the 4Hs were released. Isaacs, however, remained engaged both with labour issues and unemployment, which would become a central concern. Soon, he was also in conflict with Bustamante.

Disruptions in trade due to the war exacerbated Kingston unemployment, already heightened by economic depression and rural-to-urban migration. Census figures for December 1942 record that, in total, 28.6 per cent of males and 24 per cent of female wage earners had no work. Rates exceeded 20 per cent in general labouring, manufacturing, construction and transport, and 18 per cent in personal services. The unemployed in each cohort steadily increased as adults reached middle-age, and was acute in Kingston.[40]

In June 1943, the *Gleaner* reported on Isaacs' endeavours among the unemployed on Kingston's wharves. Working in collaboration with the Labour Department, he sought openings for around fifty workers, most of them union members. He stated: "I will not say that the policy of trade unions in Jamaica of keeping their work to the orthodox channels of bargaining for better wage and working conditions is not a good one, but special conditions call for special effort [...]. No opportunity for creating employment should be overlooked."

During the following weeks, it transpired that the employment Isaacs had found was not suitable for the workers concerned. The men who had asked for help were coal heavers, not longshoremen. However, Isaacs' move was a canny one. He had focused on unemployed men who were still expected to pay their union dues. But what assistance did the BITU provide? Angered by his interference, the union proposed to the Labour Department that in future the majority union, not employers, should fill vacancies on the docks. Effectively, the union asked for a closed shop. The proposal was rejected, but moved the TUC to respond. On 7 August 1943, the formation of a newly organized Jamaica Port Workers' League was announced. The officeholders were Isaacs (president), Ken Hill (first vice president) and Noel Nethersole (treasurer). The JPWL was a passing phenomenon, but it foreshadowed further competition between the two union-party blocs.[41]

Six days after the JPWL launch, notice was given of a mass meeting at the corner of King and Beeston Streets in downtown Kingston. The *Gleaner* report read:

> The first sharp clash between the two admittedly most powerful political parties in the island, the Jamaica Labour Party and the People's National Party, occurred yesterday evening [...] when noted Trade Union and political figures like Messrs. F.A. Glasspole, K.G. Hill, Wills O. Isaacs and St William Grant for the PNP took up the challenge thrown down by the head of the BITU, daring the rival party to hold a successful meeting in the Corporate Area and for nearly two hours and a half withstood the boos and catcalls and songs of the BITU supporters. [...] the rival factions [were] lined up by about 50 members of the Police on opposite sides of the streets.

A man was struck down and taken unconscious to hospital. One week later, a second port workers' meeting briefly brought Bustamante to the scene. His appearance was followed by further clashes between rival unionists.[42] Tensions simmered as Isaacs continued to agitate for "artisans and other socialists of labour". A few days later, he received a violent threat from two men who accosted him on the street. They warned him to leave Bustamante alone. Isaacs was armed and told the men that violence would bring a like response. The B&ATU sent a resolution to the Colonial Secretary, en route to the Governor.[43] It alleged that the BITU was "seeking dominance by a policy of terrorism" aimed at its opponents. More verbal sparring followed. Isaacs defended himself against various charges and also warned Busta: "Whatever Bustamante may say, there are two facts that he dares not deny and the first is: that there exists within his Union dissatisfaction that is fast growing and will soon engulf himself and his aides. Fact two, that until I began to do something for the unemployed workers in his Union, he did not think them entitled to any consideration."

At a PNP meeting chaired by Isaacs, he digressed to speak of Bustamante. He remarked that while some "instigators" stayed at home and sent their "henchmen" out, he was prepared to bear the blows of bricks and iron pipes. Moreover, "If Bustamante does not behave, I, Wills Isaacs, will flog him myself." Bustamante responded with characteristic panache: "I am unruffled, unperturbed and undisturbed at the rapid vapourings of this irresponsible upstart."[44]

One month later, on 14 September, Isaacs placed the following advertisement in the *Daily Gleaner*:

> **PORT WORKERS OF KINGSTON,**
>
> Port workers of Kingston, did you know that as long as MANLEY, NETHERSOLE, BUSTAMANTE OR MYSELF are connected with the public life of this country not one worker will dare attack or beat any of us? The only people that are being beaten are workers like yourselves. Anyone who teaches you to hate your fellow worker, anyone who encourages you to attack and flog your fellow worker, is not only an enemy of the workers of this country, but an enemy of the race from which we all come.
>
> WILLS O. ISAACS
> 21 Port Royal St, Kingston[45]

The hyperbole of these exchanges reflects most the inability of either Isaacs or Bustamante to achieve much for the unemployed under a wartime colonial regime. Nonetheless, Isaacs' ability to harry opponents of the TUC buoyed organizers' efforts. The union council grew.

The period during which Bustamante and Isaacs tested their mettle also saw the PNP's fifth annual conference in August 1943. Manley reviewed the previous year's activities. He noted the advent of constitutional change. Universal adult suffrage accompanied by an island-wide census had been confirmed in 1942. Further changes, to be in force by October 1944, involved an elected Lower House, a House of Representatives. Five standing committees would be established: on agriculture and land, education, social welfare, communications and general purposes.[46] These committees foreshadowed a ministerial system of government. However, the Governor's broad veto powers remained. For Manley, the changes were a disappointment. Responsible government was yet to be achieved. Nonetheless, the changes were indicative of a worldwide shift. The major nations opposed to Nazism were now seen by their colonial subjects as imperial powers which were nothing less, in Manley's words, than a "disgrace to civilization".[47]

This more assertive style informed the PNP's statement on international affairs. It called for a continuing "unity of purpose" among the progressive forces of the war, and endorsed socialist principles. A revised party platform, the *Plan for Security*, came with a comprehensive set of policies concerning land distribution and taxation, wages and employment, education, local industry and capital investment, housing and public utilities. It also proposed a Central Planning and Survey Authority and a state-owned bank. Already, the party was mindful of Jamaica's need for capital investment after the war. At this conference Isaacs was voted onto the PNP's executive committee.

The prospect of a general election in 1944 led to the formation of the JLP as well as the Jamaica Democratic Party. Manley described the JDP's platform as a "pale copy" of PNP plans. Bustamente's JLP was a "fascist masquerade" posing as a union and a party of the people. His thumbnail sketches belied the fact that, along with the *Daily Gleaner*, these parties would become a formidable alliance against socialism. The JDP had rural roots but found substantial support among urban capitalists and like-minded professionals who sought independence and a capitalist future. In August 1943, the JLP provided a statement of its platform. It would not reduce "beyond reason" capitalist wealth. Rather, it would bridge the gap between the haves and the have-nots. On self-government, it sought more autonomy but would not "clamour" for change.[48]

The contours of this conservative reaction to the PNP were soon revealed. In September 1943, the Legislative Council debated and approved the purchase of the publicly owned All-Island Telephone Service by the Jamaica Telephone Company, a subsidiary of a London-based firm. JTC provided Kingston's telephones and, with its purchase, intended to extend its service throughout the island. The motion proposing the sale was passed twenty-seven votes to two, the latter cast by electives Maurice Segre and Ivan Lloyd. Segre, a member of the Jamaica Imperial Association, was no socialist. He voted against the motion, critical of the private monopoly created. His concerns overlapped with those of Lloyd, who argued at length against the motion – but to no avail. The defeat came just months after a previous motion put by Lloyd – that the Government adopt a policy of public ownership of utilities – had failed. The subsequent *Daily Gleaner* editorial warned of this socialist stance and assured Lloyd that Jamaican electors did not want government control.[49]

The most prominent speaker for the sale of All-Island Telephone was Robert Kirkwood. The son-in-law of Sir Leonard Lyle of Tate and Lyle, and the representative in Jamaica for the West Indies Sugar Corporation, Kirkwood was also a nominated member of the Legislative Council.[50] He was supported by Roy Lindo, elective for St Mary and scion of an established landholding family. Lindo extolled the profit motive while E.E.A. Campbell declared public ownership a "doctrine for the lazy and the indolent". Kirkwood, however, led the debate. He proposed that the sale was a "test case of public vs. private ownership". People were alarmed because,

> [...] so much of the Island's income is going into the pockets of the Government Departments; whereas the actual producer, the Agriculturalist, is being little considered if he is considered at all. That is the feeling in this country, sir, not a feeling in favour of more Government ownership but of less Government ownership and less Government interference. There is a feeling of alarm and

> despondency about this trend to Government monopoly: this trend towards a totalitarian form of Government.

He instanced a number of government departments, including Public Works, the Central Housing Authority and the railway, all of which fell short as public services and mostly ran at a loss. He argued that only the profit motive could maintain utilities and "keep our people employed". He ridiculed Manley, referring to him both as "the honourable Member for Socialism" and as the "learned KC". Finally, Kirkwood took exception to the critique of British foreign ownership when, in his view, the British were "pouring money into this island". He continued, "The development of new industries in Jamaica is not going to lessen the need for export crops and for guaranteed quotas at generous prices. Where are we likely to get them from, Sir? Is it likely that we will get these benefits from any country but Great Britain, the 'foreign country'?"

Statements in the *Daily Gleaner* by Bustamante and Robert Fletcher, the JDP general secretary, supported Kirkwood. In a letter sent to the *Gleaner,* Bustamante challenged a remark by Frank Hill in favour of state-owned utilities. The letter repeated Kirkwood's themes and also raised a more "sinister" prospect:[51]

> The basis of Democracy is the freedom of the individual, the freedom and encouragement of private initiatives and enterprise. Obviously certain officers of the PNP, being fond students of Communism, cannot help being the real enemies of Democracy.
>
> Mr Manley has attacked me as being a fascist, but he knows well that with his emphasis on State ownership [...], should his party get into power (God forbid), the PNP would represent this all-powerful state, and he, in effect, as leader of the PNP, would control and boss the life of every individual in the country.

A second statement came from Robert Fletcher, the JDP general secretary. He drew attention to a speech delivered by Richard Hart to the PNP's Cross Roads group. Hart had described fully fledged socialism as a system that would see the "disappearance" of capitalists and the bourgeoisie, including clerks, professionals and others. Still, party members should keep a "common bond" with all classes for the present. Fletcher noted the implied dispensability of the middle class. He emphasized the following passage from Hart's speech: "Until we have attained self-government, the alliance with the bourgeois elements must be maintained."[52]

Isaacs was the first to respond to this attack. The exchange segued into a debate on the PNP and the middle class. His initial letter to the *Gleaner* was published eight days after it was written, allowing Kirkwood's reply to be printed one day later.[53] Of Kirkwood, Isaacs wrote,

> When this gentleman came out in public life in this country, he left the people with the impression that he was a radical Englishman, and there were many who believed he was competing with Norman Manley for the leadership of the Socialist movement in Jamaica. [….]
>
> May I enquire of Mr Kirkwood when was it that he began to abhor socialism, and socialists. May I enquire of him if he was aware of the fact that when he supported the candidature of Victor Bailey for St Mary,[54] that the party was then, as it now is, and always shall be, a socialist party. […] did he not know that the party then stood for Government ownership of public utilities and in supporting its candidate he was supporting its policy. Consistency thou art a jewel.

Kirkwood replied, airing his credentials as a liberal rather than a socialist. He claimed Norman Manley as a friend. A second letter excoriated Isaacs, and dwelt on Fletcher's critique of Richard Hart. Kirkwood noted the "astonishing silence" of PNP leaders and asked if Mr Manley agreed with Hart regarding the middle class. Kirkwood drew a parallel between Hart's approach and the Russian Communist Party's manipulation of small proprietors and unionists in its pursuit of power.

Isaacs responded again: "I am a typical middle-class man. I am a member of the party and my presence and work are welcome. I am satisfied and so are all the other middle-class members of the party." He noted that Kirkwood himself was not middle class but a capitalist, prepared to manipulate both Bustamante and the JDP to his own ends. However, both the masses and the middle class were awake to Kirkwood's "imperial interests".[55]

Two days later, other members of the party followed Isaacs' lead. The *Gleaner* published a letter from ten middle-class members of the PNP's executive committee. The writers extolled their party's broad appeal and treated Hart's statements as an internal matter. Manley followed with a press release. Of classes, he remarked, "We have a strong labour policy and a fine record of good solid work for the masses in Jamaica. The middle class, which is itself a working class, giving real and vital service to the community, depends on the general development and prosperity of the people as a whole."[56]

In the early 1940s, Isaacs proved to be a restless activist, moving from the Metropolitan Group to found his own Commercial Group; and then from building party groups to TUC involvement when the need was great. Along the way, he increased support for the PNP among Kingston's commercial class. His flair for populist politics emerged as he sparred with Bustamante and distilled an important point: that Jamaica's high unemployment ranked alongside wages and conditions as a central policy concern. This activity also saw the onset of enduring competition between party-union blocs, and Bustamante's right-wing, autocratic turn. Equally important, the debate about utilities showed that powerful anti-socialist forces were already aligning against the PNP. Isaacs was the first to speak up for a socialist party with multi-class support. He mobilized opinion against Kirkwood's arrogance and became the "stormy petrel" of his party.

In this period, a further factor emerged which helped to shape his career. His immersion in politics brought him into contact with a wide range of people: the unemployed, unionists, politicians and members of the commercial class. He would soon become a KSAC councillor. As an affable man and a supporter of H.A.L. Simpson, he also joined a group that met downtown after working hours. Participants included two town clerks and Sir George

Seymour Seymour, landowner, elective to the Legislative Council, past mayor of Kingston and a member of the conservative Jamaica Imperial Association. At that time, he was also chair of the Water Commission. Occasional participants included a few proprietors and various public servants. The journalist P.E. Trottman, a news editor at the *Daily Gleaner*, was involved. In later years, he would become president of the Jamaica Press Association. Isaacs would also have comparable contact with a younger journalist, Ulric Simmonds. These activities may explain the regularity with which reports about him appeared in the *Daily Gleaner* throughout the 1940s and 1950s. Overall, the publicity helped him and the party.[57]

# SECTION II
# FIGHTING FOR THE PARTY

## Chapter 3
# In the KSAC Council

*Wills Isaacs used to be regarded as a firebrand [...]. He didn't seem to care what people thought. He really believed in what he was doing.* – Lynden G. Newland (JLP), 1978.

*As a councillor on the KSAC, he was the most dramatic and dynamic figure that I can recall [...]. He took things very seriously and, if he felt someone was getting a raw deal, he would take up that case and fight it to the bitter end.* – Russell Lewars, 1978[1]

On December 1, 1943, Isaacs faced his first electoral contest as a PNP candidate. A by-election for the Kingston and St Andrew Corporation council had been called for a recently vacated seat.[2] He had two opponents: J. Coleman Beecher, previously a councillor and sometime leader of the in-house JPSC union, which had clashed with the TUC in 1942; and E.S. Barrington Williams, proprietor of the monthly *Political Traveller.* Isaacs stood to the left of both, who were aligned respectively with urban and rural conservatives. His own nomination had a politics as well.

Noel Nethersole had been elected to the municipal council in 1940, having failed the previous year to win a seat on the Legislative Council. Manley had asked the radical left to desist from open support for Nethersole in order to avoid an anti-communist reaction. In this instance the left obliged. In fact, some among them saw Nethersole as an alternative leader to Manley, whom they deemed too cautious. Nethersole was first vice president of the party and president of the TUC. In 1943, Hart proposed a comparable left alliance with Isaacs. He was a known unionist whose oratory drew the masses. He also had a record of cooperation with both Richard Hart and Ken Hill. This time, however, Hart's colleagues demurred. In fact, their hope was that Isaacs would lose the by-election and any purchase on future nominations. His links with commerce made his opposition to capitalists suspect. Edward Hanna and George Desnoes were among those who proposed him for the KSAC council.[3]

Still, they all agreed on certain issues. In an interview with the *Gleaner*, Isaacs courted the middle class, but focused mainly on the unemployed. Speaking of councillors he said,

> Their first duty is to the electorate, the people, who put them in. That, I feel, would be my first duty if I am selected. As I see it, that would mean the creation of more work for the unemployed and that before Christmas, if possible, and a reduction of all rates and taxes by the simple expedient of running the various departments of the council with less politics and more business.
>
> To create more work, the Corporation can assist in making available to the Central Housing Authority as many of the slum areas as possible, and there are also several wide expanses of vacant lands owned by the Corporation that could be better utilised [...] for building purposes.

Such projects would create work and housing. Isaacs also strongly supported more spending on public education, including the school children's lunch fund. In times of war, lower taxes were a vain hope. Unemployment, however, was a continuing concern.

The election was scheduled for 1 December. An enthusiastic Isaacs guaranteed a clean fight. He also promised to give his opponents "the finest thrashing of their lives". Before the final count was known, the *Daily Gleaner* declared the election a "ding dong struggle", in which Mr Beecher had the support of professionals, merchants and financiers. Votes were counted throughout the night and the tally finalised around 5 a.m. A total of 2,386 votes was cast. Isaacs won from Beecher by a margin of 124 votes. Barrington Williams polled poorly. In the words of the *Daily Gleaner*, "the declaration was received with vociferous and prolonged applause – as throughout the long hours of the night" the crowd of PNP supporters grew. The animated report continued: "Mr Norman Washington Manley, KC, leader of the PNP, arrived at 11 p.m. while the checking of lists was taking place and was greeted with tremendous applause. His arrival was signalled by the crowd of thousands in the street, and as he entered the hall the applause was taken up to an extent which caused cessation of the checking."

Bustamante was also present, along with other members of the Corporation council, including the PNP's Nethersole and William Seivright, the deputy mayor.[4]

In his victory speech, Isaacs forthrightly declared his loyalties and identified his foes, including Beecher, Bustamante and the Federation of Citizens' Associations, many of whom opposed his anti-British stance. He also paid tribute to his union comrades, and Manley.

> [Mr Wills Isaacs] wished to offer his heartiest congratulations to Barrington Williams, who had fought one of the cleanest elections that could have been fought in Jamaica (applause). When this contest started [...] he learned that Beecher had lent himself to the capitalist class of this country, he decided that he would beat him at the polls, and he had found great happiness in flogging him that morning (applause). He was happy at his victory because his party had defeated the efforts of this dead Federation of Citizens Associations (applause). He could not close without referring to Alexander Bustamante who had also given his help and assistance to Coleman Beecher. They had defeated his efforts, and next year at the General Election they would defeat him again.
>
> He could not close without thanking first of all, Mr Norman Manley, his friend and leader of his party, who during the five years

> that he had been a member of that party, had extended to him his patience and his tolerance, as if he had been his own child. Like the artist, he took the rude bit of stone and he fashioned the model that he wanted (applause). He had also to thank his comrades in the party who gave their all. They worked without thought of self. They worked without remuneration. He thanked also the members of the Builders and Allied Trades Union, who gave him the most loyal services he had ever seen. [....].

Finally, Isaacs thanked the Almighty, who had cared for him throughout his life. As he took up "the cudgels of the working class" against "the capitalist class of this country", he placed himself under "God's protecting wing".[5]

His success in the municipal race did little to quiet manoeuvring in the party. At issue by February 1944 was the provisional list of candidates for the approaching general election. Members of the left, including Frank Hill and Roy Woodham, wished to see both Isaacs and Richard Hart dropped from the Kingston-St Andrew list. Ken Post reports that their tactic was to accuse the two of taking money from the JDP. The spurious charges were deflected by both men. Hart protested to the executive and Isaacs raised Hill's propensity to nurture cliques. Tired of the unrest, Manley acted. At a meeting of the PNP executive he put a motion, "that factions, cliques and secret associations" were contrary to the party's constitution. Hart affirmed in writing that such groups had no place in the PNP, whether they were left or right wing. For his part, Isaacs withdrew his complaint against Hill.[6]

Isaacs assumed his role as a councillor for the KSAC. One set of tasks concerned the committees of council, a number of which he had been assigned to: Roads and Works, the Bournemouth, the Building Committee, Cart Stables (which included sanitation and street cleaning), Poor Relief, and Gas and Lighting. The committees met periodically and reported to the council every month. Some managed job-creating public works, funded in part by the corporation and in part by the government. Another duty was to debate central matters of the day. Usually, these debates revolved around a motion moved by a councillor. Two issues on which Isaacs consistently proposed resolutions were British appointments to government positions, and like acts, which reflected racial bias; and the poor and unemployed, including their wages, relief work, rents and the cost of staples. In a society with limited taxation and an economy weakened by war, the cost of living was a constant issue.

His first public act as a councillor came at the meeting in December 1943. He moved successfully a resolution concerning positions advertised as "whites only" by the United Services Organization, which recruited US service personnel based in Jamaica. His wording was forthright and included a proposal that the motion be sent via the British embassy in Jamaica to President Roosevelt, copies to Jamaica's governor and to the Secretary of State for the Colonies. In part it read: "Resolved that this Council records its emphatic resentment and public dissatisfaction at the offensive advertisements issued by the United States Authorities in the local press, inviting applications for employment limited to white residents and protests against the insult thereby offered to the people of Jamaica [...]."

A swift response came in the form of a lengthy apology from John V. Dallin, the US base commander in Jamaica. He expressed "deep regret" for an unauthorized act and promised a reappraisal of the organization's policy regarding "persons of all races, colour or creed". At this same meeting, Isaacs also moved to alter the contractual terms under which public utility supervisors, including the superintendent of the fire brigade, were employed. Instead of renewable five-year contracts advertised in the United Kingdom, Isaacs suggested that such contracts should be renewed annually. This procedure should be maintained only until qualified Jamaicans became available. Where necessary, the government should sponsor overseas training for suitable local candidates. The debate lasted two meetings before agreement was reached. The contracts should be for two years only, and renewable. Councillor Duval proposed that the general issue be separated from the brigade position. However, this led to the following exchange:

> Mr Isaacs: "My policy is to replace every Englishman in Jamaica with a Jamaican and I am not disguising the fact."
>
> Mr Duval: "But go slowly with it."
>
> Mr Isaacs: "No, I am taking the bull by the horns."
>
> Mr Duval: "And I agree with you; but go slowly."
>
> Mr Isaacs: "The point is, we have been going too slowly."[7]

Isaacs' protests coincided with concern about the colour bar in Britain. West Indian cricketer Leary Constantine and his wife had been barred from a London hotel. News of a protest meeting in Liverpool reached Jamaica. The House of Commons, and in turn the *Daily Gleaner*, hurried to deny that a colour bar existed, either in Britain or Jamaica. A *Gleaner* editorial likened Isaacs' views to Hart's opinion of the middle class as dispensable. The paper sought the PNP's clarification: "If it is proposed to get rid of all Englishmen in Jamaica, we are somewhat curious as to what would be done in regard to the millions of pounds of English capital invested in various businesses in Jamaica; would the English be compensated for this, and if so, where would the money come from?"

In a rush of hyperbole, the newspaper likened Isaacs' plans to Hitler's appropriation of Jewish property in Germany. Undeterred, Isaacs raised a further example of discrimination on the home front. The Jamaican manager of the Bournemouth Baths was paid less than half the amount of the English manager of the gas works. Though the latter was an engineer and working in an essential service, and the first was neither, Isaacs still called for greater parity. Where the gas works made an annual loss of around £3,000, the Bournemouth Baths made an annual profit of £8,000. The profit of one helped to subsidise the other. Was there no reward for Jamaican initiative?[8]

Isaacs' opposition to racial bias was equalled by his concern for the poorly paid and destitute. Hence his strong support for Nethersole over a matter of property tax. Government had regraded the wages and bonuses of the corporation's "subordinate" or service workers. In early 1944, a recommendation from the city treasurer and the town clerk was adopted by the council to raise the property taxes collected by the corporation. In conjunction with war bonuses paid by the government, the higher rates would allow the council to meet the wage increase. On all urban and suburban property in Kingston and lower St Andrew valued at or over £1,000, rates would be increased by three shillings for every £10. On rural property in St Andrew valued at or over £300, the increase would be one shilling for every £10. Rates on properties valued at less than £1,000 (urban and suburban) and £300 (rural) remained unchanged. The intention was to make property taxes more progressive.

As chair of the council's finance committee, Nethersole drafted a submission to government and led a deputation to the Privy Council. The submission was rejected. Instead, the council ruled that the tax increase be spread uniformly across all properties. Moreover, the ruling was gazetted immediately and without further reference to the KSAC council. The new tax rates were already fixed in law when they were published in the *Daily Gleaner*.[9]

A council meeting was called for 14 March where, to a packed gallery, Nethersole moved a resolution critical of the Privy Council and also confirmed his resignation from the KSAC council. His plan was to recontest his seat to underscore the affront to the poor caused by the Privy Council's action. His motion referred to the hardships incurred on "the lower income groups in the Corporate Area" and on "the tenants of small houses and apartments and tenements". "Skyrocketing" rentals were a major cost for these groups. Isaacs also tendered his resignation. Along with Deputy Mayor Seivright, he remarked on the "repressive" nature of the government's decision. Normally measured, Seivright, like Isaacs, was outraged. As it turned out, only Nethersole resigned. The PNP executive ruled that, given Isaacs' limited time on the council, they could not risk losing both seats. The by-election took place on 12 April and Nethersole was victorious.[10]

Isaacs continued to agitate. He sought unsuccessfully to have Glasspole and Ken Hill, as leaders of Kingston-based unions, co-opted to the finance committee. They would constitute a strong voice for labour. He encouraged protests over exorbitant rents and wretched living conditions in West Kingston and parts of St Andrew. Between late January and mid-March, three large public meetings took place, with Manley on the podium as well as W.A. Domingo, and Balfour Barnswell representing the Rent Payers League. Leftists, including Winston Grubb and Sam Hinds, also came. Speeches targeted the under-valuation of Kingston commercial property, the ineffective nature of the Rent Restriction Act, and the failure of the Central Housing Authority, which more often evicted tenants than housed new applicants. The meetings raised the PNP's profile.[11]

As 1944 reached its mid-point, Isaacs maintained his more mundane council work. He addressed himself to "the damnable condition" of lanes and streets. He restructured the Street Cleaning Department, introduced a new truck fleet, and selected priority areas for lighting. Most important of all was his role in a Corporate Area land reclamation and gully draining project. Put together in July 1944, the project was the council's central effort to provide both continuing employment and relief work. The *Daily Gleaner* described it as follows: "a programme of construction works comprising paving and protection of all gullies in the Corporate Area and other works of permanent improvement from funds to be raised by loans over a period of 18 years". Isaacs provided the financial estimates. The project continued throughout the 1940s, creating employment and saving "millions in valuable land and human life".[12]

The recently appointed Governor John Huggins received the final draft of a Jamaican constitution in January 1944. He convened a meeting of the three main political parties and some smaller groups, including the Federation of Citizens' Associations. As the principal policy-making body, the Executive Council remained problematic. It would have five nominated members and five elected by the House of Representatives. However, the governor would still preside, be able to initiate policy, and retain a casting vote. Moreover, though the five elected members would be assigned portfolios, they would have no legislated power over departmental heads. On 11 July, Roger Mais, writer of note and member of the PNP, published an article in which he called out the draft constitution as a "piece of hypocrisy" and remarked, "What we are fighting for is that [. . .] the sun may never set upon [. . .] the insolence and arrogance of one race to all others [...] *Now we know.*" Following his arrest and conviction for a "seditious attack" on Britain's war effort, he became a hero throughout the land.[13]

The PNP turned to the prospect of a general election. A meeting in July of forty-eight groups in the Corporate Area nominated eight candidates, ultimately trimmed to six, who would run in Kingston and St Andrew: For Kingston, Glasspole in the east, Isaacs in central, and Ken Hill to run against Bustamante in the west. For St Andrew, the line-up was Manley in the east, Nethersole for central, and Edith Dalton-James for the west. In Jamaica, formal declaration of the new constitution came on 20 November 1944. The election date was set for 14 December. The JLP stood twenty-nine candidates and the PNP only nineteen. The party's view was that a democratic choice of candidates was possible only in constituencies where they had established groups.

On 30 November 1944, the PNP published their *Plan for National Prosperity*, a shorter version of the earlier *Plan for Security*. The preamble stated clearly that the socialist party condemned capitalism "because capitalism has had a long innings and it does not work".[14] However, specific aims were described in more neutral terms: equal opportunity, a planned economy, and control of the public utilities central to production. Public ownership was downplayed; likewise, land redistribution. The role of private capital remained unspecified, although the money for development would come from a state bank. Better health and education with "no class distinction" was promised. This plan was more accessible than the previous one. It was also more cautious in the face of an anti-communist smear campaign launched in concert by the JLP, the JDP and the *Daily Gleaner*. But caution was to no avail. 'Socialist' had come to mean communist for many small proprietors, workers, and both rural and urban capitalists.

Bustamante swept to victory with twenty-two seats and 41.4 per cent of the vote. The JDP received a miniscule number of votes and no seats. The PNP won only five seats, three in country parishes. Only Glasspole prevailed in Kingston and St Andrew, supported by a middle-class suburban vote. In Kingston Central, JLP lawyer Frank Pixley won 58.5 per cent of the vote to Isaacs' 30.5 per cent. Bustamante won West Kingston. He became Minister of Communications and Chief Minister. In a brief summation, Munroe notes that the PNP's nationalism, in fact, was not especially popular. And the PNP's socialism "was largely unintelligible to the masses. The party too easily assumed a level of awareness which simply did not exist."[15]

Isaacs' response to defeat was to throw himself into his work as a councillor and party activist. The PNP's William Seivright had become mayor of Kingston. His deputy was Sir G.C. Gunter, an alderman and retired financial controller for Jamaica Railways. The JLP's five MHRs for Kingston and St Andrew became *ex officio* councillors, as did the PNP's Glasspole. In February, the councillors were joined by Harry Dayes, a rising solicitor, PNP member and president of the Jamaica Clerical Workers Association. Dayes had been the successful candidate in a by-election triggered by the resignation of a JLP councillor. Dayes would become a lifelong friend of Isaacs. As the incoming mayor, Seivright revamped the council's committees. Isaacs was appointed chairman of Poor Relief and immediately embarked on a survey of conditions regarding his department and the Kingston Poor House. The Poor Relief Department and the Poor House were under the supervision of both the council and a statutory body, the Board of Supervision. The latter was charged with maintaining consistent policy and practice among the councils' Poor Relief committees across the island. In 1942, with the passage of the Poor Relief (Amendment) Act, the role of this overarching board was defined more rigorously and in accord with the Colonial Development and Welfare Act.[16] In particular, though the local committees hired and fired Poor Relief personnel, all such actions, along with budgets, had to be authorized by the Board of Supervision. In Kingston, the roles of Inspector of the Poor and the Matron or Master of the Poor House had statutory duties attached. The performance of either could be censured directly by the board, over the head of a council committee chair.

In February, Isaacs made an interim report to his Poor Relief committee. His findings supported the appointment of additional staff to assist Mr Aubrey Ballen, acting Inspector of the Poor. The committee agreed that Ballen's position should be made permanent. It was clear that the Poor Relief office was under-staffed to deal with the influx of migrants from the countryside.

Early in March, Isaacs submitted a final report to the mayor based on his survey. Overall, the report detailed the parlous condition of the poor in Kingston. Controversially, its first section took issue with directions from the Board of Supervision. Board members, Isaacs remarked, made their decisions at a distance from of the poor. For example, the board had recommended that the children of destitute mothers should be removed from a family only in "exceptional" circumstances. Isaacs noted that in the case of girls, they were often assigned to other relatives. Intended as an informal fostering, these "schoolgirls" often became unpaid labour, or worse. He also remarked on the three young sons of an ill and impoverished mother. The boys were suffering from malnutrition. The destitute mother was granted a mere 7/6 (seven shillings and six pence) per week to care for the boys. How could their health be restored when that sum was to cover both food and rent? In such cases, practicalities required reappraisal of a worthy principle; namely, keeping a family together. Isaacs proposed that the children should be placed in care while the mother was nursed back to health.

He also demurred regarding the board's views on Poor Relief staffing and, in particular, on the acting Inspector of the Poor. He noted that although Mr Ballen's predecessor had requested and had council approval for additional staff, the Board of Supervision had rejected the request. They now demanded that Ballen be sacked. Isaacs and the board did not disagree on the state of the Poor Relief office, but rather on the cause. Where he blamed inadequate staffing, the board blamed Ballen's incompetence. Isaacs' fight to retain this man became protracted.

In the second part of his report, Isaacs discussed industrial schools. They should be genuine training centres and not just jails for destitute youth. To this end, the Poor Relief committee – and not police – should assign boys to the schools. Overall, he commended the Alpha and Stony Hill schools, noting that Stony Hill, like Alpha, should have a chapel. The boys needed both material and spiritual support. Isaacs recommended: (1) better medical and teaching staff for children who were indigent; (2) two additional industrial schools to work in tandem with newly established cooperative farms; (3) a system of rotating national service for doctors in order to address syphilis and other contagious diseases; and (4) with regard to administration, that the Board of Supervision's role be advisory to the council committees.

Isaacs made the state responsible for welfare services overall, and local government responsible for their delivery. As a major financial contributor, local government should take charge of poor relief, in particular. He noted that his report was not a censure of the bodies involved. All were working in deplorable conditions.[17]

These KSAC council matters were not the only ones that commanded his attention. In the first few months of 1945, Jamaica's press and public opinion were focused on a struggle at Kingston's match factory concerning the closed-shop tactics of the BITU. Five unaffiliated workers had been dismissed. Fifty-one members of the TUC's Biscuit Factory and Allied Workers Union were next in line. On 18 January, Bustamante called his workers out on strike until these workers joined the BITU or were dismissed by management. Manley described the closed-shop demands as a "vicious attempt" to deprive workers of their jobs unless they paid their dues to Bustamante. The Chief replied that the BITU merely sought to protect trade union principles against the PNP's "political intrigues". Though each one impugned the other, the tide was running in Bustamante's favour. As majority leader in the House, head of Jamaica's largest union and, in the eyes of capital and the *Jamaica Gleaner*, virtuous anti-communist, he held the upper hand.[18]

On the night of 12 February, a Monday, an estimated three thousand people gathered in Edelweiss Park to witness a discussion of the match factory issue. Speakers included Frank Hill, Hart, Glasspole and Harry Dayes and Isaacs chaired the meeting. Hill remarked that, with 4 per cent of workers not unionized, and 29 per cent members of a TUC union, there should be "proportionate representation" on a labour-management board. The action spread to woodcutters who supplied the match factory. TUC workers in coffee production and the ports also became involved. Bustamante pulled more BITU workers out.[19]

In March, an absence from the scene brought to light the death of Samuel Marquis, secretary for the Biscuit Factory and Allied Workers Union. Active in Negro workers' education, he had also headed the PNP's Propaganda and Organizing Committee, which worked out of Isaacs' office on Port Royal Street. Marquis was interned in 1941 and detained for two years. Held without trial for political reasons, his health suffered. The funeral took place on 21 March. His body was taken to Edelweiss Park where comrades paid their last respects. A procession of more than one hundred and eighty cars followed the casket to its burial place. Isaacs delivered the oration:

> Marquis was 32 years of age this month, a young man with life before him, and the loss that our party has sustained is grievous indeed. We can testify to his zeal and energy, his devotion and sacrifice in the building up of the party structure ever since its formation.
>
> It was in 1941 when our party began in earnest its agitation for constitutional reform that Marquis was called upon to make the greatest sacrifice. For no crime, only desiring his countrymen to be free within the British Commonwealth of nations, he was taken and placed in internment camp. For two years and a day, he withstood the rigours of that life but towards the end it was evident that his health was being impaired. His comrades afforded him the best medical aid that was possible, but Marquis never regained his health. Broken in flesh, but undaunted in spirit, he came out to take up the work that he loved and carried on even unto the end.

Isaacs' moving tribute, which also made reference to Marquis' Catholic childhood, celebrated his commitment both to black nationalism and the working class.

In April, Isaacs stood in for Manley as the principal speaker at a meeting of the Water Commission Manual Workers' Association. His speech was far-reaching, rich in biblical allusions and, at times, apocalyptic. It culminated with remarks on union leadership.

> It is in the days of the final struggle, in the days of chaos that must come, that democratic unions [...] will be called upon to play their part. [....] It is the leadership you create and train within your own union and among your own working-class people that will be the pillar of cloud by day and a pillar of fire by night to the people.
>
> It makes one's heart rejoice as you present tonight your officers to the audience, everyone a worker. In them I see potential leaders of the people, who will not only lead but will teach the people to think

> for themselves; who will be a lamp unto the feet of the nation in the days to come.

Isaacs had only just returned from Hanover where his father was gravely ill. The following Sunday, he was onstage at the Ward Theatre, this time to speak at the third anniversary memorial service for J.A.G. Smith. He expressed regret that Bustamante was unable to attend and described Smith as a man of "vision" and "great singleness of purpose". Isaacs continued: "To him, and perhaps to him more than anyone else, should go the credit for instilling in our minds the thought that other people did not rule us by divine permission." Past disagreements had been put to rest.

He was too busy to care when a *Daily Gleaner* opinion piece referred to him tartly as "Comrade Isaacs". It proposed that his speech to Water Commission workers showed that he had "been drinking at the very fountain of Communism, nay, not drinking [but] wallowing in the doctrine". Conservatives feared his power to inspire the masses.[20]

He now pressed on with his campaign regarding the administration of poor relief. Having submitted his report to Mayor Seivright, Isaacs convened a conference of the chairs of Poor Relief committees on 30 April. It was opened by the mayor, who stated its purpose: to consider the relationship between the Poor Relief committees and the Board of Supervision. He noted that the Poor Relief (Amendment) Act (1942) had served to diminish parochial autonomy and thereby brought frustration concerning new rules imposed by the board. More power, rather than less, had been vested in the government. Edith Clarke, the board's administrative secretary, responded in an interview with the *Daily Gleaner*. She explained that the composition of the board and its oversight of personnel were consistent with the law. Direct action by the board would be taken only when a council failed to act as directed. Clarke observed that "[this] unfortunate duty has arisen recently in regard to Kingston. The Board has sent reports of maladministration to the Committee of which Mr Wills Isaacs is a new and energetic Chairman."

Undeterred, on 16 May Isaacs took the matter to the KSAC council. In the absence of the mayor, who was overseas, Deputy Mayor Gunter presided. A majority in council voted to send a resolution to the Executive Council. The resolution proposed that the power of the board be limited. A majority also supported a deputation to the governor and the Colonial Secretary. As a co-opted member of the Board of Supervision, Gunter dissented from the resolution and opposed the deputation. He suggested that Isaacs "did not like" the board. In the first week of June, the council received a letter from the Board of Supervision terminating Ballen's position and requesting from council a new nominee for the position. A further meeting of council was called, at which Isaacs protested bitterly. He concluded that Edith Clarke's action amounted to a "very wilful and harsh bit of injustice" to Ballen. He was supported both by his PNP and JLP colleagues (other than the absent Seivright). Awaiting a response from the governor, the debate cooled.[21]

Other matters drew Isaacs in. Not least among them was the way in which Bustamante in government secured resources by denying them to others. Throughout May tensions rose as the government's budget for 1945–46 was tabled. Revenue for 1944–45 had exceeded expectations by more than £800,000, due to tax returns on excess profits and increased customs duties. Nonetheless, the government delivered an austerity budget. Speaking to the estimates, Bustamante foreshadowed major cuts in spending for the civil service, most notably in Public Works and the Labour Department. Administered by parish and municipal councils, Public Works was the vehicle for infrastructural projects and their concomitant employment. The Labour Department, weak though it was, remained the only umpire in industrial disputes. In the House of Representatives, Glasspole questioned the government's reluctance to act on unemployment. He remarked,

> We had the seconder of the resolution acclaiming the fact that it is not the Government's business to find work for the unemployed. I suppose, Sir, we ought to wait until the stage arises where men half-starved, naked, suffering all the thousand and one ills we complain about, are forced to resort to physical violence, and then money is showered not on any proper development work, but just in order to appease the appetite of the unfortunate sufferers.[22]

On 20 June, as the debate proceeded, the TUC workers at the match factory received an ultimatum from management: They were to join the BITU or else be dismissed. One hundred and fifty employees returned to work. In addition to the five already dismissed, a further forty-six were sacked. The following day, a TUC mass meeting was fired on from a car driven by a BITU supporter. The PNP crowd retaliated with a hail of stones. Poignantly, a related notice was posted in the *Daily Gleaner* two days later. It appealed for donations to enable the TUC to organize "some form of co-operative enterprise" for the dismissed workers, mainly women. In the first half of 1945, the Bustamante union made similar but unsuccessful attempts to undermine TUC laundry workers at the Myrtle Bank Hotel, as well as workers at Jamaica Railways. Though he was not central to these events, they influenced Isaacs' politics. The sense of struggle against the state – both its appointed and elected officials – was intense.[23]

He also kept his eye on matters of racial discrimination, at home and abroad. He moved a resolution in the KSAC council concerning its counterpart in Birmingham, England. A newly appointed medical officer had been given notice when his colour became known. A Birmingham councillor had notified KSAC colleagues after his own protest had failed. Isaacs' resolution read in part,

> "Whereas it would be disastrous to mankind, and Englishmen in particular, should the coloured peoples of the empire take retaliatory measures, and whereas such actions are identical to the Nazi ideology of the 'master race', be it resolved that council protests [...]."

The experience of the war, Roger Mais' "*Now we know*", and a new constitution – along with Isaacs' constant agitation – brought a united response. JLP councillor Newland seconded the motion and a long list of speakers in favour followed. None spoke against.[24] A similar issue, brought to the notice of the council in September, was more hotly debated. It also received headline treatment in the *Daily Gleaner*:

> Denouncing a reported act of discrimination against a coloured Jamaican journalist at the Miami airport, Councillor Wills O. Isaacs told his colleagues yesterday that the American nation was devoid of culture or any of the human feeling which made for respectable citizenry. He said that if such discrimination continued, steps should be taken to ban Pan-American Airways from the island, no matter how grave the consequences – no matter if the population here starved on that account.

The matter concerned Jamaican journalist and PNP member Frank Hill, who was only identified sometime later. He had been barred from a whites-only airport diner in Miami. Wills' motion, that an expression of the council's displeasure be sent to Pan Am and to the US consul, was supported by the mayor and passed by a majority. The deputy mayor dissociated himself from the motion and JLP councillor Teddy Duval remarked that Wills was "flogging a dead horse". However, the JLP's Edward Fagan defended him: "We find that Americans do not care anything about us. They discriminate against us at the Canal Zone. You will find a policeman there saying [...]. 'Nigger, get off the sidewalk', and if you turn around to speak to him, you get arrested. I have lived in America thirty-two years and I can tell you about discrimination, especially in the South; they treat you like dogs."

Pan Am responded, stating that the discrimination stemmed from Florida state law, rather than the airline. Nonetheless, the motion stood. Isaacs said that it was "the council's duty to hold a brief for the coloured people of Kingston and the island" throughout the world.[25]

While Isaacs proved influential in matters of racial discrimination, in the shorter term at least, he proved less so with the Board of Supervision. On 21 October, he departed on a business trip to New York. In his absence, a paragraph in the *Daily Gleaner* announced that two area officers from the Board of Supervision had been appointed as Inspector and Assistant Inspector of the Poor in Kingston. Mr Ballen had been assigned to the City Treasurer's Department. Moreover, Edith Clarke had attended a meeting of the KSAC Poor Relief committee held at the Poor House.

Isaacs was quick to respond from New York. His letter, dated 8 November, was published four days later in the *Gleaner*. It deplored the appointments and criticized the mayor, who had acted in accord with the board. The action was "cowardly" and "a stab in the back". At the council's November meeting, Mayor Seivright dismissed the letter. He reminded the meeting that before Isaacs' departure for New York, he had been informed that Mr Ballen would be replaced. Seivright described as "hair-brained" (sic) the resolution passed in May to send a deputation to the governor. The governor had been displeased and the council "had no leg to stand on". Seivright also censured Isaacs for sending unauthorized letters to the Board of Supervision. It appeared that Isaacs had gone too far.

As he faced the backlash, he also learned of his father's death and promptly returned to Jamaica. He assured the press that he remained friends with the mayor. Their relations were "cordial". In order to defend himself, however, Isaacs invoked his socialism: "I am a socialist and I belong to a socialist party. And my every deed and thought on matters political is directed towards the betterment of the working-class people of Jamaica, regardless of what type of work they do. I regard it as a sacred duty to protect the worker at all times against the injustice of his employer."

He reiterated his view that the problems in Poor Relief were due to insufficient staff, not Ballen's failings. He committed to "fight this matter with all I have at my command".[26]

He would not back down, but neither would Seivright. At the council meeting in December, Seivright announced his committee appointments for 1946. The committees remained much as before. However, Nethersole, who was overworked as finance chair, would no longer chair Public Health as well. That role would be filled by Isaacs who, in turn, would vacate Poor Relief. The mayor himself would chair that committee. Isaacs declined his appointment and any other, remarking that the mayor's action amounted to a censure. The mayor suggested that Isaacs might consider resignation from the council. Some days later, on 15 December, Manley stanched the rumour that Isaacs had withdrawn from politics. He remarked that Isaacs remained a "valued and trusted member" of the PNP executive and the National Council.[27] And of the KSAC council as well, since he did not leave.

He had been acting in light of the Hill report on local government, first circulated to government members, parochial boards and the corporation in January 1944. L.C. Hill had recommended a dedicated treasurer for greater Kingston-St Andrew and a dedicated financial advisor to the parochial boards. While the report sought to streamline finance, it also proposed less top-heavy administration. Local committees of parish and municipal councils should manage the functions that concerned "the day-to-day conveniences" of a community. Poor relief was among them. In March of that year, Manley had embraced the measures when he addressed the Jamaica Association of Local Government Officers. He said that vigorous local institutions were required for democratic politics.[28]

In July 1946, Mr Ballen was reinstated in his position following agreement reached between the KSAC and the Board of Supervision. William Seivright publicly apologized to Wills as both the council and the board now agreed that arrears in Poor Relief were due to under-staffing in the face of escalating demand. The two revived their friendship. A year later, not least due to Isaacs, some aspects of the Hill report, including matters involving the provision of poor relief, became PNP policy. More financial autonomy for local government remained a vexing issue.[29]

In the course of 1946, Isaacs made shelter for the poor and inaction by the Central Housing Authority a focus of debate. In the first week of April, he put a motion passed by council that various unused facilities be used as shelters for the destitute. He noted that while the cost of rentals in Kingston had tripled during the war, the earnings of the poor employed had not, pushing many into destitution. A sub-committee chaired by Isaacs was formed to pursue the matter.[30]

On 27 April, a deputation from Kingston Pen, representing more than one hundred homeless people in Bustamante's constituency, called in turn on the Minister of Lands and the CHA. They had been forcibly ejected from Kingston Pen and their shacks had been removed. Many were now living in the open. The deputation moved from the CHA to the *Gleaner* office and there met Isaacs. He sent telegrams to the governor and the archbishop of the West Indies. He proposed that church halls across the island be opened. But this was not all. Under his direction, a council sub-committee prepared an ambitious proposal to house four thousand West Kingston working-class people. With council endorsement, the proposal was submitted to the Executive Council in mid-July. At the end of August, the government voted to allocate £65,000 for housing, citing "urgent need". The measure was rushed through the House ahead of a foreshadowed ten-year plan. To ease the situation in Kingston Pen, tenements would be built in Trench Town and Denham Town. Isaacs noted that the government's scheme, though more modest, was sourced mainly from his committee's work. They had stolen the "Isaacs scheme".[31] This plan was among the first devised for tenement dwellers in West Kingston.

## Chapter 4

# In the Streets and Lanes

*[Wills] was not afraid to fight. And in those days, they didn't use guns, but people fought with fists, you know, and rock stones. And you might have heard his famous words, 'What are a few broken skulls in the birth of a nation?'* – Howard Cooke, 2002.

*I want to be a free man in my own land. I don't want any overseer. [....] I welcome the stranger within my gate, but I don't want him to rule me.* – Wills Isaacs, 1949.[1]

Although the PNP Opposition was small indeed, the party mobilised supporters through its groups. PNP councillors in turn, especially on the KSAC council, maintained vigorous policy debate. Conflict between the two major parties occurred often – both in council and on the streets. Beginning in 1943, PNP street corner meetings were disrupted by JLP supporters. The frequency and intensity of these interventions increased as the 1944 election approached. Both the rank and file and the leaders in the PNP have testified to the role of violence in that election, especially in West Kingston, where Ken Hill lost to Bustamante. Manley later said: "I remember 1944 when in St Andrew and Kingston a reign of terror obtained on election day; the leader of the country marching, his army behind him, and PNP voters terrified and staying at home."[2]

Another factor informed the fray. This was the battle between the BITU and the TUC to extend their memberships and their representational rights at industrial sites. While the BITU commanded the larger groups of workers in the cane fields, factories and on the wharves, the TUC was successful with smaller groups. These included essential service workers in transport, hospitals and prisons. Union conflict merged with conflict between the parties. Sives remarks that JLP dominance up to 1945, "triggered the use of violence between the parties as the PNP chose to respond by organising groups to protect their meetings". Violence became increasingly common at strikes and in election campaigns. It was soon reciprocal and cyclical.[3]

Matters were made worse when Bustamante, as leader of the government, sought to intervene. He appeared to view TUC strikes as first and foremost strikes against the government. Two strikes in 1946 demonstrate this stance. Both occurred at sites where a significant majority of workers were represented by TUC unions. They involved the Government Railway Employees Union, and the Government Hospital and Prison Warders Union, the latter on behalf of employees at Jamaica Lunatic Asylum (now Bellevue Hospital). Richard Hart was president of the railway union, while Glasspole headed the hospital union. With the war nearing its end, Hart had renewed the claims of railway workers. One year later, on 3 January 1946, the governor rejected the claims. His message to the House also stated that the government would only recognize a union as a "sole bargaining agent" if it represented *all* employees. This was a blow to the under-resourced TUC, which favoured proportional representation on negotiating teams at all sites.[4]

The sitting of the House at which this message was read brought a notable remark from Frank Pixley (JLP). He said that the PNP and its allies bore "the mark of the beast". He added that deserving cases among railway workers would be heard. Should a strike occur, however, those involved were likely to forfeit their pensions and, where relevant, their seniority. In response, on 9 January, Wills chaired a large railway union gathering at which Hart spoke. Hart announced a series of meetings throughout the island to be addressed by Isaacs and Ken Hill. Soon after, a number of railway clerks were retrenched, while Bustamante rewarded the "deserving ones". The bargaining process broke down. On 8 February, at the Ward Theatre, a birthday celebration for Isaacs became a political rally as well. Manley urged those present to "gird their loins" against Bustamante's government and union.[5]

More strife came when two hundred and eighty mental hospital workers went on strike on 15 February. The workers were calling for a regrading of wages and the dismissal of the hospital's manager, known for his arrogance. Responding to the asylum strike, Bustamante telegraphed the governor, enjoining him to "take an iron hand in this matter; no sympathy whatsoever must be shown". Bustamante claimed that "the insane" had been let loose on the streets. "Only those with the mark of the beast carrying the odour of the skunk" would be capable of such action. "This is not a strike," he said. For its part, the TUC observed that the Labour Department and its advisor had become pawns of the government. By Saturday morning, close to one hundred and thirty-five nurses were on strike, accompanied by more than one hundred other staff. Pickets were formed. Bustamante, along with Pixley, inspected the pickets and were jostled by TUC supporters. In retaliation, they went to the waterfront and recruited their own force, three thousand strong. The BITU members and supporters marched through downtown Kingston and past Isaacs' office on their way to "the asylum". Accounts vary, but in the confrontation three men were killed, including John Nicholas. Isaacs would never forget this event. Bustamante and Pixley were charged with manslaughter, though not convicted. There were fifteen other deaths that day, which became known as Black Saturday. Fire had broken out on a ward, trapping inmates. The crisis compelled the Labour Advisor to meet with the TUC. Union gains were made and eventually all strikers were re-employed. But at what price? Soon after, the PNP's Noel Nethersole declared, "We will fight our attackers in the streets, in the lanes, on the housetops until we have driven them into the sea."[6]

Amid this turmoil, Governor Huggins wrote to the Secretary of State for the Colonies that Bustamante did not handle well his dual roles as "member of Government" and head of a "political union". "[He] cannot throw off the manner and method of a mob leader." Nonetheless, Huggins cited mitigating factors. Bustamante had to "carry with him an ill-educated and excitable following". Moreover, he was "baited" and "goaded" to respond. The source of this provocation was the People's National Party, which included: "a considerable range of political opinion – from well-meaning intelligentsia to violent anti-Imperialist extremists". Huggins wrote that the intention of the extremists was to wreck the self-government experiment. He ruminated on communist connections in the region, and worried that the PNP had support in the police force. A *Jamaica Situation Report* for February1946 expressed concern that the TUC's strength in essential services might be used to political ends.[7]

Mid-1946 was a turbulent time, with rolling strikes affecting the wharves and other services, and tensions among KSAC employees. Cart stable workers who cleaned the streets went on strike against their foreman, whom Isaacs defended. Bustamante brought the workers' claims to council, and the two men clashed. Isaacs vowed that "fifty Bustamantes and a thousand Labour Party members" would not prevent the streets being cleaned. On the night of 22 July, Adina Spencer, a newspaper vendor and PNP comrade, was killed on a downtown street. The shots came "out of the dark" as she turned for home. Her funeral was equal to that of Samuel Marquis. While Manley and the PNP councillors stood beside the grave, across from them "four men held the PNP flag with its blood red background and blood red rays of a red sun rising over a black Jamaica". A comrade shouted that Adina Spencer had died for "freedom, peace and justice".[8]

It was in this climate that Isaacs began his campaign for the unemployed, led by an organized group of ex-servicemen. Some six weeks after Adina Spencer's funeral, one hundred and fifty unemployed men disrupted the council chamber. They voiced their dismay at the government and cried out, "Hungry man, angry man!" Isaacs enjoined a reluctant Mayor Gunter to take their names and find them work. Angered by the incident, Bustamante voiced his intent to become mayor of Kingston following the next municipal election. On the night of 21 October, the PNP held a mass meeting at Race Course. MHRs and councillors charged the government with neglecting a wide range of policy areas, including housing and employment. The *Daily Gleaner* sought a reply from Bustamante, who said that agitators were "goading" the unemployed. They demanded relief but would not provide a "fair day's work for a fair day's pay". Isaacs responded, claiming victimization. He claimed that Bustamante's men on the council decided who should be employed.

Late in October, a small group of unemployed men called at the *Gleaner* office, saying they represented a force of five thousand jobless citizens. They would march unless they were offered work relief. Their concern was "Christmas work" that would provide their families with income for the festive season. The group denied they were idlers. Nor was their appeal a "question of politics". Marching had become their only recourse. A November by-election in Hanover brought "the angry cries of scores of marching unemployed men and women". They also invaded Montego Bay to tramp from one government building to another. In the House, Bustamante claimed that although others seemed to lead, in fact Isaacs was behind the marches.[9]

In an open reply, Isaacs wrote that Bustamante was a tool of capitalists and "our Imperialist masters… They are using you to divide the nation." Noting that the JLP government was "at a loss", he told them what to do, drawing on PNP policy planning:

> 1. With all the speed that is possible, build schools to accommodate the 200,000 children in Jamaica that are not going to school at all. If the people had education, politicians couldn't fool them and in building these schools you would give an enormous amount of work to the people of Jamaica.
> 2. You must at once set out to create permanent and new jobs for the people. This system of relief works will get you and the country nowhere. You must industrialise the country. [....] If the cost of producing the goods will be higher than the imported article, or if the industrialist will not get a sufficient return from his investment, then you must subsidise the industry. If you adopt this policy we will not have to spend £80,000 a year on pauper relief in Kingston alone. [....]
> 3. [....] Lands must be given to people who have no lands at all. At present time land settlement only benefits the middle-class land speculators. [....] You also must make available to them expert advice how to produce [and] make available to them loans at cheap interest and a market for what they produce.[10]

Demanding Christmas work, more labourers besieged Isaacs' office on 25 November. On 9 December, when a KSAC council meeting confirmed additional relief works for both JLP and PNP constituencies, the gallery cheered.[11]

In the latter part of 1946, the *Daily Gleaner* devoted two editorials to protest marches and chamber invasions regarding unemployment. In the first it remarked on a "near riot" outside the government's Headquarters House. On this occasion, one woman had said that, if there was no work, the government should return people to Africa. A further editorial in November provided an analysis. Reporting on the island's first "Labour Force Bulletin", it noted that a high proportion of the unemployed were long term, and of less than middle age. Moreover, one in seven had arrived in

Kingston since 1943. The editorial's conclusion was that this "drift" to Kingston was of those who wished to live off relief. Bustamante's "straight talk" was applauded. The unemployed should return to the lands whence they came.[12]

By 1947, protest marches, chamber invasions and the issue of Kingston unemployment were not new. On 14 January, Isaacs put the situation on record with a motion that the council submit to government a further schedule of works in the absence of industries to employ the people. In subsequent months, he continued to publicize his commitment to a socialism that involved the nationalization of public utilities, and industrialization to generate employment. As the municipal election approached, the PNP took their views to the people. At a meeting on Spanish Town Road, a gathering was stoned by unknown assailants. And on 12 May, a conflagration occurred in and around the KSAC council chamber. Inside, Isaacs debated Bustamante on jobs. As reported, "the loud-voiced damning" Councillor Isaacs, the "stormy petrel of the People's National Party", shouted at the "equally heavy-voiced Prime Minister". Outside, "thousands" of the unemployed and ex-servicemen waited on Bustamante. The crowd had arrived behind Isaacs who, earlier in the day, had been barred from entering the Executive Council. He had gone to petition on behalf of ex-servicemen. The British had promised work for them on their return to Jamaica.[13]

The next day Isaacs announced plans for an island-wide march of ex-servicemen and the unemployed. Deftly, he was using the prestige of returned soldiers to raise the standing of those on relief who were subject to denigration and abuse. Neither had continuing work. Isaacs summoned contacts in Portland and St Mary. He spoke at Cambridge and Roehampton in St James, moving on to Hanover, where he preached in the Baptist church at Gurney, and then to Savanna-la-Mar. The word went out across the island and plans were made for a coordinated effort.[14]

One week later, the *Gleaner* published a short, unattributed notice that the government was going to ban marches around various venues, including the legislature at Headquarters House, the KSAC council and the offices of parochial boards. The next day, Bustamante issued a statement that sought to distinguish ex-servicemen from those on relief. While the former was worthy of respect, the latter "savoured of lawlessness". That night, the PNP held another meeting at Race Course. The crowd was estimated at fifteen thousand. Passions ran high: Manley recalled John Nicholas, the comrade killed in the asylum strike, and spoke about government victimization. Isaacs followed, saying that he would pursue Bustamante until the "demagogue goes". The following day, 21 May, a marching bill was introduced in the House. It was passed that day, but did not preclude a Labour Day march. That night, a massive but orderly procession took place throughout Kingston.

Soon afterwards, the governor proclaimed a ban on all meetings, gatherings, assemblies and marches held without a permit in any public place across the island. In force for twenty-eight days, it precluded Isaacs' all-island march. Moreover, the date by which the municipal election should have been called – in March, long past – was pushed back further. Bustamante gloated; Manley counselled restraint. Nonetheless, he urged the ex-servicemen to place their confidence in Isaacs. No such vote of confidence came from Governor Huggins. In a telegram to the Secretary of the State on 27 May, he remarked at length on the councillor:

> Wills Isaacs, a municipal councillor and one of the most irresponsible of PNP leaders, has put himself at the head of a section of unemployed men in Kingston and has formed a new Association of Ex-Servicemen (although he himself has no war service). On 12th May, he led a large crowd of unemployed ex-servicemen and hangers-on, including criminal elements, to the Secretariat and demanded [to see] the Executive Council, which was sitting at the time. [....] Later that evening a clash between supporters of the PNP, who marched at the instigation of PNP leaders to break up a meeting at which Bustamante was speaking, was averted by the intervention of

> a large force of police. The march earlier in the day and the violent speeches made that night created a state of excitement in which serious disorders might well have taken place.[15]

The fight between JLP and PNP supporters known as the Duke Street incident was the culmination of these events. Outside Headquarters House on 28 May 1947, as the MHRs adjourned for lunch, Bustamante was "alternately booed and cheered as a crowd milled around". They carried bricks, sticks and other objects, and had arrived in small groups to avoid arrest. Bustamante, waiting for his supporters to arrive, threatened the crowd. He was known to carry revolvers. Police intervened and sought to disperse the throng. They stayed to see Bustamante stride back up Duke Street, proclaiming "I'll walk alone and let them come!" The incident lasted barely fifteen minutes. No deaths were reported. However, in yet another telegram to the Colonial Office, Huggins opined: "Criticism and opposition have goaded Bustamante into a state where he is at times unable to control himself, while Wills Isaacs, who now appears to call the tune in the PNP, is no less violent and scurrilous."The subsequent inquiry was inconclusive but established *inter alia* that politicians bore arms.[16]

Municipal and parochial elections were called for 23 October. Almost three weeks before this date, a serious fracas occurred in Rose Town. A meeting had been called to support Ken Hill's St Andrew Central campaign. JLP supporters attacked the meeting and PNP personnel responded. Reportedly, a total of eleven from both sides were injured, but it was soon clear that the PNP crowd was not done. Some proceeded to a nearby meeting in Trench Town, where two men identified as JLP supporters, were killed. In his subsequent statement, Manley noted that the PNP would not itself provoke disorder. However, the party had a duty "not to allow its own meetings to be broken up by mob violence". He proposed that the BITU, with its adversarial unionism, had "sown the wind" and now reaped "the whirlwind".[17]

The quick response at Rose Town suggested a new form of organization – one that was community-based, rather than union-based. Arnold Bertram relates that Isaacs and Ken Hill had assumed the task of organising "party militants to protect their colleagues". It was in this situation that PNP group members based at 69 Matthews Lane "established a response mechanism under the leadership of Noel 'Scarface' Cambridge. They named it Group 69." Years later, a PNP stalwart detailed its origin: "People would attack you because you were PNP. You couldn't keep a meeting on the street. You had to build a counter-force. Group 69 was part of it." Isaacs had told supporters to summon "all the roughnecks" and fight back. Other groups followed, including the Pioneers of Edelweiss Park. A former participant recalled their strategy: "We used to scout out meeting sites, make sure of refuge and assistance if the meetings were attacked, and generally provided security from attack. Soon we could hold most of our group meetings and street meetings without molestation although the violence still continued."[18]

In the municipal election, the PNP won seven of the thirteen seats on the KSAC council. Ken Hill and union activist Thossy Kelly were elected for the first time. Isaacs was re-elected. Later, Bustamante fulfilled his promise and was elected mayor of Kingston, in addition to be being chief minister. Overall, the PNP had improved their position. Island-wide, they gained more votes than the JLP, and an almost equal number of local government seats. All this did not come without personal cost. Vunnie Isaacs could not forget those torrid days. As a young man, he resided with his father on the Kingston-St Andrew border, close to Torrington Bridge. Sometimes he slept under the bed. Wedged in a strategic corner of the room, Isaacs sat awake in a rocking chair, grasping a pillow. He was called out early and often came in late. "I remember once, four o'clock in the morning. *Knock, knock, knock* on the gate. Norman Manley. He was very impatient. The old man jump in the car. Him gone to Clarendon. Next thing, hours after, one *whir* at the gate. Ambulance. They brought him out in a stretcher. A big stone lick him in him head. And he laid down on the bed beside me." Later, the wound opened up and bled profusely. The ambulance was called again.[19]

Increasingly Bustamante, the *Gleaner* and the governor assumed a consistent stance. Each implied a link between violence, the TUC-PNP, and communism. And as the JLP intended, socialism was now seen as tantamount to communism. This conflation reflected an emerging Cold War paranoia within and beyond the United States. It coalesced with a Colonial Office fear of a socialist PNP aligned with unions prominent in essential services. The JLP's local government campaign had been cast as a stand against communism and for the Church: "We want no Communism! We want Peace, Work, and Prosperity."[20] In response to this redbaiting, unionists and the PNP resolutely continued their resistance. However, it was easy for the government to inflect the tenor of events, supported by the governor. Well-organized strikes were portrayed as sites of violence and near chaos, as Isaacs learned.

Members of the Jamaica Printers and Allied Workers Union employed by the *Daily Gleaner* had been on strike since 10 November 1947. At issue was a wage claim first canvassed in 1946. When the management brought in strike breakers, the union turned to picketing. The strike dragged on into the new year. The newspaper was published by the management. A final settlement was reached in April 1948. It favoured the workers and included a retrospective rise in wages. Before the strike concluded, thirty-two pickets had been arrested. Six PNP-TUC leaders were also charged, including Glasspole and Isaacs. They had addressed pickets from a truck parked in Harbour Street. Eventually all were acquitted or fined small amounts.[21] As these hearings proceeded, a fracas occurred outside the courthouse. Bustamante appeared and was "besieged by a booing crowd". Threatened, he drew two revolvers. That night the Chief addressed his supporters, charging Iris King, Isaacs and

Ken Hill with inflaming "the mob". He threatened bloodshed in return. Bustamante also appealed to Huggins: "It is no news to the Governor that a state of disorder exists through the action of the Communistic elements. [....] It is time to declare that when I do not get protection and I am concerned I will shoot."[22]

Four days later, pitched battles raged in the streets between JLP and PNP supporters. At a disturbance in Matthews Lane, police used riot guns, tear gas and batons to subdue the combatants. Governor Huggins banned "all meetings, gatherings, assemblies of persons and all processions and marches" in Kingston and St Andrew. On the same day, however, he wrote to the Secretary of State, remarking that Bustamante had made no effort to stop his followers, while demanding protection from "lawless elements".[23] Nonetheless, the colonial state supported the chief minister.

Ken Hill, as secretary of the Tramway, Transport and General Workers Union, called a bus strike on 21 February 1948. Bus drivers parked their buses at nearby terminals and removed the ignition keys. Soon after, they returned the buses to their depots, which were picketed. In an upbeat statement, Hill confirmed that the union's preference was for a negotiated settlement.[24] The following day, the driver of a bus proceeding along Spanish Town Road was shot in the neck. Elsewhere, conductors going on duty were struck by missiles. A few days later, a bomb planted on a bus exploded. Another bus was bombed and a third bomb, possibly destined for a bus, exploded on a sidewalk. Ken Hill and Thossy Kelly were charged with sedition and unlawful assembly. Glasspole was also charged, as well as two others. These events did not involve Isaacs, although he stood surety for Hill and others. The *Daily Gleaner* attributed the violence to the PNP-TUC. Although no arrests were made for the bombings, which were contrary to the interests of the TUC, the union was blamed and the strike failed.[25]

This embattled condition extended to the KSAC council. In June 1948, JLP councillors G.S.L. Thompson and Hugh Shearer moved a resolution that the government monitor new arrivals to Jamaica – to safeguard against communists. The resolution was won on the casting vote of the deputy mayor, Lynden Newland. This political theatre was used to mask JLP inaction in other areas. Seivright expressed his frustration in the course of a debate on relief for the destitute. He raised Isaacs' 1944 drainage and gully works initiative and argued that it should be funded as a development project by central government. A register of the unemployed was required, and a definite policy on creating jobs. In August 1948, the council addressed its engineering department. There had been numerous charges of bias in the award of labour contracts and in the purchase of materials. Isaacs proposed a commission of enquiry. On an amendment, the task was given to the deputy mayor alone. In October, he returned an 'all is well' report, which was accepted on a divided vote. By this time, Newland had succeeded Bustamante as mayor.[26]

In November, KSAC procedural changes came into effect. The council's committees would retain their previous briefs, but only the full corporation council would make policy. Soon after, the new mayor announced his committees for 1949. Chairmen for the fourteen committees were drawn exclusively from elected and *ex officio* JLP members of the council. It seemed that bi-partisan governance had collapsed.[27]

Isaacs' proposal of a forty-hour work week for shop assistants in the Corporate Area of Kingston was not supported. In late 1948, he tabled a resolution that council request a government review of the ongoing lease of US bases in Jamaica. Isaacs stated that a post-war Jamaica should have regional independence. The mayor and JLP councillors voted unanimously against the motion. The Association of Parochial Boards, chaired by Rudolph Burke, met at Headquarters House in March 1949 to prepare for upcoming discussions with the Executive Council. Isaacs had spent months drafting a submission for the group. It called for an additional £1 million to fund local government across the island. Revenue would come from a range of established property and consumption taxes. In tune with the Hill report, Isaacs sought to move local government beyond perennial deficits. The outcome of the discussion with the executive was negligible. As inter-union conflict continued and victimization fuelled community violence, both British and Jamaican officials cried "communist" and pointed at the PNP.[28]

Redbaiting had now become perennial. Socialism had come to mean "communism, expropriation of private property and godlessness".[29] With relentless repetition, this JLP cant overrode the 1940 caveats on PNP socialism formulated by Norman Manley. The situation strengthened Isaacs' resolve to see the PNP wrest government from the JLP.

He was soon in strife, however, arrested for a speech he allegedly made in March 1949. The occasion was a PNP meeting at the corner of Beeston Street and Chancery Lane. He was charged with sedition, inciting to riot and inciting to assault. Arrested at 9 p.m., he called on Seivright to meet him at the lock-up, where he was bailed for £100. The trial extended for some weeks in the Kingston Resident Magistrates' Court, with Manley defending Isaacs. A verdict was reached in early May. In its front-page coverage of the arrest, the *Daily Gleaner* described Isaacs as a "socialist politician" speaking at a meeting under PNP auspices. It also stated that the councillor spoke in terms that might incite the crowd to act violently, especially towards the JLP's Madame Rose Leon.[30]

The speech had been made in response to the news that Iris King and Ken Hill had been assaulted in Trench Town by JLP supporters. It was not a JLP gathering as such. The Central Housing Authority had organized an event to mark the part-completion of the housing scheme proposed by Isaacs in 1946; the one co-opted by the government. Councillors were invited and Hill and King attended, only to be attacked by JLP supporters. They arrived shaken at Isaacs' meeting, along with comrade Gladstone Evans, chair of the PNP's West Kingston group. Evans was wounded, his head and eyes swathed in bandages.

The police stated that Isaacs had called on the crowd to "arm yourselves with cutlasses, sticks and black-jacks and attack any man you know to be a member of the Labour Party". Declaring "total war", he purportedly said that, to redress the "dirt and stones" thrown at Mrs King, on the morrow they should go to the office of Madame Rose Leon. There they should "full your hands with dirt" and "dash it in her blasted face". Other evidence was that members of Group 69 were present and made declarations of the type, "Comrade Evans' blood was spilt and blood must flow with Evans' blood tonight." Testimony was also given that Isaacs had claimed, to a superintendent, that Bustamante incited people "to murder, cut-up and bloodshed".

The prosecution's case rested largely on shorthand notes from a police witness. He acknowledged that the notes, taken over an hour and a half, were not verbatim but captured the "gist" of Isaacs' speech. The defence questioned whether the notes were an accurate record. Manley submitted that Isaacs did not speak at the time announced. When he did speak, he was often interrupted. The picture emerged of a densely packed platform and a microphone passed between speakers. At various points, Isaacs left the crowd to confer with either Evans, or Hill and King. At one point in his absence, a Mr Binns took his place. A police witness for the defence confirmed that Binns was on the platform and had a "vocal style" similar to Isaacs'. On grounds of reasonable doubt, Isaacs was declared not guilty on all counts. Saved by Mr Binns.

However, the trial was not merely perfunctory. Part of Manley's defence rested on "crudities" uncharacteristic of a practised speaker such as Isaacs. He would not say, for instance, "murder, cut-up and bloodshed". The prosecuting counsel asked, "Trained and practised speaker, who trained you?" Isaacs responded: "By practice over a period of years." "What about your schooling?" The question was derisive. Isaacs replied: "I attended an elementary school at Pond Side in Hanover. At fourteen years of age I creditably passed the Third Year Pupil Teachers' examination. I taught for one year and for three years I studied English, Theological and Roman history."

Isaacs explained that he had been preparing for the ministry, but was precluded by his need to find work. Magistrate C.G.X. Henriques declared himself unimpressed. He noted that if the charge had been proven beyond reasonable doubt, he would have passed an exemplary sentence. Instead, Isaacs left the courtroom accompanied by his son, Vunnie, whereupon supporters lifted him on their shoulders. Vunnie was described as the well-known "former centre-forward of Jamaica College". On the following Saturday night, a freedom dance was held to honour the councillor. The advertisement proclaimed: "PNP-TUC LIVE FOREVER!!!"[31]

Soon after these events, and following separate meetings with Manley and Bustamante, Governor Huggins had the two sign matching peace agreements. They were published on page one of the *Daily Gleaner*, 18 May 1949. The agreements varied only in respect of each party's name and the signature of its leader. Three weeks later, however, the governor was appointing a one-man commission to report on a stone-throwing incident between JLP and PNP supporters in proximity to the BITU headquarters. One stone had wounded a constable as he and colleagues fled the scene.[32]

Interest in this inquiry, which proved inconclusive, was soon extinguished. In the first week of July, more dramatic events played out in and around Gordon Town, on Kingston's northeast periphery. A vacancy on the KSAC council had arisen upon the death of Councillor Teddy Duval. The PNP's Allan Isaacs (no relative of Wills) was defeated narrowly by his JLP opponent. Campaigning was intense as the local seat overlapped with the one Manley would contest in the approaching general election. Each of the parties was keen to do well.

The atmosphere was tense on the day of the election, 6 July. As a PNP truck passed through Tamarind Town on its way to Gordon Town, an elderly JLP supporter, Benjamin Taylor, was beaten and left to die on the road. The culprits could not be identified so no one was arrested. Later that evening, a crowd in the Gordon Town square, around a thousand, was subdued with tear gas. The majority were PNP supporters, and their attention had been aroused by an altercation between Bustamante, Isaacs and Manley. These two events book-ended a turbulent and troubling day. Following the poll, the governor proclaimed another one-man commission, this time in the person of Chief Justice Sir Hector Hearne. Known as the Hearne Commission, its terms of reference were as follows: "First, all political incidents subsequent to 2 July and relevant to the by-election were to be investigated. Second, the commission was to explore all the events and circumstances leading up to the violence; and third, the commission was to identify the persons or political bodies who were responsible."

Though broken into three parts, the terms of reference in fact addressed two broad concerns: one was to plot the advent of violence immediately prior to and on election day. The other was to assign responsibility either to specific groups or individuals. To date, both parties had tried to avoid the latter issue by always depicting their supporters as victims. One more antecedent event could always be found. Huggins sought to stop the regress. In doing so, his terms of reference were distinctly ahistorical.[33] In the PNP's view, inter-party violence had a specific historical sequence and causality. It resided in the JLP's opportunistic use of the power of the colonial state. It began in earnest in 1944.

The commission found that on 3 July in Dallas, a small hamlet south of Gordon Town, a JLP brigade and band had marched through a PNP meeting. The account in *Public Opinion* related that the JLP group traversed the Dallas square four times, declaring "who get lick down, get lick down". Some PNP supporters were injured. Next day, in retaliation, PNP supporters disrupted a JLP meeting in Gordon Town. The disruption involved "booing, handclapping, ribald remarks and the singing of songs" that ridiculed the JLP. Later, stones were thrown and at least one JLP supporter was injured. Hearne's report stated that the incident involved roughly one hundred and fifty PNP supporters, of whom about half had been trucked from Kingston. On 5 July, the parties each held a meeting, the PNP in Gordon Town and the JLP at Mission House, just above Gordon Town. Three officers and one hundred men were deployed to maintain a roadblock between the two meetings. Overall, there was little violence.[34]

On polling day, skirmishes were frequent. Following Benjamin Taylor's death, combatants began to amass in Gordon Town square. PNP supporters engaged in lusty songs. As the morning passed, a report came that the JLP's Rose Leon, her husband Arthur, and their bodyguard were driving from booth to booth, threatening PNP voters. In response, a local constituency officer, Keith Martin, called the Kingston-based PNP general secretary, Vernon Arnett. He asked Arnett to send three trucks with supporters to patrol the booths. Also in the morning, when JLP councillor Hugh Shearer arrived at Gordon Town, a PNP crowd surged around him. Shearer drew his revolver, an act for which Arthur Leon was arrested later that day. In the afternoon, Isaacs had angry words with police officers after a PNP truck was stopped on the way from Kingston to Gordon Town.[35] Manley arrived at Gordon Town around 6.30 p.m. and Bustamante soon after. Manley was cheered while Bustamante was booed. Stepping from his car, the Chief wielded an iron pipe, two feet long. In the turmoil, there was an altercation between him, Isaacs and Manley. As Isaacs tried to shepherd Busta away, the Chief turned to strike him and Isaacs responded with a punch that missed. Prior to beating his retreat, Bustamante exclaimed to the police, "Gas Manley. Gas everybody!" In return, Manley called Bustamante "a damned disgrace". As the crowd surged, a superintendent ordered tear gas to be used. Four or five cylinders were thrown and the crowd fell back and began to disperse.

Justice Hearne found that the People's National Party, Keith Martin and Isaacs – a specific group and two individuals – were responsible for the violence on 6 July. Though he cited Martin, Hearne's invective was aimed at Isaacs, who had caused a "saturnalia of hatred, intimidation, insult and abuse, violence and even death at Gordon Town". Hearne said,

> I find that the incidents in Gordon Town were due to the mass importation of non-voting PNP supporters into the town for the purposes of forming a nucleus of aggression, and they were actually provoked to violence by the sheer unprincipled conduct of Mr Wills Isaacs. [....] It is clear that the transport of non-voting PNP supporters to Gordon Town in overwhelming numbers had been arranged with a definite object by the Party organization for the election [...]. In these circumstances the organization and instigation of violence must be placed at the door of the PNP.[36]

Hearne had also specified an additional factor outside the terms of reference. He would only be concerned with violence that was organized, rather than "sporadic" or individual. He made this distinction by treating the activity of individuals or groups trucked only within the constituency as sporadic, not organized. Moreover, his interpretation made it inconsequential that, on election day, the only figures wielding firearms or another weapon – Bustamante's iron pipe, for instance – were JLP leaders. Nor was it of consequence that JLP groups visited booths and threatened PNP voters, or that in the days before the election, some of each party's meetings had been disrupted by opponents. Hearne also put aside that, late on polling day, both JLP and PNP trucks were on the way from Kingston to Gordon Town, though the only truck apprehended was a PNP one. Apparently on this basis, Hearne dismissed Martin's evidence as "malevolently false"; namely, that his morning phone call to Arnett had been provoked by JLP attacks in the area.

Manley had, in evidence and after the judgment, disputed Hearne's account of the facts. In a statement published on 9 August, he professed his "deep regret" regarding Benjamin Taylor's death.

However, he also questioned the Hearne Commission's findings:

> I know that this particular By-Election caused an unusual degree of excitement. I know, too, that the long years of abuse and subjection to physical attack at meetings and otherwise has created the danger that people too readily remember the past. [....] Eleven years of history [since the formation of the PNP] may be ignored by those who have no concern with it. We who seek to evolve a sound political life and to achieve Self-Government for our own people know however that what exists day by day is the product of the past.

Manley rejected the report's conclusions. He was "totally unable to accept" that the PNP was entirely to blame and that the JLP had received "wholesale exoneration".[37]

But what of Isaacs? He was not present or involved in the death of Benjamin Taylor. If Isaacs was connected at all, at most it was an unintended consequence of indirect influence. Prominent members of Group 69 were identified in and around Gordon Town. However, not one 69er was linked with the death or with any other specific event. Their presence may have been significant but not decisive in a crowd of one thousand.[38] Still, Hearne remarked that, with this death, "organised violence had reached the highwater mark of callous cruelty". And he found Isaacs responsible.

The weight of evidence on which Hearne relied concerned Isaacs' exchanges with the police. As Attorney General Cundall questioned him, a consistent theme emerged: that on the day, Isaacs had queried the police's authority and did not feel compelled to hide that fact from his supporters. During his evidence, Isaacs also put forward the view that anti-colonial struggle did involve conflict and, on occasion, injury. After all, Jamaican history was replete with such events.[39]

Hearne, Cundall and the police at Gordon Town took these views to be, if not seditious, then malignant and dangerous. Cundall's questions focussed on several incidents. They included the following: A constable gave evidence that, in Gordon Town square, soon after 9 a.m. when Isaacs arrived, some PNP supporters were singing and booing JLP supporters. In response to a request that Isaacs calm the crowd, he encouraged them to even greater effort. Isaacs disputed this account. He did not, in fact, speak to the crowd. Rather, he turned to the officer and said, "My friend, let the people sing" for they were in a holiday mood. When Hugh Shearer drew his revolver in front of an officer, it seemed to the crowd that the act was condoned by the police. People called for Shearer's arrest. Cundall asked if Isaacs had discouraged their outburst. He replied that he did not because he shared their view. Cundall proposed that such a stance was "likely to engender hate". Justice Hearne cautioned Isaacs that his evidence should not include his own opinions. Consequently, when Cundall linked Gordon Town to the Duke Street incident, Hearne became even more annoyed. Isaacs called the Duke Street affair "frivolous". He remarked, "When Churchill was booed no Commission was set up". Continuing, he declared, "A broken skull or two does not matter much in the growth of a nation." At this, Hearne replied that the commission was not interested in Wills Isaacs' "philosophy of history".[40]

Questioning turned to the truck waylaid on the road from Kingston around 4.30 p.m. Waiting in Gordon Town, Isaacs complained because the truck was carrying voters. He approached a senior superintendent. The man gave evidence that Isaacs was abusive, saying that a PNP government would fire them all. Again, Isaacs questioned the account. In fact, he had said that when his party came to power "all the imported officials would be returned to England and their places filled by capable Jamaicans".[41]

The final evidence that Isaacs gave concerned the altercation between himself, Bustamante and Manley. Reportedly, Bustamante had opened his car door abruptly and, in doing so, knocked down three bystanders. Isaacs sensed that the crowd was offended, and asked an officer to help him usher "Mr Bustamante" away. Isaacs related that "he told Mr Bustamante to go back in his car and be finished away with the incident. Mr Bustamante pushed him and he swung a blow at [Bustamante] but the police intervened and the blow missed its mark." Afterwards, the police took Isaacs to stand beside Manley on the steps of the Gordon Town courthouse. Isaacs saw blood on Bustamante's face. He also saw the police remove an iron pipe and stones from the Chief's car.

Cundall confirmed that statements made by five officers supported Isaacs' account. However, Hearne's view was different: that Bustamante "distained" Isaacs' help and "pushed him aside whereupon Mr Isaacs attempted to assault him". Hearne did not refer to the remarks at the time made by either Bustamante or Manley. Rather, he proposed that the crowd's anger rose, and the gas was released. And Isaacs was the cause of it. He had made an "exhibition" of himself. His "prancing, posturing and posing" had a "definite object". "Mr Isaacs deliberately set himself the task of exacerbating [feeling] against the Police, as well as against the leaders and supporters of the JLP." As he dignified Bustamante, Hearne sought to belittle Isaacs.[42]

Though Manley was a stalwart in defence of the party, by name he did not mention Isaacs. That defence came in the pages of *Public Opinion,* which condemned Hearne's "intemperate and unbalanced" conclusions, as well as Cundall's "grotesque innuendo".[43] Isaacs was not charged with any crime. Nonetheless, the events of 1949 had an effect. In later years, his oratory and personal warmth were praised. But as he aged, the term 'rabble-rouser' was used too often to refer to his early role in the PNP. In fact, his activities in building the party were far more consequential. The truth of the matter was that the colonial state was prepared to tolerate the excesses of its JLP government, including its leader. Such largesse was not extended to a socialist PNP. In standing up to JLP members and supporters, Isaacs also opposed the state. The outcome was that, at the Hearne Commission, he stood alone.

His resignation as third vice president of the PNP was published in the *Daily Gleaner* on 10 August 1949. Isaacs acknowledged that he was not blameless, either on the day or in the course of the commission. His apology was a graceful one. It also revealed, however, that the events had wounded him. He appealed to those "closest to me" who would understand, concluding with two stanzas from Kipling's poem, *The Stranger:*

The stranger within my gate
He may be true or kind
But he does not talk my talk
I cannot read his mind
I see the face and the eyes and the mouth
But not the soul behind.
[....]

The men of my own stock
Bitter bad they may be
But at least they hear the things I hear
And see the things I see
And whatever I think of them and their likes
They think the likes of me.

An unlikely source, but the words were apt.

Isaacs travelled to New York to seek medical treatment and returned on 1 October. Met by his son, he remarked that he was well, and ready to throw his "full weight" behind the general election campaign. On 2 October, he addressed a large crowd at Edelweiss Park.[44]

# Chapter 5
# The Split of 1952

*[....] The party to which I belong declares itself a Socialist Party, and I wish to declare that I am a Socialist. I believe implicitly in the programme and policy of my own party. [....] I believe that no real progress will come to this country unless we are prepared to accept the programme of nationalisation of certain basic industries as our guide.*

*I want it clearly understood that as far as I am concerned, when there is a conflict between capitalist and worker, I am bound to take up cudgels and to fight the battles of the working people in this country. [....]*

*But when a man states what is his political creed, when you say you are a Socialist, that is not enough. If you tell the world that you are totally opposed to laissez faire capitalism and the system of exploitation you see around, that is not the only thing that the Socialist is opposed to. The Socialist is totally opposed to the Communist way of life, and [...] he has an obligation to declare himself. [....] Because no man's political faith must be a secret unto himself nor should it be shrouded in mystery. The people of our nation must know [...] what you will do and what you will not do.* – Wills Isaacs, 1950.[1]

The 1949 general election was scheduled for 20 December. Starting early, the PNP had published a policy statement following its annual conference in August. Among the notable items were: industrial development; land tax reform; nationalization of some utilities; improved education and health; labour legislation; and a continued drive for self-government and for a West Indies Federation.[2] This was but a forerunner to the *Plan for Progress* developed principally by Manley and Nethersole, and drafted by Karl Heath, an Englishman residing in Jamaica. Richard Hart assisted with wording for the conference, and the draft was endorsed by the party in October 1949.[3] It focused on the forms of development required to address Jamaica's high unemployment and low wages.

With reference to capital, the plan proposed that private investment should be encouraged, but without inducements – unless they reduced unemployment or developed natural resources. These concessions should be aimed mainly at investors within Jamaica. Surprisingly, Isaacs shared this view with Hart. They also both underlined a preference for agency loans from abroad, which could be channelled through a state bank. In the final version, however, the use of incentives – "general measures and inducements" – were allowed in order to attract foreign private capital. On the eve of the election, Nethersole, as a prospective Minister of Finance, revealed that he had already spoken with bauxite companies in Washington, DC. They were eager to progress projects in Jamaica and would "work side by side" with a PNP government.[4]

Despite this apparent unanimity in the party, during the year tension had erupted within the TUC executive, and between Manley and some TUC leaders. At issue was the TUC's affiliation with the Moscow-based World Federation of Trade Unions. Early in 1949, it became clear that there would be a split in the federation, led by representatives from Britain, the Netherlands and the United States. This fissure reflected a broader one between East and West, already termed the Cold War. Along with the Soviet Union, communist parties in the Eastern bloc had refused assistance from the US Marshall Plan. They saw it as an attempt at economic assimilation in place of a military advance.[5] As a consequence, in the West the WFTU was being identified as a Moscow group. Pushed by Manley, the TUC debated its links at some length. As months passed and the matter was not resolved,

Glasspole threatened to resign. The issue reached the public in September with a lengthy editorial in the *Daily Gleaner*. It claimed that Glasspole had resigned and warned once more of ambivalence towards communism. On 16 September, and without reference to Manley, Ken Hill published a letter in the *Gleaner* explaining his attachment to the WFTU as an international vanguard of labour. Simultaneously, the newspaper published a statement from Manley excoriating Hill for making party business public. Manley termed Hill's action "absolutely intolerable", given his senior positions in both party and union.[6]

The rift was papered over. A TUC working party presented an interim report on 19 September. It recommended disaffiliation from the WFTU for the sake of the whole progressive movement. It also showed that communism was not an issue among the TUC leadership. A statement released to the *Daily Gleaner* read in part: "We affirm positively that the TUC is not a communist organization, that no member of the TUC executive is a communist or has communist ties."[7] Glasspole resumed as TUC secretary. He noted that some differences were usual in a progressive movement. Still, reactionary columnist Peter Simple warned the PNP not to go to an election with "the millstone of Communism" around its neck. Where once the *Gleaner* had proposed that "nothing is criminal in being a communist", now P. Simple required that the party expel suspected communists. The *Gleaner*'s editorial comment also raised the stakes. In the meantime, an election had to be fought.[8]

On 8 October 1949, Isaacs and Frank Pixley jointly placed an advertisement in the *Daily Gleaner* requesting "a peaceful and orderly campaign", as well as cooperation with the police. In his constituency of Kingston Central,[9] Isaacs emphasized well-established themes: that the JLP government had governed for five years with no plan to address unemployment or the cost of living, and an incompetent administration. He noted that a vote for Pixley was merely a vote for Bustamante. Isaacs had kept his sense of humour.

He remarked that the JLP was shipping into rural areas "cases and cases of crepe-sole shoes" to exchange for votes. He was active not only in his own constituency, but also travelled to Black River in St Elizabeth, and to Christiana and New Green in Manchester. He and Glasspole spoke on each other's platforms and, along with Nethersole and Karl Heath, he supported Ken Hill in Kingston West. As polling day approached, Isaacs chided Bustamante for abandoning Kingston West to a young Hugh Shearer standing against Hill. Did the Chief feel safer in Clarendon?[10]

On 17 December, just before the election, the *Daily Gleaner* published in parallel columns statements from each of the Kingston Central candidates. Pixley invoked "the spectre of an evil ghost – of Socialism – arising from the tomb of iniquity". He proposed that socialism would mean heavier taxation, regimentation and dictatorship. Isaacs led with unemployment, the issue he had made his own:

> Unemployment is so horrible an infliction that only those in whom the 'milk of human kindness has turned sour' can regard it with unconcern. In Jamaica, this horrible infliction is overtaking an increasing number of the population. We see today youngsters, the middle-aged and the elderly, in large numbers, losing their grip on life and becoming actually unemployable through enforced chronic idleness. [....]
>
> How long can we tolerate such a state of affairs, with hordes of our countrymen, our friends and children idle and subject to the ravages of malnutrition, disease and despair? [....]
>
> The People's National Party has clearly set out how it proposes to deal with unemployment in Jamaica. No one can deny that our proposals are sober and practical. [....] Is it any wonder that from one end of the island to another there arises the cry 'It is time for a change'?

The race was described as a "runaway gallop" for Isaacs, who beat Pixley by a margin of almost four thousand votes.[11]

The party had hoped for government but was disappointed.

The outcome was good, but not good enough: JLP – seventeen seats, PNP – thirteen seats, Independents – two seats. However, Kingston and St Andrew were a triumph for the PNP. Glasspole, Isaacs, Hill, Manley and Nethersole won five of the six seats. Only Edith Dalton-James went down in defeat in a close race with the JLP's Rose Leon. In part the victory was the product of a strong group structure and the growth of the TUC among service workers. It was also due to the PNP councillors of the KSAC who, from 1945, had tested the JLP government.[12]

A new parliamentary year began on Thursday, 12 January 1950. Members of the House of Representatives assembled at noon to elect a Speaker, who then administered the oath of office to MHRs. There followed a ballot to select the five who would sit on the Executive Council. The government chose three JLP members – Bustamante, Donald Sangster and Isaac Barrant. Two independents aligned with the JLP were also elected.[13] The House adjourned at 12.54 p.m. and, as the members departed, "Mr Manley and Mr Wills Isaacs were lifted by their supporters and after Mr Manley had been carried to his car and driven away, Mr Isaacs was carried full length down Duke Street on the shoulders of his enthusiastic supporters. His feet did not touch the ground until his supporters had deposited him at the door of his office in Port Royal Street."

That night thousands gathered at Race Course in order to hear the MHRs of the People's National Party give thanks to the voters. Both Manley and Isaacs warned of likely victimization, with the latter reassuring the crowd of party support.[14]

Isaacs remained active on the KSAC council. The year began with a familiar concern – a deficit of £100,000. Councillors renewed a proposal first made by Glasspole in 1948. The entire deficit could be recouped were the council to receive the revenue from bicycle and entertainment taxes. Submitted to the government again, the request fared no better on the second occasion. The government countered with a proposal to lend the council £70,000 at an interest rate of three and a half per cent, over five years. The councillors were unanimous in rejecting the offer. Isaacs branded the proposal "impudent" and Seivright noted that the deficit was due to the rapid rise in costs handed to the council by the government – namely, poor relief and public health. Three years previously poor relief had accounted for one-fifth of the council's expenditure. It now comprised more than a third. There was comparable frustration with Kingston's failing public transport, now provided solely by Jamaica Utilities. Isaacs said that JU was not a private company but a "private monopoly". He reiterated his long-held view that the buses should be nationalized.[15]

With the new year came the election of a new mayor. The PNP councillors selected as their nominee William Seivright, indisputably the most able among them. As deputy to the mayor, they nominated Isaacs. In a remark both generous and playful, Isaacs referred to his recent activities: "Councillor Seivright has been selected by my Party to be Mayor because of his sanity, because of his ability and because of his respectability [...]. I'll be his deputy and I have been selected for that position for a particular reason, and the reason is that if the road becomes rocky and steep and no longer calls for respectability, I shall step in and take charge."

On their election, Manley praised the new mayor's honesty, loyalty and efficiency. Of Isaacs, he said, "He is a man near to my heart, renowned for his energy, dynamic and alert in his desire to preserve this council."[16] In August 1950, Seivright took leave and Isaacs became acting mayor. He continued his emphasis on unemployment, poor relief and finance. He also acted to protect squatters on Dung Hill, whom the government proposed to move. In mid-October, Isaacs took two months' leave on the occasion of his marriage to Gloria Holness. She had served for some years as a Grade 1 Clerk in the KSAC council. At forty-eight, Isaacs had become a public figure.[17]

Other significant developments occurred in 1950. In January, the Myrtle Bank Hotel, owned by the Issa brothers, had become the site of industrial strife. Hotel management had refused to negotiate with the TUC, arguing that they had previously dealt only with the BITU. The Labour Department wanted evidence of TUC support and Ken Hill suggested either a poll, or else the evidence provided by a strike. Bustamante and Shearer stalled, demanding a public ballot rather than a secret one. Eventually the strike was called on Monday, 13 February. By Tuesday pickets had formed at the hotel and at Issa stores downtown. On Wednesday the strike was over, sent to arbitration between the TUC and hotel management. The TUC had prevailed. There was celebration, but caution too. On Thursday, the *Gleaner* published the following statement: "The strike at the Myrtle Bank Hotel is over, and no bitterness exists now or has ever existed on the part of the People's National Party and the Trades Union Congress against the management of the Myrtle Bank Hotel or the firm of E.A. Issa & Bros, the proprietors of the Hotel. We feel that all negotiations with the firm will be carried through in the future in a spirit of goodwill and mutual understanding." The statement was signed by Norman Manley, Ken Hill and Isaacs.[18]

Tempers flared in March when the House sat as the Finance Committee to consider the 1950–1951 estimates. One item caught the attention of Isaacs and Ken Hill. It concerned sums of £900 p.a. and £950 p.a. for two "imports", an Assistant Commissioner of Police and an Assistant Executive Officer, CID. These appointments came in the wake of a large recruitment of police officers from England, the government's response to union conflict, communist scares and violence. Isaacs charged that the recruits had come to "keep the people down". In May, he and Hill protested again when the government prepared to make the Special Constabulary Force permanent.[19]

The simultaneous occurrence of industrial unrest and debates on policing was no accident. Following the Gordon Town riot, the Executive Council rescinded the Public Order Act (1944) in order to enact more stringent legislation. Prohibition against carrying firearms was strengthened. Cases of sedition and incitement to violence would now be heard by the Circuit Court. Penalties would be harsher. In a telegram regarding the Myrtle Bank Hotel strike, the governor had expressed his fears to Creech Jones, Secretary of State:

> Yesterday at about 5 pm a large public meeting was held in the vicinity of the hotel and addressed by Manley, Isaacs, Ken Hill and others. A strike of hotel employees was called and shortly afterwards the hotel was invaded from all sides by a considerable number of roughs wearing picket badges and some, at least, showing signs of having been drugged by ganga [sic]. The police were quickly on the spot but a crowd variously estimated between 1,500 and 2,000 remained in the vicinity listening to provocative speeches by TUC leaders through microphones and singing the Red Flag and other songs.

Of the PNP, Huggins remarked, "I have no doubt whatever that the leaders of the TUC and PNP are endeavouring to bring about a state of chaos and disorder so as to cause the fall of the present Government."[20] Interestingly, one year later, a note circulated in the Colonial Office, possibly from Creech Jones, was far less inflammatory:

> There is of course some truth in the allegation that certain prominent members of the PNP are extreme left-wing in their political sympathies and are known to be in touch with the communist party in this country.
>
> But these facts are well-known both to the Colonial Office and to Jamaica Government, and they do not amount to serious Communist infiltration [...]. They are not the cause of the trouble in Jamaica; this lies in the struggle for political power between Mr Bustamante and Mr Manley, waged in the Trade Union field [...].[21]

It was in this atmosphere that the PNP turned its attention to unemployment and proposed a legislative programme. In March 1950, Manley moved a resolution in the House:

> Whereas unemployment is steadily increasing throughout the Island, and realizing that the ruin and hardship inflicted on those who suffer this condition are aggravated by the steady increase in the cost of living and the decline in the attempts by direct action to remedy the situation;
>
> and whereas these conditions and the distresses they create involve a situation today so dangerous to the community at large as to constitute a National Emergency:
>
> Be it resolved that this House appoint a Select Committee of five to consider measures for the immediate relief of the unemployed.

Manley emphasized that "free enterprise and the unrestricted operation of ordinary economic development" would not remedy Jamaica's situation. He proposed economic planning as the answer, noting that the government's *Ten-Year Plan* (1947) had not moved beyond the recommendations of the Moyne Commission.

Speaking in support, Ivan Lloyd cited two pressing issues: One was the Agricultural Small Holdings Act (1946), which codified landlord-tenant relations, but weighted the benefits in favour of landlords. In response, small farmers were leaving the land. The other was wartime import substitution industries. Many small factories had now closed due to competition from abroad, notwithstanding the Pioneer Industries (Encouragement) Act (1949). Isaacs noted that a large pool of unemployed undermined both the union movement and consumer demand for locally manufactured goods. Both labour and capital were hurt. Clifford Campbell, for the government, responded with an amendment: the Select Committee should consist of all the members of the House, not just five. The quorum would be eleven. With this amendment, the resolution passed.[22] The committee set to work, soliciting submissions from parish boards and a range of private and other public bodies. On 11

April, the PNP followed up with a statement in the *Gleaner*. "There are probably 150,000 unemployed in Jamaica, one man unemployed for every two earning wages. Out of every four working people in Jamaica, two are wage earners, one works for himself and one is unemployed." The statement revealed that Jamaica's situation was "far worse than Great Britain in the very worst year of the World Depression, 1932, when one out of ten adults was unemployed".[23]

In July the committee chair, Finance Minister H.E. Allan, submitted an interim report. Its preamble noted that, for proposals to be more than expedients, government policy would need to change. Three new bodies were required: a Land and Agricultural Development Authority, an Industrial Development Corporation and a state bank. There were five other recommendations: (1) the provision of £1,000,000 for island-wide development works; (2) pursuit of a British government loan of £2,000,000 over fifty years to finance large-scale projects; (3) taxes on luxury goods and capital gains, along with a surtax on excess profits; (4) expediting of the hospital, school and housing projects planned by government; and finally, (5) deployment of 50 per cent of the savings bank's funds for ongoing investment in Jamaica. The interim report resembled most the PNP's *Plan for Progress*. It proceeded from the position that the island would need to industrialize and increase agricultural productivity in order to reduce unemployment. The report sought to position the government, not as an adjunct of British interests, but rather as the leader of a national economy.[24]

A message to the House on 18 September 1950 declared that the government did not accept the interim report. Letters passed between the acting governor, D.C. MacGillivray, and the Colonial Office.[25] They confirmed that the report was influenced mainly by PNP members of the House. MacGillivray explained that the JLP government had been happy to see the matter of unemployment go to a Select Committee because such entities received less scrutiny from the press. That being the case, and eclipsed by the PNP in debate, only a few JLP members attended meetings. MacGillivray continued:

> In consequence there arose a Gilbertian situation in which a committee, nominally a Committee of the House, passed in effect a vote of censure on the Government [...].
>
> Bustamante subsequently stated in Executive Council that he did not agree with the Report. [....] On the other hand, he himself and the other elected members have recently shown a marked accession of zeal in the cause of the unemployed in the country districts. No similar interest has yet been displayed by them in the People's National Party dominated Corporate Area, where the plight of the unemployed is undoubtedly more serious.

MacGillivray warned that Jamaica's unemployment was sufficiently acute to lead to "grave unrest" and that the PNP would likely exploit the situation. He wrote in a note to the Colonial Office that while politics should not dictate economics, the importance of the "constitutional experiment" meant that the British may need to pay a "toll" before "crossing the bridge" from crown colony to responsible government. He concluded that the toll should be as small as possible.[26] The outcomes from the interim report were modest. A small sum was allocated to Jamaica from the War Risk Insurance Fund. Agricultural and industrial development corporations were established respectively in 1951 and 1952. The Bank of Jamaica would come later in 1961. MacGillivray had canvassed the idea of a development plan designed by an external body. Following negotiations, the recently arrived Governor Hugh Foot sent an invitation to the International Bank of Reconstruction and Development in January 1952. The IBRD submitted its report on 19 December. The report would influence both parties' policies.[27]

In April 1950, one day after the PNP's statement on unemployment, the *Gleaner* published another statement cabled from London. It came from the chair of the Colonial Development Corporation, Lord Trefgarne. He announced that, though the CDC had failed to raise the substantial dollar loan it had sought from the World Bank, West Indian projects would proceed. He added, pointedly, that were Jamaica to "moderate its internal political controversies it would be more conducive to economic development by private enterprise". Trefgarne's statement had an immediate effect.[28] On 12 April in the House, Manley called the statement "bunk", remarking that political divisions in Jamaica were minimal compared to those in Britain. He rebuffed the suggestion that PNP policy deterred private investment.

Isaacs had a different response. At a rally that night on the corner of Laws and Hanover Streets, he declared himself a socialist and remarked that socialists were obliged to oppose both capitalist and communist oppression. Made to supporters, the speech stressed that the electorate should understand clearly what the PNP "will do and not do". The party's intent was too easily obscured by opponents' smear campaigns. Other parts of Isaacs' speech concerned the "Communist way of life". As a practising Christian, it mattered to him that the Soviet regime opposed religion and held political prisoners. He also cited the circumstance of nationalist leaders in Czechoslovakia and Bulgaria. Post-war, their movements had been crushed. How could avowed critics of British imperialism endorse a Russian version? Isaacs also noted the larger Cold War context. Was it in the island's interest to test the United States with talk of communism when its leading exponent was so problematic?

Manley's reference to bunk was made in the course of the Unemployment Committee's first meeting. Speaking for an hour, Bustamante had procrastinated, refusing to address the issue. Both Isaacs and Fred Evans had risen to their feet, demanding that he speak to the unemployment crisis. In response, the government closed the meeting.[29] Frustration was palpable and, perhaps, it was Isaacs' view that Manley could no longer simply dismiss the likes of Trefgarne, Bustamante, and their prejudicial talk. He also may have wearied of the state's surveillance of his own activities. To gain power, the PNP required more discipline on policy.

Periodic left vs right disputes now seemed a feature of the party. Hart's 1943 comments on the middle class had required a response from the PNP's executive committee. Hart instigated a further intra-party debate in 1948, objecting to statements by Barbadian Grantley Adams at the United Nations. Adams had opposed the idea that the politics of the colonies be monitored by a disinterested third party. Given the complex issues involved, he said that self-government should remain a matter between the colonies and Britain. Supporting Adams, O.T. Fairclough and Isaacs responded to Hart. The vituperative debate was pursued through the pages of the *Gleaner*. It followed a clash between the party and the *Gleaner* over an editorial on freedoms endangered by communism – in Jamaica and elsewhere. In response, the PNP executive issued a circular repudiating communism and also questioned the newspaper's own record on free speech.[30] Then, early in 1949, Ken Hill made his stance public on the Moscow-based WFTU, and Manley delivered his rebuke. Communism was hardly out of the news.

In addition, debate between Bustamante, the *Gleaner* and the PNP had assumed a further dimension. *Daily Gleaner* editorials increasingly suggested that the intellectual Manley could not control his left-wing minority. During 1948, Seivright (in January) and Isaacs (in December) had written to the paper defending Manley. Seivright remarked that the "communist bogey" had been revived specifically to undermine the leader: "Either Mr Manley is himself a communist [or] he is lenient to those of his followers who are." Having made his point, Seivright concluded, "I have no sympathy with Communism." Isaacs supported Manley's socialism with the observation that it represented a middle path between "the red shirt of Moscow and the black shirt of Rome". He remarked on Manley's ideals and Bustamante's lack of them.[31] However, perhaps by 1950 Isaacs had decided to speak more forcefully. The parliamentary party had an agenda to pursue and the PNP would not prevail unless redbaiting was curtailed.

Isaacs would have known that his speech was of interest to the press. The report suggests that the *Gleaner* received a written copy, published on 13 April. An editorial followed the next day alongside an opinion piece written by "The Sentry". Both these articles called on the PNP to heed Isaacs' call. At the PNP's April executive meeting, Ken Hill accused Isaacs of "*Gleaner* collusion" against leftists. Reportedly, Hill called for Isaacs to be disciplined, remarking that he had a "soft spot for his mercantile colleagues, the capitalist exploiters".[32] This was the same complaint made in 1943 by Winston Grubb, Frank Hill and Roy Woodham. Isaacs had left the Metropolitan Group to form the Commercial Group. In turn, they had sought to have him deselected for the 1944 election. However, he was now an elected and popular politician, a campaigner of unquestioned skill. He also worked amicably with Ken Hill on union and parliamentary matters. Manley resisted the demand to discipline Isaacs. (In private, he may have cautioned him.) Two weeks later, however, Manley spoke to a large crowd on the same Hanover and Laws Street corner. He defended Isaacs against "hatchet men" and "character assassins". Isaacs had given "yeoman service" to the party.[33]

The year 1950 had seen the TUC, now a general union, more successful than ever before. The party and the union had strengthened their affiliation, suspended briefly during the WFTU affair. The rule that the TUC could nominate ten of its members to the PNP National Council had been reinstated. With the addition of others on the left elected, the group had considerable voting strength in the election of the executive committee. The quid pro quo was that the TUC should abide by the party's policies.[34]

Manley sought to unite the party at its national conference in August 1950. He stated that the TUC and the PNP were no longer two separate entities, but two elements in "one broad progressive movement" with one programme. He added yet again: "We are not a communist organization. Every leader of this party has affirmed in writing that he has no affiliation with communist organizations in the world." He noted three further points: (1) that the PNP still saw itself as Jamaica's "genuine labour party", committed to the upliftment of the working class; and (2) that no socialist worked for divisions in society. There was, in fact, "no division between the interests of farmers who own lands, and the workers on the land and workers as such". Regarding party leaders, the left vs right distinction was "artificial" because most Jamaicans would regard the entire PNP leadership as middle-class. Finally, he emphasized (3) that the progressive movement was "a national movement based on a socialist cause". In sum, though committed to the masses, Manley saw the progressive movement as principally a nationalist class coalition that pursued self-government, rather than the demolition of a capitalist class.[35]

Tensions persisted. In January 1951, Frank Hill canvassed a motion concerning *Public Opinion* editor, O.T. Fairclough. The motion proposed that the PNP make it known that *PO*'s editorial columns "no longer express the policy of our party".[36] Criticism also came from the other side. In February, at a St Andrew constituency meeting, guest speakers Glasspole and Isaacs worked to build commitment in the groups. Reportedly, Glasspole urged comrades to "give a lead and propagandise for and not against the party". Arriving late, Wills was abrupt. He said that "non-cooperating comrades" were, by their attitudes, assisting the JLP. If they did not desist, he would call in the executive. Frustrated by negative comments from some Marxists, Isaacs reportedly said that "the communists stay behind and pull down what you build up".[37]

At this time, the TUC successfully brokered an agreement with the Sugar Manufacturers' Association for joint bargaining rights in the industry. Though still smaller than the BITU, the TUC could now claim to be a mass union.[38] In the parochial elections held in June, the PNP had substantial gains in the countryside. TUC success was flowing to the party. The results in the Corporate

Area were more mixed, though the party's MHRs still provided a PNP majority on the KSAC council. Ken Hill was elected mayor and Seivright his deputy.[39] The strength of the TUC was growing. However, its affiliate status with the PNP required commitment to a party platform that was incremental rather than radical. Soon tension heightened.

In June 1951, an eight-week strike at Ariguanabo Textile Mills was settled with an agreement for one year, after which the parties would resume talks. Glasspole and Thossy Kelly were the executives who represented workers. Glasspole acknowledged that the settlement was difficult. He thanked the labour advisor who had guided the process.[40] This strategic civility echoed the statement that followed the Myrtle Bank Hotel strike. It was not a gesture peculiar to Glasspole. Nonetheless, it became apparent that some workers were offended. Previously absent due to illness, in October Ken Hill received a written complaint from six Ariguanabo workers. They charged that Glasspole and Kelly, among other things, had shared drinks with management. They requested that henceforth they be represented by leftists Frank Hill and Osmond Dyce. As TUC president, Ken showed the letter to Glasspole and Kelly, who felt the complaints were misplaced. However, without further ado, Ken met with the workers and other TUC executives. The workers' request was granted. Intended or not, the action undermined two committed unionists. Given Glasspole's stand against the WFTU, Hill's action seemed to endorse the view that moderates on the union executive were not welcome.[41]

The party's 1951 annual conference was held on 6 and 7 October. The left gained substantial representation in the General Council and on the executive committee. The *Gleaner* reported that some on the right had expressed concern. This was matched by outspoken gestures from the conference floor by some on the left. Speakers asserted that some in the party "do not mean the workers any good". Frank Hill was more specific, referring to so-called friends who argued that wage restraint was needed to reduce the cost of living. He stated baldly that workers were always the party's priority, a rebuke understood to be aimed at Isaacs.[42] At the time, wages were not a significant part of Jamaica's inflation, which was largely imported. However, among the masses a rising cost of living had variable effects. Certainly, the interests of unionists could not always have priority over the much larger group of unemployed and non-unionized working poor. Despite the attack, Isaacs was elected fourth vice president over Frank. However, his position had slipped in comparison with Ken Hill, who remained as PNP second vice president, TUC president and mayor of Kingston.[43]

On 29 October, Isaacs took two months' leave from the KSAC council and the House for an extended business trip to New York and London. He was also seeking medical advice in New York and would return on a similar quest in 1955. He was granted leave from the KSAC on 12 October, suggesting that the trip had been planned for some time.[44]

Three weeks later, on 20 November, Thossy Kelly and W.R. MacPherson, a TUC trustee, announced that they were taking a number of members out of the Union of Bauxite and Allied Workers. They listed six other unions from which comparable groups would be drawn to form a National Labour Congress. Later Vernon Arnett, who was the party's general secretary at the time, would propose that Kelly had been encouraged by Glasspole, following the Ariguanabo affair. Kelly cited "ideological differences" within the TUC for his action. He and MacPherson remained members of the PNP, but resigned from the TUC. Its executive issued a scathing statement regarding the pair: "Their flagrant derelictions of duty resulted in the TUC losing bargaining rights for a number of important groups of workers. So now the progressive Trade Union movement has cleansed itself of these two traitors to the working class. We have no doubt that the workers of Jamaica will treat them with the scorn which they deserve." Ken Hill and Richard Hart demanded that both be expelled from the PNP. Hill charged that the Kelly and Macpherson initiative was in fact a company union. He added that with them should go "all their accomplices, high and low".[45]

Isaacs returned early from his trip, arriving in Kingston on Saturday, 1 December. On Sunday, he penned a complaint to the *Daily Gleaner*, which had claimed he was involved in these events. In the letter he related that he had first heard of the rift from Hart on that very day. Moreover, he would not be attending the PNP executive meeting scheduled for Monday night. He was not a party to these events. Munroe and Bertram, however, cite Hart to the effect that Isaacs, along with Seivright, saw Manley on the Monday and advised him not to bow to the TUC.[46] What is clear is that on 6 December, nine members of the PNP, including Vivian Blake, Glasspole, Lloyd and Isaacs, wrote a letter to Manley against the proposed expulsions. Just as clear is the fact that this situation was an escalation of long-term, sporadic struggle between the left, the centre and conservatives. All had been aggressors from time to time. However, the growing strength of the TUC and of Ken Hill on the one hand, and on the other, of the PNP Opposition in the House, provided added impetus. Each side's eyes were trained on power.

The letter was considered by the PNP executive on 10 December. It was referred to a committee consisting of Manley, Nethersole, Vernon Arnett, and Reverend E.B. Baker. A transcript of this meeting cited by Hart suggests that, at the outset, Manley favoured the TUC's position. It was in the interests of the PNP to keep party and union together. However, events soon took a different course.[47]

On 19 December, just before the committee was to begin its work, two more submissions were placed before it. The material had been provided by MacPherson. The next day Manley, as committee chair, advised the press that he had received a document implicating some party members in "teaching communist doctrines". The charge would be investigated. The committee's inquiry began in earnest on

27 December with Nethersole as the new chair. It assumed the form of a tribunal, with Ken Hill appearing for the TUC, and Vivian Blake for Kelly and MacPherson. Evidence was taken and findings made. The party's General Council accepted the committee's report on 2 March, which was then taken to a special conference of the party on 29 March 1952.

The tribunal found that Kelly and MacPherson should not be expelled from the party. Contrary to Ken Hill's claim, they had not sought to form a company union. However, if they remained as PNP members, there could be no relationship between their National Labour Congress and the PNP. The organization should be disbanded. Furthermore, Kelly and MacPherson were required to resign their positions on the PNP's General Council. It was found that Ken Hill's response to the Ariguanabo issue, though well meant, had contributed to Kelly's action. Notwithstanding, his and MacPherson's actions had "weakened and split" both the TUC and the progressive movement. A severe censure of both was in order.

These issues proved less consequential than those pertaining to a study group which involved some executive members of the TUC. The charges against them were listed by Vivian Blake. They included:

> The dissemination of communist doctrines; instruction and training of persons in the TUC, also in the PNP, in communist policy; discrediting the PNP and its socialist policies in the cause of communism; 'a smear campaign against middle class elements in the Party generally and the Leader of the Party and Florizel Glasspole in particular' in order to 'establish the TUC as the leading working class organization with intent to capture the movement for the Marxist-Communist group'.

This set of charges referred to the formation of study classes in Allman Town and other places based on a set of four lessons prepared by two New Zealand communists in Jamaica, a Dr David Lewis and his wife. The two were active in Jamaica in 1947 and

1948, when they left the island. Hart had stencilled the lessons, two of which concerned general issues of political economy and another two on steps to the formation of a communist party, drawing examples from Russia, China and France. The educational effort was furthered by an informal bookshop located in the TUC office that was run by Frank Gordon, also a PNP member. Evidence was given that the Lewises, on their departure, "upbraided" the Hill brothers, Hart and Arthur Henry for their timorous politics. Subsequently, the four resolved their differences and pledged to maintain a "secret group" devoted to a Marxist agenda.[48]

Witnesses testified that some of the lessons involved advocating for a communist group within the PNP. The class noted Lenin's view that, under bourgeois rule, it was easy to establish a communist faction that could foster a real proletarian party. This evidence echoed the incident in 1943–1944 when the JDP and WISCO's Robert Kirkwood cited similar statements by Hart. Manley had required that Hart recant. With statements made already denying communist sympathies within the party – in 1948, 1949 and 1950 – the matter had become wearily familiar. Though the Lewises were gone, Hart and Frank Hill remained with their like commitments. Other comrades were supportive. Now, with major policies in hand concerning capital development to create employment, could the party afford not to act? As Nettleford observes, by 1952 Manley was prepared to jettison comrades whom he felt had compromised the party, despite his affection for them. Not to address the matters raised by the inquiry left both the leader and the PNP exposed.[49]

The upshot of the tribunal was that Ken and Frank Hill, Hart and Arthur Henry were asked to – and in due course did – resign from the PNP. Lesser lights who were members of the executive, National Council, or both were asked to resign their positions, including Winston Grubb, Vincent Edwards and Osmond Dyce. Frank Gordon held no office in the party. Grubb and Dyce handed in their resignations, along with Roy Woodham.[50]

This description hardly captures the anger, grief, resolve and misgiving that accompanied the expulsion of the 4Hs. The process played out at a meeting of the National Council on 2 March, and the subsequent special party conference on 29 March 1952. The findings of the tribunal were read first at National Council, which accepted the committee's recommendations on a vote of twenty-three to twelve. The *Gleaner* reported that, following the vote, Isaacs "burst into loud sobbing", followed by Edith Dalton-James and others, at which Ken Hill charged Isaacs with crying "crocodile tears". Until a new executive was selected, a caretaker committee of ten was appointed to manage the party. In addition to the tribunal members, this committee included Glasspole, Isaacs and Seivright; Leslie Alexander from the TUC; and organizer Ken Sterling. Alexander had made an impassioned speech on the 4Hs' behalf, though he was also conciliatory. When the decision was confirmed at conference, cries of "Traitors!" were aimed at those who did not support the left.[51]

The PNP turned away from the TUC and determined to build a new union: the National Workers' Union was formed on 2 April 1952 and formally registered in October 1952. Its leaders at the outset were Glasspole and Stirling, with Isaacs assisting. A youthful Michael Manley, son of Norman, became a union organizer and was provided with generous support and advice from Isaacs. Despite disagreements, Isaacs would maintain avuncular, life-long relations with Michael. The NWU grew from an initial membership of 5,025 to 66,013 in 1957.[52]

It was tragic that the PNP was forced to lose the talent of both Ken and Frank Hill. In Ken's case, it concerned a matter in which he was only tangentially involved. Study groups were not his priority. And it seems a deal to retain him, and others, had been forged behind closed doors. Both Hart and Leroy Cooke relate that it was Hill's abusive attack on Isaacs and Glasspole at the special conference that sealed his fate. Manley could not condone it. Left accounts charge "the twins", Glasspole and Isaacs, with the cynical pursuit of power, propelled by the prospect of declining influence. Certainly, Isaacs was on the road back, following his 1949 departure from the executive after the Gordon Town events. In addition, there seems little doubt that Glasspole, Isaacs and their allies took advantage of the Cold War climate.

However, over the years, the tireless union work of Hart and others, including Frank Hill, had come with vocal attacks – even on the moderates. The end result was that the left's demand that "traitors" be expelled from the party, along with their "accomplices", was matched by charges that "a Marxist-Communist" group sought to "capture" the TUC. Each side's hyperbole fed the other.[53]

Where policy was concerned, Ken Hill and Hart were willing to cooperate and compromise. This was evident during parliamentary debate when Hill and Isaacs sometimes worked together. It was also evident in debate on the *Plan for Progress*. Though Hart and Isaacs voiced their concerns regarding foreign private capital, in the end they endorsed the measures proposed. However, at the union and constituency level, the rumble of more radical ambitions – of groups within groups and mobilization against the party – persisted. The situation fed an antagonistic press, and government, leading to destabilisation within the PNP. Just one year earlier, Manley had made forthright statements regarding the party's rejection of communism. Those who moved against the left were no doubt aware of this. Where the left was concerned, perhaps the Hills and Hart might have enjoined their comrades to be more mindful of Manley's position.

At the national conference in September 1952, Nethersole called for "an alliance with the dollar". He said it was Jamaica's only realistic way forward. He advocated that bauxite earnings be paid in dollars and coupled with earnings from the tourist trade. From these two items, Jamaica could build substantial dollar reserves and develop more trade.[54] Isaacs agreed, though with the caveat that beyond bauxite, industry should be Jamaica-owned as far as possible.

In 1954, delivering his final speech to the House of Representatives, Ken Hill allowed that the issues were difficult. He remarked on his previous assumption that,

> [O]nce the people showed intolerance of economic hardship all you had to do was to form trade union organizations and political parties and speed on happily [...] to progress and prosperity. Those of us who have grown up from the start have acquired the experience and knowledge to understand there is no short-cut to progress, to prosperity. It is a long road [...] and there are vehicles that must carry us no matter what our brand of politics might be.

He appealed to the Parliament to put aside its differences and grasp the power that came with independence. Frank Hill had also changed his opinions by 1957; Hart, not totally. However, in 1967, Hart wrote to Manley proposing that Jamaica's "alarming" post-war unemployment, and its impact on any party in power, had changed both Manley's and Nethersole's views on foreign private capital.[55] The ailing leader confirmed Hart's conjecture. Even with a planned economy, an independent Jamaica needed capital from abroad.

Very few in the PNP were as explicit as Isaacs regarding communism, though his views were not uncommon. His opposition to religious persecution and to imperialism, including the Russian type in Eastern Europe, informed his position. Where policies for Jamaica's future were concerned, he was in accord with many, including Nethersole and Manley.

# SECTION III
# MINISTER OF TRADE AND INDUSTRY

# Chapter 6
# Assuming Government

*The PNP has always insisted that it was necessary to build our economy on the twin pillars of Agriculture and Industry. On that basis alone can we hope to deal with unemployment. Plan for Progress*, 1955

*It is not easy for men who have known the easy way to amass wealth to turn their backs on that way, to take the harder road [...].*
– Wills Isaacs to the Jamaica Chamber of Commerce, 1955[1]

In the early 1950s, the PNP Opposition sharpened its attack on the government. Donald Sangster's 1951 budget speech was one of many notable occasions on which the opposition challenged the government's economic performance. Nethersole addressed the need for government to attract capital to the island: "[T]he two most serious things we have in economic terms are the awful realization that over the past twelve years production has decreased while our population increase is something alarming. [....] With an unemployment situation such as we have, it is idle and nonsensical to believe that the private sector of investment capital can possibly cope with the situation." He cited pressing infrastructural needs, including more extensive irrigation, an industrial estate and a major road-building programme.

Isaacs followed with a focus on consumption. He provided an overview of products imported into Jamaica, including car parts, furniture, codfish and textiles. The last had been stockpiled by merchants at the behest of their English agents, wary of sterling's unstable status. Isaacs addressed the government: "You are short a thousand and one things to develop national resources; but yet you can have three years' supply of textiles in your country." He called the situation "socialism for the privileged few" and suggested government collusion. Owing to the government's dependence on customs duties, the tax on staples had never been higher. Not only were these duties regressive, with them came rent-seeking practices, including almost automatic renewal of import licences. Restricted during the war, licences were now the possession of a privileged few. This led Isaacs and others to term the House majority a "merchant government". Both the merchants and the government gained from taxation, which was a burden mainly on the poor.[2]

Unemployment and the cost of living for the masses were Isaacs' main concerns, followed by a commitment to industrial development and particular views about the economy. Like many of his colleagues, Isaacs did not see agriculture as the main site for industrial development at the time. His interest was manufacturing and construction, the latter propelled by tourism and housing. Whereas Nethersole looked to capital from abroad, Isaacs focused on Jamaica's entrepreneurs. He did not deplore capital per se, but rather foreign ownership. It seemed to him that the government had "no real desire" to support Jamaica-owned industries: "I don't see it. You have the cement factory. Who owns it? You have the Tate and Lyle sugar factory. Who owns it? You have the [Ariguanabo] Textile Mills. Who owns it? You have the Condensery. Who owns it? You have Jamaica Public Service Company. Who owns it? May I ask, Mr Speaker, what is it that my countrymen control?"

Isaacs was first and foremost an economic nationalist. "I am not against foreign capital coming into my own country, but I want to warn this country, you can have any type of Constitution or Self-Government you want – if you are unable to control the economy of your own country you are not the masters of your own country.[3] He believed that the government should protect fledgling industries. He also hoped that the merchant capitalists – those whose wealth came mainly from distributing imported goods – could be persuaded "to take the harder road"; to invest at home in industries to employ Jamaicans. The government had its role to play, but so did the commercial class.

Sangster's budget also introduced tariff regulations, making way for a Caribbean customs union in the event of a federation. In August came an extended debate on federation as the route to dominion status for Jamaica and other British islands. The report of the Rance Committee was tabled and the House was invited to show its support.[4] Along with the Opposition, the JLP government voted in favour, reflecting a more positive stance on federation and self-government. The debate made clear that some members of the House on both sides saw federation not just as a constitutional advancement, but also as a path to economic growth. Glasspole was one. He instanced Britain paying more to Cuba for sugar than it paid to Jamaica. A federation could lobby more effectively for markets. Isaacs was sceptical. He suggested that "freedom" via federation was "like the bone the master throws to the dog". His belief was that Jamaica's future lay elsewhere: "America is our market. There must we buy and sell."[5] His view would prove correct in the longer term. By the mid-1960s, the United States had become Jamaica's major trading partner. Within a decade, its proportion of trade with the United States compared to the United Kingdom was far greater, though foreign corporations were still preeminent in the economy.[6]

Isaacs did not agree with Glasspole and Manley that an island federation would greatly assist Jamaica's economy. The increase in population and land mass was insufficient to make a major difference. And Jamaica's distance from the eastern Caribbean could be a disadvantage. He worried that a Caribbean customs union would undermine regulations to protect domestic initiatives. And he hinted at the British intent that, in a federation, the wealthier islands would take up the burden of the smaller and poorer ones. As the imperial power had shown in trade, Britain acted in its own interests. Cheaper dollar imports were denied to Jamaica, while UK producers exported all they could. The upshot was as Isaacs described: "[the British] sold us £4 million more than they bought from us – a country as pauperized as we are." In 1953, he attacked the role of Crown agents and London brokers in loan negotiations with the British government. Their transaction fees and their delays pushed interest and indebtedness ever up. Manley rebuked him, asking where else would Jamaica secure loans.[7]

Later in the year, both Isaacs and Ken Hill spoke against a bill that would permit a federal constitution. Hill objected to the exclusion of the mainland territories of British Guiana and Honduras.[8] Isaacs concurred, and criticized the fact that ultimate power would remain with Britain's Privy Council in the first five years. This was simply more imperialism. He supported the stance of Edwin Allen (JLP), who declared that nothing should be done regarding federation that would impede Jamaica's progress towards self-government. "Now you are talking," Isaacs said. "You are right. I don't like federation."[9] As a Member of Parliament, Isaacs maintained the practice he had crafted as a councillor. Although he always voted with his party, he still spoke his mind robustly, which sometimes annoyed his leader. Federation was a case in point. He deferred to Manley on constitutional issues, but was always ready to advise him on the implications for trade and industry.

Concern over federation was fuelled by disappointment at the slow pace of Jamaica's own constitutional reform. On his appointment, Governor Foot had sought to hasten the process, conferring with relevant parties through the latter part of 1951 and in 1952. A new system of ministerial responsibility was introduced in 1953, involving seven ministers recommended by the chief minister, himself confirmed by a vote of the House. The eight would assume responsibility for one portfolio each, supported by a department of the same name: Local Government, Finance, Agriculture and Lands, Education and Social Welfare, Trade and Industry, Communications and Works, Health and Housing, and Labour. The governor would still appoint a Colonial Secretary, an Attorney General and a Financial Secretary, the last to advise the Minister of Finance. In principle, the governor retained a right of veto in the Executive Council.[10] Creeping closer, the changes still did not confer self-government. Of interest to Isaacs though, was the advent of a Trade and Industry portfolio. He spoke increasingly of industrial development and of the cost of imported raw materials, food staples and articles of clothing.

The approach of a general election was signalled by the *Gleaner*'s Political Reporter on 30 June 1954. He remarked that were the PNP and its union affiliate to lose for a third time, the survival of both the party and Jamaica's democracy would be in question. The journalist implied that the parties' respective positions – free enterprise and socialist – were now mere gambits. Both embraced a planned and thereby mixed economy. Both had been influenced by the IBRD's 1952 report. As Donald Sangster described, the report was the basis for a new government five-year plan, foreshadowed in April 1954 and released in October.[11] The PNP's updated Plan for Progress was released earlier, following a large election rally. Both plans shared the IBRD emphasis on increasing rural production and fostering industrialization. At the same time, neither addressed major land reform or the role that domestic savings should and must play in development. There were, however, differences. One was their respective views on raising loan capital. The PNP's determination to escape the sterling area was marked, whereas the JLP still turned to Britain. Another difference was the PNP's far more detailed approach to social services. As stated in the plan, the aims of the PNP were to increase wealth and employment opportunities; reduce the cost of living; extend social services – especially education;

provide honest government; and achieve full self-government. The last would come in conjunction with federation and dominion status for the British Caribbean. Nationalization was downplayed and statements on private capital and loan finance – foreign and domestic – were cursory.[12]

For this election, the PNP mobilized its experienced campaigners island-wide. Vernon Arnett and Isaacs were given a roving commission in the western parishes. Around this time, Isaacs wound up his business on Port Royal Street. On behalf of Wills O. Isaacs & Son, he had sought an import licence to purchase textiles from the United States, committing commercially to the path he thought that Jamaica should follow. His application had been rejected by the Executive Council and, therefore, he no longer worked as a commission agent. Not much later, he retired as vice president of the Association of Parochial Boards. Electoral politics had become his all.[13]

Early electioneering saw him and Glasspole speaking up for Noel Nethersole in St Andrew Central. At a meeting in Jones Town in early October, Nethersole said that the PNP could not offer "sudden great prosperity", but could deliver a nation with hope and a better economy. Isaacs, who had just returned from Cornwall County, reported that the urban enthusiasm of 1949 was now present in rural areas. He described the PNP as "a light in the darkness" and recommended Nethersole to the crowd as "even more important" than Manley. Not only did his remark reflect a focus on economy over governance; it also revealed an affinity between him and Nethersole that stretched back to 1942 when Nethersole had lectured to the PNP Commercial Group.[14]

On 25 October, Manley formally launched the campaign with his speech at the annual conference. He traced a history of PNP success, including the attainment of a ministerial system, "a long stride forward in the march to national freedom". He also cited the formation of the House Unemployment Committee and its resolution requiring "the whole House" to address the pressing issue, moved in the face of a government bereft of specific development plans. Manley's speech was filled with Christian idiom. He began "on a note of confidence" in God, "on a note of humility", charity, faith and "in the spirit of harmony". He concluded with "confidence" and in "humility" and enjoined those present to "go forth" and "ask before God that we be worthy of the task that confronts us".[15] The Bishop could not have said it better.

Isaacs launched his own campaign with a bit of humour, using the idiom of a referee in a boxing match, with a fleeting bow to federation:

> I want to conduct a clean campaign because the other West Indian islands are watching us [...] I want it clean because the United States of America will be watching us and as a people, we want to earn their respect. When the People's National Party gets into power, although we propose to remain always within the British Commonwealth of nations, we would desire to draw closer economically to the United States of America and expand our trade in that country.
>
> I want it clean because the people of Great Britain are watching us to see if we are fit for full self-government [...] and any man who would conduct himself in this election as to hinder our victory is a saboteur in the election. [....] But I would not be human if I did not sound a note of warning that those who abuse my flesh and blood without just cause, I shall not forget and I shall not forgive.

At a massive meeting on Spanish Town Road a week before election day, Manley introduced Isaacs to the crowd. "Stormy Petrel" noted that new JLP candidates could claim seven pounds a day in campaign expenses. This meant that, as candidates, they often received more than their previous earnings. "Bishop" reached for a biblical viewpoint: Rather than feed themselves, the PNP would feed the people. By the Sea of Galilee, Jesus had directed Peter to "Feed my lambs, feed my sheep." Isaacs assured those present that, likewise, the PNP would feed the young and the old, the untutored and the wise.[16] The party also emphasized corruption on the government side. Two former ministers, L.L. Simmonds and J.Z. Malcolm, had been convicted of criminal charges. In its campaigning, the PNP used the broom as a symbol and its slogan was "Sweep them out!" Cartoonist Leandro portrayed Manley rising skyward over Bustamante on a flying broomstick.

On 12 January 1955, the PNP was victorious. It mattered that the *Gleaner* did not campaign against the PNP, agreeing perhaps with overseas observers, that its front bench was the more talented.[17] The PNP won eighteen seats to the JLP's fourteen – a clear victory with a workable majority. Rural candidates did better than before, while Kingston-St Andrew, formerly the PNP stronghold, weakened. In St Andrew Central, Nethersole won well against former mayor Lynden Newland. In West Kingston, however, the seat was lost to the JLP's Hugh Shearer. Ken Hill, and Iris King for the PNP, had split the anti-JLP vote. Isaacs, Manley and Glasspole all won comfortably, although Isaacs' majority had decreased. His JLP opponent was Ernest Rae, a well-known businessman and former Test cricketer who had been deputy mayor of Kingston between 1938 and 1940.

In the days that followed, Manley announced that he would leave soon for the United State in search of an expert with practical experience to guide his development initiatives. The man he chose was George Cadbury, who would preside over Manley's Central Planning Unit. It was also agreed that when the new government met for the first time in the House, the party anthem "Jamaica Arise" would be sung – not "The Red Flag".[18] On Wednesday, 2 February, from opposite directions, the government and the Opposition converged in columns on Headquarters House. B.B. Coke, the Member for St Elizabeth South, was confirmed as Speaker and swore in the members of the new parliament. A message from the governor nominated Norman Manley as chief minister. He was elected by the House without division. Eight portfolios were distributed among eight government members, including Manley who, at the outset, took Agriculture. As expected,

Isaacs became Minister of Trade and Industry. Glasspole became Leader of the House and Minister of Labour. Finance, of course, went to Nethersole.[19] The government's first business session would commence on 9 March.

In the interim, Isaacs went to work. On Thursday, 3 February, he greeted his staff at the ministry. Among the guests was Father Sydney Judah, who blessed the gathering. He was the brother of a prominent lawyer and conservative member of the Legislative Council, Douglas Judah. Another guest was Robert Lightbourne, an accomplished inventor and businessman. Governor Foot had invited him home from England in 1952 to be the IDC's founding general manager. He would remain with the corporation for another year. Later on, he would join the JLP and become the minister himself. Between them, he and Isaacs oversaw Trade and Industry for more than fifteen years. On Saturday, 5 February, Isaacs called on the Trade Control Board and its chair, the Trade Administrator. Ten days later, he declared a moratorium on the importation of "skirts, jumpers, cotton sweaters, pullovers, vests and singlets" with a landed cost of less than 220 shillings per dozen. These low-cost basics could be made in Jamaica. The measure came in the wake of a previous inquiry into garment manufacture. On the same day, a similar release addressed the importation of car batteries, an item also assembled in Jamaica. Henceforth, all government departments would be directed to purchase local batteries for their vehicles. The ministry noted that these measures were designed to "encourage and develop local industry". Quantitative restrictions were imposed in the interest of Jamaica's import substitution.[20]

As March began and the parliament sat, Isaacs also reached out to various organizations, such as the Jamaica Chamber of Commerce, the Jamaica Manufacturers' Association and the newly formed Incorporated Master Builders' Association. On Thursday, 9 March, he was guest speaker at the annual lunch of the Chamber of Commerce.[21] He remarked that many of them had known him for years. Humorously, he described his progression from commission agent to city councillor, to member of the House, to Minister of Trade and Industry. He assured them, "Fear not, it is I." A regular critic of Jamaica's merchant class, Isaacs reminded exporters that the sale of agricultural goods was now largely in the hands of producer groups. He encouraged them to develop new exports, not least among them straw products, potentially worth £2 million a year. Turning to importers, he noted that his party had come to government in order to bring down the cost of living and create one hundred and fifty thousand jobs. And here the point of his address became clear. So far as merchants were concerned, "unnecessary profits must go". The cost to the consumer must be reduced, including the "commission for the commission agent, a distributor's profit, a wholesaler's profit and also a retailer's profit".

> Jamaica is suffering from over-trading. If we could sit down and add up the amount of capital that has been invested in trading, I think it would be enormous, and if there was a possibility of directing much of that capital into productive enterprise, we would not have to be running around the world inviting foreign capital to come into our country to exploit our resources, not to mention the fact that the profits out of such undertakings would remain to enrich Jamaica.

And on that point, corporate saving and subsequent investment should be in local production, not merely in distribution. He added, "It is not easy for men who have known the easy way to amass wealth to turn their backs on that way, to take the harder road [...] but at this stage of our country's history, it is vital and imperative that each and every man must ask himself, 'What part am I going to play [...] in the building of a new nation?'"

Concluding, he remarked that "materialism of the right" did not fail to produce "materialism of the left". The merchants and others would have only themselves to blame if they failed to act in the people's interest.[22]

His address to the JMA included some central concerns about policy priorities. He noted that agricultural and industrial expansion was the government's main concern. In the case of industry, this expansion would involve building export manufacturing, which in turn required greater efficiency in production and standardization in relevant industries. With regard to productivity, Isaacs called for greater worker participation:

> It is full time for the employer to realize that a bit of work done by the skilled hands of his worker may be good, but it will never be the perfection we seek until the worker is so treated that [...] his heart goes into the work also.
>
> I believe that if industry is to succeed the employer must begin to pocket his pride and his conceit and to bring in his worker around the table to hear what he thinks is best for the industry, and let him feel that he has a stake in that industry.

Isaacs stressed the need for Jamaica's modest dollar reserves to be used wisely. Dollars allocated to an industry must be spent on the stipulated goods, and raw materials imported under licence should be used to produce a finished article. To this end, the government would introduce factory inspections.

Manufacturers voiced their own concerns through their president, Aaron Matalon. He emphasized the need for tariff protection, remarking that even the United States built its progress on tariffs.[23] He requested that if there were to be a Bureau of Standards, its operations should embrace the quality of both locally made and imported goods. He noted that the IDC required as much collateral as the commercial banks for its modest loans. This practice deterred small producers. Matalon also questioned the amount of IDC resources deployed as incentives for overseas investors. Isaacs pointed out that protection was available for domestic pioneers as well. Moreover, loans for small business were coming. Lee Gore thanked the minister and remarked that, though they might quarrel from time to time, the JMA supported Isaacs. He replied, "I am not going to quarrel at all. We all have the same aim. The industrialization of Jamaica is paramount."[24]

On 25 March, he spoke at the inaugural dinner of the Master Builders' Association at the Myrtle Bank Hotel. Governor Foot proposed a toast to the guests, who included Bustamante, Glasspole, Lightbourne, and the lawyer and businessman Neville Ashenheim. Aaron Matalon was there in dual capacities as a manufacturer and as a prospective director of new housing initiatives.[25] Isaacs proposed a toast to the association and spoke about the shared commitment of all those present to a national plan: "I, together with my colleagues in the present government, and our supporters, and indeed all Jamaicans of goodwill are engaged in planning this nation's future – and how to relieve poverty, distress and unemployment; how to reduce the cost of living; to reduce illiteracy; to improve the national economy; and to construct a healthy and vigorous nation upon the solid foundations of good government."

He noted the contributions that master builders had made to the task. One was a more orderly tendering system, which should provide a better deal to both builders and prospective owners. Nonetheless, he asked that the association be vigilant in keeping construction costs down. He also addressed the pivotal role of master builders in promoting and expanding the apprenticeship system. Such a system was "as indispensable to improved standards in the building industry as it is to the cause of technical education". Finally, he underlined the centrality and reach of construction in Jamaica's economy. The construction industry provided both skilled and unskilled labour and linked to other industries providing raw materials. He concluded that he had "the greatest admiration for his hosts as builders but they should never forget that the real Master Builder was He who built not for time but for eternity".[26]

Each of these overtures demonstrates Isaacs' commitment to a class accord within the framework of a nationalist movement. Without it, he doubted that domestic capital could be mobilized for industrial growth. Most importantly, both savings and the resources of commercial banks needed to be redirected away from distribution – the easy road – and towards manufacturing.

By March, however, Isaacs had turned his attention to another industry. Jamaica's post-war tourism had evolved as a single season, luxury trade, not least at the Myrtle Bank Hotel. Located on the Kingston waterfront, the Myrtle Bank had become a meeting place for wealthy, mainly foreign, white socialites. Reconstructed after the 1907 earthquake and acquired by United Fruit in 1918, the business declined during World War II. In 1943, Abe Issa and his father acquired the hotel and its extensive grounds for the modest sum of £35,000. As Suzanne Issa reports, "Its doors were thrown open to Jamaicans", albeit well-heeled, brown- and fair-skinned ones. This purchase was an early move in Abe Issa's illustrious career as a tourism industry developer. In January 1949, he opened the Tower Isle Hotel in Ocho Rios, establishing a new tourist destination on the north coast outside Montego Bay. He had financed and constructed the hotel without foreign help, an effort which earned him a 'Man of the Year' award from Evon Blake's *Spotlight* in 1948.[27] In 1950, Issa hosted visiting US travel agents at his hotels, assisted by his Myrtle Bank manager, Sam Levy.[28]

By the time Isaacs became Minister of Trade and Industry, it seems very likely that he and Issa had already discussed the prospects for Jamaican tourism. The link between him and the Issa family can be traced back to the 1920s when, as a struggling migrant to Kingston, Isaacs was employed by Issa's father. In later years, Issa would recall, "I spoke to Busta. I talked with Sangster. I discussed it with Manley. I pleaded with Nethersole. They all said the same thing: tourism could only be small fry. I kept telling them they were wrong; tourism could be our biggest industry. And when they asked me why? I told them, 'The world is our market.'"

Suzanne Issa continues, "Finally, in 1955, Abe caught the ear of the then Minister of Trade, Wills O. Isaacs." He put the case that Jamaica's tourism assets surpassed those of other islands, including the Bahamas. However, what these other resorts had was "a more wide-awake and business-like approach", while Jamaicans "have been sleeping".[29] This view resonated with Will's assessment of Jamaica's merchant capitalists.

Acting on a Tourist Board Act of 1954, the pre-existing Tourist Trade Development Board was reorganized as the Jamaica Tourist Board. Its twenty members would represent a range of interests and make policy for the industry's stakeholders, including hoteliers, guesthouse owners, local merchants, airline and shipping representatives, travel agents and taxicab proprietors. The new JTB met for the first time on 18 March 1955 and was addressed by Isaacs. On 1 April, Abe Issa was elected chairman, with an executive of ten members. They would meet weekly but receive no remuneration. The *Daily Gleaner* reported that the reorganization came from the agitation of various branches of the industry for "a greater share and voice in the shaping of policy". Issa would prove dominant in this respect. Many procedures, including marketing, became more effective. On 19 March, a short but pointed article in the *Gleaner* announced that, "One of the most delightful places in the world is Negril. This remote potential resort is the focus of interest by leaders in the tourist trade and local buyers." Nearby oil exploration had brought attention to this westernmost region of the island.[30]

Isaacs would take up a major interest in other industries, including textiles and knitted goods, garments, tanning and leather shoes. As a young man and then in his later years, he gained a lot from Edward Hanna's insights into the dry goods industry. His relations with Hanna were longer lasting and more intimate than those with Issa, although he worked well with both.[31] He would have long debates with beef producers and with the suppliers of cement and lumber. The monopoly position of the British-controlled Caribbean Cement Company would be a source of continuing vexation. It is telling, however, that in his first months in office, tourism was at the forefront. As the industry grew, it stimulated Jamaican construction and the domestic production of building materials. Together, tourism and construction became major drivers of the economy. Manufacturing expanded to become a major employer.

Trade and its impact on consumers were also on Isaacs' mind. On 9 March, he reintroduced a Trade Board bill that was passed by the House in 1954, but rejected by the Legislative Council. Merchants had objected to the bill, which gave the Minister of Trade and Industry power to revoke an import licence. Determined to protect their interests, merchants had briefed various members of the council. Now, with further amendments, the bill was brought back to the House. Isaacs negotiated with Richard Youngman of the Legislative Council, and president of the JCC. Agreement was reached: the Trade Board would revoke licences, rather than the minister. However, prior to a final decision, the board would need the minister to certify that it was acting in the public interest. Isaacs signalled his intent to rein in merchant government.

Another month passed and by the last week of April, Isaacs had settled into his job. He departed Jamaica for two weeks on his first trade trip – to Canada. His objective was to review the impact of the price of Canadian flour on Jamaica's baking industry. The PNP was facing an early political challenge. Bakery workers, represented by the BITU, were preparing to strike. Their claims were justified. However, the government's intent was not to pass the cost of a wage increase on to consumers. The price of bread should not rise. Isaacs used Jamaica's growing demand for flour to negotiate a lower price from Canadian producers. *Inter alia*, he also addressed the price of Canadian salted codfish, which was a major protein source for Jamaica's masses. This negotiation would prove to be long-term and turbulent. The status of Jamaican domestic service workers was another issue. Isaacs insisted that they have a pathway to permanent residence in Canada. He also made television appearances promoting Jamaica both as a tourist and investment destination. En route to Ottawa, he stayed some days in New York, working with Jamaica Tourist Board members to extend steamship services to Jamaica.[32]

Isaacs also used his status to influence public debate. He took time out to canvass for a full Easter weekend holiday for workers in the commercial sector. Within a week, the *Gleaner* reported that "Most drapers, wholesalers, and general shops have agreed to close on Saturday. Garages and factories are likely to agree [...]. Professional offices for many years have closed over the Easter weekend." On a more sober note, it was at this time that he co-operated with police in the arrest and ultimate conviction of Eric Condell, who had sought to offer Isaacs a very substantial bribe, which would be lodged in a US bank account. He wanted Isaacs to influence a decision concerning the government purchase of new diesel engines for Jamaica Railway. With police cooperation, Isaacs tape-recorded Condell making his proposition. In light of previous corrupt ministers, this event was a fillip for the PNP. Members campaigned even more forcefully on the theme of an open and honest government.[33]

These were Isaacs' first months in office. What was his place in the PNP government? The industry component of his role was to promote production and employment, especially in manufacturing, tourism and smaller rural export industries. The last included ginger, cocoa, pimento and coffee. His portfolio did not include either sugar – sold mostly to Britain under the 1951 Commonwealth Sugar Agreement – or bananas, which were managed mainly by producers and the Jamaica Agricultural Society. He encouraged local capitalists to diversify at home and worked with the IDC to seek private capital abroad. The IDC would facilitate development in Kingston by constructing an industrial estate where factory space would be provided under various terms to producers.[34] Jamaica being an export economy, the trade component of Isaacs' role involved diversifying export products and locating markets for them. The tourism and dry goods markets were mainly North American, but markets for some other products extended to Europe. The trade component of his portfolio also involved various forms of regulation. Tariffs and quantitative import restrictions were used to encourage import substitution at home. Price controls on imported staples, including milk solids, flour and codfish, were central to the cost of living. Moreover, though housing was outside his portfolio, Isaacs attended to the price of raw materials for construction – major factors in housing and rental costs, especially in Kingston. Other infrastructural issues also had implications for employment. Frequency conversion and further electrification were crucial for all industries and for locating factories in rural areas. These matters involved extensive negotiations with the Canadian-owned Jamaica Public Service Company, another firm with which he grappled over time. This and other industrial initiatives in a small economy were plagued by monopoly and near-monopoly interests, which could hold a reforming government to ransom. He was an outspoken critic; experience had confirmed that some nationalization was desirable.

Isaacs was important to the PNP government for another reason. When it came to industry, he had a particular role to play as the interface between the private sector and a nominally socialist government. Nethersole's interest was finance, including major agency and bank loans, as well as heads of government agreements. He also focussed on capital markets and fiscal policy. He produced the annual budget, albeit with his colleagues' input. Supported by Manley and the Central Planning Unit, he negotiated with the bauxite corporations.[35] Especially with regard to legal agreements, Manley was central to many initiatives. Increasingly, though, he was also preoccupied with the course of federation. As the PNP's 'Bishop', Isaacs had become the party's communicator with the masses. Now, he was handed a related role – to recommend government aims to the commercial class. In particular, he would try to persuade those with sufficient capital and acumen to enter manufacturing. He would soon have regular dealings with Abe Issa and Edward Hanna, as well as Moses and Aaron Matalon, the Levy brothers, Lee Gore, and Luis F. Kennedy and Carlton Alexander of Grace Kennedy.[36] There were many others. Behind the humour and the bluster, Isaacs was an adept negotiator. He was also passionate. His basic commitment was not to the commercial class. His youth had been spent among small farmers, shopfront manufacturers, workers, tradesmen and clerks – not among the wealthy. He believed that Jamaica's producers – from labourers to the skilled workers and the entrepreneurs – could create a future for the island. He shared these views with others in his party.

Norman Manley's victory speech in 1955 demonstrated how far he and the party had moved from the socialism of 1940. Manley said,

> It is, of course, nonsense to suggest that we are other than a moderate Socialist Party and one that is not committed to any rigid set of dogmas. [....] Let me say categorically that we recognise that Nationalization is not the present answer to our problem. Our problem is to multiply and increase tremendously the opportunities for work for our people. Our land and agricultural programme need the greatest dynamic we can generate consistent with [the] co-operation of the men on the land – the farmers themselves. Our industrial programme can only be financed to a small extent, as things stand, out of local savings. I categorically invite investment from abroad and guarantee to it fair play, adequate protection and the utmost good faith in all our undertakings.[37]

The retreat from nationalization was partly due to the need to rapidly expand employment, production and, it was hoped, government revenue as well. Major government expenditure was needed to improve infrastructure to support agriculture and manufacturing, and for public education. Literacy levels had to rise in order to provide the skills required in an industrialising society. Hence, earlier ideas – including nationalization of Kingston's buses and the electricity supply across the island – were put aside. At the outset, the government could not afford these and other measures, even if they were desirable in principle.[38]

Two years into government, in 1957, Frank Hill's remarks as a journalist would confirm this direction. Manley, he said, had "foresworn" earlier theories of nationalization, while Nethersole was modelling tax incentives for investment. Isaacs was "egging on traders to be more enterprising" and "showering encouragement on new industries". Seivright was urging farmers to greater self-reliance, both in marketing and production, while Glasspole had abandoned any ideas of worker control in industry. Hill described their stance as a new "national common sense" and, with some ambivalence, endorsed it. He wrote that if socialism had proved inapt for Western Europe, even more so was it unsuited to "the young, ebullient people of the Caribbean" set on designing their own institutions. To "replace the strait-jacket of Whitehall with a stifling Jamaican bureaucracy would be to 'swap black dog for monkey'". Hill seemed to overlook that the Caribbean had no post-war Marshall Plan and limited experience with manufacturing.[39]

Two factors influenced the policy position that became known as industrialization by invitation. One was Norman Manley's visit to Puerto Rico in 1948, where he learned about that society's industrialization programme under Governor Muñoz Marin. Puerto Rico had established a development bank and sought private investment, mainly from the United States. On his return to Jamaica, Manley spoke favourably of the initiative, and especially of the "young trained Puerto Ricans" working to raise their society out of poverty.[40] His enthusiasm brushed aside a range of factors: Puerto Rico was an unincorporated territory of the United States, with citizenship rights and the potential for financial integration. The society had some tax advantages and altogether easier conditions for commercial interface. Its disadvantages included a constricted political status, limited scale and natural resources, its offshore location, and the embedded racism in the United States towards Latinos and other Spanish-speaking citizens. Yet crucially, and unlike Jamaicans, many Puerto Ricans could reside and work in the United States. This relationship would make Puerto Rico a 'high- income' society in World Bank terms – at least among its Caribbean neighbours.

A second factor that influenced policy, and Manley's view of Puerto Rico, was the work of W. Arthur Lewis. In an early article, Lewis endorsed the Puerto Rican model and recommended it as the way to address Jamaica's situation, which he judged the most adverse in the region. Lewis' ideas had first come to light in 1944, following the publication of his reply to F.C. Benham's report on Jamaica's economy. Originally, this was a submission bearing on the CD&WA, in the wake of the Moyne Commission's report. Subsequently, it was circulated in Jamaica. Benham's report saw industrialization in terms of factories established mainly to process rural products. He deemed protection for new industries inefficient and only likely to raise the cost of living. He stated categorically that "Industrialization will make very little contribution towards solving the employment problem." The report advocated more government support for agriculture, and various subsidies for farmers. Overall, his view accorded with that of a twelve-man Agricultural Policy Committee established in Jamaica in 1944. It advised that agricultural efficiency should not be undermined by efforts at job creation. Benham's view reflected an agricultural bias and a longstanding British colonial opposition to Jamaican industrialization, even during the Great Depression. Lewis opposed this view remarking that, "[…] where a country is suffering from such chronic unemployment, money costs no longer reflect real costs. What does it cost if people are set to work? Is it better that they be unemployed than that they should produce for the home market?"

He asked if Benham's group had heard of Keynes' arguments for government stimulus in the face of high unemployment and a stagnating economy. Noting that Jamaica's local capitalists had limited knowledge of manufacturing, he also recommended "a special agency" which would become the IDC.[41]

In 1949, as a newly appointed professor at the University of Manchester, Lewis gained prominence when a series of lectures for the BBC was broadcast in Jamaica. In the next few years, his articles, and discussions of them, were circulated widely. Especially in the early 1950s, it became *de rigueur* for opinion writers and influential public figures, including Manley, Nethersole, Lightbourne and Robert Kirkwood, to cite Lewis in their remarks on industrialization.[42] This effusion followed the publication of his essay on Puerto Rico and another, more general one, on industrialization in the British West Indies. Along with these came a monograph on economic planning. Increasingly, Lewis put the view that, for societies such as Jamaica, their comparative advantage no longer resided in food-producing agriculture, but rather in niche manufacturing for overseas markets. In order to revamp agriculture, the development process should be triggered by a focus on manufacturing. Industrialization in this sector, he argued, was the key to addressing the "unlimited supplies of labour" created by under-capitalization, casualization and extensive subsistence farming. In the longer term, the redeployment of rural labour to mainly urban industries would create a fillip to innovation and increased productivity in agriculture. In time, a rejuvenated rural sector would also create more jobs.[43]

Lewis had specific ideas about the types of industry suitable for Jamaica. His view was that raw materials could be imported if labour comprised a major part of production costs. Given the low cost of Jamaica's labour, goods could still be priced competitively. In time, growing markets would bring more investment in equipment, greater productivity and higher wages. Labour would become more skilled, and the sector would expand and diversify. His list of possible manufactured goods is instructive: "hosiery, leather, the garment industry, footwear, china, paper trades, glass, building materials, canning, textiles, plastics, rubber goods, electric switches, toys and electric lights." He also emphasized that scrap metal was far cheaper to import than fit-for-purpose machinery. With the former, one might produce "agricultural implements, cutlery, pins, nails, and various foundry products and ironmongery". His views allowed for numerous smaller factories, some of which could be in rural areas. He counselled against the refining of bulk products such as sugar and, presumably, bauxite. They required the importation of expensive equipment for activities that provided limited employment. In addition, where bauxite was concerned, production beyond the extraction stage required power that Jamaica could not supply at a competitive price.[44]

Isaacs was not one to cite the work of economists. Still, central positions that he took were consistent with Lewis' ideas. These included Isaacs' desire to see domestic capital invested in more diverse and productive ways. It was not that the island lacked accumulation, but its agents were risk-averse, most of all in Jamaica itself. As Isaacs also knew, Lewis' list of manufactured goods was consistent with Jamaican conditions, including the prospect of factories in the countryside. Again, like Lewis, Wills had a measured approach to federation. Customs union and a common currency brought some advantages. However, for Isaacs at least, free movement within the region could prove a mixed blessing. Moreover, when pioneer industries looked to a domestic market first, a regional market of federated islands would have only a modest impact. To raise productivity significantly, Jamaica needed markets elsewhere and, in time, greater demand throughout Jamaica itself. Lewis argued that small segments of markets for manufactured goods in the United States and the United Kingdom could bring ample returns to Jamaica. The prospect was enticing for Isaacs, who wished to turn away from dependence on Britain and towards North America.[45]

By the time the PNP came to power, these ideas had emerged as the "common sense" described by Frank Hill. Lewis wrote with authority on the British Caribbean, and his view of development was appealing to Jamaican politicians who faced testing conditions at home. First and foremost, these conditions involved historically unequal distribution of land, poor agricultural techniques and low productivity overall. With this situation came limited risk-taking among the land-rich, and among small farmers as well. The latter were caught in a downward spiral of limited markets and fluctuating prices. Dependent on preferences, both sugar and bananas had poor prospects once Britain became a signatory to the General Agreement on Tariffs and Trade (GATT). Still, a restructured agriculture required the redistribution of land, new crops and better techniques, as well as the redeployment of manual labour – both rural and urban. Such reform needed to recast the role of good land tied up in estates, while also supporting those who owned smaller and less fertile plots. In the short term, however, resources spent on agriculture could not immediately reduce urban unemployment. While the cry was "Land for the Million" who had none, the route to that redistribution was clouded by political complexity. Issues of private property, labour and the capital required made land reform a daunting task.

Such considerations burnished the prospects of an industrialization propelled in its early stages by manufacturing. Indeed, Lewis argued that it was Jamaica's most feasible course. However, the economist's blueprint perhaps underestimated the competition for capital in a post-war world, and the impact of the rise of Japan and China as large-scale suppliers of manufactured goods, not least to the United States. Where Jamaica was concerned, manufacturing (and more widely, industrial enterprise) had only ever been a small part of the economy – reflected in the limited experience of local capitalists and public servants alike. The situation was mirrored in the PNP's Plan for Progress. The space allotted to industry was dwarfed by the far more detailed proposals for transforming agriculture, albeit over the longer term. Yet, as a potent political issue, unemployment loomed large in the present and would surely grow if not addressed. Consequently, it fell to Isaacs' portfolio to carry the heavy load. The PNP hoped that with incentives for foreign and domestic producers, import substitution, and production for export, its government could substantially reduce unemployment.[46]

## Chapter 7

# Promoting Development

*His support of the JMA and the protection of infant industries [...]. Isaacs not only helped to conceptualize [the task], but in fact he was the main implementer.* – P.J. Patterson, 2003.

*Wills was very much of the belief that we needed to encourage industrial development, and indigenous Jamaican entrepreneurship.*
– David Coore, 2003

*Wills Isaacs saw an opportunity, like any smart politician, and like any man who has a certain vision, he could see that tourism [...] had the most potential at that particular moment.* – Fred Wilmot, 2002.[1]

Isaacs did not begin with a blank canvas. The processing of sugar into various products was an industry of longstanding. However, prior to the mid-twentieth century, non-sugar manufacturing had indeed been limited. The better-known firms included Machado Tobacco; Seprod (Soap and Edible Products), which was initially based in the coconut industry; the Jamaica Shirt Factory; Desnoes & Geddes Bottling for aerated waters; Kingston Industrial Works, with a core business in sugar milling and other factory equipment; and the Jamaica Match Factory. All dated as far back as the first two decades of the twentieth century. Machado Tobacco went back further. However, it was in the war and immediate post-war years that major developments occurred. With imports depleted, garment manufacturing grew, along with food processing and canning. Some such concerns proved transient, however, due to post-war competition from abroad. Others were more durable. In 1947 and 1949, Jamaica Knitting Mills and Ariguanabo Textiles Mills took advantage of early incentive laws. Tourism was also ready to expand.[2]

Politics were involved in manufacturing. Early in the twentieth century, calls were made for industrial growth in Kingston to provide jobs for both youthful school graduates and the adult unemployed. One letter to the *Gleaner* in 1910 remarked on the "dolorous cry" of the unemployed met by the equally desperate cry of "Oh, for foreign capital to open up and extend our industries!" The writer proposed more cigarette and cigar production. Three years later, an editorial deplored the position of these same graduates: "The ordinary trades – shoe-making, tailoring, dressmaking, carpentering and so forth – are already over-crowded; and factories (which play such an important part in human affairs elsewhere) are here 'conspicuous by their absence'."

In the 1920s and 1930s, it was common for both the match and shirt factories to extol the 'native' status of their industries: "Support Native Industry and Keep Money in the Island. The Jamaica Match Factory employs only Jamaica Labour." In 1936, the Jamaica Shirt Factory would describe its Maricel shirts as a "native production and a shirt of distinction". The match factory especially was assailed by competition from Swedish makers and other prospective competitors. At the same time, small producers enjoined their fellows to support cooperatives and "strangle" the monopolies. These were the days of Alfred Mends and *Plain Talk*. Isaacs looked on.

The immediate post-war JLP governments were aware of the need for development. Tourism had become a priority. The Hotel Aid Act was passed in 1944 and the Textile Industry (Encouragement) Act in 1947. Prior to the 1949 election, the government passed the first Pioneer Industries (Encouragement) Act and one pertaining to cement production. The former was incentive legislation designed to appeal to foreign and domestic investors. Imported materials would be customs-free. Moreover, in any five of an initial eight years, one-fifth of the value of capital expended could be deducted from a factory's taxable income. The second law privileged the Caribbean Cement Company as Jamaica's sole provider.[3] In 1950, the new government passed the special concessions law concerning bauxite and alumina producers. Given the accessibility and high quality of the ore, the agreement was generous. Three foreign companies – Kaiser and Reynolds (United States), and Alcan (Canada) – were involved. By 1955 they were producing 15 per cent of the world's supply of bauxite.[4] The IDC and ADC were in operation.

In 1954, the US Department of Commerce published a report on Jamaica's changing economy. It mainly concerned manufacturing and was based on IDC reports. The number of those steadily employed in manufacture (outside sugar) was 13,500. The activities involved were as follows:

> The garment industry, with 50 registered factories employing over 3,000 workers, is now producing a wide range of garments not merely for the domestic market but for export to other Caribbean countries and to the United States. The Ariguanabo Textile Mills, with 450 employees, produced 4½ million yards of cotton fabrics in 1953, representing a little less than 20 percent of the Jamaican market for these textiles. Two knitting mills, with 350 employees, supplied 75 percent of the Island's consumption of knitted underwear and T-shirts.
>
> The shoe industry with 15 registered factories and 715 workers, produced 300,000 pairs of shoes, exporting several thousand pairs to nearby markets. The ancillary leather industry, with 11 factories and 500 workers, produces sole, side, and upper leather and exports 'considerable quantities' of the latter to the United States and the United Kingdom.
>
> To supply the expanding local construction industry, local factories produce cement, tile, wallboard, concrete products, and wrought

> iron grilles, and the local paint company turns out a range of paints, enamels, varnishes, distempers, and putty.

Numerous miscellaneous products were listed. Still, the PNP had promised one hundred and fifty thousand jobs in ten years, and a reduction in the cost of living.[5]

Isaacs' legislative framework evolved over time. Numerous amendments were made to legislation concerning textiles, processed food, petroleum products, hotels, factories, wharfage and shipping, not to mention the IDC. Some more general laws, however, were among the most important. They concerned, in turn, the Trade Board, industrial incentives, electrification and small business. Early passage of the amended Trade Board Act switched the focus from its previous war emergency roles towards peacetime ones. These included the maintenance and regulation of essential supplies, both local and imported. Prices should be set to "serve the community". More specifically, the powers covered tariffs, price controls on goods deemed staples or essential, import licences, and, where appropriate, dollar allocations to importers. The power to apply import restrictions and reallocate import licences could be used to protect local industry, and to encourage more competition in domestic distribution.[6]

Where incentives were concerned, two new laws were passed in 1956: the Industrial Incentives (Factory Production) Act and the Export Industry (Encouragement) Act. The former retained the customs provisions of the Pioneer Act, but changed the emphasis in that law from accelerated depreciation to tax exemption. By providing less direct incentive to fixed capital investment, the aim was to encourage labour-intensive activity. For a period of five years or more, dividends would be tax-free, a provision applicable both to foreign and domestic private investment. Meanwhile, the Export Industry Encouragement Act offered a choice of the tax relief provided by either the Pioneer or Incentive acts. In addition, *all* materials, including fuel to maintain a factory, were exempt from customs duties. In return, the firm would produce only for the export market. This law was intended to attract foreign firms, mainly North American ones, with established markets. (It also encouraged firms to stay for the benefits and then decamp.) The tourism industry received comparable incentives.

The third form of legislation focussed on expanding the island's electrification and on frequency conversion. There were two principal acts, one pertaining to electricity (frequency conversion) in 1957, and the other to electricity development in 1958. This enabling legislation addressed, in the first case, conversion to an industrially adequate 50-cycle frequency and, in the second, a better networked power supply to towns across the island. The legislation did not resolve, however, two central issues which would cause debate: the pace of electrification and who should bear the cost of conversion. JPSC was licensed to supply electricity in eleven of the island's fourteen parishes. Its licence was not due for renewal until 1962. Consequently, the PNP government had limited leverage with the company. In rural areas, it was difficult to establish factories without appropriate power, a situation that produced a concentration of factories in Kingston.

A fourth form of legislation involved the Loans to Small Businesses Act (1956). It provided for a board by the same name to make loans of not more than £300 to small concerns across Jamaica. Although the contribution of these businesses to the national income was modest, in aggregate they were a significant employer, and deserving of support. It was an effort close to Isaacs' heart. Along with measures to provide alternative routes to land tenure, and taxation only on the unimproved value of land, the new government also sought to support small farmers. The Loans Act was amended in 1958 and 1960. The Export Industry and Incentives acts also received emendations. Legislation sought to adjust incentives and, in the case of small business, broaden the act's scope. Cooperatives and small retailers were included. Overall, the intent of the legislation was to encourage both export and labour-intensive industries. In time, tension grew between the two. Contrary to Lewis' predictions, labour-intensive production struggled to compete in export markets.[7]

As well as a legislative framework, Isaacs had an administrative one. He was surrounded by a range of organizations on which he relied, while engaging others in robust debate. First among those on which he relied were his ministerial department and its senior officials; the Trade Board and its Trade Administrator; and the IDC. In each budget speech he thanked his departmental staff, the permanent secretary and his deputy. In addition to advising the minister, one or more accompanied him on trade trips. The most influential among them was Hector White, who was his permanent secretary from 1956 until the end of 1960. He was preceded by C.V. Hill and followed by V.C. Smith. White was a distinguished Jamaica-born public servant with a background in Treasury, Finance and Local Government. He was described as one of the "old brigade" and among "the most valuable members of the Jamaica Service".[8] With this support, Isaacs developed a remarkable command of details concerning industries, products, markets at home and abroad, trade law, and the personalities involved in trade and industry. He credited his growing knowledge to early morning conversations with his permanent secretary, which enabled "a free and frank exchange on major matters of policy" and provided wide-ranging background briefs.[9] In the first year of his ministry, both the Trade Board and the IDC were attached to his department. Geoffrey Hargreaves, a manufacturers' representative and personal appointment of Isaacs, became the new Trade Administrator and chair of the board. Aaron Matalon was Hargreaves' deputy and would succeed him.

The IDC was a statutory body designed to "stimulate, facilitate and undertake establishment of industry within the island". It administered the incentive laws, consulting with Isaacs and

Nethersole in Finance. It also provided various services to industry, including the construction of factories for rent to investors. These factories were constructed mainly on the Kingston Industrial Estate, a West Kingston property of around thirty acres. When Isaacs became the minister, the IDC's activities involved a secretariat liaising with government, and a promotional arm liaising with industry. The second arm provided technological and industry-specific research and advice, along with mainly rental factory space. The latter provision was aimed at foreign investors reluctant to commit to the purchase of fixed assets in Jamaica. Albeit with very modest resources, the corporation also had a finance and budget arm. From the outset, the IDC had provided some loan finance and share purchase often, though not only for Jamaican start-ups. These measures were designed to encourage Jamaicans to enter the manufacturing sector and often involved firms producing mainly for domestic rather than export markets.[10] Consistent with PNP policy, the corporation was tasked to prioritize labour-intensive industries. In time, the corporation's income would consist of its annual grant from the government, allocations from government loan funds, income from factory leases, and interest on and repayments of loans. Occasionally, the corporation also borrowed in its own right.[11]

Robert Lightbourne remained for one year as managing director of the IDC. He resigned in May 1956, but maintained part-time involvement with the corporation. On his departure, Isaacs praised him as a "devoted officer" who had deployed his knowledge and imagination in the role. He also took the opportunity for some reorganization. Effectively, Lightbourne's position was split in two: a previous board member, Harold Braham, would become the IDC's managing director, while Vernon Arnett, also PNP general secretary, would become financial controller. Braham and Arnett would manage the administrative load. The finance role had been approved by the previous government. From Isaacs' point of view, it was important that its occupant be free from commercial interests. The appointments were welcomed by the press: "Messrs Braham and Arnett are both sons of well-known Jamaican families whose roots have been deep in this country for generations, more particularly in agriculture."[12] However, the event dovetailed with growing unrest over political appointments. Though challenged in the House, Isaacs was on solid ground. He reported that both his permanent secretary and the IDC chairman, Neville Ashenheim, supported Arnett strongly. He remarked, "If sensible people are PNP people, don't blame them. You expect us to put fools there?"[13]

When it came to interlocutors, including critics, there were many. Principal among them were the four peak organizations that Isaacs hastened to meet on assuming office: the chamber of commerce, the manufacturers, the master builders and the tourist board. Notwithstanding the 1956 incentives legislation, the JMA's Aaron Matalon and Vin Bennett assailed the minister for not providing manufacturers with even more protection and customs duty relief. They complained that too many government resources were commanded by large agriculturalists.[14] In addition to the various peak bodies, Isaacs engaged with a broad spectrum of smaller groups – from leather- and ice-makers to beef and corn producers, as well as growers of specialist export crops. Many of these were liaison groups recruited through either the Jamaica Chamber of Commerce, the Jamaica Manufacturers' Association or the Jamaica Agricultural Society.

Finally, the administrative environment around Isaacs became more complex as the government faced mounting pressure. Between May and June 1955, a Central Planning Unit reporting to the chief minister was organized. Headed by George Cadbury Jr. (as in the famous Cadbury chocolate), its role was to work with Manley and Nethersole, and the Ministry of Finance. Its brief was broad: "to take into review all social and economic questions coming within the purview of the Government of Jamaica". With Manley as Minister of Agriculture, one of its early tasks was to survey Jamaica's rural labour force.[15] A little over a year later, these arrangements changed. Manley assumed a new portfolio – Minister of Development. William Seivright became Minister of Agriculture and Land. The planning unit became a section in a new Ministry of Development involved in planning and finance for major infrastructural projects, including harbours, railways, airports and the like.

In 1956, Nethersole foreshadowed reorganization of the IDC. The corporation was limited in scope due to its modest financial base. The loans which it did extend very often proved hard to recoup. Nethersole observed that the corporation did not have the expertise to operate as a bank.[16] The decision was taken to focus on promotion of Jamaica as an industrial site: its potential and products; factory provisions and tax incentives; technical advice; and on industrial and management training. Staff numbers grew to more than eighty. Offices were opened in New York, Toronto and London. Isaacs' role was to support IDC initiatives, mediate between producers and the IDC, and relentlessly promote Jamaica's development.

Canvassed initially in 1956, but implemented only in 1959, the IDC's finance role would go to a newly established Development Finance Corporation. The DFC replaced Manley's Ministry of Development and absorbed those staff previously involved in the Central Planning Unit. The corporation anticipated a central bank once independence was achieved.[17] Manley spoke to the legislation, which was tabled following Nethersole's untimely death. With an initial £1 million of loan finance, the brief of this new corporation was to provide long-term infrastructural support, mainly within Jamaica's private sector. It would focus on tourism, middle-class housing and non-manufacturing industry. The DFC was to "cherry pick" industries that would bring high returns. The *Daily Gleaner* noted that the DFC, reliant principally on loan finance, would need to lend and borrow judiciously. It would still be dependent on Jamaican productivity to repay the loans.[18]

Distanced from high finance, Isaacs' less glamourous role sometimes rankled. In the case of the Negril development, Manley's short-lived Department of Development moved into his domain. Isaacs responded with sly humour. His 1957 budget speech reviewed tourism's rapid overall growth for which, as minister, he was responsible. He noted, however, that Manley would speak on Negril: "I look after the little things. He [the Chief Minister] looks after the big things."[19] Still, the key to Isaacs' popularity was the fact that he dealt with more concrete issues directly affecting his constituents.

From the outset many matters required his attention, not least the volatile price for pimento in overseas markets. Early in 1955, Isaacs proposed to growers and the JAS that the price of the product should not be fixed, but vary in response to demand. He undertook that the government would cushion small producers when the price dropped steeply, and authorize bonus payments when prices were high. His message was that larger growers should look after themselves. Debate came thick and fast and required that Isaacs weather the storm until a new agreement was reached almost one year later.[20]

In April, and prior to his departure for Canada to address the price of flour, Isaacs foreshadowed a conference between the IDC and tanners' representatives. Tanners were requesting protection from imported Indian leather. In fact, since the war, there had been a steady expansion in shoe production, which quickened following quantitative restrictions on imports in 1952. Tanners were looking for equivalent treatment. Isaacs made it clear, however, that protection depended on an improved product. While Jamaica's sole leather could compete with imported leather, Indian 'uppers' proved to be of finer quality, better crafted and produced more cheaply. The IDC brought an expert from the United States to advise the tanners. Techniques improved and tanning expanded as an industry.[21]

In November 1956, he officially opened a new industrial site. The factory, of "colossal size and output", would produce shoes for the British arm of Bata, a Czech multinational company. It hoped to capture the Caribbean market and export to the Americas. It is of note that, in 1955, Isaacs had acted to keep the price of pimento high by securing a sale in Czechoslovakia of thirty tonnes of the spice. There had been balance-of-trade discussions and Isaacs took the opportunity to close a reciprocal trade agreement.[22] At the opening of the Bata factory, workers demonstrated every phase of the new assembly line. In his speech, Isaacs remarked that the scale of production enabled by mechanization would in fact create more jobs. At the same time, he extolled protection for "enabling the shoe manufacturers to ensure the necessary means to produce a good product". He also urged that industries themselves institute training programmes to improve productivity and efficiency. The expenditure would prove justified. He spoke as forcefully of unions: "I could not open my heart to a concern which refuses to pay fair wages. [....] Do not attempt to deny to the workers the right to organise in unions of their choice. [....] It is an essential part of the inherent democratic right of people to organise into lawful associations to protect their own interests."[23]

Isaacs opened another front with the formation of a committee to advise on exports to Canada. He remarked that not only had ground been lost with established products but, excluding bauxite, there was "no new worthwhile trade". The decline had been brought about in part by the poor performance of the Caribbean Preserving Company. The CPC had lost its Canadian market due to substandard canned citrus fruit. While the Public Health Act addressed processed food for home consumption, Jamaica lacked standards legislation for exported food products. Isaacs acted to correct the oversight and called in the IDC for more "rehabilitation" work, as was done for tanning. The members of the new committee on the Canada trade included the permanent secretary from

Agriculture, Edward Hanna, Luis Kennedy and Aaron Matalon.[24] A major trade trip to Canada followed in January 1958.

Despite the pressure, ebullience reigned in the early years of government. The year of Jamaica's tercentenary, 1955, brought a singular occasion for Isaacs and his colleagues. In June, Governor Luis Munoz Marin of Puerto Rico made a four-day state visit to Jamaica. His main purpose was to open the JAS' diamond jubilee show at Denbigh in May Pen. Accompanied by Chief Minister Manley, he also toured various agricultural and mining sites.[25] Even more notable was the visit in mid-September of US Democrat and presidential contender Adlai Stevenson, who opened a seventeen-day JMA-organized exhibition at Victoria Market in Kingston. Manley, Bustamante, Governor Foot, Isaacs, Nethersole, Glasspole, and the chairs of the IDC and Trade Board were present. Isaacs introduced Stevenson, who won over the crowd with his address. Speaking of Jamaica, he said,

> From the ashes of barbarity, piracy and slavery have grown industry, agriculture and commerce on an expanding scale – and with them civil order, education, and a rising standard of living, not just for a few but for all – and now, beckoning vistas of an even brighter future.
>
> Along with this economic transformation, political power has migrated from the planter aristocracy [...] to the Central Government in London [...] and then, step by step back to the Island – but back to all the people regardless of race or status.

Stevenson addressed the challenges: "[No-one] could ignore the formidable obstacles that still block your road to a better life. For here one sees development handicapped by lack of capital, and all the problems that arise in a country whose population has outstripped its resources. It is hard [...] to believe that at the present rate before too long there will be some two million souls compressed into this rugged little island."

He acknowledged the rapid growth of industry and urged widespread education. He noted that Jamaica's democracy seemed "more complete" than that of other regional societies. Stevenson concluded, "Here in the centre of your capital city with many reminders [...] of an historic past, I see a new Jamaica." He was presented with a pair of custom-made shoes, crafted by Jamaican tradesmen.[26]

This was the first of a series of trade fairs in Jamaica and the larger Caribbean where Isaacs' ministry partnered with either the JMA or JCC. In May 1957, Jamaica shone at a combined West Indies trade exhibition in Trinidad, where its displays received acclaim throughout the region. In January 1959, Kingston hosted a major Canadian exhibition, which moved on to Port-of-Spain. Isaacs' cultivation of relations with Canadian groups paved the way for this initiative. An all-island Caribbean Trade and Industrial Exhibition came to Kingston in 1961. He remarked of the exhibition, "The fair has directed the attention of the public to the tremendous industrialization effort all over the country and to the variety of high-quality products which are made in Jamaica and in other Caribbean territories." The JMA foreshadowed a further fair for July 1962.[27]

In this early period, and notwithstanding the moves towards federation, Jamaica lacked the reciprocal support that would come with a progressively decolonized world. The United Nations Commission on Trade and Development (UNCTAD) would be founded in 1964. Rapidly, it would foster cooperation between Third World nations and pave the way for a non-aligned movement. In the interim, regional trade fairs and international ones – in Suriname, Portugal (Lisbon), the US (New York), the Dominican Republic and Nigeria –which individual Jamaicans attended, served to promote Jamaican industry. These fairs played an important role in opening Jamaica's newer and smaller producers to a world of trade, with Isaacs pushing the process along.

Textile and garment production comprised the larger part of the manufacturing sector, which would soon rank, as an employer, second only to agriculture. Like tanning and shoe manufacture, these industries included sites that ranged from large factories to enterprises located in small shopfronts and yards. All these industries were similar in another way. Despite the incentive legislation provided, larger producers pressured Isaacs incessantly for protection of their domestic markets. Ariguanabo Textile Mills was a prime example. Ariguanabo was the industry's major producer of cotton cloth and, increasingly, knitted rayon fabric. The factory had been planned since 1943 and opened for production in 1951. Its principal investor was an American-born resident of Cuba who had built a successful industry there. Ariguanabo's managing director was a Jamaican, Sidney Levy.[28] The initial projection was that the factory could produce fourteen million yards of cottons per year for both domestic consumption and export. Amid conflict with the TUC in 1951 and 1952, the company had asked the government for protection. As an Opposition member, Isaacs had spoken against it, remarking that the company was already receiving incentives. Moreover, the paltry wage paid to its workers suggested that the company's ample profits could accommodate a price reduction. Domestic cloth could compete with imports without further assistance. Isaacs made this speech at a time when merchants were stockpiling imported cloth. He wanted them to buy more cloth at home.[29]

By the time he became the minister, Ariguanabo's request had become a demand. Isaacs reviewed his former position, wishing both to stymie the producers' demands, and maintain employment. Many of the workers were women. Ariguanabo was already exporting to the United States and a large Canadian order was at hand. Moreover, the garment industry had by now developed growing markets in the region. In order to protect the industry at large, Isaacs proposed that the size of an import licence should be tied to the amount of domestically produced cloth a merchant purchased, mainly from Ariguanabo. Via the Dry Goods Liaison Committee, the merchants professed themselves ready to cooperate with the government's plans. However, prior overseas credit commitments prevented new cash purchases at home. Wills modified his proposal. He also introduced restrictions on synthetic imports. A further DLC submission underlined the concessions already enjoyed by Ariguanabo. Isaacs adjusted the agreement further, but kept the new import restrictions.[30]

Despite the many matters brought to his attention, a good deal of his time was spent on tourism, the "dollar earner". En route to London in 1955, Isaacs stopped off in New York. He was there to promote Jamaica's tourist sites to New York magazines and travel publications. He was also there to meet with representatives of shipping services, most of which had their head offices in New York. The aim of this and a previous visit was to increase services from the US east coast to Jamaica in both the winter and summer months. Subsequently, on 17 May, Isaacs moved a resolution for the House to approve an allocation of £7,200 to be paid as a subsidy to the Eastern Shipping Company for twelve trips between Miami and Port Antonio. Ken Jones, the JLP member for Portland East, spoke in support of the resolution, saying that the increase in tourist trips would mean "a tremendous amount to the people of Port Antonio". The intent now was to broaden this effort and expand air services as well.[31]

The strategy of the JTB was multi-pronged. The early focus was on trade consolidation in Jamaica, shipping services and paid advertising. Soon after, the JTB and its executive began holding regular meetings, and additional staff were hired, among them a publicist/photographer to service hotels outside the Corporate Area. A survey was organized to compile a complete list of all tourist accommodations on the island to be used, JTB advised, "for general publicity and promotion work".[32] This initiative was taken in consultation with the Jamaica Hotels Association and associated small hotels, resort cottages and guesthouses. This promotion of accommodation beyond the luxury hotels – and of a summer season in addition to the winter crowd – was aimed at securing a middle-income trade. Shipping services throughout the year were essential. And closely related to this aim was Abe Issa's determination to increase the number of cruise ships to Jamaica and extend the time they spent in port. Among those on shore who would benefit, Issa listed "curio vendors, individual taxicab operators, dress shops, storekeepers, as well as night clubs, and restaurants".

The JTB employed a New York advertising agency for publicity purposes. Early on, they consulted also with the manager of advertising for the West Indies division of the Dutch airline KLM, which had flights to the region from New York. In time, advertising was repatriated when Issa employed two Jamaicans, Calvin Bowen and Fred Wilmot, to write copy in Kingston. Issa personally supervised a bi-monthly mailout of three hundred letters to travel agents in the Americas. The letters provided agents with material for "masses and masses of articles in all types of newspapers".[33] Publicity was also gained through various events, both in Jamaica and the United States. Among these was a convention sponsored by Fedders Air Conditioning, which brought two thousand dealers to the island, arriving by air and holidaying in groups of around three hundred. The exercise continued from 4 October to 15 November 1955. Its timing had special significance, as Issa outlined: "Many large corporations in the US are giving employees prize vacations instead of cash bonuses; and these holiday trips, coming as they do in what has been known as the off-season, help to extend the tourist season throughout the entire year."

Issa predicted that 1956 would be a first for year-round tourism, involving steady employment instead of seasonal work for growers of local foods, as well as dairy and poultry farmers catering to hotels. Jamaican music was deployed on the US front. The Frats Quintette, with their repertoire of one hundred Jamaican songs, was invited as a feature act at Miami's Music Festival. Members of the JHA were interviewed on radio WINZ Miami for "Rhythm at Random", a nightly programme popular in south-eastern states. This appearance initiated a continuing campaign to emphasize the summer trade and highlight smaller hotels and guesthouses. The JTB also concluded arrangements for various background features on Jamaica to be broadcast on US television. One of these was a documentary on the University College of the West Indies.[34]

These activities were not free and the government, in the financial year 1955–1956, provided £50,000 to fund international publicity for tourism. Under the JLP's development plan, the sum had been double.[35] Consequently, when the Hicks' report on *Finance and Taxation in Jamaica* (commissioned by the JLP) became public in June 1955, the industry response was outrage. The report proposed that while the provisions of the Pioneer Industries Act should extend to hotels, the cost of their publicity should not be a part of the government's budget. The Hickses suggested an industry-wide hotel levy to address this cost. They made comparable suggestions for bauxite, noting that the royalties paid to Jamaica were meagre. Their view was that industries with healthy US markets – such as tourism and bauxite – should not be a further cost to Jamaica. Indeed, as an invisible export and a transfer product respectively, the Hicks report termed their benefit to Jamaica's economy "question marks". The JHA, supported by the JTB, took out a full-page advertisement in the *Daily Gleaner* to refute this part of the report.[36] The association argued that tourism was already a major export industry. It cited the Hickses' own view that, "[I]mports have to be paid for by exports. Thus, the prosperity of the Jamaican economy depends, to quite an exceptional extent, on the prosperity of her export trades. When her exports are bringing in a good income, Jamaica is prosperous; when they do not, she is bound to be in trouble."[37]

Noting that bananas and sugar were in decline and that the CD&W grants were meagre, while income tax was "dangerously high", the JHA posed the question: "Where then will Jamaica find the money necessary to finance its development plan?"

On 25 July, Isaacs spoke up in Parliament. He said that though it had its "evils", the contribution of tourism to the economy was crucial to the government. Moreover, not least due to the JTB's efforts, it seemed that the target to double the industry in five years would be achieved in just three. He also underlined the linkages that the industry created through the sale of local food, drinks and cigarettes, business for in-bond shops and local services, including transport, not to mention the land tax paid to parochial boards. He did not address the downside: profits exported, customs duties waived, imported food and furniture to suit tourists' tastes, public beaches privatized and racial slurs endured. Yet even with these evils, tourism was a wise investment. Neither did Isaacs' colleagues argue even when, in 1956, Frank Hill wrote to the Gleaner about racism in tourist establishments.[38]

Commonly known as the budget debates, the estimates and appropriations presented by the government were the annual report cards of ministers. In 1956, Isaacs maintained the enthusiasm of 1955.[39] He noted that though Britain remained Jamaica's largest market, it was now more a source of technical advice and machinery than of consumer goods. Increasingly, the latter were obtained elsewhere, from the United States, Canada, Japan and India. Despite the rising value of imports overall, imported staples were costing less. Among these were "flour, rice, codfish, lumber, Irish potato and about 40 items of hardware". The price of various garments had fallen by a third and many were now made in Jamaica. Isaacs remarked that he wished to expand trade with the United States for another reason: in order to press them to recruit more farm workers from the island.

He reported that when he became Minister of Trade, only three merchant families controlled almost 75 per cent of the import quotas. Changes to licensing criteria meant that distribution was becoming more diversified. Where exports were concerned, the news was good. Bauxite (not in his portfolio) was making its mark. Regarding a range of export crops, including pimento, coffee and cocoa, increased production had more than countered falling prices. Where manufacturers were concerned, Ariguanabo secured its order from Canada. Moreover, negotiations were in train for large-scale production of shirts for the US market. Overall, there was a significant increase in the export of garments, textiles, shoes and other products to the Caribbean region. The SS *West Indian* had doubled its cargo out of Jamaica. Referring to his known opposition to federation, Isaacs remarked, "When I see the figures here, I am wondering whether I was quite right." As for tourism, he reported major increases in both winter and summer seasons, employing an additional nine hundred and fifty, and six hundred workers respectively.

Finally, Isaacs addressed industrial development. He listed industries assisted by the IDC, remarking that this assistance was not simply financial, but often involved technical development – in canning, tanning, shoe production, cocoa powder and dried grass fodder. He noted the success stories: production in the garment industry was now worth £5 million, including £1 million paid in wages. Shoes had done extremely well, with an annual value now of £1.25 million and a production of 650,000 pairs a year. He listed factories already in the pipeline: for confectionary, aluminium blinds and windows, paint, cardboard boxes and corrugated cardboard, leather buttons and artificial flowers. He broached the fact that most of these factories were in Kingston. The government was already working on plans for industrial decentralization to rural areas with high unemployment.

Isaacs' contribution to the appropriations debate was more selective. He raised issues concerning Jamaica's balance of trade and the need to look for markets in those economies that exported to Jamaica. Where specific trades were concerned, he sought to broker barter-like exchanges; more Jamaican manufactured goods in exchange for the island's purchase, for example, of Czech and

German car parts. He worried about bank rates in London; the consequent rise in the interest rates of Jamaica's commercial banks; and the local impact as larger merchants passed on the cost to consumers. In both speeches he reiterated that protection should not lead to poor-quality goods or to lower productivity. Both would defeat the ultimate aim to increase employment. The last item in his speech involved a brief update on electrification and frequency conversion.

In March 1956, Isaacs tabled a ministerial paper concerning frequency conversion as an integral part of the project to bring electricity to towns across Jamaica. The paper was preparatory to legislation on both issues. The IBRD's 1952 report on Jamaica's economy had advised both more rapid electrification and a frequency conversion from 40 to 50 cycles. The report had noted that the JPSC provided around 90 per cent of Jamaica's generating capacity in the eleven parishes it supplied under licence. The total amount of power generated per capita was only 23 per cent of that supplied in Puerto Rico. The report averred that this reflected Jamaica's "low living standard" and perhaps a conservative policy regarding expansion. In fact, the low consumption level was both a symptom and a cause of minimal diversification in the economy, which had major implications both for living standards and employment.

When JPSC received its original franchise, the industry standard was a 40-cycle frequency, but no longer. It was essential to Jamaica's development that the frequency be raised at least to fifty cycles in order to advance industrially. Isaacs' Ministry Paper No. 4 outlined the issue: "It is becoming more and more difficult to obtain suitable electrical equipment, as fewer and fewer parts of the world operate on the 40-cycle frequency, and fewer and fewer firms manufacture such equipment." The situation was in fact even more serious, as the IBRD outlined. Owing to the dearth of 40-cycle equipment, "the Jamaican purchaser must often content himself with 50-cycle motors which can only operate at 80 per cent efficiency on 40-cycle current and therefore increase the cost of power." The report remarked that delay in upgrading would only increase the ultimate cost.[40]

Speaking to the paper, Isaacs chided the erstwhile Government for its tardiness.[41] The current Government's preparations involved a survey of the facilities that generated electricity, and of consumer installations for utilising power. The latter included residential, rural, commercial, industrial and municipal sites. He noted that refrigeration could be changed over rapidly, and that special care would be taken not to disrupt the agricultural pumps that supplied water for farm irrigation. Rural pumping and irrigation (32 per cent), along with industry (26 per cent), were the largest consumers of power in Jamaica.[42] The task would be complex with three ministries involved: Trade and Industry to oversee the task; Finance to negotiate agreement with JPSC; and Home Affairs to mediate local interests.

At the passage of the Electricity Frequency Bill in January 1957, Nethersole spoke to finance. Were the JPSC to bear the cost, inevitably it would be passed on to consumers. Government was not equipped to oversee and regulate such charges. However, were the Government to bear the cost, taxpayers with and without electricity would pay equally. This was a difficult matter. The Government had determined that, due to its industrial importance, conversion should take precedence over further electrification. It could not charge those who still lacked power for the upgrading. Consequently, the Government determined to raise loan finance to be paid for only by those who were already consumers. And hence the survey of utilization, which would take time. An Electricity Conversion Commission was appointed to do this preparatory work. A central Electrical Authority was established.[43] Still, the process was painfully slow and frustrated Isaacs' desire to see rural factories built.

FIRST BABY?

**"Dr Isaacs" brings his expertise to Manley's Jamaica (1957).**



Another project promised more immediate benefits. In November 1956, Isaacs tabled another ministerial paper detailing a programme of expansion for the Jamaica Ice Company. The ice plant had been a division of Bronstorph Industries, acquired by Government following the company's liquidation. While Nethersole and his Ministry looked after the financial arrangements, Isaacs and his ministry oversaw the appointment of a new board of management, which included Moses Matalon as executive director, and Carlton Alexander as a board member. In part, JIC's role would be to compete with Jamaica's one like enterprise, the Kingston Ice Making Company. From March through July 1957, there was heated debate both in the House and the *Daily Gleaner* concerning the propriety of the acquisition and the relative merits of public companies in general. One anonymous opinion suggested that KIMC currently met consumer demand. When that situation changed, private enterprise would respond. Therefore, the acquisition must be seen as creeping nationalization of industry by government. A less censorious response observed that the purchase was "the biggest bargain" in years. An investor confessed his "burning desire to get some shares". The failure of the private company had been due mainly to outdated engineering and poor management.

The Government, and Isaacs, had a specific intent. The paper he tabled listed a development in three stages. The first involved increasing the factory's capacity to 180 tonnes of ice per day. The second involved plans to establish sub-depots for the vending of ice throughout greater Kingston. The third, towards which profit from the second could be put, involved providing extensive quick-freeze and deep-freeze facilities. Storage depots would be built at strategic points across the island and along the coastline for agricultural and other products, including fresh fish. The inclusion of fish in this plan reflected an ongoing problem with the price of salted codfish. Isaacs was already looking for alternatives to codfish sourced from a Canadian cartel. Import substitution with fresh fish from Jamaican waters was one part of the picture. The plan would also assist with beef distribution and price regulation. Overall, there would be a positive impact on farm productivity. Here was the Government's interest in this acquisition: not simply to prevent a KIMC monopoly, but also to stimulate primary production.[44]

Isaacs was not Jamaica's first Minister of Trade and Industry. Allan Douglas (JLP) held the portfolio for just two years with the advent of ministerial government in 1953. Nonetheless, Isaacs became Jamaica's first Minister of Trade and Industry to address an economy consciously conceived as a national project, ideally sovereign and more aggressively multilateral, notwithstanding his focus on North America.[45] Regarding that focus, Isaacs' effort was framed by and contributed to departure from a stifling imperial world ring-fenced by sterling. In his work regarding specialist export crops, leather, shoes, garments and textiles, not to mention the tourist trade, he sought to bring smaller producers along with larger ones. Employment was and would not be only in the larger establishments. With the help of the IDC, he improved the quality of various products and substantially expanded production. He played a central role in the demanding tasks of electrification and frequency conversion and sought to facilitate marketing, storage and higher rural productivity through a system of improved refrigeration. He also worked assiduously to distribute import licences more broadly among the commercial class.

Isaacs' efforts underline just how demanding was the Government's task. Import substitution was not easy and came accompanied by constant demands for government protection. Expanding export production proved expensive, whether the capital involved was foreign or domestic. Infrastructure needs were great, not least in electrification and frequency conversion. The legacies of British neglect lived on. Still, during the 1950s, PNP government policies did have a significant effect on the Jamaican economy. A 1959 report from the Central Planning Unit noted that Jamaica, in the past decade, had developed a broader economic base. It was now less vulnerable to declines in agriculture due to the growth of the manufacturing, mining and construction sectors and the development of the tourist trade. Although by no means all Isaacs' work, he played a preeminent role in diversifying the economy. His relentless presence at factory sites and trade shows validated development and projected a different vision of Jamaica both at home and abroad.

## Chapter 8

# Cartels and Monopolies

*Commerce, if it is made to serve a nation, can be an extremely good thing. If it is made to become the master of the State it can be an extremely degrading thing.* – Wills Isaacs, 1958.[1]

A growing economy was good news and did bring increased autonomy. Jamaica was the first British colony to receive legal authorization for raising dollar loans independently. The 1957 Budget was the largest on record and aimed for a surplus. Manley and his team had negotiated successfully with the American corporations in order to raise the price they paid for Jamaica's bauxite. The outcome was a new 25-year contract with the total of income tax and royalty paid rising from 2/8d to 14/- per tonne. Where the bauxite revenue for the 1956–1957 financial year had been £352,000, the forthcoming year would bring £1 million in payments. By 1960, the annual income would total around £7 million.[2]

In January 1957, Isaacs expressed "high satisfaction" with the JTB. The rise in tourist spending in Jamaica was spectacular – from around £5.2 million in 1954 to £9.8 million in 1957. The increase would continue, spurred on by new arrivals and more long-stay tourists. Manufacturing was growing too. By 1960, its contribution to GDP would exceed agriculture for the first time and, two years later, it would outstrip personal services as an employer. The growth in manufacturing came mainly from non-food products, including textiles and garments, cement, metal items, and leather and tobacco goods.[3]

The bad news was that private investment in manufacturing proved expensive for government. Moreover, once secured, the Government found it hard to plan on behalf of private firms, foreign or domestic, when it came to more rural jobs, for instance. As G. Arthur Brown remarked in 1958, ministers of government could only use incentives, however generous, to "suggest" to and "encourage" the private sector.

Between the IDC's founding in 1952 and 1960, fifty-eight firms were established with its assistance. All received incentives support. Of the total, twenty-two were set up under the Pioneer Industry Act, seventeen under the Industrial Incentives Act and nineteen with the aid of the Export Industry Act. The last category involved mainly American firms, while the former two were a mix of solely Jamaica owned and joint ventures. The cost of capital was reflected in foregone taxation and in the prevalence of dividends repatriated or held offshore. The pattern for tourism was similar. Despite a substantial minority of locally owned establishments, most of the larger hotels were foreign-owned. In both cases, profits leaked offshore. This was not the only danger in the Government's attempts to attract private capital. During the 1950s, loans and share purchases, mostly involving domestic firms, became a major cost to the IDC and therefore on government. In order to maintain employment, the IDC took over some of these firms as subsidiaries. Generally, they ran at a loss, adding further to government costs.[4]

Nor were North American markets easy to find. Jamaican investors preferred to produce for protected domestic outlets. The polite term was 'import substitution'. With the introduction of the Export Industries Act, Isaacs and the IDC looked for foreign firms with established markets. A number were US garment manufacturers who came for the incentives but did not stay for the longer term. Cheaper labour was not a sufficient incentive alone. Apart from bauxite, tourism had the best chance of securing North American markets. On the downside, the industry was highly dependent on the United States – and its social and political climate.

The upshot was that Jamaica's industrial diversification had only a moderate effect on jobs in Kingston and elsewhere. Emigration had helped. The outflow to Britain reached a highpoint in the late 1950s. As a result, the rate of unemployment fell from 18 to 13.5 per cent during the PNP's two terms in office.[5] Still, the incoming government had hoped for more.

The situation raised confronting issues. In 1955, Isaacs foreshadowed a project to locate factories in rural areas zoned as "depressed". He remarked that, by that term, he meant that "the areas are extremely poor". The focus was on low-wage work and modest capital investment. He raised the matter again in March 1956 and, in July, legislation was tabled. Glasspole and Isaacs presented the bill as the Ministers of Labour and Industry respectively.[6]

The legislation was to establish fifteen factories under the Export Industries Encouragement Act. They would be "low-wage-payment industries" geared to "highly competitive" markets. The IDC-devised plan required "a settled wage schedule" for three to five years. Although there could be collective bargaining on work conditions, no excess wage claims would be allowed. It was predictable that the Government would struggle to gain union approval. Consequently, a joint House committee was formed to determine the conditions under which the initiative could go ahead. It was chaired by the PNP's Fred Evans, a former Garveyite and spokesman for the masses. The Opposition members on the committee, Edwin Allen, Hugh Shearer and Isaac Barrant, had like reputations for toughness. Barrant described the plan as "sweated labour". Still, the Opposition was compromised by the fact that, in government, they had proposed a similar measure. They supported the bill, but also stated their opposition to low wages. Tension across the House was evident.

Seconding the motion, Isaacs spoke at length. One factory would be in Hanover, his home parish. He said that the low wage, 25 to 30 shillings a week, was for a training period. He also noted that workers trained at Ariguanabo who migrated to England to work in Lancaster's garment factories were now earning up to £20 a week. Foreign investors were complaining that Jamaica's workforce was untrained. With three hundred and fifty women gone to Lancaster, Jamaica could now train three hundred and fifty more. This would be a net gain for both the economy and the women. Isaacs compared this prospect with that of women across Jamaica whose options were confined to domestic service: "[S]he has to come at 6 in the morning to get the breakfast, then she has to mop out the house, put the breakfast on the table, she has to scrub the floor, wash the clothes and cook the meals, and how much is she paid. [....] How many people, Mr. Speaker, in this country are paying the women who work in their homes 25/- a week?"

Addressing the JLP member for Hanover West, he asked if he would prefer such women in Lucea to continue as they were, or to be paid a better wage while learning a trade. The women to whom Isaacs referred were not unionized and worked in largely unprotected sectors. Given the links between the parties and the unions, unless the latter acted with despatch, demands for collective bargaining at these sites would seem disingenuous. With just one woman in the House, the project went ahead. Three factories were established in Lucea, Morant Bay and Port Maria. Respectively, they would produce woollen knit, leather buttons and undergarments. The Port Maria factory opened in March 1957. An entirely foreign initiative, it exported brassieres to the United States. Three American women came to Jamaica to train machinists. Employing forty female workers at the outset, the addition of forty more was announced in August. The American manager remarked that the Jamaican work was excellent, but urged the adoption of piecework rather than factory-based employment. Apart from the muted House debate, there was no public outcry. A like factory was installed in Kingston's Industrial Estate later in 1957. Once again experts were brought from the United States and a training regime was put in place.[7]

The struggle for factories brought some employment, but also paltry wages for most. Moreover, investors in factories that were highly capitalized proved reluctant to locate outside Kingston. In 1958, an appeal came from residents of Maggotty in St Elizabeth. They were hoping for a glass-making factory in their vicinity, on the Black River. Isaacs met a local deputation led by the PNP Member for St Elizabeth Northern. The case seemed compelling: an ample supply of sand; transport up the Black River from the coast for machinery; the prospect of an upgraded JPSC hydro-electric station; and a good road system from Maggotty to Kingston. The deputation also observed that the region had become impoverished with heavy out-migration to Kingston and England due to years of intermittent rain and land degradation. Still, the case was unsuccessful. Isaacs detailed the reasons in his speech to the House:

> When it was decided that this factory was to be built, without any request from the Member – without his knowing that a factory was to be built – I used every effort that was humanly possible to get a factory built at Black River. I used every influence, because I felt [...] that the particular parish needs the help and assistance even more than the Corporate Area needs it. [....] It is a private investor coming in to build his factory, and when I sat down to discuss the matter with him [...] the gentleman gave various reasons why it could not be a financial success [...] if it were put in Black River. Some of the reasons were – first, that there was not enough electric power in Black River. [....] The question as to when the Maggotty Falls will be harnessed and power will be available is something which neither I nor the Jamaica Public Service Company could guarantee. It means then that if he was to wait until the Maggotty Falls have been harnessed perhaps we might wait for quite a few years more. [....]

> The second reason is that the manufacturer of the bottles of that particular factory needs an enormous amount of fuel oil. There is not storage facilities at Black River. [....]
>
> Then the gentleman pointed to me – he says 95% of the users of the bottles are in Kingston. [....]
>
> The machinery is heavy equipment. The factory must run 24 hours a day. It needs servicing [of a type] you get from the Kingston Industrial Works. Such services are vital to the factory and must be on hand. If you put the factory in Black River and anything happens, where do you get services for the factory in Black River?
>
> This is a private investment of $2,500,000 coming into the country, and the gentleman says 'I cannot put it in Black River. The only place I can put it is at the Industrial Estate.' Well, what am I to do? Am I to tell him if he cannot put it in Black River don't bring it at all? Am I to do that?[8]

Jamaica's incentive legislation seemed straightforward and generous to a fault. However, the unflinching demands of capital undermined the Government's intent. If factory development proved difficult and expensive, further strategies were required. One was to address the cost of raw materials in both manufacturing and construction. Another was to keep the cost of living down for the working poor; those who provided the main support for their unemployed compatriots. Isaacs' focus began to broaden. Increasingly, he addressed the costs of production and the cost of living, as well as employment. He fought numerous battles over price. Central ones involved the supply of petrol, beef and codfish, as well as lumber and cement. Foremost in his mind were cartels and monopolies.

Early on, Isaacs had dealings with Jamaica's lumber merchants which were difficult and became protracted. Under the heading, "The axe has been laid to lumber dealers' profits", the *Gleaner* described Isaacs' plan. His intent was to lower the cost of building materials used in construction, both domestic and commercial. *Inter alia,* he hoped to slow the rapid rise in Kingston rentals. Issues of employment were also involved. At 16 per cent between 1950 and 1955, construction and installation had the highest average annual growth rate of any industry. This was due to the start-up phase of the bauxite industry and the replacement of housing stock that followed a hurricane in 1951. Subsequently, construction was buoyed by the proliferation of tourist hotels and middle-class housing schemes.[9] The raw material with which he began was an imported product, pitch pine lumber, widely used in Jamaica. Later he would turn his attention to relevant hardware and the monopoly pricing of cement.

In August 1955, Isaacs raised three features of lumber importation. To begin with, the major merchants pooled their annual purchases, buying in one bundle the total amount they required. Moreover, this pooling involved a quite small number of large dealers located in Kingston and in regional centres. This practice was endorsed by government during the war years when trade was limited and resources scarce. The merchants pointed out that the practice allowed them to buy at a lower price. Other distributors could purchase individually if they wished. Still, as Isaacs noted, their arrangement was a virtual cartel. There were two major grades of timber imported, of narrower and broader width. Roughly 90 per cent of a bundle was usually the narrower, cheaper grade and 10 per cent the broader, more expensive one. These different products were purchased in lots of one hundred, the cheaper one at 94/- per 100 and the more expensive at 102/-. When sold in Jamaica, however, the two were "married". A uniform price of 117/- per 100 was applied. Not only was this a cartel. The price of the cheaper lumber subsidized the more expensive one, mainly required by wealthy Jamaicans. Finally, the merchants maintained a 'quantitative profit system'. On these lots of one hundred, irrespective of quality or demand, importers enjoyed a profit of 22/-. Isaacs viewed this profit as excessive. The *Gleaner* columnist on business and industry agreed.

He remarked that the system came from either an "unholy pressure inimical to consumers or out of ignorance". Either way, it worked to the benefit of a "handful of lucky lumbermen". Isaacs proposed to outlaw this particular marriage, price the grades separately, and apply a percentage profit margin of 15 per cent on both grades. The change built some flexibility into the pricing.[10]

The merchants resisted. The bone of contention became the relation between wholesalers' and retailers' margins. The merchant importers argued that their price to retailers had to allow for the small man's margin. Therefore, their own margin needed to be higher than Isaacs' 15 per cent. An interim agreement was reached with separate percentage margins for each point of sale. Further consultation brought formal recognition of the fact that retailers needed to cover transport costs in their prices. The importers' wharfage costs were paid by government. The *Gleaner* reported on 6 December that the final wholesale price of timber was slightly lower than that set by the interim agreement. And even allowing for transportation, the retail price was lower than that charged for many years.[11]

That this negotiation was in fact regulation was not lost on the merchants. Neither was it lost on Isaacs that the *modus operandi* of the lumbermen fell far short of a market ideal. Passions were roused. In the Legislative Council, Richard Youngman described Isaacs' actions as "price-murdering" and inimical to industrialization. These were harsh words from a man whose company, Caribbean Preserving, had jeopardized trade with Canada and was rescued, in turn, by the IDC. However, as a member of council and the JCC's president, Youngman had influence. Isaacs' actions, he claimed, would deter individuals abroad from investing in Jamaica. Youngman argued that the incident showed that, once a pioneer industry was on its feet, there was nothing to stop "some wild Minister" from "swooping down" to control the profits. Youngman said that his remarks would go on record to every other chamber of commerce "under the Union Jack". At a subsequent meeting of lumber merchants, he proposed that Isaacs' measures be appealed via the Executive Council and thereby the governor. The meeting, called by the chair of the lumber liaison committee, Lionel deCordova, made this a "last resort".[12]

Matters escalated with suggestions of a constitutional crisis. Manley moved to rebut Youngman whom, he observed, did not understand due process. On these matters, the legal responsibility was with Isaacs. It was he who brought matters to the Executive Council, not vice versa. Manley and others deplored Youngman's hint that he would bad-mouth the Government throughout the British Commonwealth.[13]

Though Youngman withdrew his resolution, the lumber merchants continued to insist that Isaacs' cuts would render them insolvent or unable to trade. In turn, Isaacs proposed that the Government examine their books and called on Vernon Arnett to do so. This event occurred almost a year before Isaacs appointed Arnett to the IDC, but possibly prompted him to do so.[14] The merchants objected and Isaacs called in a second auditor from the private sector. Whilst the audit was in train, the lumber merchants announced island-wide credit restrictions caused, they argued, by the new prices. No longer could they offer credit to retailers. This claim brought division in the ranks. An importer, J.P. Wynne, reminded the industry that credit in the lumber trade had been an open issue since 1954. It had nothing much to do with Isaacs' changes. The *Daily Gleaner* agreed and cited Mr Wynne: "It is not a merchant's function to compete with the banks." Nonetheless, the newspaper devoted five editorials to the "lumber war" over a period of five months.[15] On 6 December, the same day that the audit was complete, new, lower lumber prices were announced. Later, in August 1956, the Trade Board extended the use of percentage margins under the Trade Act of 1955. Margins of 5 to 15 per cent were set on a range of strategic hardware. The lower margins were applied to items such as tin plate, shingles and various agricultural tools.[16]

During the dispute, Isaacs left the island for New York, seeking treatment again for a stomach ailment. The undiagnosed condition had troubled him since the late 1940s. The news that it was not cancer lifted his spirits and he joined events that marked the British West Indies Airways' inaugural flight from New York to the Caribbean. He also took the time to visit Harlem and speak with Jamaican immigrants, canvassing ideas about Jamaican exports. He had in mind increased exports of canned fruit and vegetables, ackee included. In his absence, Glasspole shadowed his portfolio and on Isaacs' behalf made a statement on the price of cement.[17]

In mid-1956, Isaacs introduced a filling station bill, sponsored once again with Glasspole. This one sought to frustrate tactics employed by foreign firms selling petroleum in Jamaica. They included the British Regent company, soon to be taken over by Texaco, and the American Esso company, a derivative of Standard Oil. In addition to their brand name stations, these importers had begun to supply micro-operators required to sell at the brand name price. By populating intersections and street corners, these sellers choked off business to small, independent stations, who sold with smaller margins at a lower price. The proliferation of micro-operators was caused by competition between the overseas suppliers. However, as Isaacs explained, the effect was oligopolistic. They intended to maintain their price range rather than reduce it. The legislation required that prospective proprietors seek a license from the Trade Board which would weigh each case. Donald Sangster (JLP) attacked the bill and argued that licensing should be done by an independent panel, not Isaacs and the Trade Board. He voiced the merchants' general unease. Manley interposed. He remarked that the Trade Board, after all, supported free enterprise. Rather than being simply perverse, the law protected the established livelihoods of small traders.[18]

The more common form of regulation was price control. By September 1958, prices of the following grocery items were under regulation: cocoa powder, cornmeal, cigarettes, codfish, Irish potatoes, kerosene oil, pickled mackerel, matches, tinned milk (both condensed and evaporated), rolled oats, bulk and packaged rice, and coarse salt.[19] Not much of this involved monopoly producers in Jamaica. A number of the items were imported and involved problems of supply because Jamaica was a tiny market. A supplier could adopt a 'take it or leave it' approach, stipulating a minimum sale at a set price. Inappropriate import licensing could make matters worse. Isaacs' aim was to create more efficient local markets through new trade agreements and domestic legislation. The need was to bring the cost to government down while still protecting consumers. Isaacs' struggles with beef and codfish demonstrate the dilemma.

The price of beef was in the news throughout 1957 and brought a stream of remarks from Isaacs. They began with reference to another commodity, codfish. On a tour of western parishes in May, Isaacs announced that were he unable "to break the stranglehold" of Newfoundland suppliers, he was perfectly prepared to substitute New Zealand beef for Canadian codfish. He observed that the cuts might not be "of the best", but the beef could be sold for less than codfish and was more nutritious. He suggested that parish councils might work with his ministry to construct "frozen stalls" in rural marketplaces. He added in mild jest, "Butchers in Jamaica have got to understand and comply with modern concepts. Jamaica is the only country in the world to eat fresh beef." One month later, Isaacs remarked on Jamaica's own producers. Unlike those in trade and industry, the "landed gentry" who raise beef, "think nothing of black marketeering". He continued, "They think they can get away with it, well let me say now that there is not one law for the whites and another for the blacks, nor is there one for the rich and another for the poor. I am going to teach these fellows a lesson they will never forget as long as they live."

The manifest theatre in Isaacs' words reflected that a partially controlled market for beef was hard to enforce, especially in the countryside.[20] A significant part of Jamaica's beef was price controlled, according to three grades of diminishing quality. Prime beef was uncontrolled and for some years had been destined mainly for the Kingston market. Live animals were sent to the city and slaughtered there. As a part of PNP agricultural policy, a prime beef project had been introduced to upgrade both cattle and their feed. The aim was to improve Jamaica's herd and increase production as well. However, as regional towns became more prosperous, prime beef producers weighed the higher Kingston prices alongside transportation costs. Consequently, there were periodic shortages in Kingston. In rural areas, some producers also manipulated grades in order to enlarge the supply of 'prime' sold at uncontrolled prices. In turn, this situation proved a disincentive to producers of lower grades.

**Isaacs tames Jamaica's black market.**

Why should they supply at controlled prices the same beef sold by so-called prime producers? Some smaller growers on marginal land were withdrawing altogether. Consequently, there was scarcity at both ends of the spectrum. Moreover, production overall had been in decline since 1954.

Isaacs "followed the market" to a degree, reducing the controlled grades to two and expanding the prime beef category. While more beef became 'prime', the two controlled grades were more closely monitored. All beef was now inspected and stamped according to quality. Some butchers outside Kingston were allowed to supply to town and suspect pricing could be reported in the regions. The black marketing was at least contained. In July 1958, the Trade Board's new chair, Aaron Matalon, fixed a maximum fine of £1,000 for offences against the Livestock Control Order. Political Reporter praised Isaacs for diffusing the issue. He cited the battle over beef as one reason for choosing him as his "Politician of the Year" in 1957.[21]

Where the minister was concerned, however, the "Year of Beef" was no more than a skirmish. The more testing issue involved a product purchased by all Jamaicans, and especially by those unlikely to consume much beef. Imported codfish was their staple. An alliance between suppliers, Canadian and Jamaican, brought manipulation of the codfish market.

Even in the early 1950s, codfish sourced from Newfoundland and Halifax had been a volatile issue, with prices raised and lowered by the JLP government. When the PNP came to power, Isaacs dropped the retail price from 1/7 per lb to 1/5. This proved unsustainable for many reasons: Freight and packaging charges had increased, exacerbated by an exchange rate moving against the Jamaican pound. Moreover, the unit price for codfish was charged on a marriage of grades; a practice Isaacs had also faced in the case of imported lumber. Though the price was set by the superior grade, the mix contained mostly "paper-thin fish". In addition, the worldwide demand for salted fish was rising rapidly. Post-war,

Canada had moved to develop its Atlantic fishing trade. A peak organization was created, the Canadian Atlantic Saltfish Exporters Association. A leading member was the group that Jamaica dealt with, the Newfoundland Associated Fish Exporters Limited. This group also purchased fish from Halifax and sold it to Jamaica. NAFEL demanded that it deal with only one Jamaican group. Eleven Jamaican importers came together as a sole importer, Fish Importers Limited. The group was chaired by G.J. "Joe" deCordova. The arrangement meant that exporters and importers had allied interests. Rather than search for alternative suppliers in Scotland, Denmark or British Honduras, Fish Importers Ltd. Coalesced with NAFEL. Both pressed for higher prices.[22]

In July 1956, retailers indicated that the supply of codfish was dangerously low. Prompted by Richard Youngman's question in the Legislative Council, "Does the Minister intend the people to starve?", the JCC telegraphed Isaacs, strongly recommending

"LOVER COME BACK TO ME"!

**"Ms Canadian Codfish" spurns Jamaica (1956).**

removal of the retail price cap on codfish. Talks between Fish Importers Ltd. and NAFEL regarding the next annual contract had collapsed. The Jamaican price was too low. Isaacs resisted: "There is absolutely no question of de-controlling saltfish. [....] To remove price control would be to expose the poorer people to victimization by unscrupulous retailers." The *Gleaner* reported his further remark that, "[C]odfish is a staple in the diet of the poorer classes who derive high protein value at a relatively low cost." Isaacs suggested that Fish Importers Ltd. invite two representatives of Canadian Atlantic Saltfish Exporters Association to Jamaica. Talks with the minister took place, but agreement was not reached. In turn, Isaacs sent Carlton Alexander and Ivan Levy, vice chairman of Fish Importers, to try again in Canada. Protracted discussions resulted in a bid from the Canadians at 1/7½ a lb being wrestled down to 1/6½. The price was below that which had prevailed under the previous government. In May 1957, Joe deCordova congratulated the minister.[23]

Throughout September and October 1957, engineered scarcity returned. New demands were made that codfish be decontrolled. Isaacs responded that the timing was inappropriate. Deadlock ensued. DeCordova remarked of the trade that NAFEL was "making less today than it was ten years ago"; further, that so small was Jamaica's market that were it to find "some other savoury", the exporter would not mind. Designed to affront, the comment brought a response in the form of a *Gleaner* editorial. It stated in part, "The Minister of Trade is making a valiant attempt, supported by many sections of experience in the trade, to combat the iron-clad cartel which the codfish industry in Canada is driving over the Jamaican consumer. [...] the fact is that a powerful bureaucracy has taken charge of the industry in Canada and [...] can dictate terms to those who wish to buy codfish."

A split occurred among the advocates of so-called free markets. While the *Gleaner* endorsed Isaacs' stand, Fish Importers Ltd.

took out a full-page advertisement on “the facts” and opened their books. When Edwin Allen (JLP) charged Isaacs with misleading Parliament on the price of codfish, the minister gave him short shrift.[24] As 1957 drew to a close, the Jamaican government called for tenders to supply 4,800 tonnes of dried salted codfish. The deadline was 8 November. By the Monday before the deadline, no tenders had been received and, reportedly, supplies in Jamaica were all but exhausted. Fish Importers made a further request for an increase of tuppence per pound on the current 1/6½ price. The government refused and itself canvassed importing fish. Isaacs also toyed with importing wet fish to be dried in Jamaica. Suddenly, on 9 November, he declared that the shortage would cease by the end of the month. From that time, the new maximum retail price would be 1/7 per lb for eight months and NAFEL was the successful tenderer. Thereafter, the price would decrease, there being now two suppliers, Canada and Iceland. In the House, Isaacs explained that NAFEL would meet the island’s requirements until the end of July 1958. He had invited a further tender for 3,000 tonnes of codfish for the period July to December. Iceland tendered and its bid was substantially less than the Canadian one, considering cost, insurance and freight. Moreover, the fish was of good quality. The Jamaican government would save £57,000 on the anticipated cost of the year’s supplies.

Later, it emerged that Isaacs had proposed a government-to-government agreement on codfish to Canada’s Minister of Trade. The Jamaican government would licence Canada to supply the entire Jamaican market, but at a controlled price. The offer was declined. Receiving no support from Fish Importers, Isaacs turned to an alternative source and alternative importers. The Matalons and Grace Kennedy jointly received the Icelandic agency. In reply to a question from Donald Sangster (JLP), Isaacs stated that no commission was paid in relation to the tenders, which, in each case, went to the lowest bidder. Canada continued to supply codfish to the Jamaican market.[25]

In January 1958, Isaacs led a twenty-man trade mission to Canada, including representatives of business and the IDC. It was the first such venture since the war made by a Jamaican government. The ten-day visit involved stops in Toronto, Ottawa and Montreal. Those involved included export manufacturers, hoteliers, importers of bulk goods, distributors and key public servants. Among the prominent names were Carlton Alexander, Herbert DeSouza, Lee Gore, Abe Issa, Dudley and Ivan Levy, and ministerial administrator, A.A. Rattray. The trip had three general aims: to encourage more Jamaica-Canada trade, to attract Canadian capital and industry, and to stimulate Canadian interest in Jamaican tourism. Isaacs conferred with Premier Diefenbaker, the Canadian Trade Minister, and the United Kingdom Commissioner to Canada. Subsequent remarks from Diefenbaker confirmed that he wished to expand Canada's trade within the Commonwealth as a counterweight to the United States. Trade opportunities were discussed at length, as well as the upcoming Canadian trade fair to the West Indies. Under a trade liberalization plan, bilateral dollar transactions would increase. Ties were strengthened and the mission was deemed a success; so much so that one columnist declared Isaacs "the leading diplomat of our present Government".[26]

With the aid of Jamaican merchants, Canadian producers of salted cod had bargained as if they were monopoly suppliers. Jamaica's Caribbean Cement Company was a monopoly supplier in fact.[27] The licencing agreement regarding the company was completed in June 1948 and enabling legislation was passed by the JLP government one month later. After a period in which capital was raised in Jamaica and the United Kingdom, followed by construction of the plant, the CCC opened for business in 1952.[28] Within two years, controversy erupted over prices when the *Daily Express* in London published an article, later reported in the *Daily Gleaner*. The article noted that while the price of cement in Jamaica was £8.14.0 per tonne, in London the price was a mere £4.16.6. It also stated that, taking all costs into account, the company's profit was 52/- per tonne on an annual output of 100,000 tonnes. The article concluded that the profit would make a UK producer "blush". The disparity occurred because the company's licence allowed it to sell cement produced in Jamaica at a price just below the landed cost of imported cement. The calculated CCC price involved reference to a UK average price, and to the costs involved in bringing the product to Jamaica. Transport aside, this agreement entirely overlooked the substantial cost advantages of local production. These included raw materials readily available and, as it happened, adjacent to the factory on Kingston's periphery. Factory land also adjoined a deep-water anchorage. The agreement came with pioneer industry tax relief. There was a statutory monopoly on supply to boot.[29]

In Parliament, Glasspole had delayed the 1948 legislation for as long as he could. He argued that the locally produced cement would not be much cheaper than imported cement. In addition, the government had forgone significant income. The financial concessions were excessive: "non-payment of customs duty, non-payment of income tax, non-payment of mineral royalties, a 99-year lease of 193 acres of land from Government at £40 per annum, despite the fact that the license would run for only 19 years." When the price rose in October 1955, Isaacs objected that, though the price rise was within its legal rights, the company should desist. Its financial situation was "very satisfactory".[30]

There was another increase in 1957. The price per tonne had risen by 16/- in less than two years. This time, the company explained that the rise was to cover the cost of importing cement to meet demand in excess of production. In any case, a lower price must wait on a new mill and increased production. Isaacs tailored his response accordingly, remarking that the price must be lowered once the new mill was in operation. The mill and a second kiln were already in construction, although the former would only be completed late in 1957. The kiln would take longer, coming on stream in 1959, by which time another kiln was already required.[31]

Some months later in 1957, Edwin Allen attacked the government. He tabled a series of questions regarding shortages of cement and failures in distribution. The latter had led to queues of trucks waiting for hours outside the factory. Isaacs pointed out that the basic problem was production, not distribution.[32] In the New Year, Robert Kirkwood agreed with Isaacs in a speech to the Legislative Council. He observed that cement could be cheap in Jamaica and still afford "delicious" shareholder profits. If the government's goal was cheaper housing, it would need to review the "extensively protective arrangements" under which cement was produced. He noted that Puerto Rican cement was much cheaper and stated, "If we're going to foster industries, they must foster us." Retired colonel C.L. Melville CCC's managing director, replied. He described the critics as "lovers of the sensational". Kirkwood countered with the comment that a company which enjoys "complete protection" has duties to consumers as well as shareholders.[33]

Both in Opposition and government, the PNP, and most of all Isaacs, was awake to Kirkwood's points. Nonetheless, possible gain was measured against possible loss. Domestic production of cement was central to Jamaica's development plans. Aside from the predictable debates around nationalization, there was also an issue of sovereign risk were the government to break the CCC agreement. It appears that a majority of cabinet was diffident to act. This diffidence brought a reaction from Isaacs. He would not go against his leader or his government. He was prepared, however, to state a personal position. The statement was a part of his 1958 Budget speech:

> [...] while the franchise has been granted to the Cement Company by our predecessors, and they are operating under a franchise which is legal, there is not a vestige of morality within that franchise. My religion [...] has something to say about the type of profits that the Cement Company is making. There is no reasonable share-holder in the world whose conscience should not be shocked by the enormous profits that the Cement Company is making while this country is in

> need of housing, and cheap housing at that. I am afraid that I will have to advise the Cabinet on the immorality of that franchise, and to suggest to the Cabinet that the franchise be re-negotiated.[34]

Responses followed. One was from Neville Ashenheim, a director of the company and lately chair of the IDC. He criticized the "irresponsibility" of Isaacs' "diatribe". It was all the more reason for the company not to "surrender any protections secured by its license". However, one day later, the Master Builders' Association published a lengthy critique of CCC. Its remarks were organised under four headings: quality of cement, quantity, distribution and availability. They observed that the company proceeded at a "snail-like pace" to address the building industry, although that industry represented "the interests of thousands of workers". They also remarked that the association had had many conferences with the minister and company executives, in which the latter had been unresponsive. The Master Builders vowed to continue the struggle. This was not the first such industry critique of CCC. In 1954 lumber companies complained that cement pricing left hardware merchants with a net trading loss. The lumbermen noted the handsome dividends received by CCC shareholders and the company's recent issue of bonus shares.[35]

The cement company's second kiln was opened in early February 1959. Governor Kenneth Blackburn spoke of the "modern Jamaica" and the "dynamic spirit of enterprise". He was introduced by Sir William Stephenson, the Canadian-British chairman of the company. In turn Ashenheim introduced Sir William and noted that the government should be gratified by the company's success. It showed the wisdom of support for pioneer industries. Champagne flowed. Isaacs attended but did not partake. Following subsequent discussions with Stephenson, Isaacs announced a reduction in the price of cement effective 8 October 1959. The price per ton was reduced by 12/-. A bag of cement would be sixpence cheaper.[36]

The timing of the reduction rested on two factors. One was indeed the increasing capacity of CCC's factory, albeit at a slow pace. The other was a matter of the board's priorities. As early as 1954, Stephenson had told his Jamaican shareholders that his aim, with the help of tax concessions, was to rapidly reduce the mortgaged indebtedness of the company. In 1957, he reported that the entire first mortgage debenture stock had now been redeemed "at an accelerated rate". Liberal cash dividends and bonus shares were issued to investors. Although demand had outstripped supply within the first two years of production, the board had decided on a 'staged' expansion. Their monopoly position allowed this approach, along with hefty returns from rising demand. In sum, it appears that accelerated redemption of mortgage stock was given preference over expanding capacity. Builders and consumers bore the cost.[37]

The saga revealed some other politics, both international and local. Sir William was an accomplished businessman with other attributes. He was knighted in part for his contribution to the British war effort. He also mobilized sectors of North American business after the war to support Britain's dollar pool. He was a friend of British governments, of Churchill, and Lord Beaverbrook. During the late 1940s, he kept a winter residence in Montego Bay, like Beaverbrook. Keen to establish a cement factory, the JLP government's discussions had collapsed. The government enlisted former Governor Huggins to approach Sir William. Bargaining with an inexperienced government, the businessman had a reservoir of power and influence on his side.[38]

Neville Ashenheim, a lawyer and a businessman, was one of Sir William's directors and a spokesman for the company. Previously chair of the IDC, he had left in 1957 when his appointment was not renewed. Isaacs appointed Harry Dayes in his place. Dayes was a lawyer and a businessman too. He was also a member of the PNP who had served on the KSAC council with Isaacs, and on the party's executive. The two men were personal friends. In a public address that followed his departure, Ashenheim condemned "political appointments", notwithstanding his own well-known allegiances in both politics and business.[39]

These remarks came at a time when the government was under attack in the House. The JLP's target was the close association between some government members and the Matalon family. Aaron Matalon was chair of the Trade Board. Moses Matalon was an IDC director and executive director of Jamaica Ice Works. The attack was brought on by negotiations between the government and the West Indies Building Company, which had been formed to develop the Mona housing scheme. This major excursion into middle-class housing had both government and CD&W support. Previously owned by the Water Commission, the land for 720 houses had been made available by the government at an attractive price. Both Dayes and Mayer Matalon were directors of WIBC. Isaacs and others responded cogently to criticism in Parliament, but the issue endured.[40] In mid-1958, future JLP prime minister Edward Seaga published two articles on the award of government contracts. His main concern was the PNP and the Matalon family. Bravely, he argued that Caribbean Cement's profits were fair returns on risk. Proportionately, Seaga claimed, they were far less than those projected for the West Indies Building Company. Seaga cited neither the projections nor their source on which his remarks were based.[41]

Another explanation for the prominence of some families was that the PNP, including Isaacs, worked with merchant capitalists prepared to engage with their government. In the late 1950s, G. Arthur Brown noted that a major problem with family-based commerce was that it discouraged the spread of managerial and technical expertise. Activity was kept within the family and the able covered for the less able.[42] He might have observed as well that, while some of these businessmen had more experience than most public servants, all private businessmen had interests, whatever their political leanings. With higher education still open only to a few, these factors limited the advice to government and impeded development. In Isaacs' own terms, commerce may not have been the state's master. Nonetheless, its service to the state and society was tailored to commercial interests.

As Jefferson notes, Jamaica found it difficult to resolve the tension between the productivity that brings higher wages and the job creation that reduces unemployment.[43] The society's domestic market could not expand appreciably without higher wages, which, in turn, required more highly capitalised production. Less capitalised and more labour-intensive production was often not competitive in North American markets; or else, like the garment producers in the parishes, proved footloose once incentives diminished. Where capital was concerned, only a serious class accord within Jamaica may have produced fewer incentives and more effective fiscal policy overall. However, this was a whole-of-government matter and not for Isaacs alone.

The seven years that he spent as Minister of Trade and Industry brought some notable legacies. One was to promote and then consolidate tourism's expansion as an industry and as a major source of foreign exchange. A second was to change the position of manufacturing in the economy. Distribution, rather than industry, had been the 'easy way'; not least due to the preference of commercial banks to lend to distributors over manufacturers. As the 1960s progressed, this situation changed as manufacturing became more credit-worthy – not least due to Isaacs' efforts. Moreover, as the sector stabilized in the 1960s, its workforce became widely unionized.[44] A third legacy came with Isaacs' vocal opposition to cartels and monopolies that were contrary to the people's interest. Issues of mass consumption as well as production became increasingly prominent. The fight would continue with JPSC and the island's electrification. And in time, the idea of strategic public ownership became acceptable again. Just as Isaacs in the 1940s had focused attention on unemployment, in the 1950s he promoted the cost of living as a central political issue. The struggle with one required an equal concern with the other. In the 1970s, Michael Manley's government institutionalized public procurement of imported staples and other bulk purchases crucial to the economy.[45]

Faced with the daunting effects of British underdevelopment, depression and war, Isaacs and his comrades learnt on the job. There was much to learn. Development was just one challenge; there was also federation.

**As Minister of Trade and Industry.**
Courtesy of the National Library of Jamaica.

**The PNP Cabinet circa 1957. Back row, from second left: A.G.S. Coombs (Communications and Works), Rudolph Burke (nominated member), William Seivright (Agriculture); Middle row, from left: Vernon Arnett, Claude Stuart (Health), Ivan Lloyd (Home Affairs) and Florizel Glasspole (Education); Front row, from left: Dr Glendon Logan (Housing and Local Government). Norman Manley (chief minister), Sir Hugh Foot (governor), Wills Isaacs (Trade and Industry). Missing: Jonathan Grant (Labour) and Noel Nethersole (Finance).**

Courtesy of the Isaacs family.

**Isaacs and Abe Issa discuss tourism with members of the Jamaica Cab Drivers' Cooperative (1958).**

Courtesy of the Isaacs family.

**Isaacs tests a power-cutting machine at a garment factory in Kingston (1960).**

**As trade mission leader, Isaacs delivers Chief Minister Manley's message to Canadian Prime Minister Diefenbaker (1958).**

**Isaacs welcomes Norman Manley home from bauxite talks in Washington, DC, while Mrs Edna Manley and a ministry advisor look on (1960).**

**Wills and Gloria Isaacs host ministerial staff at their home in Sligoville (1960).**

Courtesy of the Isaacs family.

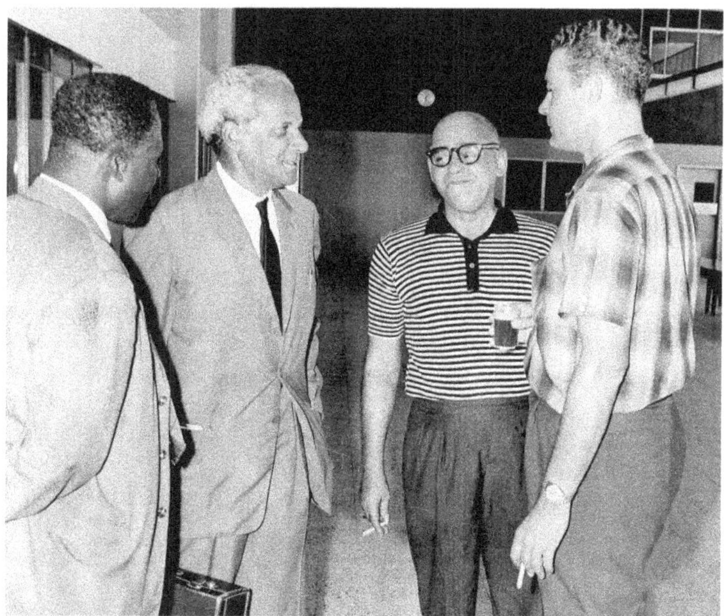

**As shadow minister for Trade and Industry, Isaacs greets Norman Manley at Palisadoes Airport. A.G.R. Byfield and Michael Manley look on (1963).**

**Isaacs presents his credentials as Jamaica's High Commissioner to Canada (1973).**

Courtesy of the Isaacs family.

# SECTION IV
# FACING FEDERATION

## Chapter 9

# Warning Signs

*Mr Isaacs was selected by Mr Manley to accompany him to Port-of-Spain. [....] He is the man the party has called upon to save its fortunes [...]. If Wills Isaacs says that he will not mind Jamaica remaining in a Federation with a changed constitution, people may begin to take heart. Wills Isaacs is the Giant-Killer, the leader of fighting popular movements, the winner of elections and – now, the dragon's paw to pull the PNP's chestnut out of the fire.* – Political Reporter, 1959.[1]

Jamaica's passage into a West Indies Federation in 1957, and its departure in 1961 to become an independent state one year later, had major implications both for the nation and the PNP. During these years, the party lost power well short of two full terms in government. The implications for Isaacs were significant. His rising popularity was augmented by his role as Minister of Trade and Industry, to which he made a total commitment. Following Noel Nethersole's death, he became the PNP's first vice president and, in the view of many, heir apparent to Norman Manley. Yet, his scepticism regarding federation, a course to which Manley was wedded, created a distance between them. Manoeuvring within the PNP grew to involve other matters as well, including tensions between rural and urban contingents of the party. Over time, Isaacs modified his stance on federation in order to support his leader.

However, by 1962 it was his view that Manley had not returned the respect he was due as first vice president. With the electoral defeat, Isaacs' thoughts of leadership faded.

These matters began to unfold in February 1956. Manley and Glasspole led Jamaica's delegation to a penultimate conference in London on the federation. They joined with other British West Indies delegates in asking for more finance. Their request was denied. Still, all agreed that the unit territories should gain independence and thereby dominion status as a federated member of the British Commonwealth.[2] Already, Jamaica was on the way to internal self-government. However, full independence depended on an autonomous financial status, which now rested on federation. It was a matter of unease back in Jamaica that Manley and Glasspole devoted their attention to a future federal government and gave less attention to regional relations. Trinidad's Albert Gomes had called for an immediate customs union with free trade. The Jamaicans, mindful of their incentives legislation and their protection of local industry, had called for a gradualist approach. Gradual was also the word when it came to introducing a federal taxation system. Tax would be paid from each unit's customs duties, a central part of Jamaica's revenues. More to the federation meant less to Jamaica for its own purposes. These were issues of concern to Isaacs and his ministry.

Speaking to the Jamaica Coconut Producers Association late in March 1956, he assured them of their importance to the government. The growers and their associates employed six thousand workers in agriculture and 550 in manufacturing. Despite its vulnerability to disease and hurricanes, the industry had grown significantly since its beginnings in 1931. In particular, Isaacs noted the growing export market for desiccated coconut, a pioneer industry. He also remarked, "You will of course appreciate that with Federation in sight and the corollary of a customs union at a later date, local industries might have to face the consequences of free trade in the federated area. Meantime, it is my personal hope that sensible and practical measures will be worked out to ensure that the change towards free trade will be gradual, so as not to disrupt the economies of the territories concerned."

Ever the party man, he continued,

> I should like to say a few words about the decision recently taken in London – an event of truly historical significance.
>
> When Federation was mooted, I was strongly opposed to it [...] but now that the London Conference has decided to take this step, we must all as good and loyal Jamaicans wholeheartedly support the idea and work towards its fulfilment [...]. This will be no easy task: it will call for all the power, resource, imagination, hard work and integrity of which we are capable as a people. I want to emphasize integrity, because [...] it is not easily bought in the market place of the various countries.

These were prescient words.[3]

Isaacs had been in the job for eighteen months. His life was full of factories and hotels, refrigeration and electrification, and the markets for this and that. He was also subject to the attentions of Edwin Allen, the JLP Opposition member for Clarendon North Western. Allen was known as "Mr Opposition" for his nonstop questioning of ministers. In every sitting week, queries came from the Honourable Edwin to the Honourable Wills.[4] This is not to say that the role was an agony. Isaacs was a publicist and a relentless advocate for the government. The role could be exhilarating, and one that brought the attention of Leandro, the Gleaner's cartoonist, who captured his efforts. The bronco-buster who tamed Jamaica's beef black market was also the nimble Isaacs who lured "Miss Codfish" back to Jamaica from an international stage. Indeed, he had become the expert on pigs, citrus, cattle breeding, milk marketing, cocoa and much more that made him a reliable resource for his leader.[5] Despite this publicity, the job was often behind the scenes and practical – as it was on that day in March when he spoke to the coconut growers. Manley and Glasspole had recently returned from London.

In June 1956, Manley went to Barbados for further talks and the founding of a Federation of Socialist Parties. The signatures of eight Caribbean leaders were emblazoned on the *Gleaner*'s front page. Their statement read that both West Indian nationhood and a "dynamic and purposeful" economy should involve a politics based on party principles. On 1 September, Manley attended the inaugural conference of a renamed West Indies Federal Labour Party. He was acclaimed the party's first president.[6] Two weeks later, at the PNP's annual conference, the gathering approved a resolution put by Manley that measures be taken to ensure the WIFLP's "vigorous growth". Fraternal greetings had been sent from socialist parties around the world.

In his address to the PNP, Manley deemed it a year of achievement. He cited the growth of the NWU and a maturing ministerial system. Nethersole reported on the Plan for Progress, Lloyd on educational policy and Glasspole on the parliamentary group.[7] Notwithstanding his election as third vice president, behind Nethersole and Lloyd, and in front of Seivright, Isaacs may have felt sidelined. He was now periodically ill, in part through exhaustion. Were all his efforts for local producers and consumers to be subject now to a regional plan? The situation rankled. Though Glasspole lacked a strong following in the party, he was close to Manley. In comparison to Isaacs, he was less impulsive and an accountant with a union background.[8] As leader of the government in the House, he was also Manley's second-in-command at federal meetings. The draft constitution stipulated that no one could occupy both a federal and a local seat simultaneously. This clause had implications for Manley and Glasspole. Where the latter was concerned, it was clear that he would stay in Jamaica and thereby become a possible contender to lead the PNP.

A petty incident at the conference in 1956 led Isaacs to threaten Glasspole that he would "wipe the floor" with him. And he did, easily defeating Glasspole for the third vice presidency. The two stopped speaking and Political Reporter made the larger context explicit: "Both would like to be Chief Minister" if Manley chose to lead the federation. As Christmas approached, the *Daily Gleaner* wished Nethersole, the "sphinx of them all", a pot of gold in his pursuit of foreign loans. For the "dissident twins", Isaacs and Glasspole, it wished for better relations. Political Reporter also urged a resolution, for the two were like rice and peas. The one's mass following was as important as the other's efficiency. Moreover, Isaacs' presence had been missed at two parish by-elections. Détente was reached on 21 December. Witnessed by Manley, the two shook hands at Drumblair, his residence.[9]

There was much to do. In April 1957, a notable Ministry Paper was tabled by Ivan Lloyd. It detailed a New Deal for education. Overall, spending would be doubled to £4.8 million by 1962. One aim was to attain the full attendance of all children aged seven to eleven. Additional schools would be built. This was an urgent reform focused in turn on basic literacy, high school entry and an upskilled workforce.[10] Lloyd was no stranger to policy. A medical doctor and MHR since 1944, in that year he had drafted a PNP pamphlet on land reform. The pamphlet, *Land for the Million*, stated that a mere 807 holdings occupied nearly half of Jamaica's arable land, and the better half. Moreover, a system which taxed all income from improvements left little incentive for small farmers to develop their land. On election, the PNP government altered the focus of taxes on small farmers to the unimproved value of their land. In terms of leadership, Lloyd was a rural counterbalance to the likes of Isaacs and Glasspole, and his efforts were acknowledged in country parishes.[11]

The federation was proclaimed on 31 July 1957. One stipulation was that constitutional changes could only be made after five years. Three initial steps would occur forthwith: the federal governor general would assume his role; a federal election would be called on 25 March 1958; and thereafter, the federal parliament would sit.

Another significant event occurred on 11 November 1957. Within the framework of a still colonial order, Jamaica received internal self-government under a council of ministers led by the chief minister. The change was something less than its description: the council of ministers replaced the previous Executive Council. The governor and official members were removed from the new elected body. However, the governor still retained significant reserve powers, and defence, foreign affairs and constitutional change were "outside the purview" of the new council.

Prior to the federal proclamation, Isaacs took the opportunity to pay tribute to Manley. He remarked that they often disagreed. However, Isaacs also praised him for obtaining both self-government and the support of the Jamaican people: "[I]t was a long struggle and let me say here and now there was nobody in this country that had the stature or had the ability to demand Self-Government at the time but the present Chief Minister of Jamaica."[12]

With the previous year's peace between the twins, the urbanites did well in the PNP's 1957 election for vice presidential roles. Nethersole's position was not contested, and Isaacs beat Ivan Lloyd for the second vice presidency. Seivright took the third as a two-way candidate, urban aligned but also the incumbent Minister of Agriculture. Lloyd took the fourth slot but resigned in protest. The election took place on a Saturday morning, too early for some rural delegates to arrive from the countryside. So wide was Isaacs' margin that these votes would have made no difference. Manley was mortified, however. Lloyd had toured country schools to acclaim, following passage of his education bill.[13]

Manley expanded and reshuffled his Cabinet after the conference. As a successful minister, Isaacs retained his portfolio. His popularity had increased among some, due to his support for reducing the voting age from twenty-one to eighteen.[14] Lloyd took the Ministry of Home Affairs, an advance on Education that would mollify him and also acknowledge his standing in the countryside. Glasspole moved to Education. There he would oversee the PNP's expansion of high school education, aided by the introduction of a Common Entrance exam with two thousand free places attached.[15] Political Reporter ventured an opinion that Glasspole's shift to Education would be temporary if Manley were to lead the federation. Glasspole would likely take over as Minister of Development. As these events unfolded, Isaacs, Glasspole and Lloyd eyed each other. The columnist remarked on this intra-party struggle: "Dr Lloyd [...] has started to fight for a comeback. Mr Glasspole [...] is out to make a bid from now on and there has always been a thinly disguised struggle within the party between the supporters of intellectual leadership and the supporters of working-class leadership. The fact that Mr Isaacs is the effective leader of the working-class groups makes the situation more interesting."[16] Nethersole remained above the fray.

Earlier, Political Reporter had noted the "divine worship" accorded to Manley. The great man aside, he cited Isaacs as one of just a few politicians with "a real patriotic desire" to serve the country, a fact which explained his widespread support. The reporter proposed that were Manley to switch to federal politics, the two contenders for party leadership would be Nethersole and Isaacs. No one else had sufficient support.

On 29 December, the journalist named Isaacs as the "Politician of the Year".[17] He wrote that in 1957 the "flamboyant Mr Isaacs" had played his politics as hard or harder than anyone else, and with an overt ambition to lead. This had brought closed ranks among those in the PNP who deemed him too outspoken and impetuous. Yet, after Manley and Nethersole, Isaacs had the most scope for action, especially where trade was concerned. The reporter cited the codfish war, where Isaacs saved the government a large sum of money, and pimento where he finessed a £1 million profit. His dealings had required "bravery and courage":

> "Mr Isaacs has had to risk the political fortunes of his party and himself; and while he has not been one hundred per cent successful,

> his shrewdness has paid off and his practical approach [...] has brought results, for Mr Isaacs is today a most popular Minister and the reputation of the PNP in trade matters has improved among an appreciative public."

Equal to his activity in trade was his support for industry, including a booming tourist trade; US$6 million earned in hard currency at a time when the sterling area was struggling for dollars. Moreover, a successful agreement with Sheraton regarding a hotel lease in Kingston – with the option to buy – showed both persistence and intelligence. These actions were backed by a refusal to be pushed around by merchants and public servants. Isaacs had taken charge of his ministry: "The Chairman of the Trade Board must see him every Monday. The Marketing Administrator is required to see him every Tuesday. The Chairman of the IDC must see him once per week. In other words, the Minister wants to know what is happening to the departments for which he exercises cabinet and parliamentary responsibility."

And with all this, "the mass of the people recognize in Wills Isaacs the common touch"; a man responsive to the ordinary folk. Political Reporter noted that Isaacs had now reached the party's second vice presidency. However, his ambition could be thwarted were Manley not to become the federated territories' first prime minister.

Manley did not go to the federation. On 3 January 1958, the British West Indies ceased to exist as a political entity and became simply the West Indies Federation. On 15 January, the PNP held a public meeting chaired by Glasspole at Half Way Tree in Kingston. Along with Nethersole, he spoke on aspects of federation. They were joined by Norman and Edna Manley around 8.30 p.m. The leader rose to speak after 9 p.m. and was greeted with a roar of approval when he announced that he would stay in Jamaica and nominate Sir Grantley Adams, premier of Barbados, as the first prime minister of the West Indies. Manley gave three reasons: first, a "conspiracy was growing" in Jamaica to derail federation; second, the federation was crucial to the island's economy; and third, in the first five years of federation, all the islands needed to achieve constitutional parity. In the interim, the two wealthiest islands (Trinidad and Tobago, and Jamaica) should do their utmost to strengthen their economies. These factors made it clear that he should remain in Jamaica to serve both the island and the federation.[18]

A youthful David Coore stood next to a friendly businessman, who remarked that Manley's decision would doom the federation.[19] This concern was not new. It had been aired some months before by Frank Hill, reporting on regional politics. In a lively column, he proposed that Manley had "bullied" his ministers into line despite their diffidence, including Nethersole, Glasspole, Isaacs, Lloyd and Coombs. Hill wrote of Manley's dilemma (to stay or go), conceding either decision was fraught. However, local politics compelled him to stay: "You can convince your hearers with the promise of more jobs and more land settlements and lowered living costs. You can't persuade them to accept an act of faith like federation, which no words can describe. So, Manley hugs his faith and there are few to share it with him."

Political Reporter had a different view: that Manley could either please the home crowd, or go to federation "against the wishes of most Jamaicans and become the historic father of a new nation". Manley should go. A third summation came from Gordon Lewis, a political scientist based in the eastern Caribbean. Though he had hoped that Manley would take the lead, he also argued that the politics of federation had been misconceived. The people who stood to gain the most were middle class, not working class. Therefore, the masses were sceptical.[20] These views did not exhaust the possibilities. Unionists, including Richard Hart and Ken Hill, saw federation as rooted in the Caribbean labour rebellions of the 1930s. They shared the vision of a powerful, union-based federation of socialists married to a regional nationalist movement. As a newly minted unionist, Michael Manley also took this view.[21]

At Half Way Tree, Isaacs stood with friends to hear Norman Manley's speech. A small group met nearby and shared some conversation before they joined the crowd. By all accounts, Isaacs was surprised and likely dismayed; and not only because of his own ambitions.[22] The decision to stay at home left untouched Manley's deep commitment to federation as the only route to Jamaica's independence. This route now rested on the five-year trial period, ending in 1963. To a degree, Jamaica's independence now depended on federal – not local – decisions on fiscal policy, trade and finance.

Isaacs kept his peace. Later in January, he departed for Canada, leading a group of twenty prominent Jamaican businessmen on a mission to increase reciprocal trade. The talks would also cover purchases that Jamaica might make from Canada, rather than the United States. The trade mission visited Toronto, Ottawa and Montreal.[23] On the same day that Isaacs left for Canada, Manley tabled a ten-year development plan in the House. It was devoted to sectors of the economy where government had a developmental role to play, paving the way for private enterprise. The plan proposed an expenditure of almost £79 million over a decade, though it detailed only the first three years. For this period, finance in excess of that provided in annual budgets would be drawn from CD&W grants and loan finance. Increasing income from bauxite buttressed the plan. Projects listed included bridges and additional road construction, acquisition of mechanical equipment, refurbishing the railway, port development, airport construction at Palisadoes and Montego Bay, new parliament buildings and other capital works. Also included were the recent advances in education. In the longer term, the projects would support a wide range of industrial activity.[24]

Though this plan was tailored to Jamaica, Manley looked to federation as a geopolitical advantage; one which would facilitate larger inter-agency loans requiring long-term government guarantees. Sherlock summarized his view: "[Manley] did not think of Jamaica going it alone, for he recognized that in a world dominated by power politics and multi-national corporations, small, heavily populated countries with limited natural resources cannot support independence and secure a reasonable standard living for their people without external aid."

From Manley's point of view, political and economic paths were converging. Colonial development and welfare projects had proceeded on a regional model; as had labour union aspirations and now those of the WIFLP.[25] Manley surmised that regional and extra-regional transactions would further Jamaica's cause and that of all the other territories. While Isaacs welcomed regional cooperation and trade, his diffidence regarding federation remained. Supported by better equipment and infrastructure, Jamaicans themselves needed to produce more – both for domestic and overseas consumption. It was this investment, on all fronts, that would bring more jobs, and allow Jamaica to repay its longer-term loans. Tourism had found a niche, while growth in manufacturing was steady, but agriculture remained an issue. The benefits of federation, in his view, would not cancel out the cost of a federal administration and parliament – providing mainly more jobs for a regional middle class. Moreover, Isaacs also may have been annoyed on learning that the Colonial Office favoured a federal development corporation over Jamaica's now well-established IDC.[26]

The federal election was scheduled for 25 March 1958, to be followed by a first parliamentary session in Chaguaramas, Trinidad.[27] Jamaica had been allocated seventeen seats; one each for its fourteen parishes and three counties. The two major parties were Manley's WIFLP and Bustamante's Democratic Labour Party of the West Indies, which was formed in May 1957. They were soon identified as the PNP-FLP and JLP-DLP. Two months prior to Manley's decision to remain in Jamaica, Bustamante had also opted to do the same. Few candidates were outstanding, and federation was barely canvassed – except in the negative by the JLP.

The election year began with a volley of comments from the JCC and JMA. Federation would bring uniform customs duties among the unit territories, as well as free trade between and beyond the territories. This would follow from the federation becoming a signatory to GATT, now inevitable if Britain joined the European Economic Community. The EEC made provisions for its members' dependent territories. However, as an independent nation, the West Indies was no longer a dependency. The federation's inclusion in GATT would mean the end of quantitative restrictions on selected imports to protect Jamaica's industries. These matters would affect jobs as much as profits.[28]

"Taxation without representation" became the JLP's rallying cry. Though Jamaica's population was more than half the federal total, the island had been assigned less than half of the Lower House seats. It was a matter of concern that the island could be readily outvoted by other territories, especially when Jamaica would be paying the largest part of federal revenue. As election day approached, the JLP distilled its message: federation meant more taxes and more unemployment. The party emphasized the cost of living and ran a scare campaign concerning GATT-imposed free trade: important industries, including garments, shoes and knitted fabrics, would be "diminished or abolished" as the result of "unfair competition from foreign goods". "Thousands of Jamaican men and women who now find gainful employment in these industries will be thrown out of work and left to starve." Voters should reject "Mr Manley and his Socialist Comrades".[29] To combat these sallies, the PNP ran on its record and avoided the subject of federation. If there was a positive theme, it concerned solidarity. "We federate or remain perpetually in economic slavery. [Federation] simply means unity, which is strength." Campaigning in sugar areas for the NWU, Michael Manley argued that the federation would give workers a chance "to link up" with comrades in the other islands.[30]

Isaacs' participation was largely confined to radio broadcasts and supporting two PNP candidates. One was Balfour Barnswell, a long-time PNP associate, and the other was Ralph Brown, a group leader and constituency secretary for Isaacs. Both were KSAC councillors. Following service in the Royal Air Force and his return to Jamaica, Brown joined the PNP and became active in the group structure of the Kingston Central constituency. He was increasingly prominent as a builder of PNP groups. Some of these became notable and even notorious, in the style of Group 69. They included Great Group Resistance, with its leaders, "Fisherman" Nelson and "Honey Boy" Hamilton. Group Determination was another founded by Brown. In the federal race, Brown stood for the Kingston parish seat and won narrowly against the JLP's George MacFarlane, also mayor of Kingston.[31] Barnswell had less luck. He stood for the county seat of Surrey in the east, where Ken Hill, who had joined the JLP, defeated him.

The 1958 federal election brought the acrimony that was now well-established at election time. A JLP supporter remarked of Brown, "Isaacs tek 'im up like rubbish heap an' throw pon us – Isaacs himself is a rubbish heap." For his part, Isaacs was drawn to fulminate against the middle class. He was charged with racist remarks when he rebuffed JLP claims that the PNP would raise the pay of household help by 50 per cent. He remarked that "those Jamaican mulatto people believe anything you tell them". They were just "too foolish", "the most gullible set of people in the country". Isaacs had wearied of the middle class, whom he now found to be self-indulgent. Two weeks earlier, he had berated hotel operators in Montego Bay: "These people in Montego Bay think themselves a little feudal republic." The House had just passed an amendment to the Hotels Aid Act, removing a number of previously tax-free items, including furniture, which was now being produced in Jamaica. Tax-exempt imports were not warranted.[32]

The WIFLP won the federal election and formed a government led by Grantley Adams. But in Jamaica, the PNP-FLP lost to the JLP-DLP. Manley attributed the loss to the JLP scare campaign on taxation and a poor turnout in rural areas, due to lack of interest in federation. He said that some voted JLP thinking that they might avoid the "carefully invented" but "imaginary burdens" of federation. The defeat was a shock to the PNP. The party had lost ground in the sugar parishes. More generally, its win in only five of the fourteen parish seats, one of which was Kingston, and its loss in all three county seats, suggested trouble in the countryside.[33]

The PNP responded. In both rural and urban constituencies, the party's group structure had weakened not only with the loss of the 4Hs, but with Isaacs and Arnett otherwise occupied. Isaacs' portfolio was a heavy one and required overseas travel. Arnett's IDC roles as the finance officer and a director were demanding. Though he remained the party's general secretary, he had withdrawn from organizational tasks. In June, Manley called in Allan Isaacs, with whom he had a long association through both the PNP and Jamaica Welfare Limited. The JWL was founded by Manley in 1937 as an extension programme for small farmers, and Allan had been a JWL educational officer since 1955, following time spent as an organizer for the Farmers' Party. A stalwart in earlier years, now he reengaged with the PNP. He became a special assistant reporting to Manley.[34] When his appointment was announced, he was already at work across the island arranging meetings between farmers and Manley. His impact was evident at the annual conference in September. The contest for second vice president between Ivan Lloyd and Allan was much closer. Allan prevailed by just six votes in the face of a strong rural presence. This is not to say that he lacked widespread support. He was nominated for his position by Manley and Nethersole, and his win reflected pockets of votes right across the island.[35]

At the 1958 annual conference, Manley addressed two major issues. One was a worldwide recession affecting Jamaica's three biggest trading partners – the United Kingdom, the United States and Canada. He noted that, after three years of growth, this recession had brought adverse effects. Exports of bauxite had been cut and workers laid off. The second issue was a federal customs union, now a priority in view of the recession. What was needed was "a policy for the whole ten islands in regard to their trade, trade among themselves, trade with the rest of the world". He continued, "We will be a third-class area of the world if we don't industrialise – and that will be our policy; and obviously if we have a bigger country for our industries, ten islands instead of one, that is a challenge to our [own] industry for efficiency, for hard work and for expansion."[36]

Manley believed firmly that ten islands "instead of one" would benefit Jamaica. Isaacs was not so sure and in fact Manley's speech pointed to a looming electoral vulnerability: crucial aspects of the federation had not been settled – free trade, a customs union and taxation – while representation was settled but problematic for Jamaica. The situation opened the government to JLP attack. Further developments made the PNP's position seem even more difficult.

For some time, Isaacs had harboured an interest in industrial products that could have widespread use in diverse industries. Varieties of glass and plastic were one, petrochemicals relevant to agriculture were another. In 1957, he began discussions with an American, Frank St Hilaire, who headed a recently formed Jamaica Oil and Chemical Company. His aim was to build a refinery in Jamaica. By mid-1958, Hilaire was seeking to secure both capital investment and oil supplies from the United States. Following a public announcement by Isaacs in June, objections were raised. One concern was that the domestic price of fuel would rise because the refinery would be producing mainly for the home market. Export prospects were limited by Trinidad, a large-scale producer with its own oil reserves. A related contention was that larger customers, including bauxite companies, could be involved in additional costs. The ministry's response was that the matter was commercial in confidence.[37]

Soon, St Hilaire turned his attention elsewhere, and Jamaica turned its attention to the Esso Corporation as a more reliable partner. The intent was to establish oil refining in Jamaica, with a consumption tax on petrol collected by government and paid for a period to Esso.[38] Although distributors were free to obtain their product elsewhere, the subsidy paid to Esso would give the refinery a price advantage, albeit for a set period. Even Isaacs was susceptible to such an arrangement, since he expected further off-shoots from the development.

Jamaica was aware that a future customs union might exclude such an agreement with Esso. Still, the company intended to invest US$5 million. Where else would the federation obtain this type of investment? In August, Isaacs went to Trinidad to speak with Manley's counterpart, Dr Eric Williams. Later, as a private individual, Williams stated that he was averse to "harmful duplication" in the federation. A *Daily Gleaner* editorial supported Isaacs. After all, Trinidad had built a fertilizer factory over Jamaica's objections. The IDC's Harold Braham had accompanied Isaacs to Trinidad and taken notes. They showed that Williams had not objected openly. In fact, discussion with Williams had been minimal. Instead, he had foisted his own Trade Minister on the pair. Back in Jamaica, Isaacs dealt with Williams' private complaint: "I do not see what the Chief Minister of Trinidad is squealing about. Jamaica takes only 11 per cent of Trinidad's petroleum output and [Trinidad] has to import crude oil to supply that 11 per cent." Morris Cargill, a DLP member of the federal parliament, was "solidly behind Mr Wills O. Isaacs". Later, the refinery project was handed to the Ministry of Development for its fuller contractual and financial specification. As the 1959 general election approached, Manley would cite it as a showpiece achievement of his government.[39]

In the context of federation politics, however, the issue remained contentious. On 8 September 1958, Prime Minister Grantley Adams raised it as an integral part of his concerns about the federal government. At a press conference in Trinidad, Adams acknowledged that he had written to Manley about the refinery plans. He said that speaking "theoretically", a unit territory should not cut across federal policy. He stated that if the federal government "felt strongly enough, we could [...] make abolition retrospective say to the start of federation". In sum, a unit territory's tax concessions to an investor could be overturned and retrieved by the federal government. In England to advise and mediate during the Notting Hill race riots, Manley was unable to respond immediately. In his place, he sent Nethersole to Trinidad to speak with Adams. Nethersole was especially vexed because he was negotiating a long-term US dollar loan. In these negotiations, the projected Jamaican refinery was being regarded as a relevant future asset. Adams' response appeared sympathetic.

Returning from a trip to Canada at the end of October, Prime Minister Adams stopped over in Jamaica. He had a private meeting with Manley and an "amicable" meeting with Manley's Cabinet. Isaacs was present, though he remained in the background and made no comment. All seemed well. However, Adams met the press just prior to his departure from Kingston. It proved an incendiary event. First, Adams raised the issue of taxation. He needed more income from the unit territories. Custom duties should be the source. And regarding Jamaica's refinery proposal, he said that his reference to retrospective legislation – to terminate an agreement – was just a "suggestion". He had made it merely to avoid future "embarrassment". The Jamaicans were not reassured. His comments amounted to a threat that, in the area of industrial development, unit governments should not act without prior federal consent.[40]

The response in Jamaica was immediate. The very next day, the *Daily Gleaner*'s headline shouted: "Adams' Talk of Income Tax and Retroactive Power of Federal Government Draws Trenchant Disagreement from Manley, JAMAICA MAY LEAVE FEDERATION." Bustamante entered the fray with a three-point policy statement on taxation, representation and protection for workers from a customs union. He called for the federal constitution to be rewritten.

On 13 November, Manley made a statement to Parliament. He noted that the government had entered federation in good faith, but now was compelled to make some undertakings to the people: first, there would be no ad hoc constitutional changes (such as that foreshadowed by Adams); second, there would be no changes to the concessions and taxes established to aid Jamaica's development; and third, the government would insist on a customs union that "preserves and encourages" development for all the unit territories. Manley then remarked that, for five years, Jamaica "did not have the right or power" to withdraw from the federation. During that period, however, the constitution must be changed. Soon to be known as the "unless clause", Manley added: "Jamaica will withdraw from Federation *unless* the Federation is so changed as to suit the special circumstances of the West Indies and the maintenance and development of the life of Jamaica and of the Unit territories themselves." Federation had become conditional.[41]

The columnists had a field day. Political Reporter, always mindful of intra-party matters, noted that during these events Isaacs had been "meticulous" in maintaining a distance. Still, events could only strengthen the body of opinion he spoke for in the PNP. From his base in Port-of-Spain, Frank Hill produced a series of acerbic articles. Following an informal talk with Adams, Hill confirmed that Adams wanted "no back seat drivers". He would not brook interference: "But Sir Grantley, never having to deal with investors in his pint-sized Barbados, and never having to come to grips with the problem of development, which his Socialist mouthings rule out of practical consideration [. . .] scoffed at Mr Manley's complaint of 'serious damage' to the Jamaican economy." Hill now saw Manley's decision for federation as a "fateful" one. There was little advantage in it for Jamaica.[42]

This was the context in which Isaacs went with Manley to the inaugural meeting of the Regional Consultative Council of the West Indies. Formed and chaired by Adams, the RCCWI would consider federal economic policy. On this occasion, the council was to discuss its constitution and receive a statement from Adams. With delegates' approval, the statement would be released to the press. The meeting was set for 12 January 1959, extending over two days. As Minister of Trade and Industry, Isaacs was the appropriate inclusion on the council, which would deal with customs union and related issues. As the minister who had instigated and sustained negotiations on the oil refinery, he was especially relevant. Moreover, since 1956, Isaacs had been active on a previous regional economic committee convened by producers and consumers of rice. The aim was to see that all the rice consumed in the Caribbean was also produced there. At the time, Jamaica, like Guyana and Trinidad, was a rice producer, and Isaacs had welcomed Guyana's Cheddi Jagan to Jamaica on more than one occasion. High hopes for rice eventually were dashed in the mid-1960s, due to US tariffs but, at the time, Jamaica was still optimistic.[43] Isaacs was also deeply involved in organizing and promoting Caribbean trade fairs. He was familiar with both the economic challenges of the region and local trade aficionados.[44] Owing to his experience, in Political Reporter's view, Isaacs was the man most likely, with Manley, to negotiate an acceptable federation. In the eyes of the public, he would be Manley's "dragon" and the one to save the PNP from "the island's anti-Federation attitude". Moreover, his presence signalled to other unit governments that Jamaica's stance had stiffened.

The two left Jamaica with a brief: they would not immediately discuss the newly submitted *Croft Report* on customs union. Neither would Jamaica agree to any constitutional change that would allow the federal government to tax unit territories prior to 1963. Further, there must be agreement that Jamaica would retain "unfettered freedom" to determine its own industrial policy. Moreover, this freedom should extend to agreements even when they involved a prior unit territory monopoly – such as oil refining.[45]

On the first day, Adams' draft constitution for the RCCWI was discussed, clause by clause. And later in the day, he introduced a draft press release on their conclusions. In the interim several issues were dealt with successfully, including the all-island rice agreement. However, discussion of Adams' two drafts raised problems. And far from being an outlier in these matters, Jamaica was supported by the other islands for the most part. Where the RCCWI's constitution was concerned, debate centred on procedure. Although unit territories could request that the council meet, and propose agenda items, the convening of meetings and provision of agendas would be the prime minister's prerogative. To add insult to injury, territories would bear the expense of their representatives' attendance. Both Isaacs and Manley attacked these clauses, which made the federal government supreme over units. When council turned from the draft constitution to the draft press release, Manley's response was brutal. He dismissed Adams' effort, proposing that it be "consigned to the wastepaper basket". The day ended on a sour note and back in Jamaica headlines celebrated Manley's and Isaacs' move against "Federal Government Supremacy".

Next day, the meeting became a hubbub of protest, led by Jamaica. Manley rose above the throng to give a detailed critique of Adams' proposed statement to the press. The statement allowed that customs union would take time. Yet it proposed that new measures inconsistent with free trade and uniform tariffs should be referred to the federal government. Consultation would follow. The statement noted the islands' wide range of investment incentives and confirmed that there would be no "arbitrary" federal interference. Still, prior to 1963, units should strive for "maximum possible uniformity".[46] These remarks were as problematic as the ones Adams had made in Jamaica. They provided no reassurance for prospective investors in Jamaica or elsewhere in the federation. The conflict between the federal and unit governments was not resolved.

Adams' response was truculent. He referred to the uproar he had caused in Kingston, suggesting that the issues had been magnified by Jamaica's approaching general election. He implied that the Jamaican delegates then and now were simply playing to the home crowd. Manley responded that Adams' words were "beyond endurance". Collecting his papers, he stood and prepared to depart. Ever mindful of his leader, Isaacs rose as well, equally enraged. He interrupted Adams to declare him "offensive, impertinent and rude". As reported in Jamaica, the two men, with "bitter thrusts", strode out of the room, followed by their advisors.[47]

Manley's eloquent speech and Isaacs' flair for performance carried the day. The dragon's paw had rescued the chestnut from the fire, for Adams had come close to the truth. Isaacs understood that the PNP's federation stance was an electoral liability. For a while at least, the walkout in Port-of-Spain neutralised the issue. This respite gave Manley, the statesman, time to reflect on federation's feasibility. It provided Isaacs, the pragmatic politician, with a more attractive electoral prospect.

In February, Political Reporter remarked that the party's intellectuals had been pushed aside. Glasspole and Isaacs, "the old warhorses", were "back in harness". At a mass meeting in February 1959, Isaacs referred to federation, vowing that the party would "fight this thing out". He would not let his leader down: "We will take the Constitution and change it to our hearts' desire and make the d____ thing work."[48]

# Chapter 10
# The Hard Work of Politics

*The truth of the matter is, of course, that Mr Isaacs takes his politics seriously. [....] He wants to win and he wants his party to win. And since he wants his rivals to lose, he goes for them hammer and tongs.*

– Political Reporter, 1960.

*Nethersole had died and Arnett came in, so that it was Arnett, Wills, Florizel [and] Alan Isaacs trying to make his run.*

– Michael Manley (on the PNP, circa 1960), 1978.[1]

A general election was due in 1960. As 1959 began, the battles that Isaacs chose to fight showed that he was mindful of electoral success. They also involved disagreements with Norman Manley. One concerned appointment to the Legislative Council, which were made formally by the governor, but on the advice of the chief minister, since federation designated as premier. Manley nominated two new members in February: Edward Hanna, now a leading manufacturer, and Harold Cahusac, general manager of WISCO and long-time manager of the Frome sugar estate. He was also described as an enlightened agriculturalist. Given Cahusac's associations, Isaacs' objection is not surprising. However, he also opposed Hanna's nomination. He knew Hanna well and had worked with him, but Isaacs' view was influenced by appearances as the election loomed. Bustamante noted the nomination of a second "giant" of sugar interests to join Robert Kirkwood on the council. A letter to the *Gleaner* asked why the government had not appointed a unionist. Was the PNP "really a working-class party as they love to boast?"[2] Post-election, Manley heeded the call, nominating to the council Thossy Kelly (NWU), alongside Hugh Shearer (BITU) for the Opposition.

Two other issues required decisions that were part of Isaacs' brief. Against Manley's wishes, he held the price of codfish down, though the Canadian government had asked for an increase. He also delayed revision of the tax incentives for hoteliers, though competition for investment was intense from both Cuba and Puerto Rico.[3] These disagreements hardly matched the tensions over federation. Isaacs' February message that the party should make "the damned thing work" played in his favour. The people's view was that he could take or leave the federation, whereas Manley was committed. Isaacs was included in Jamaica's delegation to the first inter-governmental conference on the federal constitution. Revisions were expected and he wished to be involved. Manley acceded, but kept him at bay. Some years later, Edna Manley recalled her husband's view. In a diary entry for December 1969, she cited a discussion between friends: "And the talk drifted on to Norman and why he didn't go Federal, and someone said: 'I know why he did not go; he wouldn't leave Jamaica to Wills Isaacs'." She continued, "This Norman had said himself. [Governor] Foot had thought that Jamaica would have been safe with Glasspole, but Isaacs would have split the Party [...]. And if all this had happened, as it would have done, Busta would have walked in, as he did, and taken over Jamaica and taken Jamaica out of Federation."[4]

The party and the government were already in danger over federation. And Busta would accomplish his aim. If Manley's main concern was Isaacs, he may have misjudged both issues – namely federation, and Isaacs' acumen. Isaacs knew that his support within the party, though widespread, did not include some influential comrades. On the one hand, Glasspole and Manley favoured federation, while Arnett, like Isaacs, did not. But on the other hand, Arnett and Manley were more at home with and interested in agriculture than industry. At Manley's invitation, they had now been joined by Allan Isaacs, a rural specialist and Manley's acolyte, also known to be ambitious. Federation would intertwine with these factors to complicate Isaacs' life.[5]

Politics was put aside in the face of tragedy. The sphinx, Noel Nethersole, died of a heart attack at 11 a.m. on 17 March 1959. He had been preparing budget estimates for 1959– 1960. Oxford-educated and undoubtedly one of Jamaica's elite, he was mild, approachable and admired. In government, Nethersole's finance portfolio also included taxation, banking, currency and exchange control. He was influenced by his father and John Mordecai, the senior Jamaican public servants of their generations. In office, he drew on the advice of Financial Secretary Edgerton Richardson and G. Arthur Brown. He was, in Isaacs' view, the most important person to elect to a PNP government. Just prior to his death, he had secured Jamaica's first large, long-term dollar loan on the US money market. This new source of funds, to be channelled through the DFC, was his alternative to both expensive British finance and rapacious private capital. The loss to the party and Manley was inestimable. Manley declared that he loved him like a brother and wept. In his sorrow, he was joined by both sides of the House. As the tributes flowed, Manley and Isaacs stood on either side of Nethersole's now-empty seat. In future budget debates, Nethersole's presence would be sorely missed.[6]

Vernon Arnett was plucked from the IDC to run for Nethersole's seat, St Andrew Central. Manley made it clear that Arnett would take Nethersole's place as Minister of Finance. Implicit was the view that Manley also intended Arnett to become first vice president and his new heir. At this time, Arnett was seen as an all-party man, unlike Lloyd or Isaacs, with their respective rural and urban support. His general popularity exceeded Glasspole's. Owing to the federal election defeat, a nervous PNP went to the by-election on 19 May. Arnett won comfortably from D.C. "Clem" Tavares, a lawyer and the JLP's general secretary. Buoyed by the outcome, the government decided to return to the people early. The due time for the general election was April 1960, but now the government brought the date forward to 28 July 1959.

There was reason to sacrifice up to eight months in government. Jamaica would assume internal self-government on 6 July 1959. Ministers would formally comprise "a Cabinet" for the first time, and the chief minister would become a premier in the federation. The achievement could be presented as both Jamaica's and Manley's. Moreover, a date would be set for the unit territories' review of the federal constitution two months later, in September. Why squander a celebration while waiting for the constitutional review? Its outcome was uncertain.

Jamaica's proposals for the inter-governmental conference included a rapid move to federal dominion status and thereby control of all external affairs. However, a reduction of federal government powers over unit territories was imperative. There would be no single central control of economic policy or taxation. Progress towards a customs union should be slow, and Jamaica's electoral representation should be in proportion to its population. The innovation in the PNP's proposals was that unit territories could have "closer" or "looser" relations with the federal government. This would allow an island such as Jamaica "to take care of itself". Jamaica's position was crafted as a compromise between federal and Jamaican interests.[7] Nonetheless, it was safer to go to a national election first.

Jamaica's economy seemed strong. In Parliament on 8 April, Manley reported that Jamaica's access to loan capital abroad was no long a problem. Overall, revenues for 1959– 1960 would match the previous year, which had shown a surplus. Manley extolled the Farm Development Scheme, an extension programme with continuing CD&W support. Land tax reform had commenced with pilot programmes. The new policy was that land would be taxed on its unimproved value. In conjunction with small business loans and agriculture's Revolving Credit Fund, these initiatives were designed to raise productivity among small farmers.[8] Trade, construction, tourism and manufacturing experienced "upswings". National income was rising each year and average per capita income had reached £100. The economy looked good – if unemployment, repatriated profits and the cost of incentives were kept in the background. A *Gleaner* editorial predicted "take-off" for the island.[9]

Following Manley, Isaacs gave a more sober speech, beginning with a reference to the PNP's election in 1955. He observed that agriculture was crucial to a stable economy. However, Jamaica could not depend "wholly and solely" on agriculture. "The policy of this Government is that the industrialization of Jamaica is a matter of life and death to us." As usual, he listed several successes. New goods were being produced, including domestic and commercial refrigerators, aluminium shingles and ceramics. Many factories had increased their output. Jamaica now produced a million pairs of shoes annually. In the last twelve months, the Export Industry Act had brought four more factories to Jamaica and another four were subject to negotiation. He reported on continuing efforts to place factories in rural areas. The Jamaica Public Service Company was now servicing thirty-one districts and eight housing estates with electricity. In areas that were difficult to service – St Elizabeth and Westmoreland – the government had stepped in. Frequency conversion had begun. Isaacs mentioned the showcase agreements concerning the Kingston Sheraton Hotel and the Esso Standard Oil refinery, both his initiatives. Tourism continued to expand, and 29 per cent of dollars paid out in Jamaica went directly to local workers.[10]

In this and other speeches, Isaacs also sounded a note of caution. Factories could take two years or more to negotiate, establish and start production. People who desired better living standards, he said, "need to face up to the hard facts of life that the mainspring of any progress must come from within the nation". He noted that "long range economic growth" requires stability, responsibility and financial integrity. Better and wider education was imperative. With these ingredients came the "gradual spread of benefits to a widening circle of people". He stressed that Jamaica's progress would be incremental.[11]

In July, and as the election drew near, he opened the new Montego Bay airport. Soon after, Manley set off the "inaugural blast" for the Negril roadmaking project. Just days after the election, Isaacs foreshadowed a local flour mill and a rebuilt Palisadoes airport. Along with the Harbour View housing scheme and the oil refinery, Kingston's waterfront would be transformed.[12]

A common summation of the general election in 1959 was that the PNP ran its campaign on the economy, while the JLP rallied against the federation. The parties' respective policy statements reflected these emphases. The PNP government produced a thirty-page booklet on its achievements. It was heavily oriented to the economy and social services. Advances in secondary education were underlined. The trade and industry section noted that the government had kept the price of basics down, including sugar, flour, codfish, rice and cornmeal. The JLP's advertisements were more succinct. Where industrial development was concerned, both parties were beginning to turn to a combination of local private capital investment and overseas agency loans. For electoral purposes, however, the JLP's focus was elsewhere. Its plan was to leave the federation.[13] Manley, meanwhile, made only passing mention of federation.

The PNP also introduced an equally important issue. Early in July, on behalf of the government, Isaacs announced that Jamaica was banning trade with South Africa. As a British dominion, South Africa's goods had free entry to Jamaica. The ban went against this arrangement – and the interests of some merchants. Initially, the party's stance had been prompted by a request from its National Executive Council.[14] Though two years in the making, Isaacs' statement was short and to the point: "Due to the racial policy of South Africans which is revolting to the conscience of all decent peoples throughout the world, this Government has decided to discontinue trading with that country." The Trade Board would place goods from South Africa on "specific licensing". No general import permits would be issued. The measure received widespread support.

Jamaica was the first country in the world to take this action against apartheid. Soon Ghana and Barbados followed and the movement grew.[15] The ban was also consistent with Manley's intervention in the Notting Hill riots. With these acts Manley and Isaacs had begun to define a role for Jamaica as a voice in pan-African affairs. Just six days before the election, Isaacs spoke to a large crowd at Kingston's Race Course. He called on Jamaicans to set an example in the Western Hemisphere: "There are thirty million Negroes in the United States and in our fight for full Self-Government [we] don't only seek to govern ourselves, but do it in such a way that the United States will give civil rights to the thirty million Negroes of that country, because [...] our duty is not only national, but international."

The ban had an interesting constitutional dimension. With only internal self-government, Jamaica's foreign policy was still formally dictated by Britain. As Minister of Trade, however, Isaacs was empowered to speak out on trade-related issues. It was he who censured South Africa, in terms of trade.[16] None of this should obviate the fact that neither Isaacs nor Manley nor the PNP had remarked very much, if at all, on a clash between Rastafari and police at Kingston's Coronation Market on 7 May. It would be more than a year before the government began to address the resurgence of Jamaica's own black nationalism.

The 1959 election was fought with redrawn boundaries following a new enumeration of constituencies. Isaacs' Kingston Central was divided into two – Kingston East Central and Kingston West Central. He stood for the former, while Mayor Iris King campaigned for the latter. By various additions and deletions, Isaacs' old constituency was redrawn. Where once it had been a compact downtown area, it now assumed a curious, meandering shape. These changes made both seats more marginal and, in 1967, would facilitate a further manoeuvre by the JLP.[17]

This time though, the PNP won well. The returned government was jubilant and, once the formalities were done, Glasspole and Isaacs gave vent to their feelings. Referring to unsubstantiated charges of PNP violence, Glasspole remarked, "They caan take a ticking. That the whole trouble." And Isaacs interposed, "When 'im lose he bawl yu know." Glasspole added that the early election was a "master stroke". The result seemed impressive: twenty-nine PNP seats to the JLP's sixteen in an expanded electorate – better than the 1955 result. However, the differential between votes cast for each party hardly changed and the PNP's improved performance in rural areas would not be sustained.[18]

In the person of a newly elected Ken Sterling, Isaacs received a parliamentary secretary to assist with his burgeoning portfolio.[19] Both Agriculture and Communications also received parliamentary secretaries, reflecting the workloads of their ministers. Allan Isaacs assumed the secretarial position in Agriculture. In a notable move, Manley also nominated him to the Legislative Council. Taxed by the press, Manley ascribed the new procedure to a period of constitutional transition. A formula was used: eleven and six nominations respectively for the majority and minority parties, along with four nominations reserved for the governor, who would confirm all appointments. Various restrictions were dropped. Previously, nominations had been confined mainly to ministerial positions, and could not involve unsuccessful electoral candidates.

The changes allowed the appointment of Isaacs and, for the JLP, Hugh Shearer. The former was not required in Cabinet, while the latter had lost Kingston West to the PNP. Regarding government members, Manley also stated that the premier was able to name persons "as of right". They were his personal appointments. Prior consultation, save with the governor, was not required – a view that Isaacs would struggle with.[20]

The date set for a federal inter-governmental conference to address constitutional revisions was 28 September 1959. Apart from Manley, the government delegates were Arnett, Glasspole and Isaacs. Robert Lightbourne and Donald Sangster represented the JLP. A mandate from the House on 15 September prioritized two revisions: the first concerned Jamaican seats in the Lower House, which should be "not less than half" the total of forty-five; and the second addressed limits on the power of the federal government to "interfere in the economic and industrial development of Jamaica". Three further aims were stated: to see that customs union was "not hurried"; to seek dominion status for the West Indies Federation "as soon as practicable"; and to establish an option for closer or more distant relations with the federal government. Representation was deemed to be the primary issue.

Government members of Jamaica's delegation spoke to the mandate in the course of a "crisis" debate in the House. Arnett spoke against "loose talk" about secession. Glasspole was blunt: He allowed that the reason for federation was to get international recognition. But that reason should not override "the welfare and well-being" of one and a half million Jamaicans. Isaacs was reassuring: "These demands are minimum demands and there is no compromise." Manley cautioned that the process would "take a long time". He declared that failure would involve a "historical disaster" for all concerned. This forewarning, however, re-ignited controversy. The *Gleaner* reminded him of his "unless" clause of November 1958. Having made himself open to secession, Manley could not now ignore the option.[21]

In his opening speech at the conference, Manley raised a matter which he and the party (including Isaacs) had declined to raise during the general election. He noted that while Jamaica's economic aggregates were good, distribution mattered – especially when it came to unemployment: "We have the highest level of unemployment in any country and we have vast areas of poverty hidden behind the vigorous and healthy signs of growth which meet the eye […]. We are on our own engaged in the very task [to modernise] our economy whereby material conditions will continue to overtake the increase in our population and the increase in the legitimate demands of our people."

Therefore, it was unreasonable to expect Jamaica to discard its plans and operations for a new federal machinery. "Workable solutions" must be found.[22] But all to no avail. Discussion at the conference went no further than the issue of representation. The proposal for 50 per cent of federal seats was rejected outright by Eric Williams, who marshalled the support of the smaller islands. On the second day, Manley stood to reiterate Jamaica's concerns, but Williams' interjections made him tear up his papers. As he did so, Manley quietly said that if unit territories wished, they could proceed alone. On the third day, Wills tried to force a decision on representation and failed. The Jamaicans exploded, with Manley saying, "We are not buying anything. This is our stand; this is where we stay." Isaacs followed, condemning those present. He vowed to sleep the next night at his home in Sligoville. Later, at the conference hotel, he declared, "Manley came into this thing, Jamaica came into this thing, to save you, to help you, and you are a bunch of ungrateful parasites. Me, I wouldn't have a thing to do with you or your federation." Diplomacy had withered on the vine.

A concession on the fourth day was that representation would be referred to a committee for reconsideration. A change would be made in Jamaica's favour. However, Jamaican disillusion grew. Writing from Trinidad, Political Reporter observed: "[A] new note has seeped into the Jamaica delegation's demands, and it does not appear now that there is any wish to remain in the Federation." He noted that Robert Lightbourne agreed with Isaacs, Arnett and Glasspole, the last having done a 180-degree turn on federation. Only Manley and Sangster were more restrained. Two committees resulted from the conference: one to discuss constitutional issues, including representation, and the other to discuss trade, taxation and industry concessions. Both would report in the New Year.[23]

On their return to Jamaica on 7 October, the delegation was met by PNP supporters. Questioned on the conference outcome, Manley said it had not failed altogether. Asked if Jamaica might leave the federation, Manley replied: "No. It would be a tragedy for all the islands, for all of us." Still, he would not bend, claiming that regions around the world were all forming associations: Europe, Scandinavia, Central America and the United Kingdom. The JLP released a statement on 15 October. It would not support Manley's commitment to remain in the federation.[24]

Other matters commanded Wills Isaacs' attention at the PNP's 1959 conference. The conference, held late in October, was the first one since Nethersole's death. The position of first vice president of the Party open. Following his election to Parliament and appointment to the finance portfolio, the assumption had been that Vernon Arnett also would become first vice president and thereby Manley's successor. But prior to the conference, Arnett decided to remain as PNP general secretary. When he declined to be nominated for the first vice presidency, Isaacs put himself forward. Glasspole also toyed with the idea.

However, both men became aware of a circular sent by Allan Isaacs to groups across the country. In effect, it was an electoral ticket. Allan's plan was to make Ivan Lloyd first vice president, and retain Wills as second vice president. For third vice president he would nominate the newly appointed Legislative Council member, Dr Herbert Morrison, from Montego Bay. He himself would take the fourth position, brushing aside both Seivright and Iris King. Allan Isaacs' strategy rested on the assumption that Wills and Glasspole would run against each other, thus making way for Lloyd. Rural momentum would complete the plan. However, there was reluctance among the NEC. Some believed that Lloyd avoided constituency work. Others resented Manley's patronage of Allan Isaacs. It seemed to go against Manley's studied distance from intra-party manoeuvrings. Still, Allan had worked hard for the party. With significant growth in the countryside, the number of groups island-wide had increased to twelve hundred.

Once apprised of the strategy, Isaacs and Glasspole did not oppose each other. The upshot was that Wills clearly won the top position, though Lloyd beat out Glasspole for the second vice presidency. Seivright won comfortably over Morrison and Allan Isaacs beat Iris King. Wills Isaacs and his namesake were not friends, and a tension existed between their respective responsibilities. The needs were great in both town and country. Isaacs stood in Parliament each year and reported on his portfolio. Unemployment remained too high. Still, by 1960, manufacturing and construction together accounted for 23 per cent of the labour force, a growth of close to 5 per cent since 1943. Tourism was a striking success. On the other hand, decreasing rural production had become a major issue. The JAS, and Allan, argued that farm production would increase only with guaranteed markets, both overseas and at home. Wills Isaacs and his Marketing Board resisted this proposal. This resistance came as Isaacs also rebuked shoddy manufacturing behind tariff walls. Within the PNP, these sectoral matters were becoming personal. "The battle of the Isaacses" reflected the two men's relations with their leader. While Wills and Manley sometimes disagreed, Allan seemed to have Manley's ear.[25]

As 1959 neared its end, debate on federation quickened. Bruised by JLP critique, Manley remarked that a strong federal government of the type desired by the eastern Caribbean would destroy Jamaica's economy. No Jamaican government could continue in the federation on such terms. Manley was bending now, but Bustamante wanted more. At the JLP's annual conference, he intensified his scare campaign. Trinidad's shirt, shoe and cement factories would dump their products in Jamaica, while Barbados would saturate the market with her rum. Worse, the cost of food would rise, due to federal consumption taxes. Then came an unwelcome event. For the first time, CD&W allocations to the unit territories were handled by Adams' federal government. The total grant for the federation was £9 million, extending over five years. Previously, Jamaica would have expected to receive about 35 per cent of that total. This time the grant was a mere £250,000. Jamaica had been penalized for monies as yet unspent, but committed to projects finishing in 1961. The penalty exacted by Adams contravened past practice. Bustamante demanded Manley take Jamaica out of the federation.[26]

On 8 January 1960, Manley and Arnett hastened to London to clarify Britain's stance. Met by the press, Manley said that the West Indies Federation had reached a "crisis". He stated that his government was prepared to proceed alone. The CD&W grant may have been the precipitating cause, but there was another reason for the trip. Adams and Williams were now urging the British to confirm independence by the end of 1960.[27] Manley returned to Jamaica with an assurance that if the unit territories could not agree, Jamaica might secede without prejudice. One month later, Manley tabled in the House his government's list of essential requirements for Jamaica to remain in the federation. These issues could only be resolved at an inter-governmental conference.[28]

A further federal meeting was called for 3 May in Trinidad. The two committees appointed in September were submitting reports. The parliamentary members of Jamaica's delegation were Manley, Arnett and Isaacs, and Sangster for the JLP. Isaacs had been in hospital and travelled with a private nurse.[29] Developments were positive. It seemed that Manley's tougher stance had made both the federal government and the unit territories more amenable to compromise. Back in Jamaica, Manley reported to the nation: Jamaica would receive thirty-one out of the sixty-four seats in the federal parliament, near enough to a majority vote. Where financial and economic issues were concerned, two model constitutions would be produced; one based on the Jamaican stance and one on Trinidad's. The period for the implementation of a customs union was extended from five to seven years. Regarding industrial development, the federal government would concede autonomy for units that desired it. As Prime Minister Adams floundered, the question was asked: Would Norman Manley now go to federation and guide the way to independence?[30] On 13 May, more good news came for the government: Arnett announced that a loan for £4 million floated on London's stock exchange was "oversubscribed within five minutes". The news attested to Jamaica's high credit rating.

But Bustamante marred the enthusiasm. In an open letter to Manley on 6 May, he demanded that Jamaica come out of the federation. On 30 May, he resigned as leader of the federal Democratic Labour Party, and JLP secretary Clem Tavares announced an "irrevocable" decision: It was now the JLP's policy to secede from the federation. Tavares' announcement came in conjunction with a statement that the JLP would not contest a federal by-election in St Thomas. Robert Lightbourne had resigned his federal seat, having gained one in Jamaica's Parliament. The federal vacancy provided a convenient moment for the JLP to wrest the initiative from a government growing in confidence.[31]

The announcement was made late in the evening and Manley's response came the very next morning, as he described it later:

> I want to tell you it did not take me one hour to come to that decision. When I woke up one morning and saw in the newspaper

> what Bustamante had said about Federation, I went to my cabinet meeting at 9.30 and I accepted the challenge that we will fight and we will win.[32]

In short, he made the decision at once and alone for a national referendum. It would be called to determine whether Jamaica would remain in the federation, the date to be set once the revised federal constitution was approved. When the referendum was done and Jamaica's position decided – in or out – the British would pass an Independence Act.

Mordecai notes Manley's haste. With general and parish elections behind them, the PNP had four more years in power. They could have simply faced Bustamante down. Manley also miscalculated: first, the level of support in rural areas for a pro-federal stance; and second, the time it would take to finalize the federal constitution. The referendum finally took place more than a year later, on 19 September 1961. Manley, step by step, did address the points that most troubled Isaacs. However, many changes also undermined the very idea of the federation. Meanwhile, the JLP were on constant attack.

These events forced Isaacs to pivot more. Already he had called federation a bi-partisan initiative. By March 1960, in his estimates speech, the approach was even more strategic. He began with a general observation: "If the real statesman is nothing without the support of the masses, badly led masses in times of crisis are totally powerless." He cited two recent periods of crisis in Jamaica; one marked by 1938, and the other by 1955. The period of 1938 involved a desire to overturn colonialism and gain the vote. With constitutional change in progress, the Jamaica of 1955 required development. The people wanted more, and the government was faced with the "stark reality" of creating jobs. Bustamante led the anti-colonial thrust and, by dint of personality, gave it direction. Subsequently, Manley, the "man with the plan", addressed the people's material wellbeing. Each man played his role.In his speech, Isaacs gave his usual positive report on industry and trade. He returned to history for his conclusion, referring to Napoleon, who once said that without the revolution, he would never have become a Marshal of France, and subsequently emperor. Surely this was also true of Bustamante and Norman Manley. They too were "born in the right place and at the right time". The speech was met with wild applause throughout the House and was deemed statesmanlike.[33]

Two months later, Isaacs said in a radio broadcast, "If we get the sort of federal constitution we think is good for us, and good for the West Indies, all will be well." An acceptable constitution would include: "(1) freedom to control our own development; (2) freedom from taxation; [and] (3) freedom to raise money for ourselves in the world's money markets." These may not have been his only thoughts on federation, Jamaica and the PNP. He did, however, support his leader and these three conditions became his position henceforth. Political Reporter noted his stance, but suspected that his underlying doubts, shared by colleagues, remained.

"The truth of the matter is, of course, that if Mr Manley did not believe passionately in Federation, the People's National Party would not believe in Federation. It is only Mr Manley's strong advocacy which has made it possible. [....] And the strength of his advocacy stems from the present weakness of Mr Wills O. Isaacs in his own constituency and the deals which are reported being made." Isaacs did indeed have problems in his constituency, made evident in April 1960.[34]

In his absence, a meeting of Isaacs' constituency committee had voted for his removal as chair. The person elected in his place was Ralph Brown, his former protégé. Political Reporter explained the situation with an implicit reference to Group 69 and other such entities: "His own original constituency of Central Kingston has been noted for a number of things, not least among which is the predilection of certain of its groups to violence and intrigue. But Mr Isaacs has always managed to hold a firm grip on the PNP organization in this constituency, until recently when the responsibility of high office has in fact separated him from many of his lieutenants."

The complaint was Isaacs' lack of attention to constituency matters. Some of his comrades were also annoyed that, as a minister, he refrained from allowing them to have more than their "fair slice" of the "national cake". This situation concerned in particular Marcus "Honey Boy" Hamilton. A PNP group leader in Kingston East Central, Hamilton had been elected recently to the KSAC council. The constituency committee had charged Isaacs with victimizing Honey Boy's supporters, while also failing to support his election. The anti-Isaacs campaign had both local and extra-local aspects. The latter involved some senior PNP figures acting in the interests of Allan Isaacs. Political Reporter put it bluntly: "Arrangements were made between the *ambitious* and the *disaffected* and the anti-Isaacs campaign was on and grew as others who wanted concessions from the Minister (and were refused) sought concessions elsewhere and then climbed on the anti-Isaacs bandwagon."

The account cited the following developments: group stacking, finances mysteriously boosted, new groups formed, others shifted and existing groups "fractured".[35] The journalist was circumspect but indirect evidence supports his account. The *Gleaner*'s Meetings and Services column was used by the political parties to advertise campaign gatherings. The columns show that, both before and after the council election on 1 March, Isaacs seldom appeared at Honey Boy's meetings. By contrast, Allan Isaacs was a surprisingly prominent speaker.[36] And, far from being just a local skirmish, it was also a national one. At a January conference of the JAS, President Rudolph Burke had asked Allan Isaacs, the guest speaker, to address the discord between Trade and Industry's Marketing Department and the farmers.[37] Burke suggested that his fellow member of the Legislative Council intervene at a Cabinet meeting. Burke was a minister without portfolio, but Allan had no such standing and no right to address the Cabinet, though he did have

Manley's ear. This proposal continued the argument between Wills Isaacs and the JAS concerning guaranteed markets. Wills' stance was that both manufacturers and farmers must look to their own productivity before they called on government support. When he heard of Burke's proposal to Allan, Wills expressed his disgust. His highly competent Marketing Department should not bear the blame alone for unsatisfactory levels of farm production. At best, the move was mischievous. At worst, it suggested that both men sought to undermine him.

Neither the PNP's executive committee nor the National Executive Council endorsed the constituency move. The NEC would investigate. Manley offered to intervene, but Isaacs declined his help. Instead, in the months that followed, he mustered his support in Kingston East Central, held rival meetings to those supporting Honey Boy, and replenished his grassroots contacts. Both Seivright and Glasspole fell in behind him. In September the NEC gave a ruling. The constituency motion was ruled unconstitutional and the constituency committee was dismissed. A caretaker committee would be appointed with Wills as its chair. At the NEC meeting, it was notable that Allan Isaacs objected to the finding. He proposed that the council leave the decision to Manley. The NEC, however, was unmoved.[38]

Allan Isaacs was not deterred. He continued his courting of small farmers whom, he allowed, were inefficient and under-producing on their land. However, much of this could change with an all-island water supply. More and better marketing was required and three hundred thousand houses should be built. In a Legislative Council debate on future government loans, he demanded "boldness" for the sake of Jamaica. His projected expenditures had not been endorsed by Cabinet or even the new Minister of Agriculture.[39] However, having raised the issues first in 1959, Isaacs canvassed them throughout 1960. Though known since his days in the Farmers' Party to promise much and deliver less, his advocacy brought results.[40] He approached the PNP's national conference with substantial rural support.

Following the constituency fight, a contest around the PNP's four vice presidencies was expected. Now that Manley had opted for a referendum on federation, the issue of succession loomed again. Manley had realized that if Jamaica were to remain, he must lead the federation – for its own sake, and Jamaica's. As a consequence, at the party's 1960 conference, the contest was not merely for the first vice presidency, but also for a purchase on the leadership.[41]

The most striking indication of Allan Isaacs' resolve was his invitation to Vernon Arnett to run for the third vice presidency when Dr Morrison withdrew from the contest. Arnett declined on the grounds that he would not contribute to the formation of factions. But that process had already begun with the constituency tiff, the Burke-Isaacs marketing demands, and Allan's election-like overtures to farmers. Matters escalated in November due to a series of Cabinet decisions: beef was decontrolled, and the prices of coconuts and imported milk solids raised. No further government support would be given for construction of a large grain elevator, or for rice cultivation. Wills Isaacs had a hand in all these decisions, albeit advised by the Marketing Board and the IDC. But, as Manley stressed in a statement to the press, they were Cabinet decisions, taken after lengthy discussion. They were not Isaacs' decisions alone, as implied by farm affairs columnists. Obliquely, Manley also rebuked Rudolph Burke, a Cabinet member and JAS president, who had criticized the decisions in public. Such remarks, Manley said, encouraged the view that decisions were made in terms of "Industry versus Agriculture".[42]

Allan's invitation to Arnett had confirmed his desire for a ticket. In the event, he stood for the first vice presidency and Ivan Lloyd for the second. Hanoverian councillor Roderick Francis was listed for the third, though he did not run on the day. Wills also had a ticket, relying on his allies in the recent constituency fight. While he stood for the first vice presidency, his ticket included in turn Glasspole, Seivright and Iris King, nominated for the second, third and fourth positions respectively. In a surprise move, Arnett was a late inclusion in the contest. He nominated for all four positions as a sole candidate. He said that his act, endorsed by Manley, was a protest against all factions.

By polling day, printed tickets had been distributed. For the first time, booths were constructed outside the conference hall. Manley, the sole nominee, was acclaimed as president and leader. Then the voting began. Wills Isaacs clearly won from Allan, although his vote was, for the first time, a minority one due to Arnett's participation. The tally for each of the candidates was 503 _ 451 _ 77. Effectively, Arnett split the town vote, a manoeuvre that, in the second contest, produced a narrow win for Lloyd – by twenty-six votes from Glasspole. The tally for each of these candidates was 499 _ 473 _ 43. Allan Isaacs contested both the third and fourth positions without success. Seivright and Iris King each secured more than five hundred votes. The sentiment of delegates was clear. Wills thanked his party "from the bottom of my heart". His supporters "jumped for joy all over the floor and platform, dancing and singing and waving flags". He had donned a bright floral shirt for the day. A female supporter grabbed his hand and they danced the "mashed potato", moving to the rhythms of James Brown.

The candidates shook hands with each other, as would be expected. But as the count began, Arnett joined Ivan Lloyd and Allan Isaacs. The three sat stolidly throughout the celebrations. Moreover, on the following day, Manley made a statement apparently referencing Allan Isaacs' position on the Legislative Council. He noted that a premier of the federation was appointed by the governor on the advice of MHRs. By contrast, a president or vice president of the party did not need to be an elected member of Parliament. His implication was that delegates had misunderstood the PNP's constitution, to the disadvantage of Allan Isaacs. However, it seems that the views that led the NEC to support Wills in his constituency also influenced the conference vote. In the opinion of a significant majority, Allan Isaacs was "out of order".

From this perspective, Arnett's intervention was not quite that of the all-party man. He sought to curb Isaacs' and Glasspole's strength. His move was manipulative, though undoubtedly astute. Without it, the twins might have achieved a landslide, and for town as opposed to country. Manley had approved the move, and perhaps this meant that there was something more to the war between the Isaacses. Arnett, Allan Isaacs and Manley shared an interest in small farmers who, as it happened, had not come out for the PNP in the federal election. Perhaps all three were inclined towards Allan's "bold" proposals for farmers, which entailed a major resource commitment not yet canvassed by the Cabinet. Though publicly supporting his leader, Wills Isaacs may have looked to a more immediate measure to influence the farmers: a change in the PNP's federation policies.[43]

It was with these and other matters in mind that Political Reporter named him "Politician of the Year" again. Throughout 1960, a significant number of his articles had been devoted at least in part to Isaacs. The journalist had traced the intra-party battles and Isaacs' considerable achievements. Political Reporter remarked that Wills Isaacs was not only respected as a minister at the national level, but also for his increasing role in federal affairs. The "stormy petrel" played the role of statesman as well.[44] Political Reporter's award carried a further message. It was now assumed that Manley would contest the prime ministership at the next federal election. Owing to Isaacs' support across the island, and his position as the PNP's first vice president, he had become the obvious successor.

Michael Manley's subsequent views give weight to this interpretation. He remarked that, in the PNP at this time and apart from his father, Isaacs was "quite a ways the strongest person". Moreover, there were only four "strong Federationists": Vivian

Blake and Glasspole, in addition to himself and his father. Had Manley Sr. gone to the federation, Isaacs would have succeeded him. Or would he? Isaacs' son, Vunnie, also Michael's friend, related a conversation he overheard at the time. It suggested that his father was an astute politician. Some had grown tired of Norman Manley's sometimes peremptory ways. Many did not favour the federation. They asked Isaacs to run for PNP president. His reply was a considered one: "I can oppose him, and I can beat him, you know? I have the delegates, but I'll be leader of a party without a party." Within the PNP, federation was the most immediate issue. However, as Isaacs knew, agriculture and small farmers remained an extremely serious concern and a difficult one to address. In 1960, Isaacs did his duty as first vice president and nominated Manley for president of the party.[45]

Manley's annual conference address followed these events. He suggested difficult times ahead, listing four great issues: the socio-economic question, the back-to-Africa movement, racialism, and the referendum on federation. Such was the challenge that the party re-elected in 1959 would be in trouble by 1961.

## Chapter 11

# Referendum and Electoral Defeat

*I think to this day Wills will not forget the Leader Norman Manley's decision to hold the election, which was announced while the Leader was away […]. I do not think that he was in agreement with the decision, and he was not consulted.* – Ralph Brown, 1978.[1]

For Isaacs, 1961 began with a signal event. Sensing storm clouds ahead, he went to the Holy Land, and to Rome to meet Pope John XXIII. He departed on 15 January. The trip to Israel was a state visit. Isaacs went as the guest of the Israeli government to "observe methods being used by the Jewish Republic in industrial and agricultural development". And he did. In his reports back home, Isaacs instanced a factory that assembled radios and argued that Jamaica could do the same and supply to nearby US states. At some length, he also discussed a wine-making rural cooperative of seven hundred farmers. He emphasized the scale of production and the communal organization that underpinned it. In a testing natural environment, here was success due to adequate investment, and good organization and management. He observed archly that his word might not be enough: "My Premier and some of the technical officers of his government must come to Israel and see for themselves." He remarked *inter alia* on the socialist spirit of the society; and endorsed Israel's system of compulsory youth service for two years. He had meetings with Prime Minister Ben-Gurion, and his ministers of trade, agriculture and foreign affairs. He praised the society for its productivity, nationalist commitment, and the intelligence of its leaders. At the time, Israel still appeared to Isaacs, and to many others worldwide, as a leading socialist society.[2]

Sammy Henriques, a member of a wealthy landed and commercial family, accompanied Isaacs, having paid his own way. Commercial interests may have connected the two men. Henriques was also known as a benefactor with a social conscience. Most notable among his efforts was his role in fundraising for Jamaica's first rehabilitation centre for the disabled. He facilitated the work of orthopaedic surgeon John Golding, whose initiative came in the wake of the 1954 polio epidemic.[3] Henriques helped to broker the Israel visit, while the Catholic bishop of Kingston, the Rt. Rev. John J. McEleney, assisted Isaacs in arranging an audience with the pope.

The visit was also a pilgrimage. Among many other sites, Isaacs visited the Garden of Gethsemane, the Jordan River and the Sea of Galilee. He flew to the Port of Eilat at Israel's southern tip, often identified as the point at which Moses left Egypt and crossed the Red Sea. Isaacs reported highlights in the *Sunday Gleaner*, including his visit to a synagogue where he became aware of the many youths already killed in Israel's wars. His visit to the Holy See on 7 February was brief, but no doubt restorative. The Holy Father asked him "to convey greetings to the Premier of Jamaica and all members of the Cabinet".[4]

Israel clearly influenced Isaacs. He took what he had seen and sought to apply it at home. He returned from Israel just hours after Manley returned from a federal meeting in Trinidad, where Manley witnessed the signing of a regional defence pact between the WIF and the United States. The pact allowed the United States to maintain "defence areas" in the islands.[5] Describing the march past, Manley declared it "inspiring" to hear the roar of applause as the federal flag rose beside those of other nations. To the masses, flags in Trinidad may have seemed remote. Still, Isaacs' more practical talk of Israel would have seemed equally remote. Each politician was also grappling with issues made manifest in 1959 and 1960.

Black nationalism had made a dramatic return to Jamaica in a series of clashes between Rastafarians and the state. In December 1958, Claudius Henry had established his African Reformed Church, which canvassed the prospect of a return to Africa. In 1959 came the Coronation Market melee, with its police violence against Rastafarians. Many were beaten and more than fifty arrested. John Maxwell reports that Isaacs, as acting premier, sought to make a broadcast on JBC radio enjoining the public to "round up" Rastafarians. Manley backed Maxwell's refusal to air the speech. However, in 1960, when Reynold Henry, son of Claudius, led a Castro-inspired uprising, it was Manley's turn. The manhunt centred on Sligoville, where Isaacs had his family home. During these events two soldiers were killed. The following day, Manley made a broadcast to the nation. He encouraged his listeners to report Rastafarian activity. Informants' names would not be disclosed. Manley feared that Reynold Henry, a naturalized American, had US associates. In Parliament, he remarked that both peoples deplored Henry's "vicious" activities. Subsequently, Henry and others were tried for murder and treason. He and three associates, two of them Americans, were hanged in March 1961. Claudius Henry was also tried for treason and sentenced to ten years.[6] Soon after the initial event, Manley commissioned a report on Rastafarianism, compiled by academics and others. One recommendation was a fact-finding trip to Africa, which included Rastafari delegates and various community leaders.[7] As it exercised the power of the state, the PNP government sought a way to incorporate Rastafari into their "multi-racial" society. In 1955, Adlai Stevenson had praised the society's integration. But now Jamaica looked different. The PNP's celebration of creole society seemed out of place in the face of a restless black majority and disaffected Rastafari.[8]

The events involving Reynold Henry overshadowed a further expression of black nationalism. In April 1961, barrister Millard Johnson launched the People's Political Party. He was deeply influenced by Amy Jacques Garvey (Marcus' second wife), with whom he toured Africa. His intention was to bring black nationalism into the party-political process. The party appealed to artisans, manual workers and the self-employed.[9] Candidates contested the 1962 general election, but were unsuccessful. The PPP soon petered out, but not before Vernon Arnett made a comment. He alerted comrades to the fact that the unemployed and under-employed could be attracted away from the major parties.[10]

These developments were indicative of a new "modern blackness" inspired by a society more urban and polarized, and by post-colonial movements in Africa.[11] Ideological currents addressing the state and nation were intersecting with social conditions becoming endemic. High levels of unemployment, caused initially by regional and structural change, and the impact of the Great Depression, had become a permanent feature of the island.[12] With the benefit of hindsight, Arthur Lewis remarked on the modest decline in unemployment. He noted that, in the 1950s, "the whole economy mechanized excessively" across the domains of mining, agriculture and factory production, and in offices and homes. In addition, there was an over-reliance on foreign capital due to limited domestic savings. The IDC was now carrying substantial bad debt, mostly incurred when factories failed. Finally, these brakes on industrialization included the slow pace of change in agriculture. Despite more available finance and changes to the tax regime, growth was limited. Agricultural and food-based products still comprised only a small proportion of manufactured and processed goods.[13] The government had worked hard, but it was vulnerable on the economic front. In turn, it became vulnerable to new political currents expressed in terms of pan-African dispossession. The PNP government was also distracted by issues surrounding the federation.

Arnett's budget for 1961–62 contained two major innovations. The ministry of Housing and Social Welfare would be split in two to create a Ministry of Welfare and Culture, and a Ministry of Housing. The latter reflected the fact that housing construction had become a major part of the economy, although little so far catered to the masses.[14] The marrying of welfare and culture showed that Rastafarian and other protests had captured the government's attention. Provisions regarding youth would not be far behind.

The second innovation concerned job creation and involved revamping an age-old measure. Beyond the outlays for development, Arnett announced £2.25 million invested in "special projects"; a "crash programme" as the *Gleaner* termed it. The projects included labour on roads and irrigation, swamp reclamation and the expansion of established works, such as the Sandy Gully drainage scheme. Another set involved low-income houses for purchase; and finally, work that responded to "dislocations and rehabilitation". Arnett instanced Vere and its Monymusk sugar factory, where mechanization had caused unemployment. In protest, men and women had burned the cane. The search for forward-looking projects that employed unskilled labour echoed the KSAC council of the mid-1940s. At the time, the council's cry was for development, not relief. Some of Arnett's proposals, however, were thinly veiled relief. The government's dilemmas may have seemed familiar to Seivright, Glasspole and Isaacs.[15]

Soon after Arnett's speech, Manley toured Kingston Pen, where dire poverty prevailed. He knew the conditions were "unbelievably bad", but wished to view them again in the context of government planning. Afterwards he remarked, "You see a man and his wife and seven children, ranging in ages from 10 to a baby in arms, living in a little tattoo with a cardboard roof, sleeping on the earth on a crocus bag, nine human souls living in an area seven ft long by six ft wide and six ft high. I am glad that we are now determined to bend all our resources to tackle this great and urgent problem."[16]

The response to these efforts was not what the PNP expected. The JLP portrayed the budget as a rushed response to unrest by a government that had lost the people's trust. This loss was attributed to federation and inadequate expenditure. Clem Tavares, elected to the House in 1959, chided Manley for only just discovering the plight of the people. He proposed a national housing project for all poor people, rather than Arnett's "stop-gap" measures. He maintained that the estimates reflected panic, "It is fear, fear!" he claimed.

To deflect the critics, Manley raised the danger of Reynold Henry's communist leanings. The JLP should not encourage those who would undermine society. Robert Lightbourne, now a member of the Opposition, turned the tables on Manley. He noted that Jamaica's only communists were foolish academics and political failures: "I submit that our people are not Communists." He remarked that, if a growing number wished to rid themselves of the current government, this was due to their discontent, and rightly so. Jamaica faced "racial hatred" fomented from below and, "Above that, what do you see? Desperation, cynicism, apprehension." Lightbourne's more substantive remarks concerned Jamaican productivity and the cost of living. Yet he provided no alternative plan.[17]

Isaacs' contribution to the debate came later than usual, more than a week after Arnett's speech. He had been hosting a trade mission from the United States and was busy with the follow-up. In his speech, he aired some problems. A prominent one was the government's always difficult relations with the JPSC. The company's electrification of rural areas was too slow. Ruefully, he said that "in every progressive country in the world electricity is publicly owned", listing liberal, democratic and republican societies. Tavares taunted him. Why not mention socialist countries? Weren't they progressive too? Isaacs also announced that, in future, the IDC would seek private sector cooperation to build more factory space for rent. On its own, the government could not afford it. He raised a further challenge. The United States had reneged on an agreement to purchase Jamaican sugar to the value of £1.25 million. It appeared that the order had gone to Cuba, whose sugar cost less. Isaacs' speech involved a lengthy preamble. He echoed John F. Kennedy's inauguration speech, remarking that young Jamaicans studying abroad should ask what they could do for their nation. He also had Israel in mind. Isaacs was now falling ill periodically, exhausted by trade and industry, and federation. For the first time, his speech was a weary one.[18]

A few days later, in the Legislative Council, Edward Seaga continued the attack. In a long speech, he detailed many issues concerning cost-cutting, priorities and waste, and some constant JLP demands, among them guaranteed markets and prices for agricultural products. He began with the observation that the annual budget focused on aggregate figures, whereas distribution was equally important. Manley had said as much in Trinidad. Such a practice, Seaga continued, disguised the fact that, with limited taxation on savings, wealth was growing among the fortunate, "the rich becoming richer and the poor becoming poorer". To demonstrate, he chose £300 as a dividing line between incomes and showed, using taxation records, that the gap between those above and below the line – the "haves" and the "have-nots" – was increasing. He added that unrest as a result of the gap was now being expressed in terms of race.

Manley replied in the House and foreshadowed a Ministry Paper to rebut Seaga's claims. Others in the Legislative Council, including Kirkwood, David Coore and Abe Issa, criticized Seaga's simplified sums. Still, the haves and the have-nots trope, used by the JLP as early as 1943, was compelling. More telling still, Seaga had aired this critique a year before, to little effect. This time it had widespread impact.[19]

These domestic events preceded two decisive conferences for the federation; an inter-governmental meeting in Port-of-Spain, followed by a final London conference on the federal constitution. The London conference would review and endorse the Port-of-Spain decisions. The first conference was scheduled for 1 May 1961 and the second for 31 May. Jamaica's referendum would be held soon after. Its decision to leave or remain in the federation had to be determined before a West Indies Act of independence could be passed in the United Kingdom. The meeting in Port-of-Spain was the PNP government's last chance to reach agreements on the issues that mattered most.

The team was once again Manley, Arnett, Glasspole and Wills, with a plethora of support staff. Ministerial advisors on trade and finance were at the forefront. Manley left Jamaica somewhat demoralized, given the conflict unfolding at home. Nonetheless, the delegation came home triumphant. Their central points had been addressed: increased electoral representation; no federal interference in Jamaica's industrialization; no federal claims on income tax; and, finally, a customs union phased in gradually over nine years. In addition, the decision was made that, for the purposes of central banking, the federation would divide into two regions – each with a bank, one in Jamaica, the other in Trinidad. Seasoned now and with much to lose, the Jamaican delegation had argued the issues with determination. The conference extended over twelve days. Following the return of other delegates, Manley came back to be met by a hostile JLP crowd, led by Tavares, Lightbourne and Seaga. The smaller PNP crowd, with placards reading "Welcome Manley" and "Jamaica Delegation Done It Again", was overwhelmed by a hostile Opposition with their own placards, which declared "Federation Means Slavery" and "Free Us from Other Islands".[20]

The turnaround time between one conference and the next was short. However, the PNP held a party meeting, attended by group delegates, to endorse the constitutional amendments. The mood was upbeat. Manley declared that the referendum would soon be held, and he would win. He was given strong support by others, including Isaacs, Vivian Blake and Leacroft Robinson. On the same day, Manley made a broadcast to the nation, telling the people that "we must learn to think a little in terms of History" and with a view to a future "beyond our day and generation". With Arnett and Glasspole to follow one day later, Manley flew to London on 26 May. Isaacs stayed at home to deputise for the premier. In London, Jamaica obtained "an almost permanent power of veto" over issues of income tax and development. Manley declared himself "very happy". The delegation returned in June to a triumphal welcome at Palisadoes Airport. A civic reception was planned at Victoria Pier, where Manley would be greeted by the mayor. But a massive JLP crowd gathered, voicing their hostility towards the approaching motorcade, throwing bottles, stones and pieces of wood. The police called on Isaacs to disperse the crowd, and reached for teargas, which Manley countermanded. Isaacs was outraged that the premier had been subject to such abuse.[21]

As the referendum loomed, Isaacs was everywhere, supporting his government. In March 1961, at a JMA luncheon, he surveyed world events. With apartheid and the United Nations in mind, he advocated for a federation "so that we can make our voice heard at the councils of the world with sanity". He especially noted the suffering of Africans in the Congo. With the major powers spending so much on defence, where was the aid for Africa? He challenged the JMA, asking, "What are you all doing to bring peace into the world? What contribution are you making?" He suggested that they should play roles beyond simply "making money". Troubled by the financial implications, he had found a role for the federation in international affairs and, increasingly, he also referred to the island and its people. Later in the year, he addressed the alumni association at Excelsior High School, putting forward the view that the recent upsurge in race-based protests required a response from all who cared about Jamaica. He enjoined those present to embrace technical training and employment in agriculture for the society's sake; and to put aside arrogance. Turning again to international affairs, he suggested that, were the premier to lead the federation, he would speak out for peace and against the Cold War. Manley would urge the richer nations to support the development of poorer ones; better than "wasting millions of pounds on armaments".[22]

In Parliament, Isaacs introduced a bill to amend the Small Business Loan Act. It addressed the procedural costs to small business applying for loans from the government. He remarked that, apart from the loan itself, his government had the right and obligation to assist small people on the threshold of economic independence. The JLP's response was to demand – again – guaranteed prices and markets for most agricultural goods, as well as an end to all duties on codfish, rice and frozen meat. Given the importance of duties to government revenue, and the cost of subsidies in agriculture, these demands lacked feasibility.

Nonetheless, they kept coming as the JLP confronted Isaacs with the PNP's 1955 promises. News that the United States had made a full-crop purchase of Jamaican sugar for 1961 brought some joy to the hard-pressed minister. And, in June, he opened a new head office of the Royal Bank of Canada on Duke Street. Isaacs underlined the close cooperation between the government and the bank, and took the opportunity to answer critics. Referring to tense relations with JPSC regarding electrification, he asserted the government's right to oversee central utilities and decide what "best safeguards the public interest". Hostility to government regulation, he observed, flowed from "the top to the bottom"; a jab at not only the capitalist class, but the JLP.[23]

With Manley away in London, Isaacs deputized at the queen's birthday parade. Two weeks later, accompanied by the chair of Sheraton International, he broke ground for the Sheraton-Kingston Hotel in New Kingston. Operational profits would come to the government, and after construction, hotel conventions would bring other avenues for employment. He was off the island briefly, in the second week of July, when he travelled with Arnett to Trinidad. They and other federal delegates were meeting with the UK Under-Secretary of State. He updated them on British negotiations with the EEC. Back home in the same month, Isaacs spoke at another ground-breaking ceremony. The US-based Johnson and Johnson, a manufacturer of toilet products, with extensive markets in the US, was building a factory in Kingston. It would operate "for the benefit of Jamaica, its economy and the working-class peoples of the country". Four days later, at Coronation Market, Isaacs joined Norman and Michael Manley, and Dudley Thompson at a warm-up rally for the referendum. Isaacs' activities were interrupted by ill-health at the end of July. Returning to duty on 14 August, he attended the opening of Jamaica Pottery Limited in St Catherine. The British investment totalled £500,000. Isaacs remarked on the project's benefits: "Its size, the employment it will provide for many hundreds of people, the fact that it signals yet another breakthrough in the use of Jamaica's own resources, the contribution it will make to our economy – are all reasons for us to be glad on this occasion." In August, another factory producing garments for export with a floor space of 37,000 square feet was opened on Homestead Road, just west of Spanish Town.[24]

Norman Manley had already announced that Referendum Day would be 19 September 1961. The campaign would last around six weeks. He also offered himself for election to the federal parliament were the Jamaican people to vote for federation. Predictably, the JLP accused Isaacs of supporting federation only in order to be free of his leader. However, another rationale was that his efforts were just as much concerned with avoiding a general election if the referendum failed. The government must not lose.[25] The PNP produced a pamphlet, *Federation Facts*, which was circulated widely during the campaign. The pamphlet's list of the federation's roles was remarkably distant from the people. The roles included defence and the maintenance of a customs union, along with administration of the University College. Issues of development, industry and employment were placed under "foreign affairs". Emphasis was placed on loans and lending agencies, including the World Bank, with its adjunct, the International Monetary Fund. Manley's commitment to the federation was founded on his belief in a West Indian people. It was also based on the view that Jamaica's economy required loan capital from these agencies for development. However, a pamphlet focused on finance and major institutions was not one to sway constituents – either rural or urban. The PNP campaign relied on Manley himself to bring the voters out. He was portrayed as "Mr Federation", nurturing the "Tree of Life" for both Jamaica and the region.

On 13 September, as Manley returned to Kingston from an arduous rural campaign, Isaacs left for the countryside. He declared that he was confident of retaining the support of his own constituency. Starting at Lucea in Hanover, he campaigned every day and night throughout the island's west, as he and Arnett did in earlier days. On 19 September 1961, the PNP lost. It was not so much a swing to the JLP, but a further failure to win the rural vote.[26] The defeat was dispiriting, especially for Manley, who had physically supported the crusade. Isaacs' campaigning had been interrupted by ill health – not only his own, but his daughter's. Following his return to work in August, the toddler developed a life-threatening reaction to a smallpox vaccine. She was cloistered with her mother at Sligoville and then hospitalized in Kingston, but not even a specialist sent by the vaccine's US makers could assist. The little girl became very ill. Still, these matters were put on hold during the campaign. Then, by chartered plane – she was too contagious for a regular flight – the child was flown to Denver for treatment. She survived, and following the referendum, the family's trials were front-page news.[27]

Manley's government moved quickly. On 20 September, the Cabinet met and planned a delegation to London to depart within two weeks. Along with the Secretary of State for the Colonies, the delegation would explore the steps to be taken for secession from the federation and for Jamaica's independence.[28] Subsequently, a committee would be assembled to draw up Jamaica's independence constitution. Once done, the constitution would be taken to London by a bipartisan delegation. On their return, and when a new date for independence had been set, an election would be held. despite Manley's quick response, opinion writers of all persuasions were calling for an immediate election. The JLP opened its campaign one week after the referendum with "the big guns firing" for freedom from a PNP government.

While these matters unfolded, Isaacs returned to everyday business. The IDC issued public statements regarding new export figures that reflected an improved balance of visible trade. Three major manufacturers were expanding, and the Caribbean Cement Company was about to commence further capital works. Isaacs also met in Kingston with all the overseas managers of the Jamaica Tourist Board. He remarked that Jamaica's decision to "go it alone" meant that they now had additional burdens. Still, "[T]he Jamaica which you have been serving in the past remains the same Jamaica that you [will serve] in the future." He wished them well for "a bumper winter season", expected to be the largest yet. With returns from tourism increasing and industrial output climbing, Isaacs sought to relieve the despondency.[29]

His own post-referendum mood can be gauged by a notable parliamentary speech. Tavares had moved a censure motion in the House, demanding an immediate general election. The motion was lost and brought a mighty response from Manley's lieutenants in his defence. Isaacs reminded the House that between 1947 and 1954, Bustamante's government had voted in favour of every resolution regarding federation. When the PNP came to power in 1955, the situation was such that, on the voting, Manley might have gone to Trinidad and pushed the federation through. But then came the JLP's change of mind, a cynical about-face. Referring to the referendum, Isaacs said, "I think that the Premier of Jamaica, Mr Manley, did something that will go down into the history of this country and generations will [...] praise him for the democratic principles and actions he took in the matter."

Still, Isaacs added that if he had been the leader, he would not have asked the JLP again. He would have assumed their agreement and proceeded to federate. "But Mr Manley was a democrat." At this point, Isaacs' voice shook. He referred to the fact that, during the campaign, some had attacked his absence due to illness, both his daughter's and his own. He gave the House a pledge:

> When I came back from Israel this year, I brought with me a rosary made out of the olive trees in the Garden of Gethsemane and I say it once a week so that I shall keep well during the forthcoming General Elections. I won't be sick again. I promise you I won't be sick. I promise you this time I won't be sick because I am not going to let them forget how they misled the people.

Isaacs referred to a claim made during the referendum. Seaga and Tavares had said that Britain would ban Jamaican immigrants once an entire federation was involved. Two weeks later, the ban was confirmed in any case.[30]

As the censure debate continued, Jamaica's Constitutional Committee was nominated and convened. It involved two bipartisan committees: one comprised of representatives from the House, and one of nominees from the Legislative Council. They came together in joint meetings, the first of which was called on 31 October 1961. Manley chaired these meetings, intent on producing a constitution as quickly as possible. Initially, a proposal by Leslie Ashenheim that private property rights be included in the Constitution's Bill of Rights was rejected by both Manley and Bustamante. Ashenheim came back with a personal guarantee that foreign corporations would retaliate were rights regarding property excluded from the bill. Manley and the others capitulated. Isaacs was among them.[31] However, he did object to the procedures proposed by Manley for public submissions. Manley had said there was "no time to fool around" and Glasspole opposed the publication of joint meeting minutes. Several colleagues sided with Isaacs, who spoke out. He noted that the constitution was, "[…] the people's business. It doesn't concern us alone; it concerns the people too. Give them three weeks to get together. They are not as well organised as we are. With all the legal knowledge […] three weeks would be the shortest possible time."

The committee chair ruled in the negative and Isaacs had his dissent recorded.[32] On 18 January 1962, Jamaica's constitution was published in full across eight pages in the *Daily Gleaner.* In its preamble, the document listed members of the MHR and MLC committees, chaired respectively by Manley and Douglas Fletcher. The two chairs aside, Isaacs headed the list of parliamentarians, a notable achievement for one who began his adult life solely with pupil-teacher qualifications.

Jamaica's delegation to London left the island late in January 1962. It was a bipartisan group that included Manley, Arnett, Lloyd and Glasspole for the PNP, and Sangster, Lightbourne and Tavares for the JLP. Lloyd was there due to his length of parliamentary service and his standing with rural constituents. Independently, Bustamante also flew to London, and once again, Isaacs remained in charge of affairs at home. On 5 February, it was reported in Jamaica that the independence agreement with Britain would be signed three days later. The following day it was confirmed that Jamaica's Independence Day would be 6 August 1962. A general election would be held on "some date" in April.[33]

The PNP responded to its referendum defeat at the 1961 annual conference. In his address, Manley presented the first significant reformulation of policy since 1955. It was both a response to black nationalism, at least in spirit, and an edging back towards socialism.

The four main proposals were: first, a system of national service for youth of school-leaving age to build a bridge between town and country, and between colour shades. Manley acknowledged that the idea had come from Israel, and Isaacs. Second, the party proposed mandated use of parcels of land left idle on holdings of one hundred acres or more. The land would be put to productive use and leased for this purpose by the government, with the option to purchase. Third, and relevant to the concerns of both Wills and Allan Isaacs, the government would guarantee a fair price for some farm exports.[34] Other provisions were designed to appeal to farmers and the urban poor: an island-wide water scheme – both for irrigation and household purposes, and a largescale project to provide soundly built houses for the masses. The number to be built was not stipulated, but almost certainly not three hundred thousand. Finally, there would be a Fair Labour Code that would include provisions for non-discrimination in employment, unemployment benefits, redundancy, workers' compensation, and stipulations on wages, hours and vacations. Subsequently, roads and electric light and power were added to the platform: "Every community of five hundred people can be provided with electricity in a ten-year plan on a reasonable economic basis." Two days later, and drawing on Arnett's budget, substantial relief and Christmas work was announced.[35] Another organizational response, with a general election expected within months, was to call a "no contest" regarding the leadership positions. The current occupants – Manley, Isaacs, Lloyd, Seivright and King – would be retained, and Manley spoke vociferously against factionalism.

As the PNP braced itself for the coming election, a marked thematic difference between the parties emerged. If both now recognised that race was intersecting with class to fuel popular protest, their responses were different. Manley, the internationalist, spoke of the "mission" to Africa and Rastafarianism. He described how his government was reaching out to numerous societies beyond Great Britain. By contrast, the JLP trained its eyes on "the haves and the have-nots". In Seaga's words: "We live in a divided Jamaica in which elements inter-digitate but never blend."The local and concrete vied with a broader view of Jamaica's circumstances. On his return from the London conference in February, Manley announced an election date at the Palisadoes Airport.[36] Having lost the referendum, the PNP government also lost the general election on 10 April 1962.

Isaacs played a significant role in the campaign. The matter which took most of his time was electrification. The JPSC had given notice of a five-year construction programme to cost £10 million. Early in 1962, it became clear that the company intended to raise the £10 million by increasing rates across Jamaica. On 6 March, Isaacs issued a statement that the company would not be allowed to "impose [its] will on the country". In turn, the JPSC claimed that it had no choice. Isaacs called on Arnett to release details of the extensive assistance already provided by the government to the company. On 27 March, Isaacs published a proclamation blocking rate increases for thirteen of the thirty licences held by JPSC, over which the government had some discretion. That evening, the company advised that its other licences would be subject to the rate rise, effective 1 April. With Manley campaigning in the countryside, Isaacs called an emergency Cabinet meeting. He was armed with a draft bill empowering him to limit all prices charged for electricity. With Cabinet's approval, the bill was rushed through the House without one dissenting vote. The measure also gained approval in the Legislative Council. Isaacs noted that the company's franchise was due for renegotiation on 20 June 1962. He remarked that Neville Ashenheim, an avid supporter of the JLP, had recently joined JPSC's board. He implied that the scheduling of the rate rise was in part political. On that very day, the *Daily Gleaner* carried an advertisement for Manley, the "man with the plan" who would bring "light and power" to the people of Jamaica. A few days later, Leandro published a cartoon depicting "Isaacs O" delivering a knockout blow to JPSC.[37]

**ONE . . . TWO!**

**Isaacs' one-two knockout blow to JPSC (1962).**
© The Gleaner Company (Media) Limited.

Isaacs also attended to some constituency matters. In Trelawny, men had lost their jobs due to the advent of bulk-loading of sugar at Ocho Rios and the termination of Rio Bueno as a sugar port. Deputations had come to him led by both candidates. Various possibilities for alternative employment were discussed, including deep-sea fishing, irrigation and rice farming, swamp drainage, and the siting of a factory at Falmouth. Isaacs undertook to mobilise the ADC, IDC and the Minister of Agriculture. It was telling that delegates came to him first.[38] Matters in Montego Bay were different. The seat was held by A.G.S. "Father" Coombs, the legendary labour leader. A move was made to have Dr Herbert Morrison contest the seat in place of Coombs, whose powers were diminishing. Manley had favoured the change. He attended a meeting in Montego Bay chaired by Howard Cooke, also a prospective candidate. Members of Coombs' large following confronted Manley and protested. He became angry and accused them of treating him "like a little child". Isaacs took the matter in hand, seeking to reassure Coombs and ease Cooke into the seat. Neither seat was won by the PNP, but not for lack of effort on Isaacs' part.[39]

Back in Kingston, he was active in his own constituency and in the west, supporting both Dudley Thompson and Iris King. Thompson had dubbed himself "The Burning Spear" after Jomo Kenyatta.[40] Sadly, it did not help against Seaga, though Isaacs may have warmed to the image of a burning spear in the side of the British. In a final Sunday rally at Coronation Market with Manley and Thompson, Isaacs proposed that Jamaica could be a paradise, but not overnight. More hard work was required. He had also told a trade mission from the United Kingdom that Jamaica could be a "paradise on earth" – without unemployment.[41] The remark presaged electoral defeat.

The JLP gained twenty-six seats to the PNP's nineteen. In greater Kingston, two seats were lost in the west. Isaacs and Glasspole were both returned, but with reduced majorities. The actual popular vote was 50.04 per cent (JLP) to 48.6 per cent (PNP). The remaining votes were for Millard Johnson's PPP and independent candidates. The JLP now had twice undone the PNP with scare campaigns. Redbaiting, though not dead, had been replaced by a federation bogey. Both played on fears of instability and increasing unemployment. For all the PNP's efforts, they had not been able to do enough.

Manley's dismay after this defeat is well known, eloquently described in his own words, as cited by Phillip Sherlock. Several other writers of note have testified to his grief.[42] Isaacs' dismay was also great, though barely remarked upon. He was hospitalized soon after the election, and two months later took extended sick leave from the House. In a public statement he confirmed that he would attend the opening of Parliament on Independence Day. A few also knew that he had withdrawn from his party's executive. In fact, he resigned as first vice president late in April, though this fact became known widely only in August. He participated in the June estimates debate, providing a detailed and critical speech defending his government's performance. The speech was also notable for its statements on JPSC, in which he advised Robert Lightbourne to temper his enthusiasm for a new franchise agreement.[43] Two years later, when the PNP in Opposition determined on a policy of nationalization for JPSC, it was with Isaacs' blessing. He understood well the damage the private corporation had done. Its slow progress with conversion and electrification was a brake on industrialization, especially in rural areas.

His withdrawal had an immediate cause. Following the election, Manley, as Opposition Leader, made his nominations to the Legislative Council. Some of them were PNP stalwarts, including Vivian Blake, Rudolph Burke and Douglas Fletcher. Others were candidates for the House who had been unsuccessful in the general election, Cooke and Thompson. Two were less predictable: Michael Manley, his son, and a family friend, Dr Ken McNeill. Manley had made it clear in 1959 that, as premier, such nominations were his "as of right". Now, as Leader of the Opposition, it was equally so. Isaacs first learned of the appointments when they appeared in the press.[44] Manley had good reason to nominate his son. Hugh Shearer, who was BITU vice president, was a member of the Legislative Council and a good performer. He had also produced something of a JLP electoral triumph in Cornwall. He needed to be countered in the Upper House, and Manley Jr. was vice president of the NWU. Though Thossy Kelly was also in the Legislative Council, unionist Ken Sterling along with Allan Isaacs had gone to the Lower House. Finally, Norman's defeats had made him more determined than ever to promote youth in the party.

However, in Isaacs' eyes, these nominations were consistent with other acts. As first vice president of the party, he had not been consulted personally on the referendum, or on the decision to go to an election, or on the date of the general election. When Manley was absent, Isaacs officiated as the "most senior Minister on the island" and increasingly was described as the "Deputy Premier" – but not by Manley. The latter followed his own dictates, while relying on the grassroots politician at election time. Months later, Political Reporter walked his way through these events and reported Isaacs' view on the latest issue: that though it was Manley's right to nominate to the Legislative Council, "the PNP was a democratic party democratically organised [and] the Party's First Vice President had a right to be consulted by the President".[45]

Isaacs' disillusionment had more to it, possibly implied in Edna Manley's reflection on the leadership. Isaacs could not support federation as a panacea for Jamaica's economy. Neither could he, in good conscience, offer farmers a blanket security from market fluctuations. While loyal to the party and its leader, and prepared to bend, Isaacs kept his views and expressed them, albeit often behind closed doors. He was also canny when it came to politics; prepared to grasp the moment, pick a way through debate, and use theatre when required. A brilliant orator and legal negotiator on the people's behalf, Manley had only muted respect for the skills involved in politicking – which he was inclined to equate with "trickery". Another Hanoverian, Bustamante, had these skills in abundance.[46]

# SECTION V
# THE LATER YEARS

## Chapter 12

# A Policy Conundrum

*What are the facts as we see them around us? We see a vast and growing army of unemployed people; we see young men and young women all over the land with no sort of hope of life in their own country [...]. I say bluntly we must find new roads or we are doomed to failure.*

– Norman Manley, 1964.

*[T]he challenge of the democratic world is to find a way in which you can build that dynamic for social change and avoid totalitarian methods and preserve democracy. [....] Comrades, if we could do that, the contribution we would have made to civilization and the modern world would be immense.* – Norman Manley, 1966.[1]

With these two remarks Manley captured the "stern realities" of Jamaican political life. Out of power, the PNP acknowledged that its impact on unemployment had not been as it wished. Gone was the promise of one hundred and fifty thousand jobs in ten years. Manley set the sum achieved at closer to thirty thousand.[2] Along with the double-edged sword of emigration – which lowered the number of job seekers, but leaked talent overseas – the PNP had reduced unemployment, but not sufficiently. The cost of foreign private capital had proved deleterious to both the economy and the people.

Faced with this reality, the PNP changed its narrative. In March 1960, Isaacs periodised Jamaica's advance. From 1938 to 1954, with Bustamante ascendant, the society had been engaged in the struggle to end colonialism. From 1955, with Manley in the lead, the government would embark on a planned economy. Manley now claimed independence as the party's first achievement. He and his party had done the heavy lifting. Economic reform was the second major task, not yet achieved. Excising the efforts of the 1950s, the time frame was shifted to the 1960s. Ironically, Manley's statement on unemployment in 1964 resembled Isaacs' statement in 1949. Both men spoke of the human destruction wrought by long-term unemployment. And both projected a vision of Jamaica that was more caring, responsible and equal as a nation. However, this time around, the focus turned to agriculture. Although industrialization was not put aside, if significant employment was to come from processing primary produce – Jamaica's own resources – rural productivity had to increase. Different measures were required to stanch the flow of people from the land.

A Policy Advisory Committee was appointed to devise a new platform. The policies would be considered at the annual conference in 1964. The committee was chaired by David Coore, a barrister and a former member of the Legislative Council. Other members were Vernon Arnett, Allan Isaacs, Ivan Lloyd, Dudley Thompson and Michael Manley. Arnett and Isaacs were the radicals. Lloyd had grown conservative. Both Thompson and Manley had moderate positions, centred on issues of race and class. At this time Manley, the unionist, was a social democratic bent on reconciling labour and capital. A youthful P.J. Patterson, not yet thirty years old, was *ex officio* to the committee. Word had it that Coore, Arnett, Allan Isaacs and Patterson did most of the work.[3]

In September 1962, Isaacs remained on the sidelines and saw Glasspole elected to party office at last – as first vice president. Manley expressed his appreciation for Isaacs' contribution to the "early fighting days", and for his service in a "vital" ministry. Isaacs, he said, was "a real rabble-rouser". The acknowledgement was modest. Political Reporter wrote that Glasspole was now Manley's appointed successor. Conference delegates had "made manifest what had all along been the real position". Isaacs out, Glasspole in, and the focus turned to rural production.[4]

Still, Isaacs remained active in Parliament. Being in Opposition set him free to criticize aspects of investment and trade about which he had been circumspect in government. He continued his attack on the JPSC, which was preparing to sign a new agreement for twenty-five years with the JLP government: "The Jamaica Public Service Company has brought nothing into this country and over the years it has taken a fortune out of the country. They have milched the people of this country with their electricity rates." He also made remarks on transnational trade. The government was exploring the prospect of an associate status with the European Common Market, were Britain to join. Isaacs warned against Eurocentric trade and advised alternatives: a common market with Latin America, Canada or the African states. He remarked of England that "If she has to turn her back on the Commonwealth to protect British interest, she will have no qualms of conscience to do so, and we will be in trouble." A few months later, Isaacs elaborated, foreshadowing a North-South dialogue, and raising the matter of race:

> [E]ven the infant knows that the whole European Common Market is ultimately a political union between the countries of Europe for the purpose of protecting their industries [...]. Everybody who has any sense knows that it is for the purpose of keeping the industry of Europe so that the newly independent nations will continue to supply raw materials while there will be markets for those who manufacture. [....] Those are the hard, hard facts, and there is the Minister thinking about joining these territories and becoming an overseas associated territory. It is not but six months ago that we did not want to federate with the black people in the West Indies and you want now to federate with the French [...] who have had a bad colonial record in Algiers; federate with Belgium who has had a bad record in the Congo; [and] federate with the German nation who a couple of years ago [...] agreed with Hitler that a black man was not human.

Isaacs' conclusion was mocking. The new Trade Minister, just five months in power, presumed to tell the House about "the free flow of goods".[5]

In April 1963, Isaacs made a frank admission regarding foreign investment in manufacturing. He cited Lightbourne's figures on incentives granted under the various industry laws.[6] He noted, however, that the minister had failed to mention any new factories established as ongoing concerns. It was a brief but savage attack on the pursuit of foreign private capital and the costs incurred for limited gains. Isaacs' scepticism may have increased due to an investigation instigated by the new government in 1962. It concerned a Canadian-based firm, Jamaica Woolens, which had closed down, leaving liabilities in Jamaica amounting to £600,000, including a substantial amount owed to the IDC. The Canadian company had misled the Jamaicans in a last-ditch effort to continuc trading. Isaacs and the IDC board were exonerated of dishonesty. However, the IDC was seen to have bungled the initiative and been imprudent. Following Nethersole's death in 1959, Arnett resigned from the board to become an electoral candidate. And Moses Matalon resigned soon after, leaving a memo regarding problems with the firm. The issues were not righted, however. It seems likely that Arnett – as well as Isaacs – was influenced by this experience. Responding as well to attacks on his final budget, Arnett now became more vocal on the left.[7]

At the party's 1963 annual conference, Norman Manley called on the youth to devote themselves to the country and to the PNP. He reviewed the party's history in the context of other liberation movements in India, Africa, and also among "brothers and sisters in the USA". Among the party's achievements, Manley cited the two-party system, "vital to the peace and security and freedom of our people". He remarked, "Other places may get along very well with one [party]. We don't live that way."[8] This focus on an anti-colonial struggle culminating in a democratic order was consistent with Isaacs' views and, it seems, with those of the delegates. Isaacs was nominated for the first vice presidency just one day before the conference began. He did not campaign, yet he defeated Glasspole by thirty-six votes. Ivan Lloyd supported him and became the second vice president. Vivian Blake was voted to the third position and Dudley Thompson to the fourth. Allan Isaacs lost his position and Arnett did not offer himself for nomination.

Still, radical critique was abroad in the person of John Maxwell, a broadcaster, journalist and now editor of *Public Opinion.* In 1964 he ran a series of editorials that criticised the party, and its leadership. In March, he wrote, referring to the Puerto Rican model of industrialization:

> The real weakness of our position is that we cannot pull ourselves up by our own bootstraps if we are content to allow the real economic power to remain concentrated in the hands of the few, while the masses scrabble for the crumbs under the table. The lesson of the conventional development process [...] is that it cannot change the economic, social and political relations between the mass of the people and the inheritors of economic power. The gap steadily widens [...]. Unless the people take possession of the economic power of the state, they will never be in control of their fate.[9]

His views accorded with the Young Socialist League, a group formed in 1962 and loosely associated with the party, though not formally affiliated. The YSL was committed to forging a democratic socialist course; specifically, a course which gave comprehensive control of the economy to government. Some of its members were influenced by the New World Group, founded by Trinidadian economist Lloyd Best. He coined the term 'plantation dependency' to capture the essence of the economies of the Caribbean's former slave colonies, work which George Beckford used as a touchstone. More generally, the stance drew on a range of sources – from Andre Gunder Frank on underdevelopment, to writings on imperialism and colonialism by Lenin and Stalin. Overall, the perspective was in marked contrast to that of Arthur Lewis who, in 1964, published a series of articles in the *Daily Gleaner.* Again, he addressed Jamaica's unemployment, which he described as the highest in the world. He advised a return to labour-intensive industry in both agriculture and manufacturing. Jamaica's pound should be devalued to limit imports and help exports. His solutions were market-based and once more endorsed by the *Gleaner.*[10]

Notable members of the YSL were Robert (Bobbie) Hill, a nephew of Ken and Frank, and Trevor Munroe. Both were activists who also became respected scholars. Other members included Dennis Daly and Hugh Small, two young barristers later to have stellar careers. Small was a legal advisor to the NWU. There was clear engagement between Arnett and Allan Isaacs, and this group. Still, although the YSL may have influenced policy, it did not determine it.[11]

The PNP's Policy Advisory Committee published its proposals in two stages towards the end of 1964. Agricultural policy, the clearest and most systematic statement, was published in the *Gleaner* on 12 September 1964. The rest of the draft – including statements on industry, finance and taxation, industrial relations, trade and foreign affairs, and also education and social services – followed in November. The whole would be discussed at the conference on the weekend of 14–15 November. As described by the press, the November meeting ended in "bedlam". Vivian Blake had moved that the conference declare in principle support for the draft, but postpone the final vote, pending further discussion. With time constraints on the day, a further conference in the New Year had already been scheduled. As Blake spoke, a group rushed the stage, fearing the proposals would be dismissed. Some maintain that Wills Isaacs drew a pistol in response, while Arnett declared that Blake and his like were "traitors to the cause of the down-trodden masses". Those who still opposed fundamental change should "get out of the party". Manley brought the meeting to order and, some days later, announced that the "democratic socialism debate" would resume in February or March.[12]

Proposals for agriculture in the draft included a National Land Authority that would oversee a process of land redistribution and an intensification of agriculture, leading to greater productivity. A cap was placed on land ownership. No individual, person or company would be able to own more than five hundred acres at one time. Owners of properties over one hundred acres would be required to develop their idle land in accordance with government requirements. Failure to do so would mean that the government could exercise the right to acquire the land in accordance with procedures stipulated in the constitution. Moreover, land kept idle for speculative purposes would attract a tax on capital gains. Curbs would be placed on foreign ownership. More generally, the aim was to stabilize life on the land and make land available for all who wished to farm it. Integrated production, storage and marketing was envisaged for a wide range of crops alternative to sugar. The policy on land also hearkened to a different voice: the nineteenth-century principle of cooperative society, popularised by Marx, of "each according to his ability, to each according to his need".

The substantive proposals for industry, finance and trade took their starting point from agriculture. The expected major increase in farm productivity would facilitate a radical expansion of rural factories established to "store, package and process surplus production". More generally, industry would become labour intensive and geared first and foremost to a "mass" domestic market. Nationalization was proposed, both of central services and significant private sector monopolies. This included electricity, telephone services, bus transportation and the wharves, sugar factories, Caribbean Cement and the Bybrook milk condensery. Along with the issue of nationalization came a declaration that the commanding heights of the economy would be publicly owned. Bauxite contracts would be honoured but, on their expiry, renegotiated. Effectively, the proposal was that the state would own or control minerals and large tracts of erstwhile estate land.

Regarding finance, a National Commercial Bank would be established to channel capital investment into priority areas. Foreign capital for this purpose would come mainly from international agencies and direct government-to-government aid. Other sources of aid would be explored. Foreign private investment could be arranged but at the government's behest and only for specific tasks. A range of taxes on income and wealth were deemed "acceptable and right". They included, death duties, a "super surtax" on incomes over £5,000, a surtax on company profits, a luxury tax and capital gains tax. Income derived from the purchase of national development bonds would receive tax relief. The proposals for education followed lines already established, but with a greater emphasis on regional vocational education in trades and agriculture. In trade and foreign affairs, the draft recommended non-alignment and greater identification with the "have not" nations of Africa, Latin Amcrica and Asia. Trade should be with any nation "prepared to buy on reasonable terms", including the countries of Eastern Europe.[13]

The November statement included both the proposals for industry and finance, and a summary of the policies pertaining to agriculture. The document was also studded with didactic statements giving it a particular cast: that change must be soon and absolute. It asserted that industrial development to date had been based on "two doctrines", namely private enterprise and foreign investment. It continued, "These doctrines are unsound and their unsoundness has been amply established in the record of development." Furthermore, it continued, "Private enterprise has no formal responsibility for the public good and is accountable to no authority but itself." A capitalist "simply wants to make money". The conclusion was that the government "must bear the full responsibility for industrialization" and "determine very extensively what is produced and how it is produced". The suggestion was that private property be confined to personal property, including "a man's home and landholdings within the permitted acreage and all those things that belong to people for their own use". The broad-brush statement implied the end of income from rent, and the surveillance of private lives. "[O]wnership and control of property in relation to activities that are not fundamental or basic to the purposes and welfare of the state may be permitted but within the limits [...] determined by the State itself."

In conjunction with others, this remark suggested a command economy. In turn, this implication brought another statement into question: "[...] we do not regard 'state capitalism' in which an impersonal monolithic Government is simply substituted for the private capitalist, as a preferable form of society." But what sort of society was preferred? Norman Manley's response, on 15 November, was immediate and passionate. He said, "except in a totalitarian regime", a landholding system takes time to change "without creating chaos". He added that chaos was "the only thing every totalitarian regime has created for itself". Continuing, Manley said that the PNP's socialism was committed to a two-party system and not to "Castro-type" revolution. Furthermore, the party's policies did not involve "repelling private property". He noted that Africa was a region where "private capital was being used for development along with increased public ownership".[14] The statements that brought this riposte should be distinguished from the document's long preamble, which detailed the condition of the people. It remains today a notable account of the effects of plantation dependency. However, given Jamaica's two-party system and the geopolitics of the region, its didacticism was seen as problematic by many. The document was revised and pared down. The new version, endorsed by both the executive committee and the NEC, was published in the *Gleaner* on 23 January 1965. A further conference was held on 13 and 14 February where the redraft was accepted. Manley promoted it aggressively as a socialist policy.

The notable changes included the absence of a frontal attack on private capital and capitalists as a class. The economy would be "mixed". Rather than public ownership, a diverse category of "common ownership and control" was introduced. It included nationalized enterprises, government-backed cooperative schemes in both industry and agriculture, and statutory boards concerned with "investment, prices and production quotas" for industry groups. Each enterprise would manage its daily operations. A policy for the nationalization of central services and strategic industry monopolies remained. However, the process was now avowedly gradual, starting with JPSC only. Of the new taxes initially proposed, the luxury tax on affluent housing and the super surtax on incomes over £5,000 were dropped. The changes were a sop to both the middle-class and merchant capitalists. A commitment was made to review Jamaica's incentives legislation. Overall, however, the new position on tax was a disturbing backdown.

Retentions included a National Land Authority and a National Commercial Bank. The cap on landholding remained, as did the government's right to acquire idle land. Where foreign capital was concerned, the emphasis remained on aid and loans to government. It acknowledged: "The financing of a Socialist Development Programme is a difficult matter, one which needs considerable study but we are convinced it can be done." Direct control of banking and currency transfers was endorsed. The participation of foreign and domestic private enterprise in the economy received mild encouragement, though the primacy of the government was still underlined. Plans for industry adhered to this framework:

> The need for industrialization is an accepted fact of policy for Jamaica. Until now, however, the main brunt of the work of industrialization has been left to local and foreign capitalist investment [...]. Foreign ownership has increased and the gap between the few at the top and the many at the bottom has become much greater.
>
> As industrialization is indispensable to full employment, full production, and to meet all the needs of the people, we believe that responsibility for industrialization must rest with the Government. It should be a policy of Government to initiate industrial enterprises,

having regard to the basic needs of our people for products and employment.

Labour-intensive production of low-cost goods for home consumption would be introduced across all sectors. Moreover, the government should use existing legal powers to ensure that "wholesale importation and distribution of the basic necessities of life be brought under control to reduce the cost of living".

The statement also contained innovation. It noted that the garment industry "already keeps more persons employed than any other trades or manufacturing activity in Jamaica". However, as Isaacs knew, merchants and local producers preferred to import more expensive textiles to clothe the middle class, rather than support domestic production for the masses. The revised statement proposed a foreign-domestic partnership to produce in Jamaica a variety of textiles that would satisfy the range of middle- and working-class demands. The venture would bring technology transfer and, possibly, overseas outlets for surplus production. On his 1961 trip to Israel, Isaacs had seen large collectives linked to processing and marketing cooperatives backed by the government. Later that year, Norman Manley himself visited Israel and invited Israeli advisors to visit Jamaica.[15]

Notwithstanding the modifications, the party overall supported the new policies and deemed them socialist.[16] The *Daily Gleaner* showed its usual outrage, noting that the document justified extensive interference with citizens' rights. Also, the policy was contrary to human nature: people do not work for the State, or even for their fellow man; but for their own self-interest.[17]

Undoubtedly, a politics revolved around the policy statement. The YSL had doubled down and written a rebuttal, which suggests that neither Arnett nor Allan Isaacs was entirely in tune with the group.[18] Except for his remarks on 15 November, Manley stepped back from the policy debate. He had set the framework. Between Manley's intervention and the revised policy statement,

Glasspole and then Isaacs stepped forward. Each wrote to Manley individually. In his letter, Glasspole demanded that the PNP take action against the YSL. Hugh Small, a member, had been involved in accusations of financial mismanagement against the NWU, and against Michael Manley in particular. Initially, the charges came in a circular issued by an Unemployed Workers' Council. In solidarity, Small also censured the NWU's executive. Michael spoke of "treachery" in the ranks and his father spoke of "scandalous" lies. The UWC was accused of being communist and Small was summarily dismissed from the NWU.[19] These matters hardly concerned Isaacs, who was mostly in the countryside at the time. For one week before and three weeks after the November conference, he was in charge of a by-election campaign. It involved the seat of Portland East, left vacant by the death of the JLP's Ken Jones. For all four weeks he was resident in Portland.[20] He did, however, write to Norman Manley.

In his letter, he stated that he could not support policy that excluded the private ownership of land and other assets. The original policy statement did not do this, though it did suggest that private property should be limited to personal possessions and the means required for a basic livelihood. Isaacs objected to this and to the land cap policy, though he made no public statement. In executive committee meetings in January 1965, he threatened to resign if the first draft was not amended.[21] This stance was supported by others, including Glasspole, Iris King, Ken McNeill and Keble Munn. Uncharacteristically, Glasspole threatened twice to walk out of meetings. In the event, the land cap remained, though the stance on private capital became less aggressive. Following passage of the second draft on 14 February, elections for president and the vice presidents of the party were held on 28 February. Manley was returned unopposed. In order, Isaacs, Glasspole, David Coore and Munn were elected to the vice presidencies. All were centrist politicians. Isaacs and Glasspole beat their opponents, Vernon

Arnett and Allan Isaacs respectively, by modest margins. Later still, on 11 April, there were elections for eleven members of the NEC. Although the left of the party did well on both the NEC and the executive committee, they still fell short of majorities.[22]

Members of the party clearly reacted against the Young Socialist League and its party associates. YSL was becoming active among sugar workers. In the form of a Workers' Liberation Union, they sought to challenge the party-union strength of both the JLP-BITU and PNP-NWU. This activity would hardly have endeared them to either Norman or Michael Manley. In late 1965, both Hugh Small and fellow barrister Dennis Daley, who had been a member of the NEC, were brought before a PNP disciplinary committee. Although Arnett represented Daley, both men were expelled from the party.[23] Consistent with the 1952 split, a common view makes Isaacs responsible; to some, a veritable Svengali of the right and the main obstacle to change.[24] At most, he was one among a small number prepared to speak up. The more radical appraisal of his powers should be assessed in terms of three other factors: Norman Manley's own position; YSL manoeuvring; and the interests of Michael Manley.

Norman's passionate statements on the first policy draft were an instance of his consistent support for Westminster procedures. He may also have considered his experience with Jamaica Welfare. Among small farmers who owned their plots, a cooperative spirit came with a dogged independence. Despite Jamaica's very unequal distribution of good land, the complex of small holdings linked by an internal marketing system stood as an enduring response, post-emancipation, to the plantation's oppressive regime. Radical change would have meant decommissioning the poorest land, and the redeployment of labour as better land became available. As Manley implied, rapid change would mean an autocratic approach, while incremental change required measures that could avoid capital flight, more unemployment and social unrest. Land reform was a pressing need, but linked with an attack on private property, it would not receive widespread support. Manley had wrestled with this conundrum since the 1940s. He did not need Isaacs and others to hold him to the task.[25]

On the YSL: following Hugh Small's dismissal from the NWU, Obika Gray reports that the group produced a pamphlet titled *The Desperate Men!* It drew parallels between the YSL and the 4Hs. It asserted that "Wills Isaacs and his friends" intended to displace Norman Manley. Deliberately, the pamphlet exaggerated Manley's closeness to the YSL, and the support in the party for Isaacs. The aim was to strengthen left support, though the manoeuvre showed little regard for Isaacs' realism. By the mid-1960s, his desire for the leadership had flagged due to age, ill health and family circumstances. For his account of YSL manoeuvring, Gray cites Dennis Daley, an exemplary source.[26] And where Michael Manley was concerned, given both his union and party executive roles, it seems unlikely that he would have supported the YSL. Already, he was seen as well-placed to succeed his father.[27]

The left critique aimed in a singular fashion at Isaacs is also inconsistent with the policy positions he took at the time. These included selective nationalization, not only of utilities but also of industry monopolies, such as cement; a mixed economy; reduced use of foreign private capital; government regulation of the production and price of staples; and, where appropriate, the use of cooperatives. He also supported the PNP's institutional changes regarding banking and other forms of finance. He was an early critic of merchants and their easy profits. This is not to say that Isaacs was anything other than a moderate who had moved to the left in his early days, and to the right as he aged. In September 1965, as acting leader at the PNP's twenty-seventh anniversary dinner, he spoke on land redistribution and sugar.

> Sugar lies across the road of social change and social improvement in Jamaica. Sugar it was which brought our society into being and from

> the very beginning it has meant feudal land ownerships, foreign capital, slavery and indentured labour.
>
> The Jamaican social structure evolved from the feudal ownership of sugar lands and the mass organization that sugar needed to reap large profits for its feudal owners and its hold on the Jamaican society remains as firm today as it was in the past days of official slavery.
>
> To get down to the grass roots of social change in Jamaica we have got to change production methods of sugar, and if necessary, to replace sugar with other crops more amenable to social change and to the social improvement of the masses of the Jamaican people.
>
> And aside from the need to eradicate the plantation economy and the plantation social structure in our country, where a few families hold thousands of our people in virtual slavery, there is sound economic reason for planning the obsolescence of sugar as early as possible.

Isaacs detailed the cultivation of beet sugar in Europe, and of sugar cane production around the world. He declared cane sugar to be "a sick international commodity". For that reason, as much as others, he concluded, "It is in truth the enemy within our midst. And we intend to radically change, and where we cannot change, root out a system which has condemned generations of Jamaicans to a lifetime of penury and hopelessness." In November, the Parliament debated legislation to further assist the sugar industry. Arnett and Allan Isaacs led the Opposition in the clash. The PNP proposed "reorganization of the structure of the sugar industry", "non-capitalistic" or cooperative ownership, and elimination of the estate system. Isaacs' contribution was to find market sense in his party's position.[28]

In 1966, attention turned to policy again and to a platform for an election in the coming year. The redrafted statement of 1965 was modified and shortened. It was called *A Plan for Action* and published in October.[29] It promised immediate crash programmes and a clampdown on luxury expenditure – both public and private. In agriculture, the policy was that, on all properties of fifty acres or more, idle land would be deployed for employment. New compensation legislation would be passed to enable the use of idle land, and to implement the caps on land ownership "previously announced". With these words, the 500-acre cap was alluded to rather than stated. Explicitly, the platform confirmed the re-organization of sugar and the development of new export crops. Incentives to raise productivity were at the forefront. National cooperative farms were also foreshadowed for the purposes of production, research, experiment and training. Missing from the platform, however, was an explicit legislative programme for rural reform.

Where industry was concerned, growth would be almost entirely in terms of publicly financed infrastructural work to encourage intensified domestic production in agriculture and manufacturing. Industrial space would be made available, not to private foreign investors, but rather to Jamaican craftsmen and tradesmen sharing materials and other resources. A statutory commission would undertake the transfer of utilities and monopolies to public ownership. These would include electricity, cement, textiles, telephones, condensing, wharves and city transport. It was proposed that the tourist industry could become a "national asset" by "devising means to keep more of the dollar in Jamaica". Further commitments in keeping with the times were made: additions to human rights legislation, further to those already guaranteed in the constitution, to protect citizens from the state. The document was progressive, but also reflected the constraints imposed by regional politics, the island's limited resources, and Jamaica's institutional framework.

The rise of serious violence in West Kingston and lower St Andrew meant that the PNP's mid-1960s policy debate was just one factor in the upcoming elections. Issues of deprivation came to the fore and elements of the university-based left turned their attention to post-colonial critique that focused on race and repression. Black Power advocates incensed the JLP government, notably Walter Rodney, the Guyanese academic who was refused re-entry to Jamaica in 1968 on account of his politics. Support for him aligned sections of the middle class with vocal sections of the poor and black, who were deemed by the state to be threats to law and order, requiring suppression.[30]

These events had been foreshadowed in 1960 by Reynold Henry and his allies. Now, other Rastafarians were also involved. Among them, standing with the PNP, were residents of the squatter community, Back-o-Wall, in the proximity of Kingston Pen, between the waterfront and Spanish Town Road. Beginning in 1963 and culminating in 1966, twenty-three hundred huts were removed without compensation to make way for the Tivoli Gardens housing scheme and industrial development. Edward Seaga used his position as Minister of Development and Welfare to provide not only jobs, but housing as well for his supporters.[31] Warring between beneficiaries and those displaced caused a state of emergency to be proclaimed on 3 October 1966. It followed violence described by the JLP as located in the "Western section of the Corporate Area, involving shooting of citizens, bombing of premises, throwing of dynamite and other acts of violence both against private citizens and the police".[32] Seaga and Norman Manley defended their followers and questioned each other's integrity.

This violence reached a peak as the 1967 general election approached. Its roots, however, were two decades old. Bustamante's biographer, George Eaton, notes the partisan patronage of the 1940s dispensed by the Chief as KSAC mayor, and Leader of the House. In addition, following the 1944 election, Busta had sat cheek-by-jowl with the governor on the Executive Council. The council prepared the government's budget, gave consent for money bills, and was the body with whom the governor consulted when exercising his reserve powers. Nominees to this body from the Parliament were drawn from the government side. It was this duality of roles, as first among equals in the KSAC council, but as superordinate in government, that heightened Bustamante's power – especially with only five PNP members comprising the Opposition.[33]

In response to apparently partisan decisions, PNP councillors, with Isaacs in the lead, had engaged in debate, led marches, and seen pitched battles occurring across both West and Central Kingston. Not only were resources unequally distributed. In street corner fights, police were reluctant to act against government supporters. In response, Isaacs and Ken Hill formed Group 69. The unit, and others, could be mobilised defensively, and also used to harry opponents in and beyond the Corporate Area. In the 1940s, Arnett had dispensed such groups to Gordon Town on Isaacs' request. Amanda Sives remarks that, initially, major clashes took place at street meetings and union picket lines. The 1950s saw the emergence of "loosely organised political gangs", as well as violence in and between communities. Activists among residents included party partisans, the materially deprived and petty criminals. Any of these groups could involve some Rastafarians. A new development was 'rude bwoy' gangs with their distinctive urban style. Some were also engaged in crime.[34]

Still, the advent of the garrison as a bounded and defended territorial phenomenon came with specific developments in the 1960s. One was the Tivoli Gardens scheme, which located in one place the benefits dispensed to just one party. Another was the rapid expansion of an international ganja trade in which both overseas and domestic capital was involved. Mexican supplies to the United States had been disrupted by a crackdown at the border. Jamaica became an alternative route in a multi-million-dollar business, bringing cash and guns to Kingston. Sives concludes that without the history of party-union clientelism, beginning in the 1940s, the stage would not have been set for garrisons. However, she continues, "The allocation of housing and employment in the most deprived section of the Corporate Area to only one group of supporters was guaranteed to [...] deepen the level and intensity of violence" – made lethal by the spread of firearms.[35]

Underlying all these developments was greater Kingston's unemployment. British anti-immigration laws in 1962 blocked Jamaican migration to a large extent. Unemployment climbed again as the JLP continued with policies that were less and less effective against widespread joblessness. By the mid-1960s, neither political party had proven to be equal to the task.

The JLP government looked for further ways to gain a grip on greater Kingston. Stretching across the border between Kingston and St Andrew, the urban area had been a stronghold for the PNP since 1943. Even when the 1944 general election was lost, representation on the KSAC council allowed the PNP to build an effective Opposition. Moreover, Jamaica's increasing population had provided the PNP with an opportunity in 1959. It gave the government ample justification to expand the number of seats island-wide, from thirty-two to forty-five. The number in Kingston-St Andrew rose from six to ten, with one seat added in Kingston, and three in St Andrew. In Kingston, Isaacs' seat was divided into Kingston West-Central and Kingston East-Central.[36] In 1959, Iris King was elected to West-Central and Isaacs to East-Central. In 1962, even in defeat, the PNP still won eight of the ten Kingston-St. Andrew seats. Though Seaga triumphed in West Kingston, the JLP's determination was to undo further the PNP's urban ascendancy.

PNP strength in the KSAC council was matched in parochial councils across the island. Council boards resided in towns and, irrespective of parish-wide loyalties, towns leaned to the PNP. Local elections and by-elections were used to criticize the central government. It was no surprise when – close on the heels of the Tivoli development – the KSAC and parish elections, due in 1964, were postponed. Instead, the government appointed a UN advisor to examine the relationship between central and local government. In addition, review commissions were to assess respectively, the KSAC council and the Portland parish council. The terms of reference were wide and also retrospective to 1960: to report on negligence, dishonesty and so forth across the full range of council duties. Predictably, in June 1964, the JLP government dissolved the KSAC council. In its absence, two commissioners were appointed by the government to administer the council's affairs. This arrangement remained in place until the general election had passed. The Portland council was dissolved as well, and permission for protest marches was refused. Parish elections took place in June 1966. Island-wide, the JLP won the popular vote and a slim majority of parish seats – their best performance ever.[37] At the PNP's 1966 conference in October, Norman Manley spoke of the situation:

> This Government has pursued victimization to a level where it has become the bed of corruption. It does not matter what public funds are voted for, whether it is for work or it is for housing or even the establishment of trade schools [...]. Wherever it is the Government sees to it that no one benefits but people who are active members of their party. They have undermined the authority of all the boards in Jamaica, all the statutory corporations. They have even undermined the authority of the Parish Council.[38]

The JLP government also adopted new procedures for voter registration, which amounted to voter suppression. Previously, an enumeration of the population had also produced voter registration lists. Now, registration became a separate process. Mobile units were provided by the government. Voters would be fingerprinted and receive an identity card. For certain "prescribed" areas where, purportedly, fraud was common, a photo ID was required as well. Most prescribed areas were in Kingston and St Andrew. Voter registration declined. While the decline in other parishes was 27.4 per cent, in Kingston and St Andrew it was 43.3 per cent. In the 1967 election, almost ninety-five thousand fewer voters registered in these two parishes than in 1962. It seems likely the new procedure deterred mostly the poor and less educated, and PNP supporters.[39]

A further measure involved the manipulation of constituency boundaries. These matters were reviewed periodically by the Delimitation Committee of the House of Representatives. The Chief Electoral Officer provided maps and figures; but the politicians, however, made the decisions. Committee members were drawn equally from the government and the Opposition. In the case of deadlocks, the government-appointed chair had a casting vote. This previously informal procedure was stipulated in the 1962 constitution. Both parties endorsed the procedure. Now, with population growth, various boundaries could be reconsidered, including those of seats in Kingston.[40]

An initial decision that Kingston retain four seats had been made with the JLP's Donald Sangster supporting the PNP position. Politicians on both sides were fearful of further violence in the city if the boundaries were redrawn. At a subsequent meeting, Vernon Arnett reversed his stance. He was prepared to lose a Kingston seat to gain a rural one. Arnett assumed that the reduction to three seats would be made by absorbing Iris King's West-Central seat into Kingston West. Dudley Thompson had lost narrowly to Seaga in 1962 and hoped to win in 1967. Arnett thought that King's erstwhile supporters could give Thompson the victory. He was mistaken. The reduction to three seats was made, not by redrawing the boundary between Kingston West and Kingston West-Central, but rather by redrawing the Kingston East and East-Central one. Constituents from Isaacs' Kingston East-Central were absorbed into Glasspole's Kingston East – with its surfeit of PNP votes. Kingston West and the new Kingston Central both became more difficult seats for the PNP. Arnett fell ill and Isaacs, with Glasspole at his shoulder, sought to reverse the loss, but to no avail. The government used its casting vote to confirm its changes. Other consequential changes were made in St Andrew. Though Arnett described his own seat as "easy" in 1965, he would lose it in 1967.[41]

Predatory slum clearance and clientelism; enfeebled local government; voter suppression and redrawn constituency boundaries – all became tools for the JLP. Furthermore, the PNP's informal polling showed that the new Kingston Central seat was definitely in danger. The party decided that Isaacs should step aside. When he made room for Iris King, Isaacs shifted from his downtown bastion to areas further north and east. At sixty-five, it was too much for him to contest a seat that now excluded the same votes he had courted successfully in 1959 and 1962. Michael Manley resigned from the Legislative Council and stepped forward as the new Lower House candidate for Kingston Central.[42]

In the New Year, with just three weeks' notice, an election was called for 21 February. In Bustamante's absence (due to illness), Donald Sangster, as acting prime minister, made the call. The Chief would remain head of the JLP and the BITU. However, he was not nominated for the election and it was assumed that, were the JLP to win, Sangster would become prime minister. And so it was.

There was little time for policy debate or for securing the PNP's message in the countryside. There was violence aplenty, although the candidates in the four relevant constituencies – St Andrew South and Southwest, and Kingston West and Central – signed a statement advocating peace. Two weeks later, soldiers and police were patrolling roadblocks to deter gangs armed with 7.62 combat rifles and sub-machine guns. Sightings were reported of a Ferret armoured car with firearms mounted.[43] In the campaign's final days, each party published lurid advertisements regarding the violence of the other. The PNP featured Clem Tavares, whom even Bustamante had termed a hooligan. In turn, Seaga claimed that slum clearance and the advent of Tivoli were a matter of protection for his supporters from Group 69, "the first garrison". Ire on both sides was marked such that, in his first campaign, Michael Manley proclaimed PNP refugees from the west as "my garrison".[44]

When the votes were counted, Seaga retained Kingston West. Michael won Kingston Central by a margin of forty-three votes.[45] In 1962, the JLP had won just two of ten seats in Kingston-St Andrew, while in 1967 it won five of eleven seats. Isaacs worked hard in St Ann North East. His winning margin was 984 votes. Island-wide, the JLP's winning vote barely exceeded the slim margin of 1962 and its majority in the House increased by just one seat. This ostensibly steady state had been secured by the Delimitation Committee. The addition of eight constituencies had brought the PNP just one additional seat. The JLP gained seven. The new yet old conundrum remained: how to return the PNP to power with a mandate for significant change.

# Chapter 13
# Generational Change

*Nobody knew [...] we were fighting an election in 1972 for a world that was going to disappear one year later. The world wasn't the same again and it never will be. Nobody predicted this.*
– Michael Manley, 1978.[1]

In May 1967, Isaacs was at work in his constituency, opening a postal agency in affable style, expressing his goodwill towards the visiting Minister of Communications and towards the new prime minister. Hugh Shearer had been elected by his party, following the untimely death of Sangster. Long-time friends since KSAC council days, he and Shearer shared an interest in foreign affairs.[2] Like Isaacs, Shearer had come from a modest background – albeit under Bustamante's wing. Making those present his friends, Isaacs requested more postal agencies for St Ann. He also spoke of roads, and remarked on lax unionism that had left men and women in St Ann working for a pittance. Addressing the minister, he said,

> I had hoped, sir, that after twenty-nine years in politics, I would have matured into a statesman, but it is clearly evident that now that I have come to St Ann and seen what is happening here, I will once again have to be a militant politician and a rabble-rousing politician as I have been in days gone by: for I am not going to sit and tolerate these things where extremes of riches and poverty exist in the parish of St Ann.[3]

Just a few days later at the PNP's annual conference, his comrades deemed him past his prime. The election for the vice presidencies took the form of a single vote. The four nominees with the most votes would be made vice presidents of equal rank. There would be no designated deputy to Norman Manley; rather, a rotation of roles. Isaacs did not attend the conference, although he was nominated. In a field of eleven, neither he nor Glasspole was successful, although their votes were not the lowest. Glasspole, with 141, scored better than Isaacs, who received just ninety-three. The four successful candidates were, in order: Michael Manley, David Coore, Vivian Blake and Dudley Thompson – a centrist assemblage.[4]

Isaacs focused on the interests of St Ann and, in Parliament, shadowed Trade and Industry. In February 1968, Minister Lightbourne tabled legislation to increase incentives for foreign investment in companies producing for export in Kingston and the parishes. There were now forty-four such factories in Jamaica, which employed around seven thousand workers. He proposed that tax relief be made available for up to ten years and that tax holidays for foreign factories in rural areas extend to fifteen years. This was more than twice the inducement allowed by the former minister. Isaacs protested. Although some concessions were required, surely not of this magnitude. "If we continue [...] enlarging these incentives as we go along, one day we will find that we do not own our country." Already "too many concessions to foreign capitalists" had been made. Unmoved by Isaacs' concerns, Lightbourne endorsed export manufacture as the main means to expand rural employment. He noted that the keenest competition for investors was in the sphere of export industry. Edwin Allen (JLP) remarked, "Local capital won't do it and foreign capital is not interested" – unless the rewards were great. Isaacs knew this all too well.[5]

In November 1968, Norman Manley gave his valedictory address as president and leader of the PNP. The political landscape was changing rapidly, with Busta and Norman retired, Sangster dead and Ivan Lloyd soon to resign acrimoniously from the PNP. Isaacs and Florizel Glasspole had been sidelined by their own party. Manley's speech was long, heartfelt and visionary.[6] He said that Jamaica faced a crisis equal to that faced in 1938, but not one defined solely in terms of labour politics. Although he did not mention them all, this new politics included Reynold Henry and Millard Johnson, along with an expanding Rastafari presence. Others were also involved with their 'rude bwoy' styling and engagements with a drug economy. Anti-Chinese riots took place, alongside constructive Black Power initiatives. Finally, both parties had presided over the rise of garrisons, gangs and state repression. The whole was not so much a labour rebellion, but rather a rebellion of black masses, of those "not recognised" or rewarded – even when they laboured.

Manley addressed the PNP's policies taken to the recent election. He did not reject them. Still, this agenda could be now only a part of that required. He spoke about Black Power as a constructive force – "the acceptance by the black man of his own proud place in the brotherhood of man". And this must be Jamaica's own trajectory; neither British, American, Russian nor Cuban. It must include a new aesthetic and national economy, as well as a black majority politics. "We know where we're going!" he declaimed.[7] The struggle would not be violent, communist or revolutionary. Against violence, he cited Gandhi; against communism, its "intrigues" and "contempt for democracy". Against revolution, he noted that Jamaica was a stable, two-party democracy, supported by a loyal army and police force. He also said that, in the case of insurrection, the United States and the United Nations would intervene at the behest of Jamaica's authorities. He who preaches revolution, Manley said, is "a political quack".[8] He decried the "new left-wing", some of whom dismissed the recent generation. With "borrowed gods, glimpsed over false horizons", these critics rejected the socialism "we believe in": one in which "the brotherhood of man becomes a reality and the resources of each country and of the world are developed for the good." Manley balanced commitment with realpolitik.

With what would Isaacs have disagreed? Certainly not the remarks on revolution. However, three other aspects of the speech would have been discomforting. Black Power introduced new alliances with which he was ill at ease. In particular, the centring of Rastafari brought a new vernacular that was different from Isaacs', the one he had ingested from the street corners and nationalist clubs of the 1920s and 1930s. Moreover, despite his enduring anti-racist stance, the post-colonial internationalism that Norman and Michael were embracing may have seemed commendable, but vague.[9] Now travelling between St Ann and Sligoville, he stood at a distance from these ideas.

Michael Manley was elected as party president and leader on 9 February 1969. His father lived to see this succession but, deeply tired and ill, he passed away in September. Michael's opponent was the distinguished barrister, Vivian Blake. Born in 1921, Blake joined the PNP in 1948, having returned from London where he read and practised law. In the party split of 1951–52, he represented the group supporting Glasspole and Kelly. From 1952, for nine years, he served on the party's executive committee, and between 1954 and 1959, as honorary legal advisor to the newly founded NWU. For five years from 1962, Blake was a PNP nominee to the Senate. In that year and thereafter he was elected as a PNP vice president. In 1967, he ran successfully in a by-election for the seat of St Elizabeth South East. It was widely known that Isaacs supported Blake for the leadership. To the ageing politician, Blake was a more familiar figure. Moreover, familial succession bothered Isaacs. From the father directly to the son suggested the ways of Jamaica's elite.

Michael won comfortably with 376 votes to Blake's 155. In order of the votes, the vice presidents were Vivian Blake, P.J. Patterson, Howard Cooke and Glasspole. David Coore assumed a new position as chairman of the party. Manley's success rested on electability more than left versus right. His prominence as a union leader, and his oratorical flair, were important. He was, in fact, both his father's son and a leader for a new generation. Soon after, Ivan Lloyd resigned from the party and Parliament. Isaacs and Glasspole had enjoined him to stay, but he was resolved. Lloyd's departure brought a by-election in St Ann South East, which his son contested for the JLP unsuccessfully. In October and pleading poor health, Blake retired from his executive role, though he retained his parliamentary seat. Notwithstanding the vice-presidency vote, which seemed to endorse the old guard, change was afoot.[10]

The temper of the times was given full expression in Michael Manley's speech at the PNP's annual conference in October 1969.[11] He brought a different language and some new priorities. His first remarks noted the state of the nation and the JLP government: The economy was stagnant, unemployment rising, democracy threatened and the government determined to perpetuate itself. Manley repeated his father's timeline that in 1962 the PNP, though out of power, had delivered freedom to the people. Now, however, their task must be to bring economic independence. He noted that Jamaica's adult unemployed numbered about a quarter of a million:

> Here surely is the final defeat of freedom, because the unemployed is a man to whom freedom is not even a word, certainly not an idea and at best a sordid joke. Unfortunately, unemployment is the final resting ground of the sufferer. But you, the sufferers, [...] are my true constituency in this country. You are the first object of our concern and your case shall be at the heart of our planning [...].

Manley's masterful stroke came in his reference to "the sufferers", which included not only the working poor, but also those who were unemployed, seasonally employed, or casuals. Notwithstanding his own union work, he understood that the PNP had to include others beyond the union movement, some attracted to black nationalism. Indeed, without mentioning blackness, "sufferers" referenced Jamaica's black masses, one and all.[12]

Manley advocated for an economy in which Jamaican ownership and control were pre-eminent. Jamaica's assets and raw materials would not be at the mercy of "external ownership". He declared his position "economic nationalism", as distinct from "nationalization". However, foreign policy was also integral to this plan. This was not his father's idea of regional autonomy, but rather a broader Third World alliance. Jamaica must promote revised trade relations between North and South, and among newly decolonized societies.[13] Manley conceded that no colony was allowed a foreign policy; a stricture that his father and Isaacs had faced. With independence, however, wings could spread. It was in this context that he was damning of past industrial policy:

> Over the years we have built up this delightful colonial conceit of believing that when you run cap in hand to the metropolitan masters, each with a little begging plate held out in front of you, that that is the way to national survival. But I look about me in the under-developed world and I see no national survival taking place. [...] it is time we look for some new kind of weapon to enforce our need upon the world. [....]
>
> I believe if we in the under-developed parts of the world had only the diplomatic vision to see that we could forge links of steel around the world, that would give us for the first time an opportunity to throw the begging pans away.

Issues that seemed irresolvable at home might be resolved through an international alliance. Manley spoke about follow-up visits to the wider Caribbean, Latin America and African states. An inspiring vision, it also suggested in Frank Hill's phrase, an ability "to spin a mood out of lofty words", proceeding from the "abstract to the general". Hill had used these words to describe Norman Manley's hopes for federation.[14] They could also be applied to Michael's vision and, despite his father's recent warning, he did disrespect the PNP generation that preceded him. The reference to "begging bowls" made them seem abject.[15]

Isaacs continued with everyday politics. Many matters that he pursued reflected his constituency. In January and June, he took up the issue of roads at some length. Food and other supplies from the coast could not get through to more remote hamlets. In the other direction, farmers were unable to transport their bananas expeditiously to the coast. He raged at the fact that while these roads remained unrepaired, a four-lane highway was being constructed between Kingston and Spanish Town. Worse, while the latter project was highly mechanised and employed few men, parish road repairs offered potential employment for many. Housing and rents in an expanding Ocho Rios were another issue. Workers sought housing close to their workplace but, as the tourist destination began to develop, the rising demand had an adverse effect on rents. They were rising as fast as those in Kingston. Worse, the construction of Turtle Beach and the dredging involved had disrupted drainage around Ocho Rios. Housing in the town's poorer parts was now subject to flooding. The parish council and hotel owners could do better.[16]

Not all issues were constituency ones. In March 1970, and extending through April, Isaacs drew attention to shipments of refrigerator and stove components to a manufacturer of electrical appliances. He charged that the shipments had falsified manifests. The import licence was for materials required to manufacture appliances, not simply to finish them. Under cover of the licence, the company was importing new refrigerators and parts for rapid re-assembly. This practice made the company more a distributor than a producer, augmenting profits while Jamaicans were deprived of skilled work. Corruption was at play. In April, PNP parliamentarians, led by Isaacs and Michael Manley, staged a demonstration outside the Ministry of Trade and Industry. The aim was to shame both the company and the minister. Three days later, Lightbourne was forced to make a lengthy statement to the House. He acknowledged the company's violations and referred the matter to the Director of Public Prosecutions.[17]

The first six months of 1970 also witnessed intense debate about the JPSC and both electrification and frequency conversion.

Isaacs contended that the extension of franchise legislated by the government did not contain adequate performance guarantees. His budget speech referenced his constituency and also challenged Seaga in broader terms:

> [...] the Minister of Finance spoke about the share-the-wealth Budget. I invite him to come to a place called Steer Town with some forty-five acres of hillsides, rocky lands. There are some seven thousand people on that forty-five acres of land, while on the left you drive for eight miles along the Roaring River property, which belongs to somebody who is not even a Jamaican and you will never count one hundred head of cattle on the property. These people don't want to share the wealth, they want the opportunity to produce wealth in the country [...].[18]

Policy for under-utilized land was now a major issue. However, Isaacs gave most of his attention to trade, and to the effects of Britain's 1967 devaluation of the sterling. Jamaica's cost of living had risen markedly. Building materials were affected and, as a result, rental costs. Isaacs was also mindful of the cost of imported manufactured goods, staples and processed foods. On this occasion he queried the government's choice of South Korea and Taiwan as sources of imported goods. Why would the government buy from these American allies when comparable goods from Japan were cheaper? On a related issue, he called the government to account on indirect taxation. In 1964, all customs duties had been increased by a uniform 10 per cent. Revenue to government had increased by £3 million in just one year, borne on "the backs of the unfortunate people of this country". Concluding, he noted that decreasing productivity on the home front, especially in agriculture, was also a major cause of inflation, while a flagging tourist industry weakened the economy. He urged the need for new markets beyond the United Kingdom, the European Economic Community and the United States, noting that Jamaica could expect few favours from a new Tory regime that included Enoch Powell. It was a forceful speech, met with prolonged applause from his side of the House.[19]

Isaacs' parliamentary style had three components. He mastered detail and leavened his performance with witty asides that avoided gratuitous insult. In addition, his speeches addressed PNP policy relentlessly. In September, he travelled to Canberra, Australia with Jamaica's delegation to the executive committee of the Commonwealth Parliamentary Association. Among the topics addressed were aid in the public and private sectors, race relations, and trade and economic development, especially with reference to the EEC. Jamaica opened a discussion on the challenges that youth protest and poverty posed to a parliamentary democracy.[20]

As Christmas approached, Isaacs was on hand for the lighting of the Christmas tree in tiny Higgin Town, St Ann. As MP for the area, he delivered the seasonal message while a councillor turned on the lights.[21]

The year 1971 brought preparations for the general election. At their March conference, Manley presented the PNP's other fifty-two candidates, proposing that "no finer collection of brains, experience, youth, energy, skills and training" had ever been assembled in Jamaica. Automatically re-elected as president, Manley's four vice presidents were P.J. Patterson, Howard Cooke, Glasspole and Dudley Thompson. David Coore remained as chairman. Patterson had become the chief campaign organizer. Change was the dominant theme of the conference. Manley declared: "We want all Jamaica to form a grand co-operative partnership in which all men of goodwill work together to build this our homeland into a place of justice for all [...]."

Making a comparison to the battle of Jericho, he assured those present that the walls surely would come tumbling down. "Then we shall build a city and we shall call it the City of Jerusalem where the spirit of God, of peace and justice will prevail; where men and women may live together, may work together, may raise their children together in honour and decency unto the greater glory of God."

He was soon referred to as Jamaica's "Joshua", with his "rod of correction" gifted by Haile Selassie, emperor of Ethiopia.

At the conference, Isaacs turned to more practical matters. Delegates passed his resolution to instruct the Opposition to press in Parliament for action on spiralling rents. Patterson put forward a further resolution, much in the spirit of his mentor, Isaacs: "Whereas the PNP stands firmly against racial discrimination and is completely opposed to the principles of apartheid in South Africa; and whereas the United Nations has by resolution forbidden the sale of arms to South Africa; Be it hereby resolved that the Party conference strongly condemns the recent decision of the British Government to sell helicopters and other military equipment to South Africa."[22]

By June, informal campaigning had begun with a focus on justice for the "sufferers". Manley and Isaacs were pictured in a full-page *Gleaner* advertisement. It concerned the cost of living for the masses, who also bore the brunt of taxation. Soon after this advertisement appeared, Isaacs made his budget speech for 1971. He remarked on a middle-class propensity for luxury spending: "There are many people in this country who can afford to buy a Rolls Royce motorcar but Jamaica cannot afford to buy a Rolls Royce." Referring to the need for less expensive imports for the people, he raised the prospect of importing cheap foodstuffs from China, and pharmaceuticals from Eastern Europe. His information on China came from discussions at the CPA meeting in Australia. Where Eastern Europe was concerned, Isaacs drew on past experience. Also in June, he gave notice of a private member's bill for the introduction of a five-day working week. He had first raised this issue in 1965 in the course of an address to bauxite workers.[23]

On the last day of January, Prime Minister Hugh Shearer called the election for 29 February 1972. The *Gleaner* editorial called for "realism" and the conservative Morris Cargill recommended "pragmatism". He repudiated "irrelevant theories of land tenure" and suggested that, for those offended by the "excesses of Beverley Hills or the Mercedes-Benz epidemic, it is no longer effective or even relevant to believe that either can be cured by Robin Hood taxation."[24] Manley's messaging was disciplined. He pledged good governance: an annual report on politicians' assets; an end to victimization; electoral reform; and the elevation of Parliament as a forum. In addition, he promised job creation as an economic focus, gun control, a National Youth Service and "training alongside actual work", as well as a literacy programme. The PNP campaign focused on motorcades through the counties organized by Patterson. It also involved numerous uptown professionals and businessmen, including Pat Rousseau, John Marzouca, Frank Pringle, and Eli and Aaron Matalon; the last described as "a marketing genius". The style of campaigning was called 'bandwagon' and outstripped even Isaacs' efforts circa 1949. Rallies were redolent with theme songs borrowed from local reggae stars, including Junior Byles' "Beat Down Babylon" and Clancy Eccles' "Rod of Correction". Delroy Wilson's "Better Must Come" became the campaign anthem. There was little violence, and Manley rallied the victimized with his injunction, "If the word is love, the method is peace."[25]

It was a landslide victory. The final tally was thirty-seven seats to the PNP and just sixteen to the JLP. Manley was returned in Kingston Central with a much increased majority. Rose Leon, aligned with the PNP since 1967, won St. Andrew West Rural. For his toils on behalf of St Ann North East, Isaacs increased his margin from 984 votes in 1967 to 2,829 votes in 1972. Political Reporter remarked of the final election in which he would stand, that Isaacs had brought "all his Kingston expertise" to bear on the St Ann constituency.[26]

In Manley's new Cabinet, Trade and Industry was split in two. Patterson's portfolio was Industry and Tourism; Isaacs' was Commerce and Consumer Affairs. He would work with the Trade Administrator and focus on imported consumer goods as well as the overall cost of living. As the years had taught him, these were crucial matters for a population with high unemployment. Apart from clientelism, their social safety net was no more than relatives, a church, their yard, neighbours and friends. In 1972, the unemployment rate was 23.5 per cent, the same level as in 1953.[27] The ten per cent reduction Isaacs and his comrades were able to achieve in office had been obliterated in the 1960s.

Isaacs was offered Tourism, the growth of which had stemmed from his partnership with Abe Issa. He declined the role, remarking that it was too strenuous for a man of seventy years. He had struggled with racism in the industry and, through the 1960s, its segregation had become confronting. The younger Patterson vowed to change tourism's image. In terms of Jamaica's balance of payments, its economic benefits were beyond dispute. Bauxite and tourism were the two largest contributors to the country's foreign reserves which, in turn, paid for crucial imports. As well, these reserves provided credibility for bank loans overseas.[28] Eric Bell, who had moved from the Senate to the House, took on a new portfolio – Utilities – which included railways, wharves, and electric light and power.[29] With Patterson taking Tourism, and Bell Utilities, Isaacs' role was much reduced. The redistribution underlined, however, the weight of his former ministerial role. Coore became Minister of Finance and Keble Munn continued with Agriculture. Allan Isaacs went to the Ministry of Mining and Natural Resources. Glasspole remained with Education and was also Leader of the House.

However, the Cabinet composition was not fully resolved. Informed word in private circles was that Isaacs and Glasspole would not stay. As experienced campaigners – though Glasspole was seven years younger than Isaacs – they had been required to secure their seats while the party's efforts went elsewhere. They had played their part.[30] Therefore, it was significant when, soon after the election, Manley charged a small group from the NEC to clarify the PNP's "ideology". Representatives from the centre included

Coore, Patterson and Howard Cooke; and from the more radical left, Arnold Bertram, D.K. Duncan and Anthony Spaulding. Others who became involved were the PNP's Youth Organization and the Women's Movement, led by Beverley Anderson, whom Manley would soon marry. This executive group took a good year to report on a revised party stance. Soon after his inclusion in this group, Duncan became the PNP's national organizer and later, party secretary.[31]

Manley had come to power with a particular view of the economy, enunciated in the *Gleaner*'s Electoral Forum three days before the election. He was an aggressive critic of the Puerto Rican model as a blueprint for development. Once again, his tone was dismissive: "We have seen too much of the JLP tendency to look beyond our shores to get just any kind of factory to open here. Agreed, this is the simplest way of going about things, it is also the [...] indicator of questionable economic planning. As a result, many itinerant 'screw-driver' industries have come to our shores. They manufacture 'things' – something like buttons; [and] operate and relate only to the export market."[32]

Manley's tone was dismissive, but were the ills so easy to fix? The JLP had bequeathed an economy in trouble. Failure of export income to meet the cost of imports was undermining Jamaica's balance of payments, increasing debt and running down foreign reserves. The Economic Survey for 1971 brought more bad news. An expansionary phase for bauxite-alumina had come to an end and annual investment was tapering off; 25 per cent less in 1971 than in 1970. The trend would continue. A similar decrease was also evident in hotel investment, possibly influenced by overseas reports of the violence in Kingston.[33]

These island-specific factors were magnified by international trends. During the early 1970s, the currencies of Britain and the United States became less stable. Britain effectively floated its pound which, by 1972, had devalued by 5 per cent. The United

States also affected a devaluation when it cancelled the US dollar's convertibility to gold. Both economies entered periods of stagflation which produced, as a side effect, a steep rise in their export prices.[34] As Jamaica's own exports struggled, the cost of imports – mainly sourced from these two countries – rose. The situation brought a further inflationary effect. Unsure of the Jamaican currency's future, distributors stockpiled goods in Kingston, increasing the total spend on imports.[35] These events were unfolding as the PNP took power.

In March and April 1972, two "crash" programmes were introduced.[36] The first involved a literacy programme to improve the general education of workers and a training programme to address the shortage of skills. Manley looked to undergraduate students to assist with literacy. Where skills were concerned, he appealed to the private sector for support, citing specific areas that would benefit, including textile production and horticulture. The second programme was designed to provide immediate relief. In rural areas the work would be on roads and reforestation projects; in Kingston, on programmes to improve drainage and sidewalks. Projects to paint schools and other public buildings would be introduced across the island. Action in agriculture took a little longer. Where land redistribution was concerned, direct acquisition of private land proved unfeasible. The cost of compensation was just too high. In the following year, using government-owned and leased land, Project Land Lease would begin, with more than two thousand farmers placed on forty-three hundred acres. The project would extend for three years. These and other major reforms, including free education at secondary and tertiary level, were highly desirable, long-term investments. However, they were also costs on government with little immediate return.[37]

In June 1972, David Coore delivered a budget that included some austerities. Overseas travel fares, domestic mail, cigarettes, spirits and gambling returns of any type all incurred additional charges. At least three of these were taxes on the poor as well as the rich. One month later, Manley announced a price freeze in the face of rising inflation and a worsening balance of payments. He foreshadowed a general review of prices and announced some concessions for the poor. A twenty-cent charge on hospital visits would be abolished and non-prescription drugs would be sold at cost. In November, following months of discussion, the government imposed a range of measures to control imports and foreign exchange transactions. The governor of the Bank of Jamaica provided a sympathetic overview. Facing "massive unemployment and great poverty", the government could only proceed by accepting a "trade-off" between job-creating policies and a reduction in foreign reserves. The trade-off was feasible, however, only with "massive" import regulation. Essentials would be given priority.[38]

The division of labour in Trade and Industry meant that Patterson focused on agency negotiations with, for example, the EEC, UNCTAD, and regional partners in CARIFTA and the emerging CARICOM.[39] The direction of world trade had brought a new and demanding internationalism. Isaacs stayed at home and focused on the people's most immediate needs. In 1972, he assumed two tasks that showed his commitment to both the masses and his government. The first was to organize a trade mission in pursuit of cheaper staples; the second was to work on and announce a formidable list of austerities at home.

A spiralling cost of living was reflected in the issues that Isaacs faced. Local producers of condensed milk had pressed the previous government for a price increase consequent on the rising cost of imported powdered milk. With an election due, the JLP had rejected the request. Now the company was failing and its production had declined. It was imperative that the new government protect "Betty", as the brand was known locally, and its standard price of fourteen cents a can. This Isaacs did. Distributors were also demanding that the price cap on imported corned beef be lifted. Corned beef was the most popular among an increasing range of canned meats and fish that were displacing salted codfish as a staple. They were cheaper, though less nutritious than cod. Wills continued to review the price. An embargo on imported hardware fixtures – sockets, deadlocks, gate hooks, catches and the like – had served to encourage local production. However, shortages were frustrating a range of tradesmen and self-builders. Isaacs eased the embargo a little. He was also pressured to allow cheap textiles to be imported, notwithstanding bipartisan protection for Ariguanabo. It employed a workforce of around eight hundred, but lack of competition had reduced the quality and range of its products. More talks followed.

Urbanization and decreasing rural production had increased the need for cheap, imported processed food. Isaacs remarked that prices would keep rising if Jamaica continued to rely on traditional sources overseas. The government should seek alternatives. In an April television interview, he made specific reference to China and Japan. Depending on the United States as their main supplier was his major concern, as its inflation was rising at a rapid rate.[40] This was the context in which he announced a trade mission to Asia, Russia and Eastern Europe to identify sources of cheaper goods to meet basic consumption needs. Specifically, the itinerary included Japan, Hong Kong, China, the Soviet Union, Yugoslavia, Poland, Czechoslovakia and Austria. (It did not go unremarked that a number of these societies were communist.) Isaacs chose men to go from both the private and public sectors. None were politicians. The leader of the mission was Carlton Alexander, a former president of the JCC, and chairman and CEO of Grace Kennedy. Initially, the company dealt with Jamaica Fruit and Shipping, and the Banana Growers' Association. It expanded into manufacturing, processing and shipping a vast array of goods. Other members of the mission were a former president of the JMA, a prominent dry goods merchant, and the chief pharmacist. Each of them had specialised knowledge pertaining to a range of commodities. A Jamaican diplomat from the Washington, DC embassy was recruited to mediate engagements. The mission departed on 18 June 1972 and returned on 8 August.

A year of struggle was leavened by some personal victories for Isaacs, including the reduction of the voting age from twenty-one to eighteen years and significant movement towards a uniform, five-day working week. Isaacs, along with Glasspole, had argued for the first change in 1957. Regarding the working week, Isaacs had campaigned on the issue since 1965. Speaking then to bauxite workers, he said that it was wrong that "one hundred workers should be employed six or seven days a week while others work none at all".[41] These initiatives were cause for celebration. Acknowledgement of his efforts over the years came with his appearance in the Honours List for 1972. In October, he became a Commander of the Order of Distinction, the senior order conferred specifically for service to the nation. The *Gleaner* remarked on his "unique contribution to the island's national affairs". The formal citation traced his career in politics. A short preamble affirmed his modest beginnings, noting that he was born in 1902 in Hanover. "He was educated at Pondside Elementary School and by private tuition and started life as an estate bookkeeper. He later became a salesman and manufacturer's agent" before he ran for office in 1943.[42]

As September turned into October, the strains in the economy showed. Devaluation was debated. In Spanish Town, two foreign ventures in garment manufacture for export closed down. They had struggled to retain their US markets. A ban was placed on importing motor vehicles; eased; and then tightened again. The *Daily Gleaner* editorialised against illegal foreign exchange transactions that were undermining both government and the Bank of Jamaica.[43] In November, Prime Minister Manley announced further austerities which, he observed, should have been applied years ago, such as further bans on imports and controls on the finance available to merchants and for personal loans. The proceeds of foreign receipts from all exports would be retained in Jamaica, for the benefit of Jamaicans. Isaacs followed Manley with his second task: to list fifty-six import restrictions, effective immediately. Although he tried to assure the House of a local alternative for each of the items banned, the list was disquieting. Isaacs did receive frantic applause for some items, including "crustacea and molluscs" (lobster and oysters), "brandy and whisky", and especially "revolvers and pistols". He delivered the list with sober directness. He concluded, "The government has had to decide on measures which relate generally to non-essential imports so as to ensure that our ability, as a nation, to import our essential requirements is safeguarded."[44] Along with speeches by Manley and Coore, Isaacs' speech was delivered live to the nation from the House. And indeed, for many, "the world would not be the same again" as inflation buffeted the island.

The report of the mission to Asia and Eastern Europe was not released until November 1972. It was a detailed one, which considered each country visited. Raw materials were available from a number, and China, Japan and Poland had expressed interest in investment, industrial cooperation and technical knowledge. The report opened up new horizons for Jamaica and began to chip away at the decades-long communist bogey. In terms of immediate trading prospects, the most alluring items were from China: an array of canned goods, including corned beef, beef and ham, chopped pork and ham, mackerel, and pears; and from Poland and China: an extensive range of pharmaceuticals at lower cost than their US counterparts. The quality and price of textiles from Russia and China were enticing. All prices cited allowed for cost, insurance and freight. *Inter alia*, the report provided some interesting comments indicative of Isaacs' ministerial legacy. With regard to Poland, "We import canned fish and machinery and they have been buying pimento from us. The possibilities of expanded trade, especially in the trade of canned fish, machinery, drugs and textiles, are encouraging as their government operates a shipping service to [...] South America. With sufficient inducement Jamaica could be included as a port of call."

And on the China visit, "Our visits to factories were enlightening. We saw people hard at work with a sense of dedication motivated by the desire to improve their country. [....] Our stay was made most pleasant by the consideration and graciousness of these people and their solicitude for our comfort."

At a press conference with Carlton Alexander, Isaacs cited this passage on China and remarked, "I think it is something which the people of Jamaica, all the people of Jamaica, should take to heart. [....] If we can get our people to work hard for their country, with a sense of dedication and working to improve their country, this would be the best evidence of their loyalty and responsibility as citizens of Jamaica." His comment was aimed mainly at a self-indulgent middle class. Alexander underlined the point, praising Isaacs' foresight with regard to the mission: "The business community is totally lacking in not taking such a step during the last five or ten years."[45]

The mission's report was tabled in Parliament on 23 November. By that time, a reciprocal mission from China had come to Jamaica, including representatives for producers of cereal, edible oil and foodstuff. The group met with Isaacs and Patterson. They conferred with the IDC and visited the Kingston Industrial Estate. Relations would continue.[46] The *Gleaner's* coverage of the Jamaican mission's report was published on 24 November. It coincided with Jamaica's diplomatic recognition of the People's Republic as the sole government of China. Isaacs' trade initiative had followed US President Nixon's own visit to China and therefore fell within the ambit of a thawing Cold War foreign policy. At the same time, Jamaica embraced the UN policy of one China, which the United States had not endorsed. The action allowed Jamaica to assert its independence. Patterson, with Manley and Thompson, had been preparing to put the case for recognition to Cabinet. They feared resistance, not least from Isaacs. He, however, made an independent proposal that the government recognize the People's Republic of China. The Cabinet vote was unanimous. By the early 2000s, China had become Jamaica's fourth-largest trading partner, behind the United States, Canada and the United Kingdom.[47]

Manley announced the move from Jamaica House. Then, on behalf of the prime minister, Isaacs made the announcement in Parliament. He also assumed a buffer role between Manley and the Opposition. The now independent Robert Lightbourne raised the issue of communism. Isaacs replied, "We have been hearing about communism since 1938, a long time. I have been hearing about it for thirty-four years." At his press conference on 24 November, he made a statement to one and all: "My political history in this country is well known and it is my duty as Minister of Commerce and Consumer Protection to buy from any country in the world where the prices are cheaper, regardless of their ideological convictions [...]. I want it to be known that we are importing the things that we need. We are not importing ideology into this country." He concluded with a remark that the government's literacy campaign might be of most assistance to the "jittery" middle class.[48]

Isaacs' practical approach to trade with China was a precursor of the view he would take throughout the 1970s of developments in the PNP and the government. He would counsel Michael to focus on specific policies, rather than a comprehensive ideology, however laudable the latter may be. He was aware of the trouble that ideological debate could bring not only for the government, but also for the relations between comrades in the PNP. Among Michael's nominees to the Senate was Isaacs' son, Vunnie, who had been his schoolboy friend, and a footballer of note. Perhaps Michael felt that he could trust the son as he trusted the father; not always to agree with him, but neither to sabotage the party nor its leader. In turn, this action prefigured Manley's struggle to reconcile the PNP's moderates with the growing influence of the left. And, despite Isaacs' advice, ideology would soon be at the centre of debate within the party, the Parliament, and Jamaican society at large.

## Chapter 14

# An Ambivalent Departure

*The storm is breaking! Let it break in all its fury!*
– Maxim Gorky, 1901.

*When I come home, I hope I can give you a bit of advice and I beg of you not to treat it lightly.* – Isaacs to Michael Manley, from Canada, 1975.[1]

At the end of April, Isaacs notified the Speaker of the House that he would resign from Parliament on 1 June 1973. Glasspole declared that in June a special sitting of the House would be convened to say farewell to both of them, as he would be departing soon after Isaacs. In the first week of June, Michael Manley announced that Isaacs would be assuming the position of High Commissioner to Canada. He filled the role for just two years. Glasspole, a younger man, became Jamaica's new governor general on the retirement of Sir Clifford Campbell. He remained in the role for eighteen years. On his retirement, Isaacs was awarded an Order of Jamaica, in addition to his Order of Distinction.[2]

The months that preceded his departure were not easy. The austerity measures of June and November 1972 were unpopular, especially among the urban middle class and some farmers.[3] Reactions intensified with a further statement from the government on 16 January 1973. The Jamaican currency, now converted to the dollar, would be devalued and exchanged at the rate of US$1.00 = J$1.10. This devaluation of 5.6 per cent was designed to provide a modest support to exports, while containing the cost of imports. A round of bauxite investment had come to an end and capital – domestic and foreign – was leaving Jamaica. Direct investment overall fell more than 20 per cent in 1971 and by 62 per cent in 1972.[4] Isaacs noted that the price freeze – in place since July 1972 – would remain. He urged importers to seek cheaper staples abroad. In a further comment on 8 February, he said that the government would work with all "towards our national development". He added, "People will endure austerity willingly together where they have faith in their leaders and hope for the future." His final ministerial act on 1 May was to foreshadow a freeze on rents, while levels of rental control were reset. He said that recent rent hikes were "out of all proportion to reality". The burden on low-income tenants had become unbearable.[5]

On 12 June, Isaacs and Glasspole were farewelled from Parliament. They sat to the right of the Speaker, facing their colleagues. An unusual number of members gave testimonials about Isaacs' humanity and humour. Manley recalled when a fledgling NWU was competing for workers' representational rights at Ariguanabo Mills. Isaacs invited him to join the negotiating team, and later slipped away so that Manley would be in charge. "I was thrown into the water and the rest is history both for me and him."[6] Manley testified to Isaacs's acute political insight and to the "avuncular" relation between them. Robert Lightbourne, general manager of the IDC when Isaacs first entered Parliament, spoke of the ministry that the two men had shared: "I know what a rough job it is to run that place across the road. [...] but I regard Isaacs as one of the great human beings that I know. A great human being, that is what he is." Allan Isaacs, a sometime adversary in the PNP, spoke of the 1940s. He deemed Wills to be responsible above all others for the PNP becoming a mass party equal to the JLP. Isaacs had "the ability to articulate the feelings and hopes and aspirations of the common people and to articulate them in the idiom of the people [....]." In a wistful farewell, Isaacs recalled his designation as the "stormy petrel" of Jamaican politics. He said that he would miss the life.[7]

He arrived in Canada at the end of August 1973. Following talks with Prime Minister Pierre Trudeau, he set to work. Among his first concerns was Jamaica's standing as a tourist destination. He noted that it was regarded as a dangerous place and lacked prominence as a cruise destination. He called for greater effort from his former ministry and the Jamaica Tourist Board. Subsequently, he arranged for Owen Sound, a tourist town north of Toronto, to have twin city status with St Ann's Bay and Ocho Rios. Exchange visits and publicity followed.[8] He also looked at the treatment of Jamaicans newly arrived in Canada. Without a return ticket and a demonstrated means of support, they were imprisoned and deported. Surely, Canada could make these checks in Jamaica? As well, he called on local Canadian courts to assist with orders that his countrymen pay child support back home. He attended the meetings of expatriate clubs, gathered with others of the diplomatic corps, and consulted with his regional colleagues. Periodically, he crossed the border to Hartford, Connecticut for meetings of a Jamaica Progressive League branch.[9] Nonetheless, his mind was ever on events at home and the travails of his government.

In May 1973, Coore had proposed major tax reform in conjunction with an expenditure of J$87 million on human resource initiatives. The latter included the introduction of free secondary and tertiary education. A literacy programme would follow. In debate, national service for youth was raised as an appropriate reciprocity for free education. Still, fiscal policy would need to change to support the measures.[10] The centrepiece of tax reform involved new taxes on property for all but small farmers. A basic land value tax would be replaced by a tax on the improved value of land. The latter included both commercial and residential developments on rural and urban land. A second measure discouraged speculation on arable land. Too many simply allowed their land to stand idle and appreciate. In conjunction with Land Lease and Operation Grow, rural production increased, albeit modestly. In addition, the new tax regime reduced the government's reliance on indirect taxes, which hurt the poor.[11] The new impositions brought protests from *Daily Gleaner* columnists. One deplored the new inhumanity of a "Big Brother" government able to investigate individuals "at will" and soon – if national service was introduced – able to implement "forced labour". "Communism!" was the charge.[12]

The first two years of PNP government also saw a significant change in foreign policy, one of Manley's central concerns. Very soon after the government adopted a one-China policy, Jamaica also assumed full diplomatic relations with Cuba. This initiative came barely a decade after the Cuban Missile Crisis and its confrontation between the United States and the Soviet Union. Moreover, the move came arm in arm with Manley's embrace of the Non-Aligned Movement. Many of those involved were postcolonial Third World nations. Several were socialist. In September 1973, Manley travelled with Forbes Burnham and Fidel Castro to the third summit of the Non-Aligned Movement in Algiers, where he gave a keynote address. At the summit, Manley spoke of ongoing struggles in southern Africa, and the unequal terms of trade faced by commodity producers, mainly in the south. The Algiers summit marked the beginning of Manley's advocacy for a New International Economic Order between the North and the South.

From Canada, Isaacs followed events and, in a speech to Rotarians in Kingston, Ontario in October 1973, he reinforced Manley's points. He said: "The export trade of developing countries is very vulnerable. Price fluctuations leading to economic collapse are our nightmare. [....] It is a preoccupation of my government.

Today, it takes several more tonnes of sugar than it did a few short years ago to buy a tractor. External development assistance is no substitute."[13] He was hinting at the need for major changes, which foreign investment alone could not achieve. His interest in export agriculture stretched back at least to 1965, when he described sugar as a "sick international commodity".[14] Isaacs empathized with Michael's stance.

At this exact time, Jamaica experienced a decade-defining shock as OPEC declared an oil embargo targeted mainly at the United States. The action was in response to the latter's involvement in the Yom Kippur War. The resulting oil shortage meant that the price of petroleum, and many other affected goods, skyrocketed overnight. Almost exclusively dependent on imported fuel, Jamaica's oil bill rose dramatically from US$71 million to US$195 million in one year.[15] OPEC's action was inflationary on a global scale. Isaacs wrote to Manley about inflation in August 1974. The Bank of Canada had raised its prime lending rate to 9.25 per cent. Private and commercial banks would follow. Isaacs allowed that reducing the money supply would curb inflation. Still, he worried about Jamaica's situation and its multiplicity of small manufacturers: "The great dilemma is that credit restrictions, in slowing the economy, will contribute less to a reduction of inflation than to an increase in unemployment. [. . .] If the economy is slowing dramatically for other reasons, the time is not opportune to increase the bank rate."

If producers could gain a tolerable return from money in the bank, why risk further investment? He also worried about housing mortgagors on limited incomes. For them, an interest rate spiral would be disastrous; so, too, for the construction industry. Citing John Kenneth Galbraith, he suggested that a price-wage accord between capital and organized labour would be preferable to higher interest rates.[16]

The financial implications for the government were serious, even in 1973. Expenditure on employment and wages, in conjunction with import restrictions, had fuelled inflation at home, now made worse by external events. Higher interest rates on debt added to the government's costs. Its budgets were already stretched by projects in agriculture and education, each one desirable but with few immediate returns. Jamaica was now drawing on its foreign reserves to fund these commitments. Manley's response was to turn to the bauxite industry, which represented Jamaica's "largest single capital investment, earned the most foreign exchange, and paid the most taxes of any industry on the island". As 1973 turned into 1974, the Manley government led the way in establishing an International Bauxite Association. Then, in 1974, the government commenced negotiations with the North American bauxite companies invested in Jamaica. Agreement could not be reached, and in May, Jamaica unilaterally imposed a new bauxite levy. The effect was immediate. Earnings from bauxite taxes and royalties in 1973 – US$27 million – rose to US$180 million in 1974.[17] From Canada, Isaacs sent Manley copious clippings regarding the new production levy, royalties, and taxes on bauxite and alumina. Many articles pertained to ALCAN and its subsidiary, ALCAN Jamaica. And in August 1974, Wills dispatched the text of his Canadian broadcast on the twelfth anniversary of Jamaica's independence. The speech included these remarks:

> It is not necessary to recall the events throughout the world during the past year, but it is clear from the convulsions and confusion, we are sure that there will emerge a new world order.
>
> If Jamaica is to meaningfully occupy a place in that new world order, and indeed share part of the responsibility for the shape of that order, then the Jamaica you left years ago must undergo serious change.
>
> The great bauxite story, where we increased our revenue from $25 million to $175 million, is now well known and supported by our nationals in every country. We are going to buy back the two hundred thousand acres of land owned by the mining companies.
>
> This will give our people everywhere an understanding of the meaning of *national sovereignty.*

> The expansion of agriculture and industrial production and the improvements in the quality of life are all being undertaken.
>
> Youngsters remaining in school after fifteen years of age are being increased from three thousand to thirty-one thousand. We will soon have a national minimum wage and maximum working hours.
>
> We do not intend to be a nation of beggars but that in our dealings with the developed nations there must be the basis of fairness and international social justice.

In response, Manley wrote, "Concerning tight money, you will have been pleased to see that we are easing both credit restrictions and backing off interest rates in selected areas, particularly in housing." He pronounced Isaacs' independence broadcast "Excellent!"[18] The reckoning was yet to come.

These policy shifts occurred against a background of rising tensions between the government and the private sector. The price freeze was a bone of contention. In June 1973, the Chamber of Commerce surveyed some of its members on the role of government: 75 per cent were entirely opposed both to government-controlled bulk importation and to any form of price controls.[19] Several major employers began to struggle, including Caribbean Cement, Jamaica Flour Mills, JPSC, and the Jamaica Omnibus Service. When the government took shares in three and moved to nationalize JOS, the Jamaica Stock Exchange shuddered. Its chairman, Willard Samms, embraced the idea of a mixed economy. However, he proposed that the public and private sectors be clearly delineated. Government should "take over completely" needed utilities, as well as activities that were highly capital intensive and involved external debt. The private sector would do the rest; in short, a low-risk path for local capital.[20]

Two further government initiatives received a hostile reception. The initial crash programme, renamed the Special Employment Programme, was developed more fully with the assistance of parish councils across the island. Increasingly, the scheme was seen as both unproductive and as a sop to PNP supporters inclined to lean on their shovels and brooms. An equally hostile reception was given to plans for a National Youth Service linked to free higher education. Under the rubric "compulsory national service", the *Daily Gleaner* declared the plan "repugnant".[21] Opponents linked this "socialism" to Manley's foreign policy regarding Cuba and a New International Economic Order. And, as these tensions increased, so did violence in West Kingston and southwest St Andrew.

The committee convened by Manley in 1972 to review the PNP's ideology had tabled its report early in 1974. In the interim, two of the committee's radical members had assumed pivotal positions in the PNP. D.K. Duncan and Anthony Spaulding became the party's general secretary and vice president respectively. The imprint of their influence became evident when Manley renewed the party's commitment to democratic socialism at its annual conference in September. His declaration was repeated at a mass meeting downtown, and in a long speech to Parliament on 20 November.[22] No one should have been surprised. Manley's government had already taken ambitious action towards increasing rural production, improving utilities, and instigating a wide range of social reforms. Further infrastructural work on roads and port facilities was foreshadowed. During the 1960s, both the private sector and two JLP governments had had opportunities to address these issues, including the need for a more highly skilled workforce. By and large, they had turned away as agriculture stagnated, emigration dried up and unemployment spiralled. Being right, however, did not make the PNP's course any easier. By 1974, the government's annual expenditure was rising by over 21 per cent each year, and would increase thereafter at an even greater rate. As annual deficits grew, the government drew more heavily on external funds.[23]

In a brief letter to Isaacs during the 1974 annual conference, Manley wrote, "We are going to be making tremendous efforts at re-organisation during the next year and some changes may, I fear, have to be made." In his speech to Parliament, Manley detailed his government's view of Jamaica's mixed economy.[24] The public sector should address social services and human development; basic nutrition; infrastructure and public utilities; bauxite and other mineral resources; finance to support local ownership; "salvage" of strategic enterprises; and "trail-blazing" economic initiatives. It remained for the private sector to sustain profit-making enterprises "commensurate with the skills and money invested and the risks taken". These enterprises should operate within relevant laws and regulations, and with "due regard" for both workers and the community at large. Construction, a major employer, would be among them. Manley also provided more detail concerning the Capital Development Fund, although the returns from bauxite, initially intended for this purpose, were already being diverted to recurrent costs. The specification of this mixed economy comprised just a part of the speech. And as Manley would remark, it was not especially radical. It captured a spirit of the 1970s common among Third World societies and even some wealthier members of the Commonwealth.[25]

Initially, the press was restrained but hackles soon rose.[26] A coincident event may have been influential. Also in November, the government announced a 51 per cent acquisition of Kaiser Bauxite. The purchase was portrayed as a major step in buying back Jamaica. A marked advantage of the acquisition was that large tracts of bauxite land lying idle could be used as leased land for cultivation. It also emerged, however, that with the purchase Kaiser had withdrawn a challenge to the new bauxite levy lodged with the International Centre of Settlement Disputes. On Kaiser's part, the sell-off may have been an early warning sign; that in view of the persistently high cost of oil, Kaiser and other producers in Jamaica were looking for alternatives to their refineries in the Louisiana gulf. Other refineries using hydro-electric power, for example in Washington State, had become attractive, along with producers located on the Pacific rim.[27] If a bauxite cartel proved hard to sustain, and government debt continued to mount, where would the capital for further development come from?

Manley needed to define deftly his government's stance on local capital; to cajole, perhaps, but not disparage. His speech on democratic socialism struggled with the task. In an effort not to impugn individuals, Manley spoke in terms of systems: a capitalist one driven by individual acquisition, and a socialist one driven by care for one's fellow citizens. While he linked capitalism with past slavery and current deprivations, socialism was linked with Christian values and the future. He remarked that were right-minded businessmen to play their role, Jamaica's people could reach that future together. However, businessmen who remained simply bent on accumulation would not be acting in the national interest. Such people, Manley suggested, had no place in socialism or Jamaica's future. These comments jarred with a significant segment of the JCC and JMA, local investors and the *Daily Gleaner.*

In January 1975, Isaacs made a short, private visit to Jamaica. Returning to Canada in February, he opened correspondence with Manley concerning the government's position. He began by congratulating Manley "on the very bold steps you have taken in solving the problems of our country". He also wrote that Manley should "go to the country as early as you can". The party could "drop a couple of seats" and be returned to power easily. Isaacs wrote of "very strong forces" aligning against Manley and reports that "the CIA is working against you". He cited elements in the Catholic Church and some prominent capitalists. He concluded on a personal note, sending birthday wishes for Manley's one-year-old daughter.[28] A month passed and Isaacs wrote again: "Forgive me for writing to you about this but, as you know, I am an old party man and being away from Jamaica I am worried." He related the view of Carlton Alexander that it was "an error" to declare democratic socialism. Why not just instigate the policies? Isaacs made further remarks on "huge sums of money" being collected for the JLP. "My own observation is that you have completely lost the middle class." Moreover, "the man in the street" was worried about the cost of living. He noted that the Matalon family was divided in its views on the PNP's prospects. Moses was distributing contracts to JLP supporters.

In April, Manley replied to both letters, remarking that the party was unanimous in its commitment to democratic socialism. Moreover, it was not the middle class that it had lost. "What we have lost is the upper class." Still, Manley was confident:

> Our real problems are not to do with Socialism but to do with the cost of living. In this you are a shrewd politician as always. This is our real problem, along with a certain but not decisive effect that will flow from JLP money.
>
> Our country is in a deep socio-economic crisis and needs bold leadership which, while polarising society, gives the masses a clear sense of identification and purpose. I personally believe in the bold, but naturally risky road that we have taken. It has turned on our young cadres and, even more importantly, it has ignited levels of passion and enthusiasm in me I had thought long since dead. [....] Objective observers note that I still have a strong rapport with the poor, the sufferers and the masses.

Then he built a bridge to his elder, a mentor and the father of his schoolboy friend:

> In the end, all political leaders have to follow their instincts as much as their reason. There were many people who told me that you lost the PNP middle classes in your heyday when you led street fighting, riots, demonstrations and spoke of breaking skulls. I thought then that they were wrong and history proved me to be right. I believe in well-thought-out Government policy, but in bold politics. If I am wrong, we will find out.

Isaacs thanked Manley for a "most refreshing" letter and requested something comparable every month or so. He urged, "Do try and take things a little easy and try and relax as much as you can."

In April 1975, he wrote to Leslie Ashenheim, chairman of the Gleaner Company, reminding him of past conversations. Notwithstanding, it was now "abundantly clear" that the *Daily Gleaner* was "hell bent on destroying the People's National Party", using right-wing columnists as its tools. He urged a more constructive approach. He also wrote to a Jamaican financier in response to his contention that revolution was imminent:

> Have you ever thought that the alternative to the Prime Minister's declaration on Democratic Socialism could be a revolution far more catastrophic than the one you have envisaged? Time is against all of us in Jamaica. This, the Prime Minister realises, and he should be encouraged and supported by all men of goodwill in the formidable task that lies ahead.
>
> The safest guarantee to achieving the objective which we all share, is first of all to recognise that the methods tried in the past have miserably failed, and that new and drastic steps within the parliamentary democratic process must be taken to alleviate the plight of the masses. This, in my view, is what democratic socialism is about.

In a further letter to Manley, Isaacs underlined the reliability of Carlton Alexander, who was "doing everything possible to convince the private sector of their responsibilities". As he wrote, Isaacs already knew that he would be returning home. Concluding, he remarked, "Accept all that is good for you and your family and looking forward to seeing you once again."[29]

During this time, Isaacs had another priority: the treatment of Jamaican immigrants in Canada. In September 1974, it was reported in the press that the Canadian High Commission in Jamaica had recently imposed a six-month waiting period for work visas. This action appeared to be in response to rapidly increasing Jamaican immigration. A Canadian Green Paper was in the making. By no means unrelated, in October came a one-man Royal Commission into the Toronto police force regarding numerous charges of brutality, with Caribbean immigrants among the victims.[30] In

February 1975, Isaacs reported to Manley on consultations with his diplomatic colleagues from Trinidad, Barbados and Guyana. Anticipating Pierre Trudeau's visit to Jamaica for a Commonwealth heads of government forum, the four had raised the treatment of immigrants. Isaacs suggested that Manley speak directly to Trudeau.[31]

In April 1975, Isaacs received a detailed letter from a widowed fifty-year-old nurse, Lilith James, a Canadian citizen born in Jamaica. She lived with her children in Toronto. The letter described an ugly incident in which Toronto police and immigration officials had forced their way into her house without a warrant. Mrs James had protested and was choked and knocked to the ground. The men had been in pursuit of her sister-in-law for a minor breach of her entry permit. Mrs James herself was not involved and, following a complaint, the matter was closed. However, there was no redress for Mrs James. Isaacs wrote to the Canadian Secretary of External Affairs, and sent a copy to the premier of Ontario. In his letter, Isaacs said that, as Jamaica's High Commissioner, he could not tolerate "this sort of brutality by uncivilized immigration officers and policemen". He sent copies of the correspondence to Manley and again requested that he speak with Trudeau.[32]

Isaacs had also received verbal reports of police profiling and of black men under arrest who had been tortured, including the use of a technique called "the claw", where officers wrapped wire around their genitals and dragged them across the floor. Then in May, fifteen-year-old Michael Habbib was shot dead by a white man in a Toronto shopping centre. But for the fact that the victim was black, the shooting seemed random. It emerged that a white supremacist group was active in Toronto and that police officers were potentially involved. Isaacs attended the funeral, which drew four thousand mourners. His remark, that the police were "extremely racist, uncultured and inhuman", was reported in both Canada and

Jamaica. The *Daily Gleaner* deemed his comment undiplomatic.[33] Barely four weeks later, he received an enigmatic letter from Manley thanking him for his contribution to a highly successful tour of Canada by Jamaica's National Dance Theatre. Manley noted that "under separate cover" he would write "formally about the future". Vunnie portrayed the matter lightly. He noted that his father had been outspoken about the police. "And when him start to lick them 'bout the colour prejudice, Pierre Trudeau called Michael and beg him to take Wills home. And Michael took him back home."[34]

On his return, Isaacs wrote three columns for the Gleaner on Canadian racial discrimination. The Royal Commission report on Toronto police brutality was handed down in October 1976. Justice Morand's findings were bland. However, he deplored the extent to which police evidence was changed "to suit the circumstances" or was sometimes "entirely and deliberately false". He confirmed charges of brutality against some officers, and the use of the claw was corroborated.[35]

The Jamaica to which Isaacs returned in August 1975 was on edge. Foreign affairs made tensions at home and in the region more acute. In July, Manley had visited Cuba, where he had hinted that Isaacs might join him on his way home from Canada. Isaacs did not respond. He would have been an awkward witness to Michael's fulsome praise of Cuba, and his later support for Castro's pledge of troops to Angola's liberation struggle. Michael's stance was consistent with the PNP's long opposition to racialized oppression in southern Africa. The context, however, gave his speech not so much a non-aligned inflection, but rather a radical socialist one. Intolerant of socialism – both at home and in its spheres of influence – the US State Department was not impressed. A telegram sent from the US embassy in Jamaica, dated 17 July 1975, noted Manley's "unrestrained praise for his Communist neighbor and scorn for anyone who would criticize the Cuban model". On returning to Jamaica, the telegram continued, Michael addressed those gathered at the airport. Of Cuba he said, "No people in the world have such a feeling of happiness and contentment." As reported, he also said that for those who sought "palaces" or to be "millionaires", "there are daily flights to Miami where there is a different kind of society", amenable to capitalists.[36]

Edward Seaga had replaced Hugh Shearer as JLP leader. In a public speech soon after, Seaga claimed that the PNP government was laying the foundation for one-party rule.[37] Redbaiting and downtown violence seemed to go together. The violence was marked by partisan and criminal acts against a background of more and more guns in circulation. With or without CIA help, destabilization had begun.[38] Following horrific events downtown, including a fire on Orange Street that left ten dead and hundreds homeless, Manley declared a state of emergency in June 1976. A club frequented by PNP supporters had been machine- gunned just before his declaration.[39] The emergency would last for almost a year but, well before its end, Manley called a general election for 15 December 1976. Despite a vehement JLP anti-communist campaign, the masses came out for Michael. The government was returned with an increased majority.

In a 1975 by-election for Kingston East, Vunnie was elected to the Lower House, and returned in 1976.[40] Soon after his initial election, he was sworn in as a member of the House and a Cabinet minister without portfolio. He would assist Manley in the anti-inflation fight and liaise with Wills on commerce and marketing. Later, he became Minister of Labour. Vunnie joined a significant group of moderates whose influence was waning. Allan Isaacs had done them no favours. Suspected of leaking information to the JLP, he was excoriated and forced to resign early in 1976. In the general election, D.K. Duncan won the seat of St. Andrew East Central. Arnold Bertram and Hugh Small, the one originally from Abeng and the other from the YSL, were also elected to the House. Along with Anthony Spaulding, they formed a group in tune with

Michael's policy stance. The tenor of the times seemed to have turned left, but the victory was deceptive.[41]

By the end of 1976, the economy was not just under pressure, but already in dire straits. The foreign exchange reserves with which Jamaica purchased its imports were virtually exhausted, and international commercial banks had ceased to lend to the island. Soon, the Bank of Jamaica was assisting the government by manipulating the money supply to finance its social programmes and maintain minimal foreign reserves. In January 1977, G. Arthur Brown, head of the BOJ, called on local commercial banks to offer more support to the government. Albeit quietly, the Jamaican government had commenced talks with the IMF in March 1976 and, by December, had agreed on a standby facility for additional credit. However, in the wake of the general election, Manley returned to the Parliament with a mandate from the masses and, in January 1977, he opted for "bold politics". He renounced the standby agreement and described the IMF as "the central lending agency for the international capitalist system". His speech reflected the emerging position that his socialism was not "pro-communist", but rather "anti-imperialist" – against the hegemonic political and financial power of the United States. Yet, despite the strong words, Manley's stance towards the IMF proved indecisive.[42]

He outlined a package of economic measures, including a moratorium on wages, a higher sales tax on petrol, and tight restrictions on foreign exchange; the last to be used only for essential items. He rejected a devaluation of the currency and foreshadowed an Emergency Production Plan to increase Jamaica's productivity. The EPP taskforce included the UWI's Norman Girvan and George Beckford among others sympathetic to Manley's stance. Their focus was on self-reliance, a significant reduction in foreign capital investment, and the deployment of Jamaica's own resources. The centrepiece involved radical reform of agriculture. However, the EPP had a sticking point. Without IMF assistance, up to twenty-five thousand jobs could be lost in manufacturing. This was a third of the sector's labour force and would be disastrous for the PNP. In any case, the unions rejected the wage moratorium. Manley returned to the IMF in May. An agreement was reached in July for a loans package totally US$74.6 million over two years. Assets tests would measure the agreement's progress. Jamaica failed the first test in December, albeit by a small margin. The negotiated loans were placed on hold.[43]

During 1977, increasing tensions were evident in the Cabinet. A *Sunday Gleaner* column drew attention to the fact that the new Cabinet was not only large, but also involved parallel structures: the first, which included the traditional ministries such as Mining, Agriculture, Education and Labour; and a second, with two overarching ministries – one involved with National Mobilization and the other with Parliamentary Affairs. The former would focus on productivity across all sectors and on mobilizing youth. The latter would seek to keep portfolios consistent with each other. Under Ken McNeill, Parliamentary Affairs was uncontroversial. As Minister of National Mobilization, however, the forceful and articulate D.K. Duncan ran into trouble. His new ministry reflected the government's ambivalence towards the IMF. An IMF opponent from the outset, Duncan became wedged between a commitment to mobilize youth in the cause of self-reliance, and the view of some cabinet colleagues that the IMF's demands must be met. Several of D.K.'s initiatives regarding strikes, schools, and land reform were at cross purposes with those of other ministers. Moreover, although ostensibly aligned with Manley, some saw him as a threat to the leadership. During 1977, he was often ill and, increasingly, youth activist Leroy Cooke acted as his deputy. In September, Duncan resigned from Cabinet and from his party position. Subsequently, Ralph Brown replaced him as the PNP's general secretary.[44]

This did not stanch a stream of remarks from the backbench, the party's youth, and its women's movement. Manley himself had distinguished between progressive and reactionary businessmen, a distinction he retained even when speaking of flights to Miami. But the remarks of some comrades were far more radical. In June 1977, Minister of Housing Anthony Spaulding proposed that Jamaica's struggle was to "obliterate capitalism" and "the naked ruthlessness of the rich". And, in October, Duncan, from the backbench, said that the times would see the party either become a "liberation movement" or "regress" to the "plague" that enslaved Jamaica's people. During his visit to Jamaica, Castro and Manley discussed economics. Castro may have noted the unwillingness of the Soviet bloc to be involved with Jamaica financially. Darrell Levi records that Castro counselled against a path for Jamaica independent of the IMF. Leroy Cooke recalls that Castro joined a chorus that included envoys from the United States, a previous advisor from Cuba and others urging Manley to stay the course with the IMF. Such advice from those on the left may have reflected the view that Jamaica's economy, when compared with Cuba's, was both small and under-resourced. Moreover, the life of a socialist island state within the US sphere of influence was not easy.[45]

Negotiations resumed, and this time the IMF proved unforgiving. Its position was that the government persistently refused to rein in deficit spending, while the view from the PNP's left was that spending cuts would only erode advances already achieved. The IMF's new conditions revolved around two basic issues: the exchange rate for the Jamaican dollar, and the government's income policy. Both these factors were central to the competitiveness of exports, and it was through more production for export that Jamaica's balance of payments would be righted, and foreign reserves replenished. Therefore, the recommendation was for a devaluation of Jamaica's dollar and a comprehensive freeze on wages. The two factors were closely linked, as Norman Girvan observed: "The greater the degree of wage increases allowed, the higher the devaluations would have to be; the lower the devaluations the Government wanted, the more restrictive the wages policy it would have to impose."[46]

In March 1978, at Manley's behest, David Coore resigned as Finance Minister and from Parliament. In Manley's view, he could have done more to appease the IMF. Eric Bell took his place and at the end of April settled on a three-year programme. Nonetheless, the IMF demanded immediate action: a 15 per cent devaluation and price liberalization that would guarantee a 20 per cent return on private sector investment. Moreover, real wages should be reduced substantially. Bell called the demands "unduly harsh".[47]

As both the government and the masses struggled with the IMF conditions, the strain showed on Manley's Cabinet. In addition to Coore, Vivian Blake (Industry and Commerce), Ken McNeill (Parliamentary Affairs) and Ernest Peart (Works), as well as A.G.R. Byfield resigned from the Parliament. Although their reasons were diverse, the combined effect was to undermine good governance.[48] The year 1979 brought widespread violence in Kington; further rises in the price of oil; tropical storms and floods in June; an economy unable to recover; and loud criticism from the private sector and the *Daily Gleaner.* Two events sharpened these critiques. At the end of August, Manley attended the Sixth Summit of the Non-Aligned Movement, which was held in Havana. In his address, he said that the struggle against imperialism, though long, remained strong – both in the Caribbean and Latin America. That strength was due to "a movement and a man: […] the movement is the Cuban Revolution, and the man is Fidel Castro".[49] In September 1979, D.K. Duncan was re-elected as general secretary of the PNP. His early and consistent opposition to the IMF had elevated his standing among comrades.

As 1979 drew to a close, Eric Bell and his advisors had finessed almost workable relations between the IMF and the government. Then, in December, Jamaica failed another IMF test, even though the fund agreed that external factors were involved. To many it seemed that the IMF's stance was political.[50] Bell advised that the IMF's new targets would be hard to meet, and Manley paused negotiations in February 1980. In March, a report from the PNP's own Economic Affairs Commission concluded that the party had lost mass support and must change course. Once again, an alternative path of self-reliance was chosen. The party's NEC issued its own declaration: "Without development there is no future. If there is no future, who needs the IMF?" Soon after, Bell resigned and Manley trimmed his Cabinet further. The leader took on Agriculture, Hugh Small, Finance, and Vunnie became minister of both Labour, and Industry and Commerce. Duncan resumed as Minister of Mobilization.[51] Vunnie would soon resign his ministries and move to the backbench.

By this time, public opinion was deeply polarized, with few voices left in support of a combined national effort. In January 1980, the Public Sector Organization of Jamaica gave majority support to a JMA resolution calling for the PNP government to resign. The one dissenting public voice was founder and president of the PSOJ, Carlton Alexander, who had led Isaacs' 1972 trade mission to China and beyond. In December 1979, Alexander had called on the government to review its budgeting and turn the focus back to capital development. Too many non-income-earning projects had loaded the island with enduring inter-generational debt. And, at the meeting which passed the JMA resolution, Alexander called on the PSOJ to "set its own house in order". Business could do much more to replenish Jamaica's foreign exchange.[52] His voice was barely heard.

Just as the opinion-makers went to war with each other, so did the parties' supporters on the streets, but with far more brutal results. Amanda Sives reports that the "most blatant" politics that heightened the violence occurred in Kingston's west. Between

1972 and 1976, houses constructed by the government were distributed on a partisan basis. The intention was to encircle the JLP's Tivoli Gardens with the PNP's own neighbourhood enclaves. Organization on the streets became more systematic, not least in the acquisition of firearms. Politicians from both sides were involved. Moreover, the opposing groups imbibed the rhetoric of socialism versus capitalism, each one associating violence with the other. The length of the campaign almost certainly made the mayhem worse. Manley foreshadowed an election in February, but a new enumeration took more than six months to complete. Effectively, the election campaign ran from February to 30 October. The official number of murders for 1980 was 889, more than double that of the previous year. Significant injuries, as well as other murders, probably went unrecorded.[53] Overwhelmingly, the carnage was in Kingston. Downtown, destruction was widespread, with residents displaced to the city's fringes. Prior to the election, the PNP had a parliamentary majority of forty-seven seats to the JLP's thirteen. The returns for 1980 were JLP fifty-one seats and nine for the PNP – with 87 per cent of those registered turning out to vote.

Jamaica's balance-of-payments and foreign reserve problems involved domestic as well as external factors. And where social effects are concerned, neither side can be absolved. Over many years, both succumbed to clientelism and victimization. Still, Manley's statements on a world stage, more radical than his actions at home, played poorly to local interests and a US audience hostile to socialism. Both foreign and local capital took flight, and the economy all but collapsed. Moreover, the oil shock had an enormous impact. Between 1974 and 1982, the terms of trade for less developed countries, including Jamaica, worsened by 15 per cent. Worldwide inflation, and depleted export markets, meant that Jamaica's budget and current account deficits rose inexorably. For the ideologically inclined, it was easier to blame socialist mismanagement than world markets which had gone awry.

Writing of Jamaica, Sharpley argues that the IMF's "pro-market bias" was a matter of economic efficiency, rather than politics. However, she also notes that, though claims of "anti-socialist bias" are "questionable", "the conditions required for [IMF] credit were out of all proportion to the resources made available". In fact, since the 1970s, it has been accepted that IMF conditionalities can destabilize – rather than stabilize – a vulnerable society. It was just such a circumstance that forced Michael Manley to an early election.[54] Still, was the PNP's grasp of the resources at its command, and of the structures of power it faced, sufficient to support an alternative path? A party plagued by anti-communist cant since the 1940s seemed to lose its way in the 1970s, as "bold politics" prevailed over "well-thought-out government".

## An ambivalent departure...

Wills Isaacs sat on the sidelines as these events unfolded. His last years were spent in Gordon Town at his residence, Clifton Hill, just outside Kingston. Vunnie, who did not stand for re-election, kept Isaacs informed. Moreover, a retired Hugh Shearer lived nearby. In the course of 1976 and 1977 some developments occurred that Isaacs would have welcomed. His friend and associate, Carlton Alexander, established the Private Sector Organization of Jamaica in March 1976. Alexander planned to guide the sector in a more constructive direction – working with governments, rather than against them. In the 1950s and 1960s, the commercial class had proven highly risk-averse, keen to pursue government protection, unwilling to rein in luxury consumption, while avoiding its tax obligations. *Both* the private and the public sectors could do better. This was Alexander's thought, described at the time by Carl Stone as "a very lonely road of counselling, reason, tolerance, national commitment and responsibility". Though not always in the spirit that Alexander hoped for, the PSOJ would endure as an influential organization.

Years later, Arnold Bertram and Trevor Munroe, doyens of the left, would remark on his "principled leadership" at the time.[55]

In 1977, the PNP government introduced the State Trading Corporation to focus on imported items required in quantities large enough to warrant bulk purchase. Effectively, it would have a monopoly on these goods. The aim was to "lower costs, save foreign exchange, and provide a cheaper 'basic needs basket' to consumers".[56] The STC incorporated Jamaica Nutrition Holdings Ltd., introduced in 1974 specifically to import bulk staple grains, milk solids, edible oils and the like. The new and larger STC would also address the importation of pharmaceuticals, textiles and industrial equipment. With his experience in trade, Isaacs would have welcomed the development and recalled the years of struggle to contain the cost of staples and ensure fair dealing among the merchants. The STC was soon attacked by the IMF and, later, by the PSOJ.

On 15 February 1978, Isaacs became a life member of the People's National Party. At the PNP's fortieth anniversary conference, he was presented to the faithful at the Ward Theatre, along with Vernon Arnett, Florizel Glasspole, Ken Hill (now returned to the fold), and Ken Sterling, his fellow unionist. Manley recalled Isaacs' campaigning: "When Wills Isaacs came on stage, he was not only Wills, but he was also the embodiment of a spirit of resistance." At a further meeting, Howard Cooke spoke of the early days and of comrades like himself and Isaacs, who had suffered "the outcasts and half-educated" sent by the British to rule the colony. Around this time, Isaacs himself wrote about Black Saturday, when BITU workers invaded downtown Kingston in retaliation for the TUC's asylum strike. Isaacs remarked that his escape was God's will alone. He also recalled his trial for sedition in 1949, and Norman Manley's successful defence. Isaacs remarked as an aside, "None will ever know how deep were the waters crossed, nor how dark was the night that some of us passed through in building the People's

National Party." These words referenced Norman Manley's and Isaacs' favourite hymn, "There were Ninety and Nine".[57]

The counterweight to these memories was the parlous state of both the government and Jamaican society. Isaacs may have felt relieved to bequeath trade and industry matters to P.J. Patterson and then, briefly, to his own son. The plethora of international agencies involved may have seemed formidable and consumer affairs had become a farce in a failing economy. Moreover, when it came to a sovereign Jamaica, the US press, surly banks and the IMF may have seemed an external force equal to the British. Still, Isaacs was more indirect than his comrades of a younger generation. In the last few years, he barely remarked in public on intra- or inter-party politics. However, when anti-imperialist rhetoric was at its height, he did publish a short piece in the *Daily Gleaner*, titled "God Bless America". It recalled the serious illness, in 1961, of his youngest daughter, due to a bungled smallpox vaccination. Close to death, the last-minute flight to the United States had saved her life. He could not dismiss the country – if only for its medical advances.[58] But neither could he overlook the widespread suffering among his fellow Jamaicans, which he had fought so hard to alleviate. Munroe and Bertram report that between 1972 and 1980, Jamaica's GDP declined by more than 20 per cent. Worse, "unemployment stood at 35 per cent as a result of the decline in private sector employment, which had fallen from 57 per cent to 34 per cent" of the labour force. Most who were still employed worked in the public sector or were "part of the 46 per cent engaged in petty trading and petty manufacturing".[59] Isaacs could have wept.

The man known as Jamaica's "Stormy Petrel" died aged seventy-eight on 3 January 1981. He received a state funeral, attended by Prime Minister Edward Seaga, Leader of the Opposition Michael Manley, and his mother, Edna, whom Isaacs knew well. A requiem mass was held at St Peter and Paul Roman Catholic Church, and he was interred in Calvary Cemetery. Carlton Alexander gave the eulogy, while Hugh Shearer and P.J. Patterson each read a lesson. Alexander said:

> He was first and foremost a Jamaican and all other loyalties and considerations were secondary to that fact. It was his strong sense of nationalism that impelled him to resist the imposition of foreign ideologies on the Jamaican political system and to oppose the submersion of the Jamaican identity in a wider political grouping.
>
> He had an instinctive feel for the needs of people and his innate sense of justice and fair play were reflected in his concerns that while the 'trade' should get on with the task of providing the goods, the rights of the consumer should be protected. The arena of politics afforded him the opportunity to display the commitment to service which was the hallmark of his life.

Michael Manley, as president of the PNP, had issued a statement:

> Wills O. Isaacs was one of the great figures of the Independence movement in Jamaica and one of the main architects of the People's National Party. He played a significant role, both in the building of the Party and the establishment of the democratic process in Jamaica. With his passing Jamaica has lost a great son.
>
> As Minister of Trade and Industry he played a tremendous part in the early industrialization process. He had a great gift as a speaker and was powerful in communicating to the ordinary people.
>
> He was intensely human, felt issues deeply, and was quick to anger, but equally had a great sense of humour. All of this combined to make him one of the most loved figures in the modern political history of Jamaica.

Vunnie remarked that he had hoped that Manley might give the eulogy. However, the family was vexed. Michael had not rebuked D.K. Duncan when he said that "like my father, I was trying to turn back the Socialist process". It was also known that in his final year, Isaacs turned to friends outside the party, several in the private sector. In his tribute, Abe Issa wrote of a long-time friend who, suffering serious illness, had wearied and become a little disheartened. Still,

Isaacs was PNP to the end. Those he admired in the private sector – Aaron Matalon and Carlton Alexander, in particular – had always been ready to work with him and the governments he served.[60]

Michael Manley did see Isaacs shortly before he died. Vunnie described the scene:

> The old man had a few hours that he asked me to fill and Michael had said he had to go and see Wills. So I took him up. And he was on the veranda, lying downstairs. So I shook him. I said, 'Pops, Michael is here to see you.' See him here. [Vunnie enacts his father sitting up slowly from a reclining position.] He said, 'Sonny', he used to call Michael 'Sonny'. He was the only person in the Party who could get away with it. He said, 'Sonny' …

Michael received some advice from an old party man on the future of the PNP. Following the funeral, public accolades were legion. Ken Hill had attended on behalf of the KSAC council and, at its next meeting, moved a motion of regret. He said that Jamaica felt a "deep sense of loss". In words that described his comrade's generosity, and reflected his own, Hill said that "unlike many of us, he kept no malice and his opponents suffered no recrimination or revenge". He remarked that Wills "loved life abundantly and the people more"; that here was a person who "transcended the normal ambit of human endeavour".[61]

# Conclusion

Wills O. Isaacs was a dedicated man, committed to both the people of Jamaica and his party. Volatile, but not vengeful, he pursued his role with a humour that echoed the ebullient Dr Mends. He was astute and held strong beliefs. These dual aspects of the man meant that he could compromise; though not all shared his views on when to bend or stand firm. However, the longevity of his influence and the respect he commanded at the end confirm that he did not stand alone.

His career reflected both his personality and his upbringing. Isaacs was an optimist, but practical as well. Born to the rural middle class, he faced the barriers imposed by modest means and limited schooling. Early on, his engagement with sugar workers in Westmoreland left a lasting impression. The death of his first wife and four of his five children almost unhinged him. Nonetheless, he found a path through commerce to a better life. His practicality was honed by that environment, and the cut and thrust of politics. He was neither a worker nor of the elite, hence he suffered from time to time a mild, but galling opprobrium derived from the British, and aimed at the "shopkeeper" class. The attitude is suggested by the *Daily Gleaner*'s eulogy: "Quick-tempered and fiery in nature he was of a different nature than the rest of his colleagues. Where they were for the most part, calm and deliberate in their actions, he was given to acts of impulse. But he was a patriotic Jamaican first, and a loyal party-man second, and it was with passion fierce and strong that he served both causes."[1]

Isaacs was his own man. Those he assisted or felt akin to, even when they quarrelled, often came from similar backgrounds. They included Carlton Alexander, Bustamante, Edward Hanna, Alfred Mends, P.J. Patterson and Hugh Shearer. Aaron Matalon was also in this group due to his modest formal education. Early in his first term as minister, Isaacs put his trust in Matalon as his Trade Administrator. In a local capacity, he also intervened when the PNP, in 1962, had failed to secure a seemly departure for labour hero A.G.S. Coombs. Isaacs understood the fear of retirement on meagre means.

Like many in his party, he identified as a socialist and never repudiated that position. But where, truly, did he stand on Jamaica's political spectrum? During his career, it is fair to say that Isaacs adjusted his position according to events. Early on, in the late 1930s and the 1940s, his stance was framed by the dominant opposition between fascism and socialism that informed debate on the Spanish Civil War, the rise of Nazism, and evolving knowledge of the Soviet Union. He was at home with the critique of laissez-faire capitalism and the language of exploitation. From this period, he also carried through a staunch opposition to totalitarian regimes of the right and the left. In them he saw racist intent and the propensity to violence. His opposition to British imperialism was in accord with his broader view of the politics of nations.

Once the PNP was formed, and embraced socialism, Isaacs was ready to call himself "socialist" and did so often, defending his position against more radical versions. His statement in 1950 was defining. He acknowledged that, as a young man, he identified Christianity with communism. Later, however, he distinguished between socialism and communism, branding the latter – in Stalin's hands, at least – authoritarian and oppressive.[2] Like Norman Manley, and even Michael, he continued to see an affinity between socialism and Christian communalism. In 1961, he embraced Israel as a socialist society, not least for its use of cooperatives in agriculture and industry. He also returned to Jamaica with a proposal for youth brigades. In Israel, he had seen the importance of committed youth to the well-being of a nation.

On becoming Minister of Trade and Industry, Isaacs changed his emphases. He enjoined capital – domestic and foreign – to work with the state for the people's benefit. He accepted both the fact of private capital and the need for incentives. He would talk to Jamaican capitalists as part of the nation and exhort them to do better. Together with the IDC, he courted those abroad. It was only after his period in power that his economic nationalism was given free rein. He questioned aggressively both the extent of government incentives to foreign firms and their benefits when profits were sent offshore. Isaacs' attempts to establish factories in depressed rural areas underlined the dilemmas of dealing with capital not controlled by the state. And for all his efforts, manufacturing failed to play the role that Arthur Lewis had assigned it: to be the leading sector in a widespread industrialization. By the 1970s, albeit in private correspondence, Isaacs was able to acknowledge the shortcomings of the Puerto Rican model. Still, in doing so, he admonished Michael to focus on the policies that the government had announced, and not the much broader agenda of democratic socialism.

Wills Isaacs left two notable legacies: One was Jamaica's tourist industry, with its linkages, which is now a major employer. The other was his heightened awareness of market failures. He sought to confront monopolies in an economy where competition often remained hypothetical. With regard to Caribbean Cement, the political forces arraigned against him were considerable; and where the JPSC was concerned, other factors intervened. The government's pressing need to expand public education competed with the need to electrify the island. Where would the capital come from to embark on both tasks? It is striking, however, that for the period 1964–65, the nationalization to which the PNP gave priority was JPSC, the company that Isaacs sparred with over six long years. Closely related to these monopolies were the cartels that burdened both industry and the masses with inflated prices. A number involved inter-linked firms. Isaacs' efforts evolved into the State Trading Corporation of the 1970s and a continuing governmental focus on the cost of living. These two legacies also had significant offshoots: a fillip to the construction industry via tourism and, with less costly raw materials, greater diversity in manufacturing. Certainly, Isaacs worked with capital, but it is unjust to suggest he was merely its servant.

He was flexible, but also principled. First and foremost, he was deeply anti-racist and opposed to British colonialism and its exploitation of the subject peoples of its empire.[3] His antipathy to white racism extended to Nazi Germany, South Africa, Rhodesia and to both the United States and Canada. He was a nationalist throughout his life, moved most of all by the aim of independence for Jamaica as a sovereign state, with command of its trade, resources and production. Economic nationalism was central to his vision. These commitments led him to oppose federation as "the bone the master throws to the dog". In his view, the cost of a regional administration would outweigh the benefits of economic integration. He was an advocate for regional trade with other island and mainland states, but federation involved much more.[4]

The right to private property was another of his core principles. There is no evidence to suggest that he thought there was an alternative to capitalism, though he clearly favoured a mixed economy. And, although he acknowledged the conflicting interests of capital and labour, there is no evidence that he thought beyond government regulation of one and unionization for the other. At least on the public record, he seldom expressed views about taxation, either of income or wealth, including land. Still, his early solidarity with Nethersole over the issue of property taxes for Kingston-St Andrew suggests that he favoured progressive taxation and the PNP's tax reforms of 1973. He was unsympathetic to *rentiers* of unimproved land, especially those who relied chiefly on appreciation for their wealth. However, the greatest tension between his beliefs probably concerned landed property. P.J. Patterson recalls that Isaacs resisted the caps on individual ownership that became PNP policy in 1964–65 though, in Patterson's view, his resistance was pragmatic, rather than ideological.[5] It is possible that Isaacs concurred with Norman Manley that, in Jamaica, rapid change in land ownership was not feasible. Subsequently, the moment passed and neither Isaacs nor his comrades found an alternative route to major rural reform.

Finally, he was religious. At some point between departure from his natal Presbyterian home, and his first marriage, he became a Roman Catholic – in his view, a world church rather than a British one. He was a practising religionist throughout his life and raised his children in that faith. While he remained a practical man and an astute politician, his world was not secular. He invoked God the Father, and the Son, as readily in Parliament and among master builders as he did when speaking to the masses. Although he said that the Church – no less than capitalism – was guilty of atrocities, he opposed the Soviets' persecution of religion. His faith shaped his politics in other ways too. His direct engagement with the unemployed, the homeless and the indigent, suggests an affinity with the work of religious as much as a leftist orientation.[6] He admired priests who worked with the poor and, when it came to KSAC Poor Relief, his concern was not just for workers. He also looked to the domestic sphere and the care of children.

His extensive religious study as a boy allowed him to deploy, without artifice, a biblical idiom on political platforms. His religion made manifest his openness to the people, and to their precarious world. For this reason, he was indispensable in PNP campaigns. Portrayed in the main as an urban politician, it is often overlooked that, throughout the 1950s, Wills had strong support in the countryside, as reflected in delegate voting at annual conferences. His populism inhered in his performance in "the streets and lanes". Among rural folk, it also inhered in his religion, his respect for private property, his vernacular, and his concern for labouring women as well as the men.

Wills Isaacs was a nationalist and a social democrat with a populist style. From the centre, he leaned to the left and then to the right, though he maintained consistent policies. His reputation among some as an entrenched right-wing politician reflects the party debates in which he was involved. Two factors seem to have shaped this assessment: Isaacs, like his leader Norman Manley, did not aspire to mass mobilization, rapid change or a command economy. Moreover, in the 1960s his social conservatism, greater than Manley's, distanced him from Rastafari and Black Power. However, these aspects of his stance must be placed beside his deep commitment to industry and trade. No one in the PNP of the 1950s was more engaged than he in the mechanics of creating jobs and reducing the cost of staples for the masses. His correspondence with Michael Manley between 1973 and 1975 suggests that he maintained these commitments. On the other hand, his suggestions that Michael consult with Carlton Alexander show that he did not see a course for Jamaica independent of private capital. He preferred local capital to the foreign kind, though Jamaica's capitalists were more often antagonists than allies. And herein lay the PNP's policy conundrum, which Norman Manley stated in 1966: How to realize a mixed economy that could address both infrastructural and social needs within the framework of Westminster democracy. In the end, both Isaacs and Norman rejected mass mobilization as an alternative to two-party politics.

Isaacs was not alone in being wedded to various institutions of the transatlantic Anglosphere. Indeed, and ironically, a muted British bias was reflected in some of his most notable remarks. On his treatment by Chief Justice Hearne, Isaacs quoted Rudyard Kipling; and on receiving his PNP life membership, William Blake's poem, "Jerusalem". Even so, his resort to these passages showed a man searching for the precise words to express his heartfelt emotions for his people.[7] And despite this leaning, his stance was very different from leading figures on the right, with whom he contended over decades. They included Robert Kirkwood, Richard Youngman, the boards of Caribbean Cement and JPSC, and the Gleaner Company, as manifest in its *Gleaner* editorial platform, to name a few. He may have gleaned a lot from early chats with Sir George Seymour Seymour. However, that did not persuade him to align with the JIA or become merely a mouthpiece for the JCC and JMA. Isaacs' life course equipped him to converse and negotiate, as best he could, with Jamaica's merchant capitalists and their supporters. The PNP, and not least Norman Manley and Nethersole, needed and accepted his voice.

In general orientation, Isaacs differed markedly from his leaders, Norman and Michael Manley. His relations with Norman were complex. It is likely that during 1957, and again in early 1961, Isaacs hoped to become PNP president. However, as Vic Reid suggests, his aspirations always had an 'if'. In the case of the first vice presidency, *if* Nethersole lost interest, he would run. Over the years, Isaacs made desultory efforts, but nominated for the first time – and won – only after Nethersole's death. Regarding the leadership, *if* Manley went to federation and Nethersole proved diffident, Isaacs would nominate. He may have succeeded, even in competition with Ken Hill who, on his resignation, took just a few comrades with him.[8] Citing Vernon Arnett as his authority, Reid describes a long-term plan by Isaacs to displace Nethersole and then Manley. This account also grants that the left's plan was to dispose of Isaacs as quickly as possible. Ken Post cites another such plan in earlier years to see Nethersole replace Manley.[9] From time to time, the PNP experienced fevered factionalism, and subsequent accounts tend to denigrate one player or another. As such, they obscure the fact that, in the long march to independence, Manley was a commanding figure. Whatever the designs of individuals, it seems unlikely that in the 1940s and 1950s, the PNP would have chosen another leader. Isaacs truly admired the man he referred to – always – as "Mr Manley".

However, with respect came ambiguity. The two men's views diverged and, while Isaacs honoured Manley, he did not always think him wise. The ambiguity was evident in Isaacs' self-deprecation. In the company of Seivright and Manley, Isaacs remarked that he was the man for the task when "the road becomes rocky" and "no longer calls for respectability"– an allusion to Gordon Town. It was January 1950. Seivright had been elected mayor and Isaacs his deputy.[10] Speaking in Parliament in 1957, Isaacs observed that he looked after the "little things", while Manley looked after the "big things"; a reference to his concern with manufacturing, while Manley addressed high finance. In his much-heralded 1960 estimates speech, describing both Manley and Bustamante as giants born to their historical roles, Isaacs placed himself among the "littler ones" who also had a part to play. And finally, paying tribute to Manley after the referendum loss, Isaacs praised his leader's principles, but questioned his politics. Referring to the series of bipartisan votes on federation prior to the JLP's volte face, Isaacs confessed that he would not have called a referendum; "but Mr Manley was a democrat" and chose that ill-fated course.

Manley, in turn, was effusive regarding Nethersole and the young men of the left whom he reluctantly asked to resign. Regarding Isaacs, he was tight-lipped. A significant class and status gap existed between them. For all the influence imputed to Isaacs on policy, and as elections brewed, Manley was restrained in his praise. Moreover, following the referendum debacle, and as electoral defeat loomed, he failed to consult his first vice president. Thereafter, Isaacs had his dissent recorded when Manley brushed aside his request that submissions on Jamaica's independence constitution be open to the people. He was outside the circle of Manley's closest confidantes and sometimes seemed to feel it. Both visionaries of sorts, it may be that the Manleys saw Isaacs as a man of limited scope. Despite his urbane interest in trade – with contacts established beyond the Anglosphere in Poland, Czechoslovakia, Israel, Iceland and China – Isaacs' feet were planted firmly in Jamaica. He was not by nature an internationalist, which both the Manleys were, though in different registers. Norman's eyes were trained on federation as the destiny of the West Indian people. He also believed that the large, long-term development loans that Jamaica required would be commanded more readily by a federation than by one small island. On the other hand, Isaacs noted in 1959 how the islands wrangled over a federal grant, a sign perhaps of things to come. Where Michael Manley was concerned, his internationalism addressed non-aligned states politically, and the peripheral economies, mainly of the South, which sought a New International Economic Order. On the latter point, Isaacs agreed. However, by 1977, Michael's very public embrace of Cuba was clearly not in Jamaica's interest. Castro cautioned him at the time. And, in their retrospective account, Stephens and Stephens note that "The direct attack on US economic interests entailed in the bauxite offensive generated nothing like the reaction that the Cuba connection did. That the charges of Cuban subversion of Jamaica [. . .] were almost entirely groundless is beside the point. Jamaica still lost more than she gained by the relationship."[11] On these matters, Isaacs fell silent as Manley, angered by the IMF, continued to poke the US bear.

Called "a rabble-rouser" by Norman, and a "resistance" figure by Michael, Isaacs preferred the term "stormy petrel" himself. He withstood the years in Opposition and on the streets. In

Parliament, he used his breadth of knowledge and rhetorical flair to shape debate. In trade and industry, as well as consumer affairs, he deployed his grasp of commercial life to advance the well-being of the masses. Wills Isaacs was a different man from the Manleys, yet he was loyal to them as leaders of his party.

Wills Isaacs' story sheds a light on Jamaica and its political economy, past and present. The century in which he lived brought Jamaica both great rewards and great trials. Following crown colony rule, the island became independent, built its own social, political and financial institutions, developed a more diverse economy, and became renowned for its stand against racist regimes, and its achievements in sports and the arts. However, the global, regional and domestic pressures with which this story began brought suffering and violence to many in Kingston and across the island. With it came further social and economic grief that few could have imagined, even in 1938. Jamaica's internal and external migrations were indicative of a plantation and small farmer economy which, underdeveloped by Britain, had reached its limits. Industrialization by invitation failed in the 1950s and 1960s, due in part to the cost of capital and to the growth of mass production in much larger, low-wage societies. Principally in Asia, and often with levels of investment that Jamaica could not command, these societies rode the wave of industrialization. The advent of highly efficient container shipping swept away Jamaica's previous advantage of proximity to the United States. Subsequently, extended quarrels over trade – especially regarding textile and garment exports – hurt Jamaica. Negotiations involving the General Agreement on Trade and Tariffs and the World Trade Organization, in conjunction with preferences denied, due to the North American Free Trade Agreement and the European Union, have deprived the island of much-needed overseas markets.[12] Consequently, the range of manufactured goods for export has narrowed, while the volume and value of Jamaica's commodity exports have declined. Bauxite and sugar are no longer a core strength, while tourism – the main employer – is subject to fluctuations based on both internal and external factors.[13] As the twentieth century turned into the twenty-first, these challenges came with other, equally formidable ones.

Jamaica's relationship with the IMF, which began in earnest in the 1970s, has proved to be a continuing saga. The financial crisis of 1996–97 exacted a heavy toll on the government, numerous firms other than financial ones, and on individuals – many of modest means. The government issued a deposit guarantee that ensured the savings of some, but by no means all of those involved. The guarantee helped stabilize civil society but, in conjunction with high interest rates at home and abroad, added to Jamaica's debt. By 2009, that debt had reached 142 per cent of GDP. A circumstance that was unsustainable led to Jamaican Debt Exchanges (JDXs) in 2010 and 2013. Domestic financial institutions, and numerous individuals, agreed to lower interest rates and extend existing periods of debt repayment. The government avoided financial collapse, but not without resort to the IMF. Agreements were secured in 2010, 2013 and 2016. By 2019, government fiscal restraint – with minimal spending on infrastructure, education, housing and health – had reduced debt somewhat. However, celebrations were cut short by the arrival of the Covid pandemic.

The government response sought to assist workers, businesses and the markedly disadvantaged, but at an inevitable cost. Further IMF assistance came in 2020 and 2023. Dryly, the fund reported that the rule against deficit budgeting had been suspended for one year. The deadline by which the island's public debt had to be reduced to 60 per cent of GDP was extended by two years. All the while, 23 per cent of Jamaica's people were living below the poverty line.[14]

Can one compare the post-war world that Isaacs faced with that which emerged following Jamaica's financial crisis? Certainly, the contours of international trade and finance, which Jamaica cannot escape, have become clearer – and herein lies a connection. Isaacs, like his comrades and their leader, Norman Manley, were nationalists; albeit, as Manley made explicit, with their major focus on the masses. Although some see this nationalism as opposed to a working-class and a black nationalist politics, it can be viewed in another way: as an understanding that Jamaica, facing perennial challenges, needs a whole-of-society approach.

Ironically, Jamaica's financial crisis impressed this fact upon its private sector – since their own interests were now at stake. A pioneering effort, the Acorn Group, comprising trade unionists and some business leaders, was formed in 1997. Focused on industrial relations, it addressed, among other issues, the impact of globalization on "every facet of the Jamaican community". Trevor Munroe, from the radical left, was a speaker on this topic. Commencing in 2003, the Partnership for Progress included representatives from trade unions, private sector organisations, agriculture and NGOs, including the human rights lobby group Jamaicans for Justice. And during the 2013 Jamaica Debt Exchange, the National Partnership Council and the Economic Programme Oversight Committee emerged; the former chaired by the prime minister and bipartisan, the latter co-chaired by the Minister for Finance and a representative from Jamaica's private sector. In 2010, both the JMA and PSOJ gave early support to the debt exchange and urged the financial sector to cooperate. Jamaica Money Market Brokers signalled their support in January, and Jamaica's two largest banking groups – NCB and Scotia Jamaica – followed suit soon after.[15]

Critics of 'the businessmen' spoke up. In 2008, Robert Buddan published a comment on the government and capitalists both, noting that members of the private sector talked mostly about what "Government should do", and very little about their own responsibilities. These businessmen, he remarked, said nothing about "how to improve the education and training of employees, what is needed to conserve energy and other costs, how to take advantage of CARICOM [...] how to make business more efficient and globally competitive, and how to bring the diaspora market more fully into our economy."[16] In 2010, columnist Wilberne Persaud took up comparable themes. With reference to Wall Street and the global financial crisis, he remarked on Jamaica's own financiers: No "wealth-holder" who could earn "17 per cent off government paper" would bother to build a factory or find markets for manufactured goods produced in a rural parish. However, having brought the crisis on, self-interest triumphed over interest rates. Anxious financiers agreed to lower the rates. Persaud took aim not simply at the finance sector, but at capitalists in the round. He warned that the debt exchange alone would not bring the type of growth that Jamaica required. That growth would need to be "soundly based, [...] equipping the unemployed with skills and making wise, prudential and innovative use of natural, cultural and proven resources". Such growth, he suggested, had been hard to achieve because "Jamaican capitalists enjoy a kind of almost-monopoly or oligopoly situation", expecting high returns on their capital, and protection from competition.[17]

"It is not easy for men who have known the easy way to amass wealth to turn their backs on that way, to take the harder road." So said Wills Isaacs in 1955 as he sought to speak with both the masses and the merchant capitalists. That harder road was required because foreign private capital would prove not simply "footloose" but, in the longer term, largely indifferent to Jamaica's modest human and natural resources. In view of regional and global constraints, the finance to address Jamaica's intractable inequities must come in part from those with some affection for their homeland; a local class which, by virtue of its interests, will come into conflict with government over wages and profits, taxation, industry protection, raw material subsidies and, at times, the movement of capital in and out of the island.

Nevertheless, a whole-of-society approach needs a workable relationship between local capital and government to obtain multilateral development finance. Agency funds are required to foster innovation and assist with basic services, public works and workforce skills. Among Jamaica's diasporic communities, social impact investing linked to sustainability could contribute. Without the gains in productivity that investment brings, it is hard to see Jamaica's two-party politics moving beyond clientelism to address a further challenge: the widespread disaffection among youth who lack the skills to secure a future in Jamaica. Their deep and abiding discontent is fuelled by the conspicuous consumption of the wealthy, and by the failure of governments to fulfil their promises. Spoken on behalf of kin as the 1970s neared its end, the words of a friend still ring true: "It's like promises, promises, and after promises, excuses, and after excuses more excuses [….] Nothing coming up, and he is tired and frustrated and he don't see no way out." In the 2010s, a new generation of youth justified a turn to crime with the observation, "Me na work fe monkey money" – the pittance paid to unskilled black youth living downtown.[18]

Following Jamaica's financial crisis, Kari Levitt noted that social stability requires much more than fiscal and monetary policies. Left to these means alone, stabilization falls mainly on the poor. Politically, the policies fail. They also need, she remarked, "a more egalitarian, participatory and co-operative relationship between the major classes and interest groups in society." Some years later, Michael Witter wrote that "until Jamaica fashions an appropriate social compact to guide, facilitate and direct focused productive activity by the society as a whole, economic conditions will continue to deteriorate." Their views on change may diverge, but there is a common theme – the need for a whole-of-society approach, which goes beyond the ambit of market economics and partisan politics.[19]

For some, the term 'mass mobilization' connotes a command economy, possibly leading to a one-party state. Today, such a prospect has become remote; due not only to US influence on the region, but also to the international structures of trade and finance that bolster a global order. Still, the nationalism of Wills Isaacs' time, with its British-derived institutions, also falls short. In Jamaica, it has tended to produce a non-inclusive politics in which the more privileged still hold sway, with deleterious results. In his discussion of Jamaica's Westminster system, Bryan Meeks suggests a starting point for change. He notes that the 1962 Bill of Rights included in the independence constitution effectively privileged property rights – foreign and domestic – over the rights of the propertyless for employment, shelter and health supports. He called for referenda and a convention aimed at constitutional change.[20] While governments need adequate resources with which to work, focused productivity – by and for a whole society – needs well-crafted politics. A more inclusive Bill of Rights might provide leverage for further debate about levels of taxation, the democratic process and the social state. Jamaica's non-compulsory, first-past-the-post voting system does not encourage independent candidates or newly formed groups unaligned with the major parties. In view of Jamaica's marked and persistent inequality, campaign funding targeted at diversifying the political field could also help. Lastly, both recognition of Britain's historical debt to the West Indies, and fairer relations between North and South would facilitate constructive constructive change in Jamaica, and other like states.

Wills Isaacs assumed that socialism, of the type that he embraced, could align with enterprise to serve the people. He understood that, in his cherished land, better could come from the cooperative spirit of farmers and the determination of workers, supported by more local investment. Powerful interests would remain, but could be blunted in service to the nation. He and his comrades presided over significant changes, but in the longer term their efforts did not realize all that they had hoped for and worked towards. Since that time, the tendency has been to denigrate their generation far more than to praise it. Wills Isaacs' story invites a more positive response.

In recent years, the struggle between the social responsibility of elected governments and the reach of financial capital bent on profit has become increasingly unequal. This circumstance reveals that even wealthy democratic states, and especially those riven by race, consistently fail groups that they claim to represent. Moreover, the steady flow of economic refugees, often from the South and heading north to Europe or the United States, underlines the truly international dimensions of this inequality. When it comes to Jamaica, the issue may not be those who have worked for change but, rather, the structures of power that make their task so difficult. An appreciation of this fact brings respect both for those who went before and for those who continue the struggle.

# Appendix: In His Own Words

Though many have remarked on the power of Wills Isaacs' oratory, few records of his speeches remain. Three examples follow. Together, they are indicative of his ability to move an audience, and to win arguments using passion and wit. The first example is a speech that he delivered in 1950, which addressed the fact that the PNP was a socialist party, and rightly so – rather than capitalist or communist. Delivered in his Kingston Central constituency, the speech was one of several developments that culminated in the split of 1952. In a dramatic passage, Isaacs instances Eastern European nationalists and socialists sidelined or forced out of power by communists loyal to Moscow. In the case of Jan Masaryk, son of Tomáš Masaryk, his cause of death is still disputed – murder or suicide. The truth may never be known. Still, Isaacs' reference to nationalist heroes pushed aside by secretive communist forces was, perhaps, a none-too-subtle reference to PNP cliques and their purported designs on Norman Manley's leadership.

The second and third examples, one in 1956 and the other in 1978, reach back to the 1940s, and to the years of struggle to establish the PNP as a mass party. The 1956 parliamentary speech came during debate on an Opposition motion deploring political appointments made by the newly elected government. Some of the appointments were to public service positions and others were at worksites in Kingston and the parishes. Where the latter were concerned, issues of clientelism and victimization were involved. The Opposition also cited Isaacs' appointment of Vernon Arnett to a new position as financial controller of the IDC. Previously, Arnett had been the PNP's general secretary for some years. As Minister of Trade and Industry, Isaacs no doubt preferred someone in the IDC position whom he felt would resist the pressure of private sector interests. In his response to the Opposition, he addressed two issues. One was clientelism and victimization. Dating these practices to the formation of Jamaica's first elected government, he deplored the JLP's hypocrisy. Left unsaid was the PNP view that police and unelected colonial officials allowed the JLP's victimization of PNP supporters to go unchecked. Regarding his appointment of Arnett, Isaacs was on firm ground. His choice was strongly supported by both his permanent secretary and the IDC's chair, Harold Braham. Nor did the *Gleaner* raise any objections. The third example of Isaacs' oratorical skill was on the occasion of the party's fortieth anniversary, and his PNP life membership. An emotional reflection on the 1940s, he also honoured the leadership of Norman Manley. Given at a time when Michael Manley's government was under increasing pressure, his words demonstrated his deep commitment to the party.

## Socialism, Capitalism and Communism

April 1950, reported in *The Daily Gleaner*[1]

"In Jamaica today, we are so taken up with our own troubles and difficulties and poverty that we seem to forget that we are part of the world and that what happens in the world will sooner or later affect us. At the present time there are grave and serious differences between the Eastern and Western Nations of the world, and although you and I don't know it, there are feverish preparations being made for war.

"Now, in a situation such as this, where do we stand? It is the duty, the grave and solemn obligation of every public man to direct the thoughts of his own people to this most important subject. In trying to direct thoughts, I must say that there has been much loose thinking amongst our people in believing that Socialism and Communism are the same thing. I am not going to blame them for that loose thinking, because I myself did much loose thinking at the beginning, when I came into public life. There was a time in my life when I thought so too – when I thought that Communism and Christianity were one and the same thing. It was only after years of reading and study that I realized that I was making a mistake.

"In trying to direct the thoughts of his people, it is necessary for the public man of any importance today, to state his own public views. The party to which I belong declares itself a Socialist Party, and I wish to declare that I am a Socialist. I believe implicitly in the programme and policy of my own party. I believe in the nationalization of certain basic industries. I believe that no real progress will come to this country unless we are prepared to accept the programme of nationalization of certain basic industries as our guide.

"I want it to be clearly understood that as far as I am concerned, when there is a conflict between the capitalist and the worker, I am bound to take up the cudgels and to fight the battles of the working-class people of this country. And I want to state very clearly that if an employer wishes to use the power of his money to take advantage of the worker, if an employer refuses to listen to reason, I will have no qualms of conscience in using force in fighting him. I may be criticized by many for that decision, and I am not going to quarrel with my critics. They have a right to disagree with me. My only answer is, my conscience is clear on the point and I am not going to change that decision.

"But when a man states what is his political creed, when you say that you are a Socialist, that is not enough. If you tell the world that you are totally opposed to laissez-faire capitalism and the system of exploitation you see around, that is not the only thing that the Socialist is opposed to. The Socialist is totally opposed to the Communist way of life, and when a man declares himself a Socialist, he has an obligation to declare himself not only against the Capitalist exploitation of mankind, but also against Communism.

"I say without fear of reasonable contradiction that failure to make such a declaration leaves people with a sense of insecurity and with a sense of fear. Because no man's political faith must be a secret unto himself nor should it be shrouded in mystery. The people of your nation must know you as they know themselves. They must know what you will do and what you will not do.

"Having said that, I know that there are a few people who will say it does not make any difference if the Socialist and Communists work together. Events have proven throughout the world that that is a total impossibility, because in every country where the Socialists have co-operated with the Communists after a while there begins, first of all, a smear campaign against the Socialist and assassination of his character. History has shown to us very clearly that wherever that co-operation takes place, the Socialist will either have to run for his life or be assassinated. That is what happened to Kostov of Bulgaria, to Masaryk of Czechoslovakia, who was leader of his people, responsible for the movement against Hitler. Benes of Czechoslovakia died of a broken heart and Masaryk was foully murdered.

"In Jamaica our stand must be clear. My party is a Socialist Party, and we must see that it remains a Socialist Party. There can be no co-operation with capitalist elements who have exploited the people for a long time. But there can also be no co-operation with the Communist. Our party in Jamaica is a queer combination of being Nationalist and Socialist at the same time. Our position as part of the Colonial Empire seems to force this upon us, but I want it to be clearly understood that this party is not going to be any open sesame for Marxism and Communism, for if ever this begins I am going to warn the working-class people of the danger. I am going to warn the nation of the danger. I have promised the people of this country that if ever I see anything wrong, I am going to tell it to them.

"I want to be perfectly frank and tell you that I am seeing things at the moment that I don't like. I am hearing things I don't like, and I promise you that I am watching it very keenly and I am going to come back to you again very shortly to speak to you, the people. For there is no man in this country too high, too lofty or too rich, that if the necessity arises, I will not oppose publicly."

## Victimization and Democracy

July 1956, recorded in Proceedings of the House of Representatives (Hansard)[2]

"Mr Speaker, I think the Opposition should be the last people to charge anybody with political appointments. I can speak perhaps with greater authority and deeper emotion than anybody on political appointments and political victimization in this country. During the years, Mr Speaker, of 1944 down to perhaps 1946 and 1947, I have seen political appointments, political victimization in this country that would touch the hardest hearts. I have seen, Mr Speaker, in the KSAC during those years where men were hounded down as if they were criminals, because of their political views.

"There is one man that stands out very clearly in my memory, who was run out of his job. He walked the streets of Kingston hungry for two years, starved, fell into tuberculosis, because of malnutrition, and his last words upon his dying bed were, 'I am sorry I will not live to see my Party in power.' It was done when that side was in power, Mr Speaker.

"The brutality and victimisation of our people during those years are very fresh in memory, and I could never forget it. As a matter of fact, it has almost become a pattern laid down and it is a pattern from which we are suffering, because the Chief Minister has laid down that there shall be no victimisation – that we shan't interfere with employees, and we have got to obey. But it is a hard order to obey, because if I was Chief Minister my people would have to get work first. I speak freely about it. I have seen my people being beaten on jobs, and beaten off the work they get, bruised and bleeding. I have seen it, Mr Speaker, with my own eyes. It has been the most heartless party that this country has ever known, and those of our people who have suffered over the years are looking to us at least to satisfy them now, and because, with all the honour to the Chief Minister who wants to build up a democracy, something worthwhile that is decent in this country, we have to suffer and take it.

"I have not forgotten the case, Mr Speaker, of the railway. When those men showed that they did belong to a union that was not affiliated to the party in power, hundreds of them were dismissed. Men who had served for years and years, one day they were thrown out of work on the streets, with their wives and children not knowing where they would earn the next month's salary. And many of them have walked the street for long periods without getting work. [....]

"And we are told now about political victimization. I don't know how anybody on that side could have so much brass in the face to talk about that when the Chief Minister has had the guts and courage to have done what he has done and has laid down a course that we have to follow. A course that is hard. It is because I am of a disciplined party, and I have got to obey, but it is the hardest bit of obedience that I have ever exercised in my life. When I remember those dark days of 1944 to 1947, men were not only victimized, but brutally beaten off their jobs.

"Then I have heard them mention the appointment of Mr Arnett to the IDC. Mr Speaker, the present position he holds, the first person the recommendation came from was my permanent secretary, who sat with me on that board and said, 'You cannot find a better man' [and then] I said, if I cannot find a better man on the board, and the chairman of the board, the chairman said, 'You cannot find anybody as good in this country.' And those of us who know him know that you cannot find anybody else that can do that job; and when you enquire up there of the work he is doing to clean up that place, as he is cleaning it up – if sensible people are PNP people, don't blame them (laughter). You expect us to put fools there? I don't know any sensible Bustamante people [...]"

The Speaker cautioned Isaacs, though Bustamante said that he did not mind. Isaacs continued:

"I don't mean to insult. I only mean that I don't know them (laughter). Go downtown, Mr Speaker, and ask the people with whom [Arnett] worked what a loss it has been to them that he has been appointed to that post in the IDC, then you will understand what the man's ability is. Not to mention the man's integrity, which is vital in any corporation of that type. We on this side, Mr Speaker, have got to put the two things together, ability and integrity. We cannot take any chances, and I feel very strongly about this talk of political appointments."

Isaacs' contribution to the debate was almost at an end. He returned to the theme of party patronage, or clientelism in government; a practice he ascribed to the Republican and Democratic parties in the United States which, he suggested, Bustamante had copied. The latter protested; Isaacs did not waver; and the Speaker did not intervene.

## Struggle, Trouble and Loyalty

February 1978, reported in the *Sunday Gleaner*[3]

"Comrades, forty years in the life of any organization is a creditable span. It is the more creditable when the role of such an organisation at its onset was a pioneering one. It is a wonderful thing that such an organisation, dedicated to the cause of its fellow men, has striven to break down barriers which enslaved the people politically, economically and socially; and as I look back along the years we have trod I rejoice with you today that we have been able to pave the way out of a slough of despond to a brighter and better day for our generation and the next.

"As I have said, it has been a long hard road. I remember the turbulent days. I remember the days when it took courage, yes, great courage, to lift up your head and be counted as a member of the People's National Party. I remember the harassment of our leadership. I remember the internment of the Hill boys, Domingo, Samuel Marquis and others. I remember the shooting of Adina Spencer in cold blood because she espoused our cause. I remember the persecutions of some of us – Thossy Kelly, myself and others.

"Oh yes, I remember the bloody battle of Gordon Town and more than all, I remember Black Saturday and the slaying of John Nicholas.

"And I recall, my Comrades, how when as I gave evidence before the Hearn [sic] Commission, how I was badgered when I told the stern judge that a few broken skulls were nothing in the growth of a nation. Those of you who have travelled along these years of our struggles are witnesses to the fulfillment of that statement, or was it a prophecy?

"And if I had to live my whole life over again, I am sure that I would travel along the same road and do the same things I have done alongside my colleagues.

"Comrades, it was my great honour and pleasure to have been a close and constant aide of my late beloved leader, Norman Washington Manley. I recall his sincerity, his devotion, his integrity, his unfailing love for his people, and his sacrifice for his party and the cause of Jamaica. Many were the long days and the long, long nights which he toiled. And those of us who stood beside him and walked beside him were inspired by his genius and his great knowledge, and I say to you who carry on in the traditions set by him, and who are privileged to walk in the footsteps left on the sands of time of this great party, revere his memory and honour his name.

"Finally, my comrades, I remind you that it is your solemn duty as the party which is the custodian of the welfare of the people of Jamaica, that you have the inescapable responsibility of dedicating yourself anew to the cause you serve. To work unstintingly no matter what the cost, in order that you can help to fulfil the dream of Norman Manley and those of us who toiled before you, of building Jerusalem in Jamaica's green and pleasant land."

Notwithstanding his own life and politics, Isaacs' conclusion cites "Jerusalem", a British nationalist poem. Assuredly Jamaica, not England, was Wills Isaacs' "green and pleasant land".

# Notes

## Preface

1. For my major works on Jamaica, see *Urban Life in Kingston, Jamaica: The Culture and Class Ideology of Two Neighbourhoods* (Abingdon: Routledge, 2018 (1984)), and *Jamaica Genesis: Religion and the Politics of Moral Order* (Chicago: Chicago University Press, 1997); and on Australia, *Arrernte Present, Arrernte Past: Invasion, Violence and Imagination in Indigenous Central Australia* (Chicago: University of Chicago Press, 2008), and *A Different Inequality: The Politics of Debate about Remote Aboriginal Australia* (Sydney: Allen and Unwin, 2012).

## Introduction

1. Elsewhere in Westminster democracies, these groups are often known as "branches".
2. *Sunday Gleaner,* 26 March and 2 April 1978. Notwithstanding the frictions between Bustamante and Isaacs, his relations with JLP members were often cordial. The full text of Isaacs' address to PNP comrades is contained in the Appendix.
3. The term 'social democrat', used mainly in Britain and Western Europe, has a different connotation from the American 'liberal'. While the latter – especially in recent decades – has come to stand mainly for individual freedom, the former references the reforms associated with the welfare or social state, including the redistribution of income via provision of public education, health and housing services. Consequently, social democrats

and liberals can have conflicting views on fiscal policy and the role of the state. See also Donald Robotham, "Liberal Social Democracy, Neoliberalism, and Conservatism," in *Rethinking America: Rethinking the Imperial Homeland in the 21st Century*, eds. J. Maskovsky and I. Susser (Boulder, CO: Paradigm Press, 2009), 213–33, and Thomas Piketty, *A Brief History of Equality* (Cambridge and London: Belknap Press of Harvard University Press, 2022).

4. As a political position, socialism is intimately linked with the socialization of capital and therefore can come in more or less radical forms. The socialization of capital includes both nationalization of industries and services, and redistributive measures, including taxes on profits and wealth as well as incomes. Such redistribution can be realized through expanded public services. It can also involve other provisions for the unemployed, the landless, and the aged and disabled. Socialization can be more or less rapid and extensive. Though in early twentieth-century Russia and Germany, both terms were used to describe radical socialist positions, the terms 'social democrat' and 'democratic socialist' are best conceived as right- and left-leaning positions, respectively. In Jamaica, a stand for socialism was taken to be akin to endorsing the socialism of the British Labour Party which, in government between 1945 and 1951, pursued widespread nationalization of services and some industries. In 1940, Norman Manley endorsed a centralized and planned economy. However, Manley and others, including Wills Isaacs, struggled to reconcile this strategy with Jamaica's post-war need for capital, and the institutional dictates of Westminster democracy. In government, their stance was social democratic. Also see Michael Harrington, *Socialism: Past and Future* (New York: Arcade Publishing, 1989), and Michael Kaufman, *Jamaica under Manley: Dilemmas of Socialism and Democracy* (London: Zed Books, 1985): 78–81.
5. Isaacs died of lung cancer. He had been a heavy smoker throughout his adult life.
6. The sobriquet "Stormy Petrel" has a history. In 1901, Maxim Gorky published his well-known ode to the storm petrel, a sea bird that heralds tempestuous weather. Albeit metaphorical, the song was intended as praise for those in the vanguard of radical change. The usage spread beyond Russia, and its initial revolutionary framework. In Britain, the outspoken Welsh Labour

politician Aneurin Bevan became known as a "stormy petrel" – for being passionate, outspoken and brave. And in Jamaica, Alexander Bustamante was called Stormy Petrel in 1938. However, following the 1944 election, when Bustamante came to power, the term was used both by comrades and the press to refer to Wills O. Isaacs. He embraced the name which followed him throughout his life.

7. Michael Manley interview (1978), 1–2.
8. Anthony Payne, *Politics in Jamaica,* 2nd ed (London: Palgrave Macmillan, 1995), 64–65. For populism in the region, see Carlos de la Torres, *Populist Seduction in Latin America,* 2nd ed (Athens: Ohio University Press, 2010)
9. For the distinction between creole and the new black nationalisms, see Deborah Thomas, *Modern Blackness: Nationalism, Globalization and the Politics of Culture in Jamaica* (Durham: Duke University Press, 2004); and for a portrait of the type of culture with which Isaacs was familiar, see Brian Moore and Michele Johnson, *Neither Led nor Driven: Contesting British Cultural Imperialism in Jamaica, 1863–1920* (Kingston: University of West Indies Press, 2004).
10. See Hilary Beckles, *How Britain Underdeveloped the Caribbean: A Reparation Response to Europe's Legacy of Plunder and Poverty* (Kingston: University of West Indies Press, 2021). On Britain's failure during the Great Depression, see Richard Bernal, "The Great Depression, Colonial Policy and Industrialization in Jamaica," *Social and Economic Studies* 37, nos. 1& 2 (1988): 33–64.
11. George W. Roberts, *The Population of Jamaica* (Cambridge: Cambridge University Press, 1957), 43, 139–40, 144–49; Colin Clarke, "Population Pressure in Kingston, Jamaica," *Transactions of the Institute of British Geographers* 38 (1966): 165–82; and W. Arthur Lewis, Foreword, Gisela Eisner, *Jamaica, 1830–1930* (Manchester: Manchester University Press, 1961), xv-xxiii. Also see Olive Senior, *Dying to Better Themselves: West Indians and the Building of the Panama Canal* (Kingston: University of West Indies Press, 2014).
12. For a periodization of these years and subsequent decades of the twentieth century, see Donald Robotham, "Transnationalism in the Caribbean: Formal and Informal," *American Ethnologist.* 25, no. 2 (1998): 307–21.
13. See W. Arthur Lewis, "An Economic Plan for Jamaica," *Agenda* 3, no. 4 (1944): 154–63; "Industrial Development in Puerto Rico," *Caribbean Economic Review* 1, nos. 1&2 (1949): 153–76; "The

Industrialisation of the British West Indies," *Caribbean Economic Review* 2, no. 1 (1950): 1–61 and "Economic Development with Unlimited Supplies of Labour," *The Manchester School* 22 no. 2 (1954): 139–91. Also, see Mark Gersovitz, ed., *Selected Economic Writings of W. Arthur Lewis* (New York: New York University, 1983). Lewis' stance is often described as a 'the dual-sector model' of relations between traditional agriculture and an emerging modern manufacturing sector.

14. W. Arthur Lewis, Foreword, xv-xxiii, and "Unlimited Supplies of Labour," 155–60.
15. See Walter Rodney, *How Europe Underdeveloped Africa* (London: Verso, 1972); and George Beckford, *Persistent Poverty: Underdevelopment in Plantation Economies of the Third World* (New York: Oxford University Press, 1972).
16. These banks included the World Bank as well as foreign commercial banks. The most comprehensive account of Jamaica's experience with the IMF from the 1960s to the 2010s is *Contextualizing Jamaica's Relationship with the IMF* by Christine Clarkson and Carole Nelson (Cham: Palgrave Macmillan, 2022). Also, see below, Chapter 14 and Conclusion.
17. On the 1970s and 1980s, see Omar Davies, "An Analysis of the Management of the Jamaican Economy: 1972–1985," *Social and Economic Studies* 35, no. 1 (1986): 73–109; and Michael Manley, *Up the Down Escalator: Development and the International Economy – a Jamaican Case Study* (London: Andre Deutsch, 1987).

    In 2009, Jamaican government debt – domestic and foreign – amounted to 142 per cent of the GDP. For the financial crisis, see Clarkson and Nelson, *Contextualizing Jamaica*, 195–216. Also, see Martin Naranjo and Emilio Osambela, "From Financial Crisis to Correction," in *Revitalizing the Jamaican Economy: Policies for Sustained Growth* (DB, 2004), 119–52; and Wilberne Persaud, *Jamaica Meltdown: Indigenous Financial Sector Crash, 1996* (Lincoln, NE: iUniverse, 2006). On structural adjustment, see John W. Robinson, "Lessons from the Structural Adjustment Process in Jamaica," *Social and Economic Studies* 43, no. 4 (1994): 87–113); and Elsie LeFranc, ed., *Consequences of Structural Adjustment: A Review of the Jamaican Experience* (Kingston: Canoe Press, 1994). Also, see Conclusion.
18. In the past forty years, the engagement of Russia and China with an increasingly global capitalism has been influential. On the

impact of China, see John Gittings, *The Changing Face of China: From Mao to Markets* (Oxford: Oxford University Press, 2005). On the diverse policy responses to a broadly shared situation in post-colonial Africa, see Stefan Dercon, *Gambling on Development: Why Some Countries Win and Others Lose* (London: Hurst and Company, 2022). For a different (Caribbean) perspective, see Dave Ramsaran, ed., *Contradictory Existence: Neoliberalism and Democracy in the Caribbean* (Kingston: Ian Randle Publishers, 2016).

19. Giovanni Arrighi, "The Developmentalist Illusion: A Reconceptualization of the Semiperiphery," in *Semi Peripheral States in the World Economy*, ed. W.G. Martin (Westport, CT: Greenwood Press, 1990), 11–42; and Manley, *Up the Down Escalator*. The concept of unequal exchange contests the idea that each society's economy has a natural comparative advantage. Rather, advantage is manufactured, especially through unequal trading relations. Arrighi takes his terminology pertaining to the periphery from Immanuel Wallerstein's world systems theory. Oliver C. Cox, the noted Trinidadian sociologist, pre-dated Wallerstein's world systems' view by some years. See his *The Foundation of Capitalism* (New York: Philosophical Library, 1959): 15ff.
20. See Kari Polanyi Levitt, *The Origins and Consequences of Jamaica's Debt Crisis, 1970–1990*, revised ed. (Kingston: Consortium Graduate School of Social Sciences, 1991); and the Fifth Sir Arthur Lewis Memorial Lecture, "The Right to Development", Eastern Caribbean Central Bank, St Lucia, 2000; Norman Girvan, "W.A. Lewis, The Plantation School and Dependency: An Interpretation," *Social and Economic Studies (Special Issue on Sir Arthur Lewis, Part 1)* 54, no. 3 (2005): 198–222; and Norman Girvan, "Sir Arthur Lewis – A Man of His Time; and Ahead of His Time," Distinguished Lecture, "Year of Sir Arthur Lewis," UWI St Augustine, 20 February 2008; and Carl Stone, "Political Aspects of Post-war Agricultural Policies in Jamaica (1945–1970)," *Social and Economic Studies* 23, no. 2 (1974): 145–75.
21. Political biographies in Jamaica have mainly concerned party leaders. They include works or collections on Marcus Garvey by Amy Jacques Garvey and Robert Hill; on Alexander Bustamante by George Eaton and Frank Hill; on Norman Manley by Rex Nettleford, Victor Stafford Reid, and Phillip Sherlock; on Hugh

Shearer by Neita Hartley; and on Michael Manley by Michael Kaufman, Darrel Levi, and Godfrey Smith. Edward Seaga and P.J. Patterson have written autobiographies.

## Chapter 1

1. Gisela Eisner, *Jamaica, 1830–1930* (Manchester: Manchester University Press, 1961), 187; and Sydney Haldane Olivier, *Jamaica, the Blessed Land* (London: Faber and Faber, 1935), 34–35. Lord Sydney Olivier was acting governor of Jamaica in 1902 and governor from 1907 to 1913. Later, he became a well-known Fabian.
2. These remarks on Wills Isaacs' antecedents are drawn from a number of sources: personal recollections of the Isaacs family; Jamaican historical records, including *Jamaica, Church of England Parish Register, 1664–1880, Jamaica, Civil Registration, 1880–1999, Directory of Jamaica, the Parish of Hanover, 1878, 1887, 1910, Jamaica Almanac, 1875, 1877*; and Wills Isaacs, "Things I Remember," *Sunday Gleaner*, 17 June 1973. The latter is one of a number of Isaacs' reminiscences written for the *Sunday Gleaner* between 1973 and 1975. Also, on Isaacs' early life, see Marguerite Curtin, "Wills O. Isaacs: The Early Years" (Typescript, 2006), 1–6; and Curtin's *The Story of Hanover: A Jamaican Parish* (Kingston: Phoenix Printers, 2007), 146–48. The Cridlands' estate shared its name with a number of others in county Cornwall, perhaps predictable when early allocations of crown land went to men retired from military corps. See Barry Higman and Brian Hudson, *Jamaican Place Names* (Kingston: UWI Press, 2009). Elsewhere, Higman provides a description of Greenwich, a proximate property in Hanover. See Barry Higman, *Jamaica Surveyed* (Kingston: UWI Press, 2001), 128–31.
3. *Daily Gleaner*, 29 November 1945.
4. *Directory of Jamaica, the Parish of Westmoreland,* 1878 and 1910, and *Daily Gleaner*, 25 July 1918. On 'book-keeper' and other terms, see Frederic Cassidy, *Jamaica Talk: Three Hundred Years of the English Language in Jamaica*, 2nd ed. (London: Institute of Jamaica and Macmillan, 1971), 164–65.
5. Isaacs cited in Curtin, "The Early Years," 2–5.
6. *Sunday Gleaner*, 17 June 1973. The reference to Anne Palmer concerns the myth and pantomime, "The White Witch of Rose Hall".

7. Nadine Isaacs interview (2001), 24–25; *Sunday Gleaner*, 5 August 1973.
8. Colin Clarke, *Kingston, Jamaica: Urban Development and Social Change, 1602–2002* (Kingston: Ian Randle Publishers, 2006), 52–53; and Olivier, *Jamaica*, 335.
9. Marguerite Curtin, "Wills O. Isaacs: Wills Becomes a Kingstonian" (Typescript, 2006) and *Sunday Gleaner*, 1 July, 12 August 1973. A timeline for Wills Isaacs' life is provided in a brief family portrait by Christine Gore, *For Your Information: The Life and Times of Wills O.P. Isaacs* (Kingston: n. p., 2016), 10–21.
10. Suzanne Issa (with Jackie Ranston), *My Jamaica, Abe Issa* (Kingston: Suzanne Issa, 1994); Patricia Patterson and Maxine McDonnough, *Edward Hanna: The Man and His Times, 1894–1978* (Kingston: Ian Randle Publishers, 1997). On Nathans and Co., see Ken Post, *Arise Ye Starvelings: The Jamaican Labour Rebellion and Its Aftermath* (The Hague: Martinus Nijhoff, 1978), 90.
11. Wills Isaacs, "Things I Remember," *Sunday Gleaner*, 26 June 1975.
12. Matthews Lane would be a significant locale for Wills Isaacs. See Chapter 4.
13. *Sunday Gleaner*, 9 February and 22 July 1973. On the epidemic, see *Daily Gleaner*, 11 November 1931. Wills Isaacs remarried twice following Ivy Lucille's death; to Ivy Pringle in 1942 and to Gloria Holness in 1950. On his death, nine surviving immediate family members were listed (*Daily Gleaner*, 9 January 1981).
14. Some family members recall these events as mainly involving Ivy's death in childbirth. William's account underlines the epidemic (William Isaacs interview, 2001) 17.
15. *Daily Gleaner*, 5 October 1930 and 2 August 1932. The quoted passage is based on I Corinthians 1:28.
16. *Sunday Gleaner*, 10 June 1973.
17. William reports that he grew up with Gloria Samms, almost as a sister. As Gloria Knight she would head Jamaica's Urban Development Corporation from 1968 to 1989 (William Isaacs interview, 2001), 1–2; and Nadine Isaacs interview (2001), 25–26.
18. Clarke, *Kingston, Jamaica*, 62, 75.
19. Marguerite Curtin, "Wills O. Isaacs: Staving Off Trouble in the Capital (Typescript, 2007).
20. On the Legislative Council and Jamaica's crown colony constitution, see James Carnegie, *Some Aspects of Jamaica's Politics: 1918–1838* (Kingston: Institute of Jamaica, 1973), 15–19.

21. See Carnegie, *Some Aspects*, 97–99. Mends was addressed as "Doctor" by his followers, though his local training was not recognized by the authorities.
22. At the time, a dollar was worth four shillings (4/-), a unit of value possibly devised by Jamaican workers in Panama and Cuba. For early trade unionism, see George Eaton, "Trade Union Development in Jamaica," *Caribbean Quarterly* 8, nos. 1&2 (1962): 43–53 and 69–75.
23. *Daily Gleaner*, 10 June 1924; and for Isaacs' comments, *Sunday Gleaner*, 7 and 14 January 1973.
24. *Daily Gleaner*, 15 May 1924. Though Probyn secured Jamaica's first trade union law in 1919, his introduction of income tax made him unpopular (Carnegie, *Jamaica's Politics*, 41–50). Tillett, a Labour MP, had visited Jamaica en route to a Labour convention in Canada.
25. *Daily Gleaner*, 17 November 1923. See also, Post, *Arise Ye Starvelings*, 212; and Eaton, Trade Union Development, 52.
26. See Robert A. Hill, ed., *Marcus Garvey and the Universal Negro Improvement Association Papers, Vol. 7* (Berkeley: University of California Press, 1983), 106; and Glen Richards, "Race, Class and Labour Politics in Colonial Jamaica, 1900–1934," in *Jamaica in Slavery and Freedom: History, Heritage and Culture*, eds. K. Monteith and G. Richards (Kingston: University of West Indies Press, 2002), 340–62.
27. Post, *Arise Ye Starvelings*, 209–12 and *Sunday Gleaner*, 14 January 1973.
28. *Daily Gleaner*, 9 March and 9 May 1925.
29. *Daily Gleaner*, 7 April, 1 December 1911 and 16 September 1912. Also, see Arnold Bertram, *N. W. Manley and the Making of Modern Jamaica* (Kingston: Arawak Publications), 38–41; Hill, *Marcus Garvey*, 21, 344; Richards, "Race, Class and Labour," 347–48.
30. See below, Chapter 2 and Carnegie, *Jamaica's Politics*, 63–95.
31. Bertram, *N. W. Manley*, 45. In 1925, Kingston and St Andrew were combined for the first time to create a municipality of greater Kingston.
32. *Daily Gleaner*, 7 December 1934.
33. See *Daily Gleaner*, 10, 23 March; 3, 21, 30 April; and 18 June 1925. Henry VIII and his wives aside, Isaacs' references seem to be to the execution of Thomas Seymour by his brother Edward, Duke of Somerset and protector of his young nephew, Edward VI.

With regard to Elizabeth I, the reference was to the mysterious death of the wife of the queen's favourite courtier, Robert Dudley.

34. *Daily Gleaner*, 4 May 1938. On Bustamante, see *Daily Gleaner*, 17 September 1936. About one thousand people lost their lives in Barcelona between 16 and 18 March, 1938. For the debate on communism, see *Daily Gleaner*, 4, 5 and 12 April; and 3 May 1938. Isaacs' letter followed.
35. For Krim's lecture, see *Daily Gleaner*, 10 June 1938. Isaacs' reply came on June 17, also cited in Post, *Arise Ye Starvelings*, 315.
36. *Daily Gleaner*, 7 July and 13 December 1938 (letter dated 12 December).
37. Richard Hart's remark on Isaacs' nickname, cited in Trevor Munroe, *Jamaican Politics: A Marxist Perspective in Transition* (Kingston: Heinemann (Caribbean), 1990), 95.

## Chapter 2

1. Dudley Thompson interview (2002), 4; and Howard Cooke interview (2002), 3. Thompson was a prominent PNP politician, especially during the 1970s. Cooke had a distinguished career in the PNP prior to his appointment as governor general from 1991 to 2006.
2. Carnegie, *Jamaica's Politics*, 98–101.
3. The LBC was founded in 1936 by Victor Gollancz, Harold Laski and John Strachey. Norman Manley was a member. See Richard Hart, *Towards Decolonisation: Political, Labour and Economic Development in Jamaica, 1938–1945* (Kingston, Canoe Press, 1999), 36. See also Bertram, *N.W. Manley*, 127; and Post, *Arise Ye Starvelings*, 222, 225.
4. In Manley's initial view, the relevant issues for the black majority were principally economic, hence his agricultural extension organization, Jamaica Welfare Limited. See Rex Nettleford, ed., *Manley and the New Jamaica: Selected Speeches and Writings, 1938–1968* (Kingston: Longman (Caribbean), 1971), cix–cxii; Horace Levy, "Jamaica Welfare: Growth and Decline," *Social and Economic Studies* 44, nos. 2 and 3 (1995): 349–57.
5. See Nettleford, *Manley*, 11–12, 19–20, 22; also, Bertram *N.W. Manley*, 169–73.
6. Eaton, "Trade Union Development," and O.W. Phelps, "Rise of the Labour Movement in Jamaica," *Social and Economic Studies* 9, no. 4 (1960): 445.

7. Hart, *Towards Decolonisation,* 24–29.
8. In 1946, the TUC would reorganize to become the Trades Union Congress with a number of affiliates and, in 1948, to become a general union.
9. People's National Party, *People's National Party Constitution,* original pamphlet, 1938. Also, see Ken Post, *Strike the Iron: A Colony at War, Vol. 1* (New Jersey: Humanities Press, 1981), 66–68.
10. Cited in Bertram, *N.W. Manley,* 175.
11. Post, *Strike the Iron,* 68–70; *Daily Gleaner,* 7 May 1940.
12. Marguerite Curtin, "Wills O. Isaacs: The Social Revolution of 1938" (Typescript, 2007), 4–6; Carnegie, *Jamaica's Politics,* 101.
13. Rachel Manley, ed., *Edna Manley: The Diaries* (Kingston: Heinemann (Caribbean), 1989), 255.
14. Trevor Munroe, *The Politics of Constitutional Decolonization: Jamaica, 1944–62* (Kingston: Institute of Social and Economic Research, 1972), 32 and passim; Bertram, *N.W, Manley,* 185.
15. Post, *Strike Vol. 1,* 197–99; Owen Jefferson, *Post-war Economic Development of Jamaica* (Kiingston: Institute of Social and Economic Studies, 1972), 8–9.
16. Established by O.T. Fairclough in 1937, the weekly *Public Opinion* became the voice of the PNP.
17. Cited in Post, *Strike Vol. 1,* 57.
18. Cited in Post, *Strike Vol. 1,* 119. Also, see *Daily Gleaner,* 29 August 1940.
19. Eleven groups in all attended, along with representatives of the JPL and the Negro Workers' Educational League (Hart, *Towards Decolonisation,* 72).
20. Post, *Strike Vol. 1,* 123; *Daily Gleaner,* 29 August 1940.
21. *Daily Gleaner,* 16 December 1939; *Daily Gleaner,* 20 June 1940.
22. *Daily Gleaner,* Friday, 3 October 1941. J.A.G. Smith died soon after in April 1942.
23. *Daily Gleaner,* 10 March and 10 June 1941.
24. *Daily Gleaner,* 29 May 1942. The advertisements for Nethersole's lectures appeared in the *Daily Gleaner* on 11 and 25 November 1942, and 13 January 1943.
25. Hart, *Towards Decolonisation,* 80–92; and Post, *Strike Vol. 1,* 129–34.
26. Hart, *Towards Decolonisation,* 89–91; Post, *Strike Vol. 1,* 178.
27. E.E.A. Campbell was president of both the Federation of Citizens' Associations and the Clerks' Association. Originally supportive of the PNP, he became increasingly conservative.

28. *Daily Gleaner,* 10 July 1941.
29. Hugh H. Watson was the US consul general. Cited in Post, *Strike* Vol. 1, 179; in Hart, *Towards Decolonisation,* 91; and in Colin Palmer, *Freedom's Children: The 1938 Labor Rebellion and the Birth of Modern Jamaica* (Chapel Hill, University of North Carolina Press, 2014), 261.
30. Also, see above, Chapter 1.
31. For this debate, see *Daily Gleaner,* 9 and 11 September 1941. Further articles and correspondence followed through September and October 1941.
32. Hart, *Towards Decolonisation,* 100–106. An accountant, Glasspole was secretary of the United Clerks Association.
33. Bertram, *N.W. Manley*, 191–94.
34. This is not an exhaustive list. See Hart, *Towards Decolonisation,* 228–32.
35. *Daily Gleaner,* 1 August 1942.
36. An example was the Kingston March Factory strike of 1945.
37. On TUC activity generally, see Hart, *Towards Decolonisation,* 228–32. On unions with which Isaacs was involved, see Post, *Strike Vol. 1*, 187, 234, 264–67; and Ken Post, *Strike the Iron: A Colony at War, Vol. 2* (New Jersey: Humanities Press, 1981), 391, 407–8, 434.
38. Cited in Post, *Strike Vol. 1*, 267.
39. *Daily Gleaner,* 9 March 1943; and Ken Hill interview (1978), 2.
40. Clarke, *Kingston, Jamaica,* 103–7; Carnegie, *Jamaica's Politics*, 20–25. Between 1921 and 1943, Jamaica's population had grown by 40 per cent from 858,000 to 1,237,100.
41. *Daily Gleaner,* 19, 26, 30 June and 7, 9, 20 August 1943.
42. *Daily Gleaner,* 14 August 1943; and Post, *Strike Vol. 2*, 391, 403.
43. *Daily Gleaner,* 16 August 1943.
44. See *Daily Gleaner,* 23, 27, 30, 31 August 1943. The meeting was called to protest the sale of the All-Island Telephone Service, contrary to PNP policy on nationalization of public utilities.
45. *Daily Gleaner,* 14 September 1943.
46. *Daily Gleaner,* 25 August 1943; Post, *Strike Vol. 1*, 299.
47. Hart, *Towards Decolonisation,* 240–46; Munro, *Constitutional Decolonization,* 26–35.
48. *Daily Gleaner,* 12 August 1943; Post, *Strike Vol. 1*, 226–27; and *Vol. 2,* 307–9.
49. The London firm was Telephone and General Trust Limited (*Daily Gleaner,* 28 May 1943).

50. Palmer, *Freedom's Children*, 249–53; Thomas Holt, *The Problem of Freedom: Race, Labour, and Politics in Jamaica and Britain, 1832–1938* (Baltimore: Johns Hopkins University Press, 1992), 372–75.
51. For the Legislative Council debate, and Bustamante's letter, see the *Daily Gleaner*, 9 September 1943. In his speech, Kirkwood also derided Norman Manley's Jamaica Welfare Limited.
52. Fletcher's statement and Hart's speech were also reported in the *Gleaner* on 9 September 1943. Hart's speech received its first report in *The Masses*, a local workers' weekly, on 21 August.
53. *Daily Gleaner* 17, 18 September 1943.
54. It was Roy Lindo who defeated Victor Bailey for the seat of St Mary on the Legislative Council and would do so again in 1944, this time for the House of Representatives (Bertram, *N. W. Manley*, 197). Bailey was the brother of the more radical Amy Bailey. Their father founded the Jamaica Union of Teachers.
55. *Daily Gleaner*, 23 September 1943.
56. *Daily Gleaner*, 30 September and 2 October 1943. The ten PNP signatories were F. Goodison, H. Dayes, R. Burke, S. Brookes, I. Lloyd, L. Leslie, C. Saunders, Amy Bailey, Edith James and W. Seivright.
57. Russell Lewars interview (1978), 6–7; personal communication, Isaacs family. Ulric Simmonds' byline was "Parliamentary Reporter", and for his *Sunday Gleaner* column, "Political Reporter". On the Jamaica Imperial Association, see the pamphlet issued at the time, *Jamaica Imperial Association: Its Origin and Inauguration* (Kingston: JIA, 1918). Its slogan was "Not Philanthropy, but Business".

## Chapter 3

1. Lynden Newland interview (1978), 5; and Russell Lewars interview (1978), 1, 5. Elected to the House of Representatives in 1944, Newland (JLP) also served as Kingston's mayor, 1949–51, but lost his seat to Nethersole (PNP) in 1949. Lewars was Assistant Town Clerk and then, from 1945, Town Clerk for the KSAC council.
2. The retiring councillor was Dr G.E. Valentine.
3. Those on the left opposing Isaacs were Roy Woodham, Winston Grubb and Frank Hill (Post, *Strike Vol. 1*, 96–97; and *Strike Vol. 2*, 433–35). Isaacs' other proposers were Arthur Henricks, E.C. McCullock, and John and Ivan Fraser (*Daily Gleaner*, 22 November 1943).

4. *Daily Gleaner*, 24, 25 November and 2 December 1943.
5. *Daily Gleaner*, 3 December 1943.
6. Post, *Strike Vol. 2*, 359, 434.
7. *Daily Gleaner*, 14 December 1943. Also, see *Spotlight Magazine*, February–March 1944.
8. *Daily Gleaner*, 12 January 1944; and *Spotlight*. As chair of Finance, Nethersole supported Isaacs (*Daily Gleaner*, 7 December 1943).
9. *Daily Gleaner*, 14, 23 December 1943 and 12 January 1944. The new law was published on 1 March 1944. The resolution, pertaining to finance, had gone straight to the Privy Council rather than to the Legislative Council. With the 1944 general election and a new constitution, the Privy Council, though still retained, would be largely replaced by an Executive Committee. For its roles, see Alex Zeidenfelt, "Political and Constitutional Developments in Jamaica," *Journal of Politics* 14, no. 3 (1952): 512–40.
10. *Daily Gleaner*, 14 April 1944; Post, *Strike Vol. 2*, 437.
11. *Daily Gleaner*, 15, 21 January and 13 March 1944.
12. Russell Lewars interview (1978). On gully works, see *Daily Gleaner*, 11 July and 11, 16 and 17 August 1944.
13. Huggins succeeded Arthur Richards as governor in September 1943. On the constitutional issues, see Bertram, *N.W. Manley*, 186–87; Post, *Strike Vol. 2*, 423–24; and Munroe, *Constitutional Decolonization*, 46–47.
14. The statement also said that "Socialism will put an end to the use of the workers by employers to secure riches for themselves [...]. Socialism condemns Capitalism" (*Daily Gleaner*, 30 November 1944).
15. Munroe continued, "The workers were only just beginning to exploit their organized power [...] when the PNP was advocating the abolition of capitalism" (*Constitutional Decolonization*, 41).
16. On Dayes see *Daily Gleaner*, 9 February 1945. The CD&W Act was passed in 1940 and accompanied the tabling of the *Moyne Commission Report*.
17. *Daily Gleaner*, 5, 12, 13, 14, and 16 March 1945. Isaacs used the press to air these issues concerning poor relief.
18. *Daily Gleaner*, 24, 29, and 31 January 1945; and Post, *Strike Vol. 2*, 510–12, 526.
19. *Daily Gleaner*, 12 and 23 February, and 7 March 1945. Previously, Glasspole and Manley had proposed a government board to address complaints from minority unionists.

20. For Isaacs' three speeches, see *Daily Gleaner,* 22 March, and 17 and 25 April 1945. The *Gleaner's* attack came on 24 April.
21. *Daily Gleaner,* 2 and 16 May, and 13 June 1945. Isaacs' protagonist in the affair, Edith Clarke, was an enlightened daughter of the planter class; see Christine Barrow, "Edith Clarke: Jamaican Reformer and Anthropologist," *Caribbean Quarterly* 44 nos. 3 and 4 (1998), 15–34.
22. *Daily Gleaner,* 10 May and 21 June 1945. In the absence of qualified JLP members, approval of the budget had been moved and seconded by independents Harold E. Allen and Roy Lindo.
23. *Daily Gleaner,* 21, 23 June 1945; Post, *Strike Vol. 2*, 523, 526. The March Factory owners were Owen K. Henriques and R.D.C. Henriques, who was also the manager.
24. *Daily Gleaner,* 12 June 1945.
25. *Daily Gleaner,* 11 and 12 September, and 4 and 11 October 1945. See Hill's reference to the incident some years later, *Daily Gleaner,* 28 January 1956.
26. *Daily Gleaner,* 2, 8, 12, 16 and 29 November, and 3 December 1945.
27. *Daily Gleaner,* 11 and 15 December 1945.
28. *Daily Gleaner,* 11 and 26 January, and 2 and 4 March 1946; and Richard Hart, *Time for a Change: Constitutional, Political and Labour Developments in Jamaica and Other Colonies in the Caribbean Region, 1944–1955* (Kingston: Arawak Publications, 2004), 42–45.
29. *Daily Gleaner*, 9 July 1946. For PNP policy on municipal and parochial administration, revised in 1947, see *Daily Gleaner,* 27 September 1947; Hart, *Change*; and Keith Miller, "Local Government Reform in Jamaica," in *Handbook of Research on Sub-national Governance and Development,* eds. H. Schoburgh and R. Ryan (Hershey, PA: IGI Global, 2017): 520–42.
30. *Daily Gleaner,* 9 April 1946. The mayor whom Isaacs addressed was G.C. Gunter. Seivright had resigned rather than order municipal firemen back to work in the course of strike activity. He remained on council as an alderman (*Daily Gleaner,* 25 February 1946).
31. On these initiatives, see *Daily Gleaner,* 29 April, 9 July, and 20, 23 and 28 August 1946.

## Chapter 4

1. Howard Cooke interview (2002, 4). Wills Isaacs' address following the Hearne Commission on Gordon Town and his resignation as PNP third vice president (*Public Opinion,* 20 August 1949).
2. Cited in Bertram, *N. W. Manley,* 212.
3. Amanda Sives, *Elections, Violence and the Democratic Process in Jamaica, 1944–2007* (Kingston: Ian Randle Publishers, 2010), 11. Also, see Deborah Thomas, *Exceptional Violence: Embodied Citizenship in Transnational Jamaica* (Durham: Duke University Press, 2011) and Yonique Campbell, *Citizenship on the Margins: State Power, Security and Precariousness in the 21st Century* (Cham: Palgrave Macmillan, 2020). These studies provide a comprehensive account of the evolution of garrison politics and state violence. Sives' study is most relevant to Isaacs' period.
4. *Daily Gleaner*, 4 January 1946; and Hart, *Change,* 28.
5. Pixley's phrase is from the Book of Revelations. Between 4 and 26 January 1946, the *Daily Gleaner* had at least seven reports on the conflict. See Isaacs' subsequent statement on the railway strike in the Appendix.
6. *Sunday Gleaner,* 24 February 1946; and Hart, *Change,* 27–40. On Isaacs' recollection of Black Saturday, see Appendix. Nethersole cited in Sives, *Elections, Violence,* 15.
7. Telegram from Huggins to Secretary of State, 21 February 1946; and Jamaica Situation Report, 22 February 1946. CO/137/864/1; Sives, *Elections, Violence,* 14.
8. See *Daily Gleaner,* 9, 15, 17, 24, 25 and 27 July 1946.
9. These marching events, reported frequently in the *Daily Gleaner,* occurred between 10 September and 7 November 1946.
10. *Daily Gleaner,* 15 November 1946. For his remarks on land, Isaacs would have drawn on Ivan Lloyd's *Land for the Million* (Kingston: PNP, 1944).
11. *Daily Gleaner,* 29 November and 13 December 1946.
12. *Daily Gleaner,* 25 and 26 September, and 13 November 1946.
13. *Daily Gleaner* 14 January, 27 February, 28 April and 13 May 1947.
14. *Daily Gleaner,* 14 and 15 May 1947; and *Sunday Gleaner,* 18 May 1947.
15. *Daily Gleaner,* 19, 23 and 29 May 1947; and *Sunday Gleaner,* 25 May 1947. Telegram from Governor Huggins to the Secretary of State for Colonies, 27 May 1947, CO137/887/6.

16. *Daily Gleaner*, 29 May 1947. Huggins' telegram to the Secretary of State, 31 May 1947, CO 137/887/6. For relevant evidence to the inquiry, see *Daily Gleaner*, 17 and 25 June 1947.
17. *Daily Gleaner*, 3 and 6 October 1947; and Sives, *Elections*, 19–20.
18. *Sunday Gleaner*, 2 April 1979; also cited in Bertram, *N.W. Manley*, 212; and Sives, *Elections*, 54.
19. William Isaacs interview (2001), 11.
20. *Daily Gleaner*, 22 October 1947.
21. *Daily Gleaner*, 27 December 1947 and 7 February 1948. Also, see Hart, *Change*, 61–65.
22. *Daily Gleaner*, 13 and 14 January 1948.
23. *Daily Gleaner*, 16 January 1948; Huggins' telegram to the Secretary of State for the Colonies, 16 January 1948, CO 137/887/7.
24. Hart, *Change*, 66–76; and *Daily Gleaner*, 27 February 1948.
25. Accounts of and comments on the strike in the *Daily Gleaner* extended from 27 February to 6 June 1948. Hart (*Change*, 66–76) notes that the strike had a further outcome, that the sixteen unions affiliated with the new Trades Union Congress were amalgamated to become a general union.
26. *Daily Gleaner* between 18 May and 15 October, 1948.
27. *Daily Gleaner*, 12 November 1948.
28. *Daily Gleaner*, 16 August and 10 September 1948, and 31 March 1949.
29. Nettleford, *Manley*, lix.
30. See extensive *Daily Gleaner* reports from 2 April to 13 May 1949.
31. For Isaacs' statement and the trial's outcome, see *Daily Gleaner*, 6 and 11 May 1949.
32. *Daily Gleaner*, 25 June 1949.
33. Sives, *Elections*, 51; and *Daily Gleaner*, 8 July 1949.
34. This account is based on two major sources: the *Daily Gleaner*'s reports of evidence published throughout July 1949 and its publication of the Hearne Commission Report on 6 August 1949; and *Public Opinion* commentary over the same period. For events on July 3 specifically, see *Public Opinion*, 16 July 1949.
35. *Daily Gleaner*, 15 and 16 July 1949.
36. See *Hearne's Report*, which also details each of the following issues.
37. *Daily Gleaner*, 9 August 1949.
38. They included Lester Mackenzie, 'Jarman' and Vincent Porteous. Lynden Newland's evidence, *Daily Gleaner*, 21 July 1949.
39. Isaacs' evidence, *Daily Gleaner*, 15 July 1949; and *Hearne's Report*.

40. *Public Opinion,* 16 July 1949; and *Daily Gleaner*, 9 August 1949.
41. *Daily Gleaner*, 16 July and 9 August 1949. Neish assumed that the truck came directly from Kingston, whereas Isaacs reported that it was carrying local voters, albeit on the road from Kingston.
42. *Hearne Commission Report*, *Daily Gleaner*, 6 August 1949.
43. *Public Opinion*, 16 July 1949.
44. Rudyard Kipling became known as a voice of British imperialism. An acclaimed narrative writer, he received a Nobel Prize for Literature in 1907. For Isaacs' return, see *Daily Gleaner*, 3 October 1949.

## Chapter 5

1. *Daily Gleaner*, 13 April 1950. For the full text of Isaacs' speech, see Appendix below. *The Split* is also the title of an unpublished manuscript on these events by Vernon Arnett, cited by Nettleford and others (Nettleford, *Manley*, xxv, fn. 2).
2. *Daily Gleaner*, 22 August 1949.
3. Personal communication, Leroy Cooke.
4. *Daily Gleaner*, 19 December 1949; Hart, *Change*, 138–40; Trevor Munroe, *The Marxist "Left" in Jamaica, 1940–1950*, Working Paper No. 15 (Kingston: Institute of Social and Economic Studies, 1977), 52–54.
5. For some interesting commentary on the Marshall Plan, see J. Bradford DeLong, *Slouching Towards Utopia: An Economic History of the Twentieth Century* (London: Basic Books, 2022): 320–25.
6. *Daily Gleaner*, 6 October 1947, and 13 September 1949; Hart, *Change*, 102–21; and Richard Hart's papers, folder 1949–50, 2/32.
7. Hart's papers, folder 1949–50, 2/37; and *Daily Gleaner*, 20 September 1949.
8. *Daily Gleaner*, 5 March 1948, and 13 and 19 September 1949.
9. Kingston Central was the name of the constituency in the area designated as Central Kingston. In 1959, the constituency boundaries were redrawn and Central Kingston became the site of more than one constituency.
10. *Daily Gleaner*, 27 October, 17 November, and 10 December 1949.
11. *Daily Gleaner*, 21 December 1949.
12. Bertram, *N.W. Manley*, 220–23. During the election, the KSAC council was deadlocked over a new mayor, reflecting the JLP's weakening position.

13. These were Sir Harold (H.E.) Allan, who resumed as Finance Minister, and J.Z. Malcolm, who was jailed in 1952. He was replaced by the JLP's L.L. Simmonds.
14. *Daily Gleaner, 13 January, 1950.*
15. *Daily Gleaner,* 21 and 28 January 1950. For Hugh Shearer's vivid account of Glasspole's 1948 request, see Neita Hartley, *Hugh Shearer: A Voice for the People* (Kingston: Ian Randle Publishers and the Institute of Jamaica, 2005), 131–33.
16. *Daily Gleaner,* 27 January and 8 March 1950.
17. "On the Dung Hill", *Daily Gleaner,* 4 August. Isaacs' wedding was on 14 October 1950 at the Church of St Peter and St Paul. Comrade Harry Dayes was best man.
18. *Daily Gleaner,* 20 January, and 15 and 16 February 1950.
19. *Proceedings of the House of Representatives, Session 1950,* 1 March; *Daily Gleaner,* 2 March and 6 May 1950.
20. Telegrams between Huggins and Arthur Creech Jones, Secretary of State for the Colonies, 29 and 31 August 1949, CO137/887/8; and 14 and 18 February 1950, CO137/902/4. Creech Jones was also a British Labour MP (1935–50 and 1954–56).
21. Internal memo, Colonial Office, 5 January 1951, CO137/902/4.
22. See *PHR, 1950,* 16 March, for Manley's resolution and the subsequent debate and amendment.
23. *Daily Gleaner,* 11 April 1950. Jamaica's population was around 1.4 million with a total labour force of approximately 609,000 (George Cumper, A Comparison of Data on the Jamaica Labour Force, *Social and Economic Studies* 13, no. 4 (1964): 430–39).
24. The party was influenced by the Puerto Rican model of industrialization. Manley visited there in 1948 (*Daily Gleaner,* 4 June 1948).
25. Governor Huggins's term had expired mid-way through 1950 and the Colonial Secretary acted in his place. Hugh Foot took office as governor on 7 April 1950.
26. Letters from Acting Governor MacGillivray to S.E.V. Luke, Colonial Office, 26 September and 9 December 1950, CO 137/899/5.
27. IBRD, *The Economic Development of Jamaica,* report by a mission of the IBRD. Chief of Mission, John C. Wilde (Baltimore: Johns Hopkins University Press, 1952).
28. *Daily Gleaner,* 12 April 1950. Perhaps Trefgarne was emboldened by the British Labour government's poor election result. A majority of three hundred seats in 1945 was cut to a mere five in

February 1950. Following extensive nationalization, Labour lost power in 1951. These events may have troubled the PNP.

29. For the parliamentary fracas, Manley's statement, and Isaacs' speech that night, see *Daily Gleaner*, 13 April 1950. See above endnote 1, this chapter.
30. The Grantley Adams dispute was pursued through the pages of the *Daily Gleaner* in October and November 1948. The *Gleaner*'s comment on free speech came on 28 April 1948. The PNP's response came in the form of a circular (Hart's papers, 1948–49, 2/1).
31. *Daily Gleaner*, 28 January and 30 December 1948.
32. Ken Hill cited in Victor Stafford Reid, *The Horses of the Morning: About the Rt. Excellent N.W. Manley, QC, MM, National Hero of Jamaica* (Kingston: Caribbean Authors Publishing, 1985), 311–13.
33. *Daily Gleaner*, 27 April 1950.
34. Hart, *Change*, 104–18, 156).
35. *Daily Gleaner*, 28 August 1950.
36. Letter from Arnett to Richard Hart in Hart's papers, 1950–1951, 2/64, 2/68.
37. Hart's papers, 1950–1951, 2/62; and 1948–1949, 2/26. Hart's papers reveal like confidential reports to him over some years.
38. In 1951, TUC membership was around 8,750 and two years later had swelled to twenty-five thousand, albeit compared with a BITU membership of seventy thousand (Trevor Munroe, *The Cold War and the Fall of the Left* (Kingston: Kingston Publishing House, 1992), 100–101).
39. Isaacs had stepped aside for Seivright. *Daily Gleaner*, 29 June and 13 July 1951.
40. *Daily Gleaner*, 11 June 1951.
41. Vernon Arnett located the roots of the 4Hs' expulsion in this TUC rift. He said that the rift was due to Glasspole, though he identified Isaacs as overall leader of the 'right'. (Vernon Arnett interview (1978), 5).
42. *Daily Gleaner*, 9 and 10 October 1951; and Frank Hill, cited in Hart, *Change*, 157–58.
43. On inflation, see *Daily Gleaner*, 7 August 1950. In 1950, Seivright stood aside so that Isaacs could return to the PNP executive, following his 1949 resignation over Gordon Town. After Manley's election to the House, he combined the roles of party and PNP

House leader. Ivan Lloyd, formerly leader in the House, became a vice president for rural areas. In 1951, Nethersole and Ken Hill filled the first and second vice presidential positions, Lloyd and Isaacs, the third and fourth.

44 *Daily Gleaner*, 13 and 29 October 1951. Isaacs mistook his abdominal pain for the stomach cancer that killed his mother (personal communication, Isaacs family).

45. Vernon Arnett interview (1978), 4–5; *Daily Gleaner*, 28 November 1951.

46. *Daily Gleaner*, 3 December 1951; Trevor Munroe and Arnold Bertram, *Adult Suffrage and Political Administration in Jamaica, 1944–2002* (Kingston: Ian Randle Publishers, 2006), 174–75.

47. The following is based principally on *Public Opinion*, 8 and 15 March 1952; the transcript of the "Marxist Charges" tribunal report to the PNP General Council, published in the *Daily Gleaner*, 3 March 1952; Hart, *Change*, 154–89; and Leroy Cooke, *Land of My Birth: A Historical Sketch of the First Forty Years of the People's National Party of Jamaica* (Kingston: Negro River Publishers, 2016), 131–53.

48. At this time, labour conditions in Jamaica could hardly recommend capitalism, and belief in a scientific socialism that predicted the rise and ultimate fall of capitalism was pervasive among the left in many societies. Increasing knowledge of Stalin's excesses would dampen this belief throughout the 1950s. Notwithstanding Norman Manley's rejection of a revolutionary path, and Isaacs' critique of Soviet Russia, the sincere conviction of some of their comrades should not be doubted. See Gareth Stedman Jones, *Karl Marx: Greatness and Illusion* (Cambridge, MA: Harvard University Press, 2016).

49. Nettleford, *Manley*, xxiv–xxvii, lii–lxi.

50. Munroe, *Cold War*, 100–104. Both Ken Hill and Richard Hart would rejoin the PNP sometime later. Frank Hill pursued a successful career in public service (Munroe and Bertram, *Adult Suffrage*, 175–76).

51. See Cooke, *Land*, 150–51; and *Daily Gleaner* 3, 4 and 31 March 1952.

52. Michael Manley, *A Voice at the Workplace: Reflections on Colonialism and the Jamaican Worker* (London: Andre Deutsch, 1975); Phelps, "Labour Movement".

53. Hart, *Change*, 181–88; and Cooke, *Land*, 151–53. On Isaacs as a mere opportunist, see Hart, *Towards Decolonisation*, 265.

54. *Public Opinion*, 27 September 1952.
55. *PHR 1954*, 2 October; *Sunday Gleaner*, 28 July 1957; and Hart, *Change*, 133–34.

## Chapter 6

1. People's National Party, *Plan for Progress* (Kingston: The City Printery Ltd, 1955); *Daily Gleaner*, 6 March 1955.
2. *PHR 1951*, 17 July.
3. *PHR 1952*, 31 January.
4. *Daily Gleaner*, 27 June 1951. The Standing Closer Association Committee convened across 1948 and 1949. Sir Hubert Rance's report addressed fiscal, customs and tariff policies, currency unification, federal finances and other matters. The Jamaica debate took place in August 1951 (Munroe, *Constitutional Decolonization*, 122–25).
5. Glasspole was responding to the British Economic Co-operation Act of 1950. Britain sought to restrict Jamaican trade, and trade with Cuba. (*PHR 1951*, 14 and 15 August).
6. See Ransford Palmer, *The Jamaican Economy* (New York: Praeger, 1968), 142–46. The US trade proved a mixed blessing, however. See Norman Girvan, *Corporate Imperialism: Conflict and Expropriation* (New York: Monthly Review Press, 1976) and Levitt, *Jamaica's Debt Crisis*.
7. Behind Isaacs' remarks was his concern that, as a British dependency, Jamaica was exempted from GATT. Federation entailed joining GATT and losing both British preferences and protection for local industry (*PHR 1951*, 15 August; *Daily Gleaner*, 29 May 1952 and 7 March 1953).
8. In April 1953, the British suspended Guyana's constitution on the election of the leftist Cheddi Jagan. Earlier, Guyana and British Honduras had considered federation, but had been ambivalent. They feared an influx of labour from the islands. See Raymond Smith, *British Guiana* (Westport, CO: Greenwood Press, 1980).
9. *PHR 1953*, 25 June; Hart, *Change*, 190–97.
10. *Daily Gleaner*, 13 January 1953.
11. *Daily Gleaner*, 24 April and 25 October 1954.
12. *Daily Gleaner*, 17 September 1954. Two other parties were also in contention: Ken Hill's National Labour Party and the Farmers' Party.
13. William Isaacs interview (2002), 14; *Daily Gleaner*, 21 July 1954.

14. From a young boy, William "Vunnie" Isaacs addressed both Noel Nethersole and Florizel Glasspole as "uncle". Like his father, he was close to both.
15. *Daily Gleaner*, 25 October 1954. During the campaign, a life story of Manley, *Man of Destiny*, was widely publicized.
16. *Daily Gleaner*, 27 October 1954 and 5 January 1955.
17. *Daily Gleaner*, 13 and 18 January 1955.
18. During the war, George Cadbury worked with Stafford Cripps. In Jamaica, he would help administer some £30 million, coming mainly from CD&W (*Daily Gleaner*, 22 and 24 January, and 4 March 1955). The PNP anthem, "Jamaica Arise", was composed by William Seivright.
19. For all the portfolios, see Munroe and Bertram, *Adult Suffrage*, 208.
20. *Daily Gleaner*, 8 and 15 February 1955.
21. Known as the Jamaica Chamber of Commerce, this group was Kingston-based. Other centres, including Montego Bay and Portland, also had chambers.
22. *Daily Gleaner*, 15 February and 12 March 1955.
23. Matalon referred to the tariff regime introduced by the United States in 1930, dismantled only in part under GATT.
24. *Daily Gleaner*, 17 March 1955.
25. See below, Chapters 7 and 8.
26. *Daily Gleaner*, 28 March 1955.
27. Issa, *My Jamaica*, 87.
28. *Daily Gleaner*, Tuesday, 27 June 1950.
29. Issa, *My Jamaica*, 113.
30. *Daily Gleaner*, 17 and 18 March 1955.
31. Personal communication, Isaacs family.
32. *Daily Gleaner*, 22 April, and 3 and 9 May 1955.
33. *Daily Gleaner*, 1 and 5 April 1955; and on the Condell affair, *Daily Gleaner*, 26 April, 20 and 26 May, and 11 October 1955.
34. For the IDC, see Stacey H. Widdicombe, *The Performance of Industrial Development Corporations: The Case of Jamaica* (New York: Praeger, 1972).
35. A youthful George Arthur Brown was a member of the Planning Unit. In 1957, he became head of the unit and, in 1967, the first Jamaican head of the Bank of Jamaica.
36. Issa chaired the JTB and Hanna advised on Canadian trade, as did Luis Kennedy and Carlton Alexander. Hanna also advised on dry

goods, while Kennedy advised on Kingston Wharves, of which he was a proprietor. Five brothers co-owned the import-export company Levy Bros. Dudley would succeed Richard Youngman as president of the JCC. Sidney managed Ariguanabo Mills and founded Jamaica Broilers. Aaron Matalon was president of the JMA and deputy chair of the Trade Board, later to become chair. Moses was a director of the IDC. The Matalons expanded into construction. Lee Gore became a president of the JMA and was an IDC director. Later, the Gores expanded into construction. While some were sympathetic to the PNP, especially Hanna and the Matalons, others were less so. These families and others were interlinked through corporate co-ownerships that effectively controlled the economy. See Stanley Reid, "Elites in Jamaica: A Study of Monistic Relationship," *Anthropologica* New Series 22, no. 1 (1980): 25–44; and Peter Phillips, "Jamaica Elites: 1938 to Present," in *Essays on Power and Change in Jamaica*," eds. C. Stone and A. Brown (Kingston: Kingston Publishing House, 1977), 1–15.

37. *Daily Gleaner*, 13 January 1955.
38. This was Manley's view, even in 1940. Nationalization would take money and effort from urgent needs in "education, health, public services and a million [other] things" (cited in Nettleford, *Manley*, lv).
39. *Sunday Gleaner*, 28 July 1957. The article's famous title, "Black Dog and Monkey", would be taken up by the Abeng group in the late 1960s to critique neo-colonial government.
40. *Daily Gleaner*, 4 June 1948.
41. Frederic C. Benham, *Report of the Economic Policy Committee* (Kingston: Government Printer, 1945), 31–32; on the Benham-Lewis debate, Widdicombe, *Industrial Development*, 81–87. On the Agricultural Advisory Committee, Carl Stone, "Agricultural Policies"; and for colonial policy on industrialization, Bernal, "Great Depression".
42. For remarks by Manley, Nethersole, Lightbourne and Kirkwood, see *Daily Gleaner*, 6 December 1952, 4 August 1954, and 20 March 1951.
43. W. Arthur Lewis, *The Principles of Economic Planning: A Study Prepared for the Fabian Society* (London: Allen and Unwin, 1949); and the following articles: "Jamaica", "Puerto Rico", "British West Indies", and "Unlimited Supplies of Labour" (1954).

44. *Daily Gleaner*, 11 May 1950.
45. *Daily Gleaner*, 17 October 1949 and 15 May 1950. Lewis did not see the federation's benefits as mainly economic (W. Arthur Lewis, epilogue to John Mordecai, *The West Indies: The Federal Negotiations* (London: Allen and Unwin, 1968, 455–62).
46. Lewis' ideas were criticised throughout the 1960s and 1970s, especially by the Plantation Dependency School, inspired by Lloyd Best's New World Group. Critics proposed that Lewis' "dual-sector" model focused on manufacturing and overlooked agriculture. Later, Levitt and Girvan argued against this interpretation of Lewis' position (see Introduction above). However, Lewis overestimated the returns from foreign private investment, and underestimated the task of finding export markets. His neoclassical idea of comparative advantage proved inadequate as the evidence grew of unequal exchange between the centre and the periphery. For an overview of critics, see Terence Farrell, "Arthur Lewis and the Case for Caribbean Industrialisation," *Social and Economic Studies* 29, no. 4 (1980): 52–75.

## Chapter 7

1. P.J. Patterson interview (2003), 15; David Coore interview (2003), 14–15; and Fred Wilmot interview (2002), 11. Wilmot, a journalist, returned to Jamaica from Canada to work with Abe Issa in the tourism industry.
2. Carnegie, *Jamaica's Politics*, 20–39; Mahood A. Ayub, *Made in Jamaica: The Development of the Manufacturing Sector*, World Bank Occasional Paper 31 (Baltimore: Johns Hopkins University Press, 1981). Also see IDRD, *Jamaica Report.*
3. Jefferson (*Post-war Development*, 130–33), remarks on the liberal provisions for CCC. Also see Chapter 8 notes below.
4. Jefferson, *Post-war Development*, 161–64; and Norman Girvan, *Foreign Capital and Economic Underdevelopment in Jamaica* (Kingston: Institute of Social and Economic Studies, UWI, 1971).
5. "Jamaica Industry Progresses," *Foreign Commerce Weekly* 51–52 (27 December 1954): 9.
6. See https://moj.gov.jm/laws/trade-act. Accessed 8 July 2020.
7. Jefferson, *Post-war Development*; and Ayub, *Made in Jamaica.*
8. White received an OBE in 1958 *(Daily Gleaner*, 5 January 1958).
9. *Daily Gleaner*, 23 July 1956.

10. Jamaican capital investment in manufacturing was limited by the commercial banks, which preferred to provide low-risk loans to distributors. This situation changed as manufacturing became a stronger sector. Also, see Chapter 8 notes.
11. Widdicombe, *Industrial Development;* Jefferson, *Post-war Development,* 132; and Alvin G. Wint, "The Role of Government in Enhancing the Competitiveness of Developing Economies: Selective Functional Intervention in the Caribbean," *International Journal of Public Sector Management* 11, no. 4 (1998): 281–99.
12. Arnett's father was a British Baptist missionary who became the JAS' Supervisor of Agricultural Instructors. Arnett's early schooling was in England. Later, he attended Calabar High School. Following his father, Braham had extensive experience in the citrus and dairy industries and with farm equipment companies *(Daily Gleaner,* 7 June 1956).
13. *PHR 1956,* 25 July; *Sunday Gleaner,* 20 May 1956. For an extended extract from Isaacs' speech, see the Appendix below.
14. *Daily Gleaner,* 9 August 1957.
15. The CPU called on the expertise of the Bureau of Statistics and the Institute of Social and Economic Research *(Daily Gleaner,* 23 May, 4 June, and 16 December 1955).
16. Jefferson, *Post-war Development,* 237–39; Widdicombe, *Industrial Development,* 213–14; for Nethersole's views, *Daily Gleaner,* 11 April 1956.
17. In fact, the relevant Act was passed in 1960 and the Bank of Jamaica opened its doors in 1961.
18. *Daily Gleaner,* 28 May, 4 June and 22 October 1959. Manley made his support for middle-class housing schemes clear in December 1956, when he opened the first such project, Hampstead Park, located in his constituency (*Daily Gleaner,* 4 December 1956).
19. *PHR 1957,* 20 March.
20. *Daily Gleaner,* 5 March 1955 and *Sunday Gleaner,* 5 June 1956.
21. *PHR 1955,* 26 July; *Daily Gleaner,* 29 April 1955. Briefly, the Gores were also interested in leather. See Marguerite Curtin, *Legacy: The Levian Gore Family – A Jamaican Story* (Kingston: Marguerite Curtin, 2004).
22. *PHR 1956,* 11 April 1956; Daily Gleaner, 16 April 1956.
23. *Daily Gleaner,* 7 and 8 November 1956.
24. *Daily Gleaner,* 28 July 1955. A related effort involved a trade mission to London led by Wills in May 1955 concerning bananas,

citrus and cigars. All three exports were in trouble, despite British preferences (*Daily Gleaner*, 26 May 1955).

25. *Daily Gleaner*, 10 June 1955.
26. *Daily Gleaner*, 14 and 16 September 1955.
27. *Daily Gleaner*, 28 April 1961. For the JMA's 1962 plan, see *Daily Gleaner*, 15 September 1960.
28. Ariguanabo was founded by Dayton Hedges at the behest of Levy (*Sunday Gleaner*, 7 July 1957).
29. The factory management wished to pay workers on a trainee basis. The TUC obtained representational rights and negotiated a limited timeframe for this status (*Daily Gleaner*, 27 and 29 August 1952).
30. *Daily Gleaner*, 17, 26, 27 and 31 August, 21 October and 4 November 1955; *Daily Gleaner*, 24 January and 3 February 1966.
31. *Daily Gleaner*, 23 April and 3 May 1955; *PHR 1955*, 22 May. Already, by 1950, air was preponderant over sea when it came to tourist travel to Jamaica. The increase of travel by sea in the 1950s was due to the growing popularity of cruise ships. On tourism, see Frank F. Taylor, *To Hell with Paradise: A History of the Jamaican Tourist Industry* (Pittsburgh: Pittsburgh University Press, 1993); and eds. Kenneth Hall and Rheima Holding, *Tourism: The Driver of Change in the Jamaican Economy?* (Kingston: Ian Randle Publishers, 2006).
32. *Daily Gleaner*, 27, 22 and 29 April 1955.
33. *Daily Gleaner*, 20 April 1955; and Issa, *My Jamaica*, 116.
34. Reports on conventions and other media promotions appeared throughout April 1955 in the *Daily Gleaner* and the US media. These rapid-fire announcements by the JTB also acted to promote tourism to the domestic market.
35. J. R. Hicks and U.K. Hicks, *Report on Finance and Taxation in Jamaica* (Kingston: Government Printer, 1955), 17–19, #28–33; and 103, #209. Jefferson notes that this sum, which he puts at J$100,000 in 1955, had risen to J$3.3 million in financial 1969–70 (*Post-war Development*, 172).
36. *Daily Gleaner*, 6 June 1955; and Jefferson, *Post-war Development*, 170–84.
37. Hicks and Hicks, *Finance and Taxation*, 9.
38. *PHR 1956*, 11 April; and for Hill's letter, *Daily Gleaner*, 28 January 1956.
39. *PHR 1956*, 22 March and 11 April; and *Daily Gleaner*, 23 March 1956.

40. IBRD, *Jamaica Report*, 109–14.
41. For Ministerial Paper No. 4, Conversion of Electricity Frequency, see *PHR 1956*, 27 March.
42. IBRD, *Jamaica Report*, 114.
43. *Daily Gleaner*, 18 January 1957 and 21 February, 16 August and 6 October 1958.
44. *Daily Gleaner*, 16 March, 5 May, 3 10 July and 16 November 1956.
45. For contemporary commentary, see Ramsaran, *Contradictory Existence*, 1–6; and Robin McAlpine, "What is Economic Sovereignty and Why is it Important?', https://robinmcalpine.org/what-is-economic-sovereignty-and-why-is-it-important/

## Chapter 8

1. *PHR 1958* 1 April.
2. *Daily Gleaner*, 18 January and 25 March 1957; and Girvan, *Foreign Capital*, 111–13.
3. On tourism, *Daily Gleaner*, 18 January 1957; and Taylor, *To Hell with Paradise*, 160–61; and manufacturing, Palmer, *Jamaican Economy*, 17, 22–28; and Jefferson, *Post-war Development*, 30, 125–48.
4. G. Arthur Brown, "Economic Development and the Private Sector," *Social and Economic Studies* (Study Conference on Economic Development in Under-developed countries 7), no. 3 (1958):103–13; Widdicombe, *Industrial Development*, 263–71; and Colin Clarke, *Decolonizing the Colonial City: Urbanization and Stratification in Kingston, Jamaica* (Oxford: Oxford University Press, 2006) 22–24. On tourism costs, see Jefferson, *Post-war Development*, 177–79.
5. Clarke, *Colonial City*, 23–24 and Jefferson, *Post-war Development*, 15–39.
6. *PHR 1955*, 26 July; *PHR 1956*, 22 March; and *Daily Gleaner*, 11 July 1956. The issue was ongoing throughout July, August and September. For the IDC report, *Daily Gleaner*, 17 September 1956.
7. *PHR 1956*, 10 July; and *Daily Gleaner*, 21 and 25 March, 9 April, and 2 August 1957.
8. *PHR 1957*, 26 September; and *Daily Gleaner*, 10 and 13 March 1958.
9. Jefferson, *Post-war Development*, 44–47 and *Daily Gleaner*, 20 August 1955.

10. *Daily Gleaner*, 26 and 30 August, and 24 September 1955.
11. For each of the pricing steps, *Daily Gleaner*, 26 August, 4 November and 8 December 1955.
12. *Daily Gleaner*, 3 and 7 September 1955. Lionel deCordova was manager of Hardware and Lumber Ltd., one of Jamaica's largest importers of lumber.
13. *Daily Gleaner*, 7 and 20 September, and 1 October 1955.
14. Isaacs' move was headlined "Show Your Books" (*Daily Gleaner*, 3 and 9 October, and 10 December 1955).
15. *Daily Gleaner*, 22 October and 10 November 1955; and *Sunday Gleaner*, 6 November 1955. Four further editorials appeared between 11 September 1955 and 11 January 1956. While the *Gleaner* rejected Youngman's specific proposals, it endorsed Executive Council oversight of the economy.
16. *Daily Gleaner*, 25 and 27 August 1956.
17. *Daily Gleaner*, 5, 15, 22, 18 and 31 October 1955.
18. *Daily Gleaner*, 12 July 1956.
19. *Daily Gleaner*, 25 September 1958.
20. *Daily Gleaner*, 4 May 1957.
21. The beef debate was reported in the *Daily Gleaner* periodically throughout 1957 and 1958. On "Politician of the Year", see *Sunday Gleaner*, 29 December 1957.
22. *Daily Gleaner* 19 July, and 10 and 12 November 1956. Lionel and Joe deCordova, the one in lumber and the other in codfish, were second cousins (personal communication, Ainsley Henriques).
23. *Daily Gleaner*, 4, 8 and 17 August 1956, and 31 May 1957.
24. *Daily Gleaner* 27 September, 18, 19, 22, 29 and 31 October, and 1 November 1957; *Sunday Gleaner*, 19 August 1957.
25. The lower price for Icelandic codfish entailed the government absorbing some "financing charges". Domestic traders were also required to make a "slight adjustment" in profit margins. See *Daily Gleaner*, 30 October, 9 and 29 November 1958, and 17 October 1959. It seems likely that Isaacs consulted both Aaron Matalon, as Trade Administrator, and Carlton Alexander, for Grace Kennedy, on this matter. See also endnote 41 below.
26. *Daily Gleaner* 21 and 24 January, and 13 and 25 February 1958. For a full list of the trade mission members, see *Daily Gleaner*, 21 February 1958.
27. In 1938, James Gore proposed to produce cement in Jamaica at a price well below the British imported price. He was rebuffed by

the Colonial Office (Hart, *Towards Decolonisation*, 107–112; and Curtin, *Legacy*, 54–57).

28. *Daily Gleaner*, 1, 12 and 15 June 1948. For the formation of CCC, also see http://www.caribcement.com.history.
29. *Daily Gleaner*, 12 June 1954.
30. For Glasspole's initial objections, see *Daily Gleaner*, 7 July 1948; for the government's 1955 response, *Daily Gleaner*, 19 October.
31. *Daily Gleaner*, 4 and 15 January1957.
32. *Daily Gleaner*, 9 May and 12 November 1957.
33. *Daily Gleaner*, 8, 10 and 11 March 1958.
34. *PHR 1958*, 1 April.
35. *Daily Gleaner*, 9 and 10 April and 1 July 1958.
36. Following the death of his first wife, Isaacs largely abstained from alcohol (personal communication, Isaacs family). For the kiln opening, *Daily Gleaner*, 10 February 1959; and for the price reduction, 9 October 1959.
37. The priorities of the CCC board are a good example of the now common view that a board's principal responsibility is to maximize returns to shareholders, called in recent times Maximizing Shareholder Value (MSV). Other stakeholders, including employees and consumers, become lesser priorities. On this issue, see Mariana Mazzucato, *The Value of Everything: Making and Taking in the Global Economy* (Milton Keynes: Penguin Books (2019), 183–85.

    Stephenson came to Jamaica each year to deliver the CCC annual report and address the shareholders' meeting. Shareholder meetings in New York were attended by Melville, Ashenheim, and another director, Charles D'Costa. Reports of these meetings were published in the *Daily Gleaner*. D'Costa's firm, Lascelles de Mercado, was the sole marketing agent for CCC. See *Daily Gleaner*, 9 and 12 June 1954; 9 April 1957; 7 and 12 June; 7 October; 12 November 1960; and 19 January 1962.
38. For background on Sir William Stephenson, see *Daily Gleaner*, 21 December 1948.
39. *Daily Gleaner*, 17 October 1957.
40. For Isaacs's exchange with Allen regarding the Matalons, see *PHR 1957*, 25 July, and the *Daily Gleaner*, 26 July 1957. The scheme was formally announced in October (*Daily Gleaner*, 22 October 1957). Harry Dayes had brought back new construction techniques from Puerto Rico. Subsequently, he and his brother, V.A. Dayes, became

successful build-developers. WIBC, also known as the West Indies Building Association, was a predecessor to the Matalons' West Indies Home Contractor. The attack on the Matalons was so vociferous that the family took out a full-page advertisement to rebuff charges (*Daily Gleaner*, 27 July 1957). In the 1960s, it became clear that the Matalons also dealt extensively with the JLP government. See Diana Thorburn, *Mayer Matalon: Business, Politics and the Jewish-Jamaican Elite* (Lanham: Hamilton Books, 2019), 69–88.

41. *Daily Gleaner*, 10 and 11 June 1958. Seaga also hinted that the government was returning favours to the Matalon family for their assistance with Icelandic cod. See endnote 25 above.
42. Brown, "Private Sector". In discussion of post-war policy, Carl Stone, "Agricultural Policies", 170, makes a similar point regarding the dependence of a progressive political leadership on the "skills and technical expertise" of planters and a middle class reluctant for major structural change.
43. Jefferson, *Post-war Development*, 12 and passim.
44. Girvan, *Foreign Capital*, 186–88; and P.J. Patterson, "The History and the Development of the Modern Labour Movement: Lessons from the Past, Prospects for the Future," Inaugural Distinguished Lecture Series (Kingston: Trade Union Education Institute, Typescript, 2018), 8.
45. See Chapter 14 below.

## Chapter 9

1. *Sunday Gleaner*, 8 February 1959. The Chinese dragon is often depicted holding a pearl but, in this case, a chestnut. As this chapter shows, Ulric Simmonds (aka Political Reporter) was an advocate for Isaacs, who quite likely gave the reporter his views on events, especially between 1959 and 1961.
2. In addition to the £1 million offered by Britain, the delegates believed that they needed a further £2 million to secure the federation (*Daily Gleaner*, 15, 16, 17 and 18 February 1956). 'Dominion' refers to a self-governing status within the Commonwealth, rather than a colonial one.
3. *Daily Gleaner*, 29 March 1956.
4. The March 1957 budget debate brought an outburst from Wills. Tired of interruptions, he called Edwin Allen "a little down grow fellow" and threatened to "beat him to a pulp" outside the House.

Good relations were restored, however. See *Daily Gleaner*, 21 March 1957.

5. *Daily Gleaner*, 14 June and 19 July 1956, and 10 August 1957. Isaacs had become more domesticated. With wife Gloria, he maintained a family residence and small farm at Sligoville, northwest of Kingston. Supervised by Gloria, the farm raised pigs, of which Isaacs declared himself most fond (personal communication, Isaacs family).
6. *Daily Gleaner*, 15 June and 6 September 1956. On the name change, see Frank Hill's comment, *Daily Gleaner*, 12 September 1956.
7. *Daily Gleaner*, 17 September 1956.
8. Glasspole graduated from Wolmer's High School and trained as an accountant. He spent six months at Oxford on a Trades Union scholarship from 1946 to 1947 (*Daily Gleaner*, 7 February 1955).
9. *Sunday Gleaner*, 23 September, and 2 and 23 December 1956; and *Daily Gleaner*, 22 December 1956. A constituency worker for Glasspole spread the rumour that Isaacs intended to dislodge Nethersole, a palpable untruth. Isaacs suspected Glasspole.
10. *Daily Gleaner*, 26 April and 2 May 1957.
11. Ivan Lloyd, *Land for the Million*.
12. *PHR 1957*, 24 October; and *Sunday Gleaner*, 27 October 1957.
13. Lloyd repaired a previous misstep. Earlier in the year, he and Manley had moved to regrade the salaries of secondary teachers, while leaving primary teachers' pay barely altered. The JUT was angry, and Fred Evans resigned from the PNP. See *Daily Gleaner*, 2 and 9 May 1957.
14. *Daily Gleaner*, 15 July 1957; and *Sunday Gleaner*, 1 December 1957.
15. At the outset, the scholarships were not means-tested, which meant that most still went to the children of the middle class. A 70/30 distribution across government and private preparatory schools respectively was introduced by the 1962 JLP government.
16. *Sunday Gleaner*, 3 and 17 November 1957. The journalist was correct to note a social class difference between Isaacs, and Glasspole, Lloyd, Manley and Nethersole. They all had attained higher education, which Isaacs lacked. Still, his attraction to the working class came from his populist style, rather than a radical left stance.

17. *Sunday Gleaner*, 29 December 1957. The designation "Politician of the Year" was an annual exercise from which the two parties' leaders were excluded; otherwise, the *Gleaner* reporter maintained, one of them would win every year.
18. *Daily Gleaner*, 16 January 1958. The seminal work on federation is John Mordecai, *The West Indies: The Federal Negotiations* (London: George Allen and Unwin, 1968). Also, see Munroe, *Constitutional Decolonization*, 116–38; and Edward Seaga, *Edward Seaga: My Life and Leadership Vol. 1: Clash of Ideologies, 1930–1980* (Oxford: Macmillan, 2009), 45–74.
19. David Coore, "The Role of the Internal Dynamics of Jamaican Politics on the collapse of the Federation," *Social and Economic Studies* 48, no.4 (1999): 65–82.
20. Lewis was a political scientist at the University of Puerto Rico. *Daily Gleaner*, 12 September 1957; and *Sunday Gleaner*, 22 September 1957 and 9 March 1958.
21. On federation and labour, see Phillip Sherlock, *Norman Manley, a Biography* (London: Macmillan, 1980),173–76.
22. Personal communication, Isaacs family. Historian Swithin Wilmot also relates a similar a story (personal communication).
23. *Daily Gleaner*, 21 and 22 January, and 7 and 13 February 1958; and *PHR 1958*, 1 April.
24. A notable inclusion in the plan was guaranteed prices for some rural producers. Isaacs had received such requests and mostly refused them, due to the cost. Such was the impact of the 1957 bauxite agreement (*Daily Gleaner*, 23 January 1958.
25. Sherlock, Norman Manley; Hart, *Change*, 52–58; and *Daily Gleaner*, 28 November 1957 and 28 March 1958.
26. *Daily Gleaner*, 5 September 1958.
27. Mordecai gives an account of the tortuous process by which Chaguaramas became the site of the federation capital in *West Indies*, 106–23.
28. *Daily Gleaner*, 10, 11 and 14 January 1958. Over the years, Roy Lindo and Robert Kirkwood had been prominent in debate. For example, see *Daily Gleaner*, 8 September 1955; and, after the election, *Daily Gleaner*, 5 April 1958.
29. *Daily Gleaner*, 17 April 1957 and 22 March, 1958. Certainly, there was no guarantee in a customs union that smaller islands would not import cheaper mass-produced goods rather than Jamaican ones.

30. *Sunday Gleaner*, 23 March 1958; and *Daily Gleaner*, 24 March 1958.
31. Ralph Brown interview (1978), 8. Brown would go on to a stellar career with the PNP.
32. *Daily Gleaner*, 17, 20 and 23 March, and 6 and 9 April 1958.
33. *Daily Gleaner*, 2 and 8 April, and 29 September 1958; *Sunday Gleaner*, 6 April 1958. Lawyer Vivian Blake's loss in county Cornwall was a narrow one, determined after recounts.
34. Horace Levy, "Jamaica Welfare: Growth and Decline". Allan Isaacs proved to be ideologically agile during his career. See chapters 12 and 14 below. He and Isaacs were not related.
35. *Daily Gleaner*, 5 June 1958; *Sunday Gleaner*, 8 June 1958 and 5 October 1958.
36. *Daily Gleaner*, 29 September 1958.
37. Mordecai, *West Indies*, 124–28 and 146–50; and *Daily Gleaner*, 5, 9 and 27 June, 8 September 1958 and 10 January 1959.
38. Various reports cited a period between eight and fifteen years for the subsidy. The refinery was not opened until 1964.
39. On the Isaacs-Williams controversy, see *Daily Gleaner*, 19, 20 and 27 August, and 10 September 1958.
40. Mordecai, West Indies, 135; and *Daily Gleaner*, 4 September and 31 October 1958.
41. *Daily Gleaner*, 1 and 5 November 1958; and Manley's parliamentary statement, *PHR 1958*, 13 November; and *Daily Gleaner*, 1 and 5 November 1958. Emphasis added.
42. *Sunday Gleaner*, 2 November 1958; and for Frank Hill's series of articles, see *Daily Gleaner*, 5 and 10 September, 4 and 21 November, and 19 December 1958.
43. *Sunday Gleaner*, 6 June 1956; and *Daily Gleaner*, 11 October 1957 and 4 November 1959.
44. Isaacs' most forthright statement on regional trade cooperation, as opposed to federation, came at a trade fair in Kingston in April 1961, and in the presence of the WIF's governor general, Lord Hailes. Having celebrated regional expansion in production and trade, as reflected by the fair, Wills added that this did not entail his support for a federal structure. See *Daily Gleaner*, 5 April 1961.
45. The *Croft Report* had been prepared by the federal government's Trade and Tariffs Commission (*Daily Gleaner*, 10 January 1959).
46. *Daily Gleaner*, 13 January 1959.
47. *Daily Gleaner*, 14 January 14, 1959.
48. *Sunday Gleaner*, 8 February 1959.

## Chapter 10

1. *Sunday Gleaner*, 13 March 1960; and Michael Manley interview (1978), 10.
2. *Daily Gleaner*, 13 March 1959.
3. *Daily Gleaner*, 9 March 1959
4. Manley, *Edna Manley*, 87–88.
5. David Coore interview (2003), 14; and Michael Manley interview (1978), 5.
6. For the DFC, *Daily Gleaner*, 28 May 1959; and for Nethersole's death, *PHR 1958–1959*, 17 March, and *Daily Gleaner*, 18 March 1959. Also, see James Carnegie, *Noel Newton Nethersole: A Short Study* (Kingston: Bank of Jamaica, 1975).
7. *Daily Gleaner*, 28 May 1959.
8. *Daily Gleaner*, 19 May 1959; and Jefferson, *Post-war Development*, 85, 122. These measures for agriculture were a far cry from the contemporaneous Cuban land reforms. For an overview, see James O'Connor, "Agrarian Reforms in Cuba, 1959–63," *Science and Society* 32, no. 2 (1968): 169–217.
9. *Daily Gleaner*, 9 April and 13 May 1959.
10. *PHR 1959*, 21 April; and *Daily Gleaner*, 22 April 1959.
11. *Daily Gleaner*, 28 July and 5 December 1958. Isaacs' speeches involved openings for Willco Shoes and Ludlow Linoleum respectively.
12. *Daily Gleaner*, 27 July 1959, and *Sunday Gleaner*, 19 July 1959. The Flour Mill eventually opened on 3 September 1968. Work on Harbour View began in December 1959 and would be completed in 1962; the Esso Refinery, in 1964.
13. *Daily Gleaner*, 20 July 1959.
14. Previously, the executive body was called the National Council.
15. In November 1962, the United Nations passed its first resolution against South African apartheid. Commonwealth Heads of Government were not successful until October 1985, when Prime Minister Margaret Thatcher was finally persuaded.
16. Steven Jensen, 2016. "Embedded or Exceptional? Apartheid and the International Politics of Racial Discrimination," *Studies in Contemporary History, Online-Ausgabe* 13, no.2 (2016). https://zeithistorische-forschungen.de/2-2016/5364. For Isaacs' statements, see *Daily Gleaner*, 2, 8 and 25 July 1959; for positive responses, abroad and in Jamaica, *Daily Gleaner*, 8, 13 and 14 July

1959. The *Daily Gleaner* published two relevant editorials on 18 and 25 July 1959.

17. Sections of the constituency bordered by West Street and Matthews Lane were deleted, as was much of the 'downtown' part of the 1944 constituency. Parts of Allman Town to the north, Passmore Town to the east, and Rae Town to the south, east of Elletson Road, were added. Although enumerations were done independently, governments controlled the drawing of boundaries. Both parties used this power to advantage.
18. *PHR 1959*, 1 September. Jamaica's non-compulsory and non-preferential voting system means that a small percentage shift in the vote can produce a very different result in terms of seats won or lost (Mordecai, *West Indies*, 223).
19. Ken Sterling was a previous island supervisor for the NWU, who had moved on to a regional role with the Inter-American Organization of Workers. On his return to Jamaica, Sterling won the seat of St Mary Central.
20. *Daily Gleaner*, 15 August 1959.
21. *Daily Gleaner*, 17 and 18 September 1959.
22. *Daily Gleaner*, 29 September 1959.
23. *Daily Gleaner*, 30 September and 1, 2, 8 and 9 October 1959; *Sunday Gleaner*, 4 October 1959; and Mordecai, *West Indies*, 173–85.
24. *Daily Gleaner*, 16 and 26 October 1959.
25. *Daily Gleaner*, 26 October 1959; and *Sunday Gleaner*, 1 November 1959. The term was coined by 'Political Reporter'.
26. *Daily Gleaner*, 6 and 23 November, and 4, 5 and 7 December 1959.
27. 'Independence' had now replaced the term 'dominion' status (*Daily Gleaner*, 3 May 1960).
28. *Daily Gleaner*, 11 and 19 January 1960; and, on the "essential requirements", *Daily Gleaner*, 26 February 1960.
29. The nature of Isaacs' illness was not disclosed. He was rumoured to have had surgery. See *Daily Gleaner*, 2 May 1960. While in Trinidad, however, he visited the Caribbean Trade Fair with Manley. The Jamaican pavilion was deemed a triumph.
30. *Daily Gleaner*, 3 and 9 May 1960; and *Sunday Gleaner*, 8 May 1960.
31. *Daily Gleaner*, 6 and 31 May 1960; and *Sunday Gleaner*, 5 June 1960.
32. Cited in Mordecai, *West Indies*, 224.

33. *PHR 1960–1961*, 9 March; and *Sunday Gleaner*, 13 March 1960.
34. *Sunday Gleaner*, 19 June 1960. For three earlier comments on Isaacs and the leadership issue, see *Sunday Gleaner*, 24 January, 13 March and 1 May 1960.
35. *Sunday Gleaner*, 4 September 1960. Emphases added.
36. These observations are based on a survey of columns between 14 January and 20 March 1960. Often, but not always, they appear on page two of the *Daily Gleaner*.
37. *Daily Gleaner*, 13 and 14 January 1960.
38. *Daily Gleaner*, 7 September 1960. For examples of Isaacs' fightback, see *Daily Gleaner* "Meetings and Services" columns for 24 and 26 July. Meetings of the competing groups were scheduled at the same time. One of Isaacs' notices carried the call, "Our Comrades turn towards the Dawn, new life!" taken from "Salute to Life", a socialist song attributed to Dmitri Shostakovich.
39. *Daily Gleaner*, 14 and 23 November 1959. Subsequent public discussion was critical of Allan Isaacs, calling for more regional-specific expenditure. See *Daily Gleaner*, 21 November and 1 and 16 December 1959. After the 1959 election, Seivright had gone to Home Affairs and Keble Munn to Agriculture.
40. *Daily Gleaner*, 1 and 27 August 1960.
41. Manley's intent seemed evident at his birthday party in July. Isaacs and Glasspole wished him well in his quest to become prime minister of the WIF (*Daily Gleaner*, 6 July 1960). 'Political Reporter' would write two further analyses of "the battle of the Isaacses", appearing in the *Sunday Gleaner* on 13 and 20 November 1960.
42. *Daily Gleaner*, 17 November and 3 December 1960.
43. *Sunday Gleaner*, 13 November and 25 December 1960; *Daily Gleaner*, 22 November 1960. See Bertram, *N. W. Manley*, 326, for a brief reference to this vice-presidential contest.
44. *Sunday Gleaner*, 25 December 1960. Isaacs' achievements included a successful negotiation with New York's First National Bank to establish a branch in Jamaica; see *Daily Gleaner*, 1 and 12 September 1960.
45. Michael Manley interview (1978), 10; and William Isaacs interview (2001), 8.

## Chapter 11

1. Ralph Brown interview (1978), 5.

2. *Daily Gleaner*, 16 January 1961; and *Sunday Gleaner*, 19 and 26 February, and 5 March 1961. Regrettably, the dispossession of many Palestinians that came with the foundation of the Israeli state would only be widely known in later decades.
3. Thomas G. August, "An Historical Profile of the Jewish Community in Jamaica," *Jewish Social Studies* 49, nos. 3 and 4 (1987): 303–16. Professor Golding was knighted for his services to Jamaica. His son, Mark, a lawyer and businessman, was elected leader of the PNP on 7 November 2020.
4. *Daily Gleaner*, 9 February 1961.
5. There had been previous bases during World War II, including Vernam Field and Goat Island in Jamaica, as well as the longer-term Chaguaramas in Trinidad. The Cuban Revolution ensured continuing US interest in the region.
6. Obika Gray, *Radicalism and Social Change in Jamaica* (Knoxville: University of Tennessee Press, 1991), 46–62. On the Coronation Market event, see http://johnmaxwellshouse-2004.blogspot.com/; for June 1960s events, *Daily Gleaner*, 6 May and 22 June 1960; and *Sunday Gleaner*, 26 June 1960. For the trial and execution, *Daily Gleaner*, 29 and 30 March 1961; and *PHR 1960–1961*, 28 June.
7. Michael Smith, Roy Augier, and Rex Nettleford, *The Rastafari Movement in Kingston* (Kingston: ISER, 1960); *Report of Mission to Africa* (Kingston: Government Printer, 1961); and *Daily Gleaner*, 19 November 1960.
8. Gray (*Radicalism*, 54–56) refers to this creole stance as "Jamaican exceptionalism". For a comprehensive critique of the stance, see Thomas, *Modern Blackness.*
9. Gray, *Radicalism*, 240; endnote 38.
10. John Cannon, "Millard Johnson and His Party: Racial Ideology in Jamaican Politics," *Caribbean Studies* 16, nos. 3 and 4 (1976–77): 85–108. Millard's PPP referenced a short-lived party of the same name formed by Marcus Garvey in the early 1903s.
11. Thomas, "Jewish Community".
12. Speaking in Birmingham, England, Norman Manley put the unemployment figure at 18 per cent, with 26 per cent for those aged sixteen to twenty-five (*Daily Gleaner*, 13 June 1961). Jefferson's unemployment figure for 1960 is 13.5 per cent (*Post-war Development*, 28).
13. *Sunday Gleaner*, 6 September 1964; Widdicombe, *Industrial Development*, 211–15, 263, 268–71; and Jefferson, *Post-war Development*, 237–39.

14. The projects at hand were Hope Pastures in Kingston and Sydenham in Spanish Town.
15. *PHR 1961–1962,* 16 March; and *Daily Gleaner,* 17 March 1961.
16. *Daily Gleaner,* 18 March 1961. The term 'tattoo', also spelt 'tatoo', refers to a makeshift shelter of cardboard pieces and other non-durable materials. Although the word seems to have affinity with military terms, it also may derive from the Portuguese *tatu,* meaning armadillo, with its multiplicity of segments. 'Tattoo' is not used much nowadays. A more common term for a slum house is 'wappen-bappen', meaning something thrown together and noisy.
17. *Daily Gleaner,* 16 March and 5 April 1961; and *PHR Session 1961–1962,* 5 April 1961.
18. *PRH Session 1961–1962,* 29 March 1961.
19. Edward Seaga, *Edward Seaga Vol. 1,* 63–74. For another view of the circumstance, and of weaknesses in the Lewis model, see David Panton, "Dual Labour Markets and Unemployment in Jamaica: A Modern Synthesis," *Social and Economic Studies* 42, no. 1 (1993): 75–118.
20. Mordecai, *West Indies,* 331; and *Daily Gleaner,* 18 May 1961.
21. *Daily Gleaner,* 22 May, 19 and 27 June 1961. It was reported that Isaacs was carrying a revolver, which seems quite likely.
22. *Daily Gleaner,* 4 March, and 5 and 6 June 1961.
23. *PRH Session 1961–1962,* 9 April 1961; and *Daily Gleaner,* 2 and 7 June 1961.
24. *Sunday Gleaner,* 11 June 1961; and *Daily Gleaner,* 7, 10, 15, 17 and 18 July 1961. For Isaacs' departure from and return to duties, see *Daily Gleaner,* 23 July and 12 August 1961. His periodic illnesses were undoubtedly real, but never described in the press. Though fear of stomach cancer had abated, he would die of lung cancer. On the industry openings, *Daily Gleaner,* 15 and 28 August 1961.
25. *Daily Gleaner,* 20 July and 24 August 1961.
26. Mordecai, *West Indies,* 411–14; and Munroe, *Constitutional Decolonization,* 129–38. A further aspect of the referendum was that the commercial class was split. Mordecai (*West Indies,* 392–93) cites evidence provided by Wendell Bell.
27. *Daily Gleaner,* 23 September 1961; and personal communication with Christine Gore (née Isaacs). The flight took Christine and her mother, Gloria, to the University of Colorado in Denver, where she was seen by Professor C. Henry Kempe.

28. At this time, Manley also resigned as president of WIFLP, while the PNP ceased to be an affiliate.
29. *Daily Gleaner*, 22, 26, 27 and 29 September 1961.
30. Isaacs' reference here was to the bill that preceded the Commonwealth Immigrants Act of 1962. For the entire debate, see *PRH Session 1961–1962*, 18 October 1961.
31. The upshot of the inclusion was that, while a Jamaican government could legally acquire private property, the court would decide the compensation involved. The impact on land reform was predictable. Also, see Bertram, *N. W. Manley*, 320.
32. Munroe, *Constitutional Decolonization*, 138–42; and Bertram, *N.W. Manley*, 319–21. Also, see Bryan Meeks, preface to *Beyond Westminster in the Caribbean*, eds. B. Meeks and K. Quinn (Kingston: Ian Randle Publishers, 2018), vii–x.
33. *Daily Gleaner*, 20 December 1961; and 18 January, 5, 6 and 9 February 1962; *Sunday Gleaner*, 28 January 1962.
34. In 1961, however, Allan Isaacs had changed his position and strongly defended Isaacs' stance on marketing. He no longer endorsed a blanket guarantee of prices and markets. The two Isaacses also agreed on the need for more productive uses of capital (*Daily Gleaner*, 29 May 1961).
35. *Daily Gleaner*, 21, 23 and 28 November 1961; and *Sunday Gleaner*, 26 November 1961.
36. *Daily Gleaner*, 12 February 1962.
37. Reporting of the dispute between Isaacs and the JPSC extended from December 1961 to April 1962. Some key reports were *Daily Gleaner*, 15 December 1961; 9 and 26 February, and 6, 14, 28 and 29 March 1962. The Leandro cartoon of Isaacs' victory appeared in the *Gleaner* on 2 April 1962. Ample support for JPSC was published in the *Gleaner* at this time.
38. *Sunday Gleaner*, 6 February 1962; and *Daily Gleaner*, 19 February, and 7 and 10 April 1962.
39. Coombs ran as an independent and attracted fewer than three hundred votes. On Isaacs' role, see *Daily Gleaner*, 13 November 1961, and 5 January and 2 February 1962; and *Sunday Gleaner*, 26 November 1961.
40. For the full story of Thompson and Kenyatta, see Bertram, *N.W. Manley*, 329.
41. *Daily Gleaner*, 14 March and 10 April 1962.

42. Sherlock, *Manley,*186–89. The other descriptions include those given by Arnold Bertram, Rachel Manley, Rex Nettleford and Vic Reid.
43. *PHR Session 1961–1962,* 6 June.
44. *Daily Gleaner,* 4 May 1962.
45. *Daily Gleaner,* 4 May 1962; *Sunday Gleaner,* 26 August 1962; and Ralph Brown interview (1978), 5.
46. For Edna Manley's comment, see Chapter 10 above. Manley used the word "trickery" at two notable points: first with regard to JLP tactics immediately prior to the 1962 election, and later in 1964 when he proposed that politics needed "great debate", not just "trickery". See *Daily Gleaner,* 7 April 1962 and 16 November 1964.

## Chapter 12

1. Manley's two comments come from a 1964 broadcast on land policy (Nettleford, *Manley,* 325); and from his 1966 PNP national conference address (*Daily Gleaner,* 16 October 1966).
2. *Daily Gleaner,* 15 May 1964. The "stern realities" of Caribbean life is C.L.R. James' term, cited by Nettleford, *Manley,* xc–xci.
3. Arnett and Allan Isaacs were considered on the left. For Michael Manley's position, see Manley, *Voice,* 70–71; and Darrell Levi, *Michael Manley: The Making of a Leader* (Kingston: Heinemann Caribbean, 1989), 111–15.
4. *Sunday Gleaner,* 23 September 1962.
5. *PHR Session 1961–1962,* 6 June, 4 September, and 7 November 1962. France vetoed this attempt by Britain to enter the EEC, a quest that was finally successful in 1973.
6. *PHR Session 1963,* 24 April.
7. *Daily Gleaner,* 28 and 29 November, 27 December 1962, and 12 February and 13 March 1963. Wills noted that he had conferred with the Canadian Deputy Minister of Trade regarding the company's good standing. The commission made its report in 1965. It was withheld until 1967 and released just prior to the general election. See *Daily Gleaner,* 25 January 1967; and Widdicombe, *Industrial Development,* 211–15.
8. *Daily Gleaner.* 19 August 1963.
9. *Public Opinion,* 6 March and 11 September 1964. In the interim, Maxwell criticized the "proprietorial hold the 1938 men" had on the party (*Public Opinion,* 26 March 1964).

10. *Daily Gleaner*, 14 and 18 September 1964; and Farrell, "Caribbean Industrialisation". For two hallmark works, see William Demas, *The Economics of Development in Small Countries with Reference to the Caribbean* (Montreal: McGill University Press, 1965); and George Beckford, *Persistent Poverty*.
11. Gray, *Radicalism*, 87–114; and Munroe, *Jamaican Politics*, 1–25, 204–30.
12. On 14 November, Marcus Garvey's remains were to be interred in his homeland. The conference was to conclude at 3 p.m. to facilitate attendance.
13. A note of Isaacs' realism came with the remark that Eastern European prices may not be the lowest. However, a reciprocal trade could bring more markets for Jamaican goods.
14. *Daily Gleaner*, 16 and 21 November 1964; and on Cuban land reform, see O'Connor, "Cuba".
15. *Daily Gleaner*, 10 August, 4 September and 1 October 1965. Isaacs' and Manley's apparent enthusiasm for co-operatives was also shared by a number of their PNP comrades. For a subsequent, sober analysis of their viability in one industry, see Carl Stone, "An Appraisal of the Co-operative Process in the Jamaican Sugar Industry," in *Perspectives on Jamaica in the Seventies*, eds. Carl Stone and Aggrey Brown (Kingston: Jamaica Publishing House, 1981), 437–62.
16. See, for instance, *Sunday Gleaner*, 17 January 1965; and *Daily Gleaner*, 20 February 1965.
17. *Daily Gleaner*, 25 February 1965. By contrast, Gray (*Radicalism*, 106) deemed the policy "tepid and ideologically innocuous".
18. Gray, *Radicalism*, 101–3.
19. *Daily Gleaner*, 8 December 1964; and Levi, *Michael Manley*, 114.
20. *Daily Gleaner*, 10 November and 16 December 1964.
21. Author's interview with P.J. Patterson, Tuesday, 23 April 2019. Patterson observed that Isaacs opposed major land redistribution in Jamaica on practical grounds. He was not committed to the protection of private property above all else.
22. *Sunday Gleaner*, 3, 10 and 17 January, 21 and 28 February, and 4 and 11 April 1965. Also, see *Daily Gleaner*, 29 March 1965.
23. Gray, *Radicalism*, 105, 109–13; Bertram, *N.W. Manley*, 350; Levi, *Michael Manley*, 114–15; and *Daily Gleaner*, 11 and 26 February 1966.

24. Bertram, *N.W. Manley*; Munroe and Bertram, *Adult Suffrage*, 320–21; and Cooke, *Land of My Birth*, 132, 239.
25. Nettleford, *Manley*, lix, 296–301. Also, see Sidney Mintz, "Caribbean Peasantries," in *Caribbean Transformations* (Chicago: Aldine Press, 1974), 131–250. Mintz sees the small farmer class as a response to the plantation's oppression. On land redistribution, see George Beckford, "Land Reform for the Betterment of Caribbean Peoples," in *The George Beckford Papers,* introduced by Kari Levitt (Kingston: Canoe Press, 2000), especially 96–97.

    Also, see Stone, "Agricultural Policies". Stone argues that Manley's position was one that simply aligned with the class interests of large landholders. His discussion does not address the debates on land reform within the PNP, including Ivan Lloyd's *Land for the Million*, and the policies of 1964–65, which also addressed agricultural co-operatives.
26. Gray, *Radicalism*, 105–8, and endnotes 80, 81 and 82 (p.250). Daley was a foundation member of Jamaica's Council of Human Rights, and an eminent human rights lawyer. Gray interviewed him in the course of his research.
27. *Sunday Gleaner*, 4 April 1965.
28. *Daily Gleaner*, 20 September and 25 November 1965.
29. *Daily Gleaner*, 8 October 1966.
30. Walter Rodney was returning from Canada to the Mona campus of the UWI, where he had a teaching position. A few years later he would publish his seminal work, *How Europe Underdeveloped Africa*. For Black Power in the late 1960s, see Gray, *Radicalism,* 144–82; and eds. Clinton Hutton, Maziki Thame and Jermain McCalpin, *Caribbean Reasonings: Rupert Lewis and the Black Intellectual Tradition* (Kingston: Ian Randle Publishers, 2018). Indicative of the changing politics was the emergence of Abeng, succeeding both the New World Group and YSL.
31. Some of the history of this tragedy was recorded in October 1963, including the squatters' requests for re-housing and the promises provided, but not kept (*Daily Gleaner*, 2 October 1963). Also, see Kevin Edmonds, "Guns, Gangs and Garrison Communities in the Politics of Jamaica," *Race and Class* 57, no. 4 (2016): 54–64; and, for a different view, Seaga, *Edward Seaga Vol. 1*, 152–58.
32. *Daily Gleaner*, 4 October 1966.
33. George Eaton, *Alexander Bustamante and the Modern Jamaica* (Kingston: Kingston Publishers, 1975); and Zeidenfelt, "Political and Constitutional Change".

34. Barry Chevannes, "The Rastafari and the Urban Youth," and Peter Phillips, "Community Mobilisation in Squatter Communities," in *Perspectives on Jamaica in the Seventies,* eds. Carl Stone and Aggrey Brown (Kingston: Kingston Publishers, 1981), 392–422 and 423–36, respectively; Gray, *Radicalism,* 23–52; and Amanda Sives, "The Historical Roots of Violence in Jamaica," in ed. Anthony Harriott, *Understanding Crime in Jamaica* (Kingston: University of West Indies Press, 2004), 49–61.
35. Sives, *Elections,* 77. For the origins and logic of Jamaica's political clientelism, see Carl Stone, *Democracy and Clientelism in Jamaica* (New Brunswick: Transaction Books, 1980).
36. *Sunday Gleaner*, 18 September 1966.
37. *Sunday Gleaner*, 22 December 1963, and 5 January, 20 May and 28 June 1964. Also, see *Daily Gleaner*, 23 June 1964. For the ban on marching, see *Daily Gleaner*, 10 July 1964; and for the local election results, *Sunday Gleaner*, 3 July 1966.
38. *Daily Gleaner*, 17 October 1966.
39. *Daily Gleaner*, 3 February and 23 March 1964. Also, see *Sunday Gleaner*, 6 and 13 December 1964. Seaga notes that, due to finger-printing, 1962 voter registrations decreased by 32 per cent in 1967 (*Edward Seaga Vol. 1*, 280).
40. On gerrymandering, see Political Reporter, *Sunday Gleaner*, 18 and 25 September, and 11 December 1966. Also, see *Daily Gleaner*, 2 November and 15 December 1966; *Sunday Gleaner*, 13 February 1972; and Cooke, *Land of My Birth,* 241–42.
41. *Daily Gleaner*, 16 November 1965.
42. These were the areas of Fletcher's Town and Kingston Gardens in the north of the constituency, and Brown's Town and Rae Town in the south. It was this longitudinal stretch which created the queer shape. In the new, even more anomalous Kingston Central, Brown's Town and Rae Town remained.
43. *Daily Gleaner*, 3 and 20 February 1967.
44. Sives, *Elections,* 67, 73–77. The JLP remarks on Isaacs were published in the *Daily Gleaner* on 19 and 20 February. Also, see Cooke, *Land of My Birth*, 242; and Seaga, *Edward Seaga Vol. 1*, passim. Author's note: For my own exchange with Orville Brown on these matters following Seaga's death, see *Sunday Gleaner*, 9 and 30 June 2019.
45. Ken Hill returned to Jamaica to support Michael Manley in the 1967 election. Following the election, Norman Manley, as

Opposition Leader, nominated Hill to a senate seat in the 1967 parliament.

## Chapter 13

1. Michael Manley interview (1978), 22.
2. Following independence, Shearer was an appointed member of the Senate (formerly the Legislative Council), between 1962 and 1967, when he then became the MHR for Clarendon South. During the Senate years, he also represented Jamaica at the United Nations.
3. *Daily Gleaner*, 11 May 1967. Men and women worked for ten and six shillings a day, respectively. Jamaica decimalised its currency and switched to dollar denominations in 1969. In 1971, with sterling effectively floating, the Jamaican dollar was pegged to its US equivalent.
4. *Daily Gleaner*, 15 May, 1967.
5. *Daily Gleaner*, 9 February 1968.
6. *Daily Gleaner*, 11 November 1968.
7. Michael Manley would use these words as a campaign slogan eight years later.
8. Norman Manley contrasted Jamaica's circumstance with that of Czechoslovakia in 1968. The United States and the United Nations stood aside as Russian troops arrived to quell the Prague Spring. They would not stand aside from a comparable event in Jamaica.
9. Author's interview with P.J. Patterson, Tuesday, 23 April 2019. Patterson allowed that Isaacs was "uncomfortable" with the ethos of Black Power, though his anti-racism was "unrelenting".
10. *Sunday Gleaner*, 16 February 1969; and *Daily Gleaner*, 10 February, and 21 and 22 October 1969. Seymour Mullings retained the seat of St Ann South East for the PNP.
11. *Daily Gleaner*, 27 October and 5 November 1969; and *Sunday Gleaner*, 28 December 1969.
12. Manley expands on these issues in *Voice*, 213–14. Interestingly, in 1966, D.K. Duncan, assigned to Browns Town as a dentist, founded a socialist group with a newssheet called *The Sufferer* (*Daily Gleaner*, 6 October 2020).
13. These comments foreshadowed the International Bauxite Association and the movement for a New International Economic

Order. A vociferous opponent of the NIEO was Harry Johnson, a leading monetarist at the time. See Johnson, *The New International Economic Order*, Selected Papers No. 49 (Chicago: Graduate School of Business, University of Chicago, 1976).

14. *Daily Gleaner*, 28 February 1959. Hill's reference was to Norman Manley's statement to parliament on 13 November 1958.
15. For some recent perspectives on Manley, see Godfrey Smith, *Michael Manley, the Biography* (Kingston: Ian Randle Publishers, 2016); and Orlando Patterson, *The Confounding Island: Jamaica and the Postcolonial Predicament* (Harvard: Harvard University Press, 2019). The latter writes of Manley's "flawed charisma".
16. *Daily Gleaner*, 30 January, 26 June and 20 November 1970.
17. *Daily Gleaner*, 22 April 1970.
18. *PHR Session 1969–1970*, 10 March and 25 June.
19. *Daily Gleaner*, 8 July 1971.
20. *Daily Gleaner*, 12 and 18 September 1970. Roy McNeill, Minister of Home Affairs and Leader of the House, headed this deputation.
21. *Daily Gleaner*, 4 January 1971.
22. *Daily Gleaner*, 1 March 1971.
23. *PHR, 1971–1972*, 29 June; and *Daily Gleaner*, 16 and 25 June, and 6 September 1971.
24. *Daily Gleaner*, 31 January, and 10 and 12 February 1972.
25. *Daily Gleaner*, 2, 4 and 26 February, and 7 March 1972. Also, see P.J. Patterson, *My Political Journey: Jamaica's Sixth Prime Minister* (Kingston: University of West Indies Press, 2018), 60–68.
26. *Sunday Gleaner*, 2 April 1972.
27. Davies, "Jamaican Economy:1972–1985".
28. Patterson, *My Political Journey*, 83–93.
29. Bell was the first minister with a portfolio devoted entirely to utilities.
30. William Isaacs interview (2001), 9; and personal communication with the Isaacs family.
31. Michael Manley, *Jamaica: Struggle in the Periphery* (London: Third World Media, and Writers and Readers Cooperative, 1982), 119–29. Also, see D.K. Duncan's statement on his resignation as party secretary (*Sunday Gleaner*, 9 October 1977). Early on, Manley did seek advice from capitalists and conservatives, including at least four of the Matalon brothers; Leslie Ashenheim; John Pringle; and Morris Cargill. See Thorburn, *Mayer Matalon*, 69–88; Levi,

*Michael Manley*, 128–54; Kaufman, *Jamaica Under Manley*, 73–81; and Michael Manley, *The Politics of Change: A Jamaican Testament* (London: André Deutsch, 1974), 83–85.

32. *Daily Gleaner*, 26 February 1972.
33. *Daily Gleaner*, 19 February, 30 June 1972; and Central Planning Unit of Jamaica, *Economic Survey: Jamaica, 1971* (Kingston: Government Printer, 1972).
34. On international monetary issues, see Norman Girvan, Richard Bernal, and Wesley Hughes, "The IMF and the Third World: The Case of Jamaica," *Development Dialogue* 2 (1980): 113–55; and Davies, "Jamaican Economy: 1972–1985". Also, see Don Kalb, "Thinking About Neoliberalism as if the Crisis was Actually Happening," *Social Anthropology* 20, no. 3 (2012): 318–30.
35. See Michael Witter, "Exchange Rate Policy in Jamaica: A Critical Assessment," *Social and Economic Studies* 32, no. 4 (1983): 1–50. Jamaica's currency had been converted from pounds to dollars in 1968, reflecting the increasing engagement with North American trade, commerce and finance.
36. *Daily Gleaner*, 14 March, 19 and 22 April 1972; and *Sunday Gleaner*, 21 May.
37. *Daily Gleaner*, 28 January 1972; and Davies, "Jamaican Economy". The new government inherited the Agricultural Incentives Act (1972), which brought relief from customs duties, and tonnage and income tax. It also provided incentives for banks to provide farmers with long-term loans of J$2,000 or more (Evelyn Stephens and John Stephens, *Democratic Socialism in Jamaica: The Political Movement and Transformation in Dependent Capitalism* (Princeton: Princeton University Press, 1986), 73–74.
38. *Daily Gleaner*, 30 June and 2 November 1972.
39. Patterson, *My Political Journey*, 69–82.
40. For negotiations on these commodities, see *Daily Gleaner*, 22 and 23 March, 29 April and 17 May 1972; and for Isaacs on China and Japan, see *Daily Gleaner*, 6 April 1972. From 1973, US inflation accelerated due to the Middle East oil crisis (Alan Binder, "Anatomy of Double-Digit Inflation in the 1970s," in *Inflation: Causes and Effects*, ed. R. Hall (Chicago: University of Chicago Press, 1982), 261–82.
41. *Daily Gleaner*, 6 September 1965.
42. *Sunday Gleaner*, 15 October 1972; and *Daily Gleaner*, 18 October 1972.

43. *Daily Gleaner* news reports, editorials and opinion columns between 11 September and 3 November 1972.
44. The speeches were delivered live to the nation from the House. See *Daily Gleaner*, 10 November 1972.
45. *Daily Gleaner*, 24 and 25 November 1972.
46. *Daily Gleaner*, 8 November 1972.
47. Patterson, *My Political Journey*, 280–81. The United Nation's China policy was confirmed in October 1971. Jamaica's response was not idiosyncratic. Australia's Labor government recognized China in December 1972.
48. *PHR Session 1972–1973*, 21 and 23 November; and *Daily Gleaner*, 25 November 1972.

## Chapter 14

1. See "Song of the Storm Petrel" by Maxim Gorky, English translation by Sally Ryan. https://ruverses.com/maxim-gorky/song-of-the-stormy-petrel/4260/. For Isaacs' remark, see
Canada Correspondence, box 2, folder 66, letter dated 28 July 1975.
2. *Daily Gleaner*, 22 and 23 May, and 5 and 7 June 1973. Both orders were conferred formally in October, just before National Heroes Day. Isaacs returned briefly from Canada for the event. Glasspole officiated as governor general.
3. *Daily Gleaner*, 24 February 1973.
4. Girvan, Bernal, and Hughes, "The IMF"; Witter, "Exchange Rate"; and Davies, "Jamaican Economy: 1972–1985". Also, see *Daily Gleaner*, 17 January 1973.
5. See *Daily Gleaner*, 17, 18, 19 and 25 January, and 2 and 12 February 1973. Also, *PHR Session 1973–1974*, 1 May 1973.
6. Also recounted in Manley, *Voice*, 30–32.
7. For all speeches, *PHR Session 1973–1974*, 12 June 1973. Allan Isaacs, on his way from a sojourn on the left back to the right, possibly sought to emphasize that it was not only leftist unionists who built the PNP in the 1940s. Three years later he resigned from the PNP under suspicion that he had leaked a Cabinet paper to Edward Seaga. See endnote 41 below, and also, *Daily Gleaner*, 22 January 1976.
8. Canada Correspondence, box 2, folder 55, letter dated 19 November 1973.
9. CC box 2, folder 54, letters dated 8 April 1974 and 19 December 1974.

10. *Daily Gleaner*, 4 May 1973; and Manley, *Struggle*, 87–88.
11. David Coore detailed the issues in a radio broadcast on 20 May (*Daily Gleaner*, 21 May 1973).
12. "Thomas Wright" in the *Daily Gleaner*, 18 May 1973. Less colourful but relentless comment on the tax reform continued throughout the year, most of it negative. For example, see *Daily Gleaner*, 26 March, 8 June, 8 August and 30 December 1973.
13. *Sunday Gleaner*, 28 October 1973.
14. See chapter 13, Isaacs' speech on the twenty-seventh anniversary of the PNP.
15. Davies, "Jamaican Economy", 81.
16. The correspondence on inflation extended from 8 August to 1 October 1974, CC box 2, folder 54.
17. Those involved were Kaiser, Reynolds, ALCOA and Anaconda from the United States; as well as the Aluminium Company of Canada; and ALCOA Jamaica. See Davies, "Jamaican Economy"; and "Economic Transformation in Jamaica: Some Policy Issues," *Studies in Comparative International Development* 19, no. 3 (1984): 40–58; and *Daily Gleaner*, 28 December 1974.
18. Emphasis in original. CC box 2, folder 54.
19. *Daily Gleaner*, 10 June, and 15 and 18 August 1973.
20. *Daily Gleaner*, 11 June and 2 October 1973. For the nationalization of JOS, see *Sunday Gleaner*, 7 April 1974; and *Daily Gleaner*, 1 May 1974. For Willard Samm's discussion, see *Daily Gleaner*, 30 April 1974.
21. On the SEP, see Robert Girling and Sherry Keith, "The Planning and Management of Jamaica's Special Employment Programme," *Social and Economic Studies* 29, nos. 2 and 3 (1980): 1–34; and Davies, "Jamaican Economy". On the National Youth Service, see Cooke, *Land of My Birth*; and the *Daily Gleaner*, 26, 27 and 29 April 1974.
22. For the full text of Manley's speech, see the *Daily Gleaner*, 21 November 1974.
23. Davies, "Jamaican Economy", 73–83.
24. CC box 2, folder 55, Manley's letter dated 26 September 1974. In addition to Manley's speech, see also Manley, *Struggle*, passim; Cooke, *Land of My Birth*; Kaufman, *Jamaica Under Manley;* and "Democracy and Social Transformation in Jamaica," *Social and Economic Studies* 37, no. 3 (1988): 45–73; Levi, *Michael Manley*; and Stephens and Stephens, *Democratic Socialism.* Compare Smith, *The Biography*, 157–67.

25. Manley, *Struggle,* 87–95. The settler societies of Australia (led by Labor's Gough Whitlam) and Canada (by Pierre Trudeau) also leaned to the left.
26. The *Gleaner* editorial showed some restraint (*Sunday Gleaner,* 24 November 1974) and "William Strong" (Evon Blake) did his best. Under a heading, "Not frightening", he interpreted Manley's stance as one which proposed that socialism and capitalism could co-exist in "a new and humane form" (*Daily Gleaner,* 22 November 1974).
27. See Davies, citing C. Davis, "Jamaican Economy", 81–82. One such supplier was Australia, with extensive reserves of bauxite at Gove in northern Australia.

    Author's note: See my own youthful contribution to the issue of bauxite, Diane Austin, "Jamaican Bauxite: A Case Study in Multi-National Investment," *Australian and New Zealand Journal of Sociology* 11, no. 3 (1977): 53–59.
28. Stephens and Stephens, *Democratic Socialism,* 134–35, 356. The authors report that, as certified by the Carter Administration, the CIA was not involved. Also, see Levi, *Michael Manley,* 168–69.
29. CC box 2, folders 53 and 66, Isaacs' letters dated 18 February, 26 March, 21 April, 7 May, and 27 and 28 July. Manley's letter dated 4 April. All letters were written in 1975. For Ashenheim's subsequent remarks, see *Daily Gleaner,* 31 May 1975; also cited in Levi, *Michael Manley,* 161.
30. *The Globe and Mail,* 12 September 1974. Back in Jamaica, Isaacs wrote of these events (*Daily Gleaner,* 11 October 1975). Justice Donald R. Morand presided over the Royal Commission into Metropolitan Toronto Police Practices.
31. The other issues dealt with at length were Canada-CARICOM trade and Canadian aid (CC box 2, folder 53, Isaacs' submission to Manley, dated 19 February 1975).
32. CC box 2, folder 53. James' assault was reported in the black community newsletter *Contrast,* 11 April 1975.
33. *Daily Gleaner,* 13 May 1975.
34. CC box 2, folder 53, Manley's letter to Isaacs, dated 6 June 1975; and William Isaacs interview (2001), 5.
35. For Isaacs' columns and comment, see *Daily Gleaner,* 27 August, 12 and 15 September, and 6 October 1975. For the commission's findings, see *Daily Gleaner,* 18 and 20 August 1976.

36. Telegram 2743 from the US embassy in Jamaica to the Department of State. https://history.state.gov/historicaldocuments/frus1969-76ve11p1/d453
37. Seaga, *Edward Seaga Vol. 1*, 216.
38. See endnote 28 above.
39. See Levi, *Michael Manley*, 169–75
40. The previous incumbent, Eli Matalon, had resigned on medical grounds.
41. It is significant that Allan Isaacs had been Manley's Minister for Mining, more than likely challenged by his leader's foreign policy stance. For his statement on resigning, see the *Daily Gleaner*, 22 January 1976. On the *Gleaner's* appraisal of PNP government support, see Levi, *Michael Manley*, 179; and on radical politics in Jamaica at this time, see Gray, *Radicalism*, 216–24 and Munroe, *Jamaican Politics*, 244–46.
42. Girvan, Bernal, and Hughes, "The IMF", 113–22. For Arthur Brown's statement, see *Daily Gleaner*, 29 January 1977.
43. For this part of the IMF drama, see Levi, *Michael Manley*, 183–86 and 189–90. Also, see Girvan, Bernal, and Hughes, "The IMF", 118–24.
44. *Daily Gleaner*, 17 March and 26 September 1977; and *Sunday Gleaner*, 16 January and 9 October 1977. Regarding Duncan's relations with other ministers, see Stephens and Stephens, *Democratic Socialism*, 156; and Kaufman, *Jamaica Under Manley*, 143. The 16 January column on Cabinet structure was written by Ulric Simmonds, no longer using his previous *nom de plume*, Political Reporter.
45. For Anthony Spaulding's comment, see Stephens and Stephens, *Democratic Socialism*, 180; and for D.K. Duncan's comment, *Sunday Gleaner*, 9 October 1977. On Castro, see Levi, *Michael Manley*, 189, 313fn. Levi indicates that the information came from a "confidential source". Carlos Rafael Rodriguez, number three in the Cuban Communist Party, also personally advised "anti-IMF holdouts" in the PNP to accept the IMF proposals. Author's note: I am indebted for detailed remarks on the foregoing events provided by Leroy Cooke (personal communication).
46. Girvan, Bernal, and Hughes, "The IMF", 124. Jamaica floated its dollar in 1983 and removed the remaining exchange controls in 1991.

47. Girvan, Bernal, and Hughes, "The IMF", 125–26. For pertinent remarks by Carl Stone, see *Daily Gleaner*, 8 May 1978.
48. Coore went to the World Bank; Blake to a senior court position in the Bahamas; and Peart became Jamaica's High Commissioner to the United Kingdon.
49. Cited in Levi, *Michael Manley*, 211.
50. See *New York Times*, 9 October 1979, "Despite IMF aid, Jamaica still lags"; a good example of how a political judgment becomes an integral part of assessing financial risk. https://www.nytimes.com/1979/10/09/archives/despite-imf-aid-jamaica-still-lags-mired-in-stagnation.html

    Also, see Jennifer Sharpley, "Jamaica, 1972–80," *The IMF and Stabilisation: Developing Country Experiences*, ed. Tony Killick (London: Heinemann, 1984), 115–63. Like some others, Sharpley describes 1970s Jamaica as a "command economy". This it was not, though a number of the general ideological statements made by Manley and some members of his government may have led external observers to that conclusion.
51. See Manley, *Struggle*, especially 169–203; and Levi, *Michael Manley*, especially 217–29. Richard Fletcher resigned from the Senate at the same time.
52. *Daily Gleaner*, 23 December 1979, 15 and 16 January, and 4 March 1980.
53. Sives, *Elections*, 107–17
54. Sharpley, "Jamaica 1972–1980", 159. Clarkson and Nelson (*Contextualizaing Jamaica*, 123–66) give a comprehensive account of finance and the IMF, including the Manley government's Emergency Production Plan (EPP).

    Jamaica's case was one of a number which involved strictly applied IMF conditionalities to peripheral or 'less developed countries' experiencing balance-of-payment problems. In addition to Manley, *Struggle*, and *Up the Down Escalator*, see ed. Tony Killick, *The IMF and Stabilisation: Developing Country Experiences* (London: Heinemann, 1984); and *The Quest for Economic Stabilisation: The IMF and the Third World* (London: Heinemann, 1984). For the continuing debate concerning conditionalities, see Graham Bird, *The IMF and the Future: Issues and Options Facing the Fund* (London and New York: Routledge, 2003); eds. Gustav Ranis, James Vreeland, and Stephen Kosack, *Globalization and the Nation*

*State: The Impact of the IMF and the World Bank* (London and New York: Routledge, 2003); and Ray, Rebecca, Kevin Gallagher, and William Kring, "'Keep the Receipts': The Political Economy of IMF Austerity During and After the Crisis Years of 2009 and 2020," *Journal of Globalization and Development* 13, no. 1 (2022): 31–59.

Several of the central issues raised in this literature were anticipated in the special issue of *Development Dialogue (The International Monetary System and the New International Order)* 2, 1980. Norman Girvan, Michael Manley, Richard Bernal, and Wesley Hughes made major contributions to this publication. Also, see Adlith Brown, "Economic Policy and the IMF in Jamaica," *Social and Economic Studies* 30, no. 4, Regional Monetary Studies (December 1981), 1–51.

55. *Daily Gleaner*, 16 March 1976; and *Sunday Gleaner*, 4 April 1976. For Carl Stone's remark, see *Sunday Gleaner*, 16 January 1977; and Munroe and Bertram, *Adult Suffrage*, 424.
56. *Daily Gleaner*, 29 May, 25 October and 19 November 1977.
57. *Daily Gleaner*, 16 February, 9 April and 26 September 1978. For Isaacs' remembrances, see *Daily Gleaner*, 4 and 9 January 1979. Regarding Norman Manley's preference, I am indebted to Leroy Cooke (personal communication).
58. *Daily Gleaner*, 13 September 1979. The relevant drug company, placed under pressure, had paid for the flight.
59. Munroe and Bertram, *Adult Suffrage*, 470.
60. Christine Isaacs remarked that her father would have been just as happy to have Matalon officiate at the funeral, but he was off the island.
61. William Isaacs interview (2001), 25; *Daily Gleaner*, 6, 7, 10 and 14 January 1981. Some forty years later, the remains of Wills and Gloria Isaacs were re-interred at St Peter and Paul Roman Catholic Church, Old Hope Road, Kingston.

## Conclusion

1. *Daily Gleaner*, 6 January 1981.
2. For Isaacs' 1950 statement on his political position, see Appendix below.
3. His notable failure perhaps, which he shared with many others around the world, was not to appreciate the injustice done to

Palestinians by the advent and subsequent course of the Israeli state. Also, see chapter 11, endnote 2 above.

4. The forms of alliance which followed the end of the Federation – CARIFTA and CARICOM – suggest that Isaacs was correct. Each focused mainly on economic co-operation rather than political integration.
5. Author's interview with P.J. Patterson, 23 April 2019.
6. Note his nickname, the 'Catholic Communist', in the 1930s.
7. For the first of these remarks, see chapter 5, and for the second, the Appendix. The point made here is similar to, though not the same as, that made by David Scott concerning the influence of Enlightenment values, and aspirations, in the Caribbean. See Scott, *Conscripts of Modernity: The Tragedy of Colonial Enlightenment* (Durham: Duke University Press, 2004); and "Political Rationalities of the Modern Jamaica," *Small Axe* 14 (September 2003): 1–22. Scott is sceptical regarding a history of progress for the Caribbean. Others are less so and focus instead on the struggle to develop suitable national and transnational institutions that support both sovereignty and development. See, for instance, eds. Bryan Meeks and Kate Quinn, *Beyond Westminster in the Caribbean* (Kingston: Ian Randle Publishers, 2018).
8. Other contenders, including Arnett and Glasspole, and even Lloyd, never approached the heights of IsaacsIsaacs' popularity among PNP delegates.
9. Reid, *Horses of the Morning*, 311–16; and Post, *Strike Vol. 1*, 96–97.
10. Seivright was a lifelong member of the Church of England and a senior brother in Kingston's Masonic Lodge, as well as being a successful businessman, most assuredly wealthier than Isaacs.
11. Stephens and Stephens, *Democratic Socialism*, 341.
12. On manufacturing, see Government of Jamaica, *National Foreign Trade Policy: Positioning Jamaica to Increase Foreign Trade* (Kingston: Ministry of Foreign Affairs and Trade, 2017).
13. An internal factor becomes an external one when media, especially in North America, focus on crime and violence in Jamaica. A further proposed pivot for Jamaica's economy has been as a logistics hub connecting island-based services with traffic through the Panama Canal. An excellent idea, it remains stuck on the drawing board.
14. The debt exchanges only involved Jamaica-based institutions. The explanation was that interest rates were higher in Jamaica than

elsewhere. It also seems likely that the Jamaican government wished to avoid the legal complications involved in tackling international banks and other institutions. For a lucid account of Jamaica's initial debt exchange, see United Nations Development Programme, *Jamaica's Debt Exchange: A Case Study for Heavily Indebted Middle-Income Countries, A Discussion Paper* (New York: Bureau for Development Policy, 2010). For Jamaica's dealings with the IMF in the twenty-first century, see Clarkson and Nelson, *Contextualizing Jamaica*, 217–89. Also, see International Monetary Fund, *Jamaica: Selected Issues, IMF Country Report No. 22/044* (Washington, DC: IMF Publication Services, 2022), which cites a World Bank poverty "headcount" in Jamaica of 23 per cent for 2010-2021.

15. For references to these various organizations, see *Daily Gleaner*, 4 March 2000, 28 August 2005, 31 October 2010, 25 July 2013 and 6 September 2020. At the time, the CEO of the JMMB Group was Keith Duncan, a son of the dentist and PNP activist, D.K. Duncan. Keith Duncan also held the position of president of the PSOJ from 2019 to 2022. He listed the concerns of the PSOJ as including private-public sector collaboration, human capital development, partnering to address crime and corruption, sustainability, digital transformation, and better engagement of both members and youth by the PSOJ.
16. *Daily Gleaner*, 3 February 2008.
17. *Daily Gleaner*, 17 and 22 January 2010.
18. When I first met Mr Patrick, he was a squatter in McGregor Gully below Jacques Road on the border between Kingston and St Andrew parishes. Over the years, he had constructed a tiny concrete block house and, with support from a community worker, he applied successfully for title to the land. He honoured Michael Manley for his good fortune, but became pessimistic in later years as unemployment increased and he worried for his children's and grandchildren's futures. A good part of his savings to build the house came from farm work in Florida. In the 1950s and 1960s he received 'tickets' for the farm work from his MP, Florizel Glasspole. Patrick cut cane in Florida and, because he was literate, wrote letters home for his workmates. The second exchange was with some youth on the corner of Portland and Windward Roads, Rollington Town, not far from the site of the TUC's asylum strike in 1946. Also, see Austin, *Urban Life;* and chapter 4 notes above.

19. Levitt's comment is cited in Owen Jefferson, *Stabilization and Stagnation in the Jamaican Economy, 1972–97* (Kingston: Canoe Press, 1999), 4; and Michael Witter, "Prospects for Jamaica's Economic Development in the Era of the FTAA," in *The Caribbean Economies in an Era of Free Trade,* eds. N. Karagiannis and M. Witter (London: Routledge, 2017), 169–86. Even the economically orthodox Inter-American Development Bank recommended a "social contract" among Jamaica's "major social partners" so that the burdens of structural adjustment might be shared; see IDB, *Revitalizing the Jamaican Economy: Policies for Sustained Growth* (Washington, DC: IDB Publications Section, 2004): 11–12.
20. Bryan Meeks, Preface, vii–x. Also, see chapter 11 notes above.

## Appendix

1. *Daily Gleaner,* 13 April 1950
2. *PHR Session 1956,* 25 February, 542. Although Isaacss recalls here the strike of 1946, troubles at the railway had begun as early as 1942. See chapters 2 and 4 notes above; and Post, *Strike Vol. 1,* 264–71. For Arnett's role in the IDC, also see chapters 7 and 8 notes above.
3. *Sunday Gleaner,* 26 March 1978.

# Bibliography


### Historical Records, Jamaica

Consulted online
Church of England Parish Register, 1664–1880
Civil Registration, 1880–1999
Directory of Jamaica, the Parish of Hanover, 1878, 1887, 1910
Directory of Jamaica, the Parish of Westmoreland, 1878, 1910
Jamaica Almanac, 1875, 1877

### Government Papers, Jamaica

Economic Council submissions and minutes consulted at the Jamaica Archives and Records Department, Spanish Town, Jamaica
1B/31/5/397-1B/31/5/491
1B/31/5/519-1B/31/5/528
Proceedings of the House of Representatives (Hansard), consulted at the Parliamentary Library, Kingston, Jamaica.
Sessions 1950–1973.

### British Colonial Office Papers

Files consulted at the National Archives, Kew, London
CO/137/885/4
CO/137/885/5
CO/137/864/11
CO/137/887/6
CO/137/887/7
CO/137/887/8
CO/137/899/5
CO/137/904/4

**Richard Hart's collected papers, 1939–1966**
Microfilm consulted at the West Indies Reading Room. UWI Library, Mona, Jamaica

**Wills O. Isaacs' collected papers**
Scanned folders provided courtesy of Christine Gore (née Isaacs).
Canada correspondence, box 2, folders 53, 54, 55 (1973–1975).
Interview files, box 1, folders 9, 16, 18, 19 (1978, 2001, 2002–2003).
Including the following:
*Interviewed by Claudette Carby (née Isaacs), 1978*
Vernon Arnett
Ralph Brown
Ken Hill
Russell Lewars
Michael Manley
Lynden G. Newland
*Interviewed by Abby Majendie-Wynter, 2001*
Nadine Isaacs
William "Vunnic" Isaacs
*Interviewed by Michael Burke, 2002–2003*
Howard Cooke (2002)
Dudley Thompson (2002)
Fred Wilmot (2002)
David Coore (2003)
Richard Hart (2003)
P.J. Patterson (2003)
Edward Seaga (2003)

**Author's interviews**
Interview with Arnold Bertram, 9 April 2019
Interview with Hon. P.J. Patterson, 23 April 2019
Phone consultation with Leroy Cooke, 15 December, 2021

**Newspapers, magazines, pamphlets**
*Daily Gleaner*
*Sunday Gleaner*
*Jamaica Observer*
*Public Opinion*
*Spotlight News Magazine*
*Foreign Commerce Weekly* (USA)
*Globe and Mail* (Canada)

Jamaica pamphlets, People's National Party. Leaflets and pamphlets, including transcripts of PNP radio broadcasts, consulted at the National Library of Jamaica, Kingston.

## Books and articles

Arrighi, Giovanni. "The Developmentalist Illusion: A Reconceptualization of the Semiperiphery." In *Semi Peripheral States in the World Economy,* edited by W.G. Martin, 11–42. Westport, CT: Greenwood Press, 1990.

August, Thomas G. "An historical profile of the Jewish community in Jamaica." *Jewish Social Studies* 49, nos. 3&4 (1987): 303–16.

Austin, Diane. "Jamaican bauxite: a case study in multi-national investment." *The Australian and New Zealand Journal of Sociology* 11, no. 3 (1975): 53–59.

———. *Urban Life in Kingston, Jamaica: The Culture and Class Ideology of Two Neighbourhoods.* Abingdon: Routledge, facsimile edition, 2018 (1984).

Austin-Broos, Diane. *Jamaica Genesis: Religion and the Politics of Moral Order.* Chicago: Chicago University Press, 1997.

———. *Arrernte present, Arrernte past: Invasion, Violence and Imagination in Indigenous Central Australia.* Chicago: University of Chicago Press, 2008.

———. *A Different Inequality: The Politics of Debate About Remote Aboriginal Australia.* Sydney: Allen and Unwin, 2012.

———. "Don't rewrite history of Wills Isaacs." *Sunday Gleaner,* 30 June 2019.

Ayub, Mahood A. *Made in Jamaica: The Development of the Manufacturing Sector*, World Bank Occasional Paper 31. Baltimore: Johns Hopkins University Press, 1981.

Barrow, Christine. "Edith Clarke: Jamaican reformer and anthropologist". *Caribbean Quarterly* 44, nos. 3 and 4 (1998): 15–34.

Beckford, George L. *Persistent Poverty: Underdevelopment in Plantation Economies of the Third World.* New York: Oxford University Press, 1972.

———. "Land reform for the betterment of Caribbean Peoples." In *The George Beckford Papers,* selected and introduced by Kari Levitt, 91–108. Kingston: Canoe Press, 2000.

Beckles, McD. Hilary. *How Britain Underdeveloped the Caribbean: A Reparation Response to Europe's Legacy of Plunder and Poverty.* Kingston: University of West Indies Press, 2021.

Benham, Frederic C. *Report of the Economic Policy Committee.* Kingston: Government Printery, 1945.

Bernal, Richard. "The Great Depression, Colonial Policy and Industrialization in Jamaica." *Social and Economic Studies* 37, nos. 1&2 (1988): 33–64.

Bertram, Arnold. *N.W. Manley and the Making of Modern Jamaica.* Kingston: Arawak Publications, 2016.

Binder, Alan. "Anatomy of double-digit inflation in the 1970s." In *Inflation: Causes and Effects,* edited by Robert Hall, 261–82. Chicago: University of Chicago Press, 1982.

Bird, Graham. *The IMF and the Future: Issues and Options Facing the Fund.* London and New York: Routledge, 2003.

Brown, Adlith. "Economic Policy and the IMF in Jamaica." *Social and Economic Studies* 30, no. 4, Regional Monetary Studies (December 1981): 1–51.

Brown, G. Arthur. "Economic development and the private sector." *Social and Economic Studies* (Study Conference on Economic Development in Under-Developed Countries) 7, no. 3 (1958): 103–13.

Brown, Orville. "Seaga 'father of political violence?'" *Sunday Gleaner,* 9 June 2019.

Campbell, Yonique. *Citizenship on the Margins: State Power, Security and Precariousness in the 21st Century.* Cham: Palgrave Macmillan, 2020.

Cannon, John. "Millard Johnson and His Party – Racial Ideology in Jamaican Politics; The People's Political Party in the Parliamentary Elections of 1962." *Caribbean Studies* 16, nos. 3&4 (1976): 85–108.

Carnegie, James. *Some Aspects of Jamaica's Politics: 1918–1938.* Kingston: Institute of Jamaica, 1973.

———. *Noel Newton Nethersole, a short study.* Jamaica: Bank of Jamaica, 1975.

Cassidy, Frederic, G. *Jamaica Talk: Three Hundred Years of the English Language in Jamaica,* 2nd ed. London: Institute of Jamaica and Macmillan, 1971.

Central Planning Unit of Jamaica. *Economic Survey, Jamaica, 1971.* Kingston: Government Printers, 1972.

Chevannes, Barry. "The Rastafari and the Urban Youth." In *Perspectives on Jamaica in the Seventies,* edited by Carl Stone and Aggrey Brown, 392–422. Kingston: Jamaica Publishing House, 1981.

Clarke, Colin. "Population Pressure in Kingston, Jamaica: A Study of Unemployment and Overcrowding." *Transactions of the Institute of British Geographer* 38 (1966):165–82.

———. *Decolonizing the Colonial City: Urbanization and Stratification in Kingston, Jamaica.* Oxford: Oxford University Press, 2006.

———. *Kingston, Jamaica: Urban Development and Social Change, 1602–2002.* Kingston: Ian Randle Publishers, 2006.

Clarkson, Christine, and Carole Nelson. *Contextualizing Jamaica's Relationship with the IMF.* Cham: Palgrave Macmillan, 2022.

Cooke, Leroy. *Land of My Birth: A Historical Sketch of the First Forty Years of the People's National Party of Jamaica.* Kingston: Negro River Publishers, 2016.

Coore, David. "The Role of the Internal Dynamics of Jamaican Politics on the Collapse of the Federation." *Social and Economic Studies* 48, no. 4 (1999): 65–82.

Cox, Oliver C. *The Foundation of Capitalism.* New York, Philosophical Library, 1959.

Cumper, George. "A Comparison of Statistical Data on the Jamaica Labour Force." *Social and Economic Studies'* 13, no. 4 (1964): 430–39.

Curtin, Marguerite. *Legacy: The Levian Gore Family. A Jamaican Story.* Kingston: Marguerite Curtin, 2004.

———. "Wills O. Isaacs: The Early Years." Typescript, 2006.

———. "Wills O. Isaacs: Isaacs becomes a Kingstonian." Typescript, 2006.

———. "Wills O. Isaacs: Staving Off Trouble in the Capital." Typescript, 2006.

———. "Wills O. Isaacs: The Social Revolution of 1938." Typescript, 2007.

———. *The Story of Hanover, a Jamaican Parish.* Kingston: Phoenix Printers, 2007.

Davies, Omar. "Economic Transformation in Jamaica: Some Policy Issues." *Studies in Comparative International Development* 19, no. 3 (1984): 40–58.

———. "An analysis of the management of the Jamaican economy: 1972–1985." *Social and Economic Studies* 88, no. 1 (1988): 73–109.

de la Torres, Carlos. *Populist Seduction in Latin America,* 2nd ed. Athens: Ohio University Press, 2010.

DeLong, J. Bradford, *Slouching Towards Utopia: An Economic History of the Twentieth Century*. London: Basic Books, 2022.

Demas, William G. *The Economics of Development in Small Countries with Reference to the Caribbean.* Montreal: McGill University Press, 1965.

Dercon, Stefan. *Gambling on Development: Why Some Countries Win and Some Others Lose.* London: C. Hurst, 2022.

Eaton, George. "Trade Union Development in Jamaica." *Caribbean Quarterly* 8, nos. 1&2 (1962): 43–53, 69–75.

———. *Alexander Bustamante and Modern Jamaica.* Kingston: Kingston Publishers, 1975.

Edmonds, Kevin. "Guns, Gangs and Garrison Communities in the Politics of Jamaica." *Race & Class* 57, no. 4 (2016): 54–74.

Eisner, Gisella. *Jamaica, 1830–1930: A Study in Economic Growth.* Manchester: Manchester University Press, 1967.

Farrell, Terence. "Arthur Lewis and the Case for Caribbean Industrialisation." *Social and Economic Studies* 29, no. 4 (1980): 52–75.

Gersovitz, Mark, ed. *Selected Economic Writings of W. Arthur Lewis.* New York: New York University Press, 1983.

Girling, Robert, and Sherry Keith. "The Planning and Management of Jamaica's Special Employment Programme: lessons and limitations." *Social and Economic Studies* 29, nos. 2&3 (1980): 1–34.

Girvan, Norman. *Foreign Capital and Economic Underdevelopment in Jamaica.* Kingston: Institute of Social and Economic Studies, University of the West Indies, 1971.

———. *Corporate Imperialism: Conflict and Expropriation.* New York: Monthly Review Press, 1976.

———. "W.A. Lewis, The Plantation School and Dependency: An Interpretation." *Social and Economic Studies (Special Issue on Sir Arthur Lewis, Part 1)* 54, no. 3 (2005): 198–222.

———. "Sir Arthur Lewis: a man of his time – and ahead of his time." Distinguished Lecture, "Year of Sir Arthur Lewis", University of the West Indies, St Augustine, 20 February 2008.

Girvan, Norman, Richard Bernal and Wesley Hughes. 1980. "The IMF and the Third World: The case of Jamaica." *Development Dialogue* 2 (1980): 113–55.

Gittings, John. *The Changing Face of China: From Mao to Markets.* Oxford: Oxford University Press, 2005.

Government of Jamaica. "National Foreign Trade Policy: Positioning Jamaica to Increase Foreign Trade." Kingston: Ministry of Foreign Affairs and Trade, 2017.

Gray, Obika. *Radicalism and Social Change in Jamaica, 1960–1972.* Knoxville: University of Tennessee Press, 1991.

Gore, Christine. *For Your Information: The Life and Times of Wills O.P. Isaacs.* Kingston: n.p., 2016.

Government of Jamaica. *Report of Mission to Africa.* Kingston: Government Printers, 1961.

Hall, Kenneth, and Rheima Holding, eds. *Tourism: The Driver of Change in the Jamaican Economy?* Kingston: Ian Randle Publishers, 2006.

Harrington, Michael. *Socialism, Past and Future.* New York: Arcade Publishing, 1989.

Harriott, Anthony, ed. *Understanding Crime in Jamaica.* Kingston: University of West Indies Press, 2004.

Hart, Richard. *Towards Decolonisation: Political, Labour and Economic Development in Jamaica, 1938–1945.* Kingston: Canoe Press, 1999.

———. *Time for a Change: Constitutional, Political and Labour Developments in Jamaica and Other Colonies in the Caribbean Region, 1944–1955.* Kingston: Arawak Publications, 2004.

Hartley, Neita. *Hugh Shearer: A Voice for the People.* Kingston: Ian Randle Publishers and the Institute of Jamaica, 2005.

Hicks, J.R., and U.K. Hicks. *Report on Finance and Taxation in Jamaica.* Kingston: Government Printers, 1955.

Higman, Barry W. *Jamaica Surveyed: Plantations, Maps and Plans of the Eighteenth and Nineteenth Centuries.* Kingston: University of the West Indies Press, 2001.

Higman, Barry, and Brian Hudson. *Jamaican Place Names.* Kingston: University of the West Indies Press, 2009.

Hill, Frank. *Bustamante and His Letters.* Kingston: Kingston Publishers, 1976.

Hill, Robert A., ed. *Marcus Garvey and the Universal Negro Improvement Association Papers, Vol. 7.* Berkeley: University of California Press, 1983.

Holt, Thomas C. *The Problem of Freedom: Race, Labour, and Politics in Jamaica and Britain*, 1832–1938. Baltimore: Johns Hopkins University Press, 1992.

Hutton, Clinton, with Maziki Thame, and Jermain McCalpin, ed. *Caribbean Reasonings: Rupert Lewis and the Black Intellectual Tradition.* Kingston: Ian Randle Publishers, 2018.

Inter-American Development Bank. *Revitalizing the Jamaican Economy: Policies for Sustained Growth.* Washington, DC: IDB Publications Section, 2004.

International Bank of Reconstruction and Development. *The Economic Development of Jamaica.* Report by a mission of the IBRD. Chief of Mission, John C. Wilde. Baltimore: Johns Hopkins University Press, 1952.

International Monetary Fund. *Jamaica: Selected Issues.* IMF Country Report no. 22/044. Washington, DC: IMF Publication Services, 2022.

Issa, Suzanne, with Jackie Ranston. *My Jamaica: Abe Issa.* Kingston: Suzanne Issa, 1974.

Jefferson, Owen. *Post-war Economic Development of Jamaica.* Kingston: Institute of Social and Economic Studies, University of the West Indies, 1972.

———. *Stabilization and Stagnation in the Jamaican Economy, 1972–1997.* Kingston: Canoe Press, 1999.

Jensen, Steven. "Embedded or Exceptional? Apartheid and the International Politics of Racial Discrimination." *Studies in Contemporary History, Online-Ausgabe* 13, no. 2 (2016). https://zeithistorische-forschungen.de/2-2016/5364

Johnson, Harry. *The New International Economic Order*, Selected Papers, No. 49. Chicago: Graduate School of Business, University of Chicago, 1976.

Kalb, Don. "Thinking About Neoliberalism as if the Crisis was Actually Happening." *Social Anthropology* 20, no. 3 (2012): 318–30.

Kaufman, Michael. *Jamaica Under Manley: Dilemmas of Socialism and Democracy.* London: Zed Books, 1985.

———. "Democracy and Social Transformation in Jamaica." *Social and Economic Studies* 37, no. 3 (1988): 45–73.

Killick, Tony, ed. *The Quest for Economic Stabilization: The IMF and the Third World.* London: Heinemann, 1984.

———. ed. *The IMF and Stabilization: Developing Country Experiences.* London: Heinemann, 1984.

LeFranc, Elsie, ed. *Consequences of Structural Adjustment: A Review of the Jamaican Experience.* Kingston: Canoe Press, 2000.

Levi, Darrell. 1989. *Michael Manley: The Making of a Leader.* Kingston: Heinemann Publishers (Caribbean), 1989.

Levitt, Kari Polanyi. *The Origins and Consequences of Jamaica's Debt Crisis, 1970–1990,* revised ed. Mona: Consortium Graduate School of Social Sciences, 1991.

———. Fifth Sir Arthur Lewis memorial lecture, "The Right to Development". Eastern Caribbean Central Bank, St Lucia, 2000. http://www.karipolanyilevitt.com/the-right-to-development/

Levy, Horace. "Jamaica Welfare: Growth and Decline." *Social and Economic Studies* 44, nos. 2&3 (1995): 349–57.

Lewis, W. Arthur. "An Economic Plan for Jamaica." *Agenda* 3, no. 4 (1944): 154–63.

———. "Industrial Development in Puerto Rico." *Caribbean Economic Review* 1, nos. 1&2 (1949): 153–76.

———. *The Principles of Economic Planning: A Study Prepared for the Fabian Society.* London: Allen and Unwin, 1949.

———. "The Industrialisation of the British West Indies." *Caribbean Economic Review* 2, no. 1 (1950): 1–61. Also published as a monograph, *The Industrial Development of the Caribbean.* Port of Spain: Kent House, 1951.

———. "Economic Development with Unlimited Supplies of Labour." *The Manchester School* 22, no. 2 (1954): 139–61. Reprinted in *Selected Economic Writings of W. Arthur* Lewis, edited by Mark Gersovitz, 311–65. New York: New York University Press, 1983.

———. Foreword to *Jamaica, 1830–1930: A Study in Economic Growth,* by Gisela Eisner, xv-xxiii. Manchester: Manchester University Press, 1961.

———. Epilogue to *The West Indies: The Federal Negotiations*, by John Mordecai, 455–62, London: George Allen and Unwin, 1968.

Lloyd, Ivan. *Land for the Million.* Kingston: People's National Party, 1944.

Manley, Michael. *The Politics of Change: A Jamaican Testament.* London; André Deutsch, 1974.

———. *A Voice at the Workplace: Reflections on Colonialism and the Jamaican Worker.* London: André Deutsch, 1975.

———. *Jamaica: Struggle in the Periphery.* London: Third World Media and Writers and Readers Cooperative, 1982.

———. *Up the Down Escalator: Development and the International Economy – a Jamaican Case Study.* London: André Deutsch, 1987.

Manley, Rachel, ed. *Edna Manley: The Diaries.* Kingston: Heinemann Publishers (Caribbean), 1989.

Mazzucato, Mariana. *The Value of Everything: Making and Taking in the Global Economy* (Milton Keynes: Penguin Books, 2019.

Meeks, Bryan. Preface to *Beyond Westminster in the Caribbean*, edited by B. Meeks and K. Quinn, vii-x. Kingston: Ian Randle Publishers, 2018.

Meeks, Bryan and Kate Quinn, eds. *Beyond Westminster in the Caribbean.* Kingston: Ian Randle Publishers. 2018.

Miller, Keith. "Local Government Reform in Jamaica." In *Handbook of Research on Sub-national Governance and Development,* edited by H.E. Schoburgh and R. Ryan, 520–42. Hershey: IGI Global, 2017.

Mintz, Sidney. "Caribbean Peasantries." In *Caribbean Transformations,* 131–250. Chicago: Aldine Publishing, 1974.

Moore, Brian and Michele Johnson. *Neither Led nor Driven: Contesting British Cultural Imperialism in Jamaica, 1863–1920.* Jamaica: University of West Indies Press, 2004.

Mordecai, John. *The West Indies: The Federal Negotiations.* London: George Allen and Unwin, 1968.

Munroe, Trevor. *The Politics of Constitutional Decolonization: Jamaica, 1944–62.* Jamaica: Institute of Social and Economic Research, University of the West Indies, 1972.

———. *The Marxist "Left" in Jamaica, 1940–1950.* Working Paper No. 15, Mona: Institute of Social and Economic Research, 1977.

———. *Jamaican Politics: A Marxist Perspective in Transition.* Kingston: Heinemann (Caribbean), 1990.

———. *The Cold War and the Fall of the Left.* Kingston: Kingston Publishing House, 1992.

Munroe, Trevor, and Arnold Bertram. *Adult Suffrage and Political Administrations in Jamaica, 1944–2002.* Kingston: Ian Randle Publishers, 2006.

Naranjo, Martin, and Emilio Osambela. "From financial crisis to correction." In *Revitalizing the Jamaican Economy: Policies for Sustained Growth,* 119–52. Washington, DC: Inter-American Development Bank, 2004.

Nettleford, Rex, ed. *Manley and the New Jamaica: Selected Speeches and Writings, 1938–1968.* Jamaica: Longman (Caribbean), 1971.

O'Connor, James. "Agrarian reforms in Cuba, 1959–1963." *Science and Society* 32, no. 2 (1968): 169–217.

Olivier, Lord Sydney. *Jamaica, the Blessed Land.* London: Faber and Faber, 1936.

Palmer, Colin A. *Freedom's Children: The 1938 Labor Rebellion and the Birth of Modern Jamaica.* Chapel Hill: University of North Carolina Press, 2014.

Palmer, Ransford W. *The Jamaican Economy.* New York: Frederick A. Praeger, 1968.

Panton, David. "Dual Labour Markets and Unemployment in Jamaica: A Modern Synthesis." *Social and Economic Studies* 42, no. 1 (1993): 75–118.

Patterson, Orlando. *The Confounding Island: Jamaica and the Postcolonial Predicament.* Cambridge, MA: Harvard University Press, 2019.

Patterson, P.J. *My Political Journey, Jamaica's Sixth Prime Minister.* Kingston: University of West Indies Press, 2018.

———. "The History and Development of the Modern Labour Movement: Lessons from the Past, Prospects for the Future." Inaugural Distinguished Lecture Series. Trade Union Education Institute, University of the West Indies, 2018.

Patterson, Patricia, and Maxine McDonnough. *Edward Hanna: The Man and His Times, 1894–1978.* Kingston: Ian Randle Publishers, 1997.

Payne, Anthony. *Politics in Jamaica,* 2nd ed. London: Palgrave Macmillan, 1995.

Persaud, Wilberne. *Jamaica Meltdown: Indigenous Financial Sector Crash, 1996.* Lincoln, NE: iUniverse, 2006.

Phelps, O.W. "Rise of the Labour Movement in Jamaica." *Social and Economic Studies* 9 no. 4 (1960): 417–68.

Phillips, Peter. "Jamaica Elites: 1938 to Present." In *Essays on Power and Change in Jamaica*, edited by Carl Stone and Aggrey Brown, 1–15. Kingston: Kingston Publishing House, 1977.

———. "Community Mobilisation in Squatter Communities." In *Perspectives on Jamaica in the Seventies,* edited by Carl Stone and Aggrey Brown, 422–36. Kingston: Kingston Publishing House, 1981.

Piketty, Thomas. *A Brief History of Equality.* Cambridge, MA and London: Belknap Press of Harvard University Press, 2022.

Post, Ken. *Arise Ye Starvelings: The Jamaican Labour Rebellion and Its Aftermath.* The Hague: Martinus Nijhoff, 1978.

———. *Strike the Iron: A Colony at War, 1939–1945, Vols. 1 and 2.* New Jersey: Humanities Press, 1981.

People's National Party. *Constitution.* Kingston: PNP, 1938.

———. *Plan for Progress.* Kingston: The City Printery, 1955.

Ramsaran, Dave, ed. *Contradictory Existence: Neoliberalism and Democracy in the Caribbean.* Kingston: Ian Randle Publishers, 2016.

Ranis, Gustav, James Vreeland, and Stephen Kosak, eds. *Globalization and the Nation State: The Impact of the IMF and the World Bank.* London and New York: Routledge, 2003.

Ray, Rebecca, Kevin Gallagher, and William Kring. "'Keep the Receipts': The Political Economy of IMF Austerity During and

After the Crisis Years of 2009 and 2020." *Journal of Globalization and Development* 13, no. 1 (2022): 31–59.

Reid, Stanley. "Elites in Jamaica: A Study of Monistic Relationship." *Anthropologica*, New Series 22, no. 1 (1980): 25–44.

Reid, Victor Stafford. *The Horses of the Morning: About the Rt. Excellent N.W. Manley, QC, M.M., National Hero of Jamaica.* Kingston: Caribbean Authors Publishing, 1985.

Richards, Glen. "Race, Class and Labour Politics in Colonial Jamaica, 1900–1934." In *Jamaica in Slavery and Freedom: History, Heritage and Culture,* edited by Kathleen Monteith and Glen Richards, 340–62. Kingston: University of West Indies Press, 2002.

Roberts, George W. *The Population of Jamaica.* Cambridge: Cambridge University Press, 1957.

Robinson, John W. "Lessons from the Structural Adjustment Process in Jamaica." *Social and Economic Studies* 43 no. 4 (1994): 87–113.

Robotham, Donald. "Transnationalism in the Caribbean: Formal and Informal." *American Ethnologist* 25, no. 2 (1998): 307–71.

———. "Liberal Social Democracy, Neoliberalism, and Conservatism." In *Rethinking America: Rethinking the Imperial Homeland in the 21st century,* edited by J. Maskovsky and I. Susser, 213–33. Boulder, CO: Paradigm Press, 2009.

Rodney, Walter. *How Europe Underdeveloped Africa.* London: Verso, 2018.

Scott, David. "Political Rationalities of the Modern Jamaica." *Small Axe* 14 (September 2003): 1–22.

———. *Conscripts of Modernity: The Tragedy of Colonial Enlightenment.* Durham: Duke University Press, 2004.

Seaga, Edward. *Edward Seaga: My Life and Leadership, Vol. 1: Clash of ideologies, 1930–1980.* Oxford: Macmillan Education, 2009.

Senior, Olive. *Dying to Better Themselves: West Indians and the Building of the Panama Canal.* Kingston: University of West Indies Press, 2014.

Sharpley, Jennifer. "Jamaica, 1972–80." In *The IMF and Stabilisation: Developing Country Experiences*, edited by Tony Killick, 115–63. London: Heinemann, 1984.

Sherlock, Philip. *Norman Manley, a Biography*. London: Macmillan, 1980.

Sives, Amanda. "The Historical Roots of Violence in Jamaica." In *Understanding Crime in Jamaica*, edited by Anthony Harriott, 49–61. Kingston: University of West Indies Press, 2004.

———. *Elections, Violence and the Democratic Process in Jamaica, 1944–2007.* Kingston: Ian Randle Publishers, 2010.

Smith, Godfrey. *Michael Manley, the Biography.* Kingston: Ian Randle Publishers, 2016.

Smith, Michael G., Roy Augier, and Rex Nettleford. *The Rastafari Movement in Kingston, Jamaica.* Kingston: Institute of Social and Economic Research, University College of the West Indies, 1960.

Smith, Raymond. *British Guiana.* Westport, CO: Greenwood Press, 1980.

Stedman Jones, Gareth. *Karl Marx: Greatness and Illusion.* Cambridge, MA: Harvard University Press, 2016.

Stephens, Evelyn, and John Stephens. *Democratic Socialism in Jamaica: The Political Movement and Social Transformation in Dependent Capitalism.* Princeton: Princeton University Press, 1986.

Stone, Carl. "Political Aspects of Post-war Agricultural Policies in Jamaica (1945–1970)." *Social and Economic Studies* 23, no. 2 (1974): 145–75.

———. *Democracy and Clientelism in Jamaica.* New Brunswick: Transaction Books, 1980.

———. "An Appraisal of the Co-operative Process in the Jamaican Sugar Industry." In *Perspectives on Jamaica in the Seventies,* edited by Carl Stone and Aggrey Brown, 437–62. Kingston: Jamaica Publishing House, 1981.

Taylor, Frank F. *To Hell with Paradise: A History of the Jamaican Tourist Industry.* Pittsburgh: University of Pittsburgh Press, 1973.

Thomas, Deborah. *Modern Blackness: Nationalism, Globalization and the Politics of Culture in Jamaica.* Durham, NC: Duke University Press, 2004.

———. *Exceptional Violence: Embodied Citizenship in Transnational Jamaica.* Durham, NC: Duke University Press, 2010.

Thorburn, Diana. *Mayer Matalon: Business, Politics and the Jewish-Jamaican elite.* Lanham: Hamilton Books, 2019.

United Nations Development Programme. *Discussion Paper – Jamaica's Debt Exchange: A Case Study for Heavily Indebted Middle-Income Countries.* New York: Bureau for Development Policy, 2010.

Wallerstein, Immanuel. *The Modern World-System: Capitalist Agriculture and the Origins of the European World-Economy in the Sixteenth Century.* New York: Academic Press, 1976.

Widdicombe, Stacey. *The Performance of Industrial Development Corporations: The Case of Jamaica.* New York: Praeger Publishers, 1972.

Wint, Alvin. G. "The Role of Government in Enhancing the Competitiveness of Developing Economies: Selective Functional Intervention in the Caribbean." *International Journal of Public Sector Management* 11, no. 4 (1998): 281–99.

Witter, Michael. "Exchange Rate Policy in Jamaica: A Critical Assessment." *Social and Economic Studies* 32, no. 4 (1983): 1–50.

———. "Prospects for Jamaica's economic development in the era of the FTAA." In *The Caribbean Economies in an Era of Free Trade*, edited by N. Karagiannis and M. Witter, 169–86. London: Routledge, 2017.

Zeidenfelt, Alex. "Political and Constitutional Developments in Jamaica." In *Journal of Politics* 14, no. 3 (1952): 512–40.

# Index

Printed in the USA
CPSIA information can be obtained
at www.ICGtesting.com
CBHW021508161024
15956CB00001B/5